Oregon's Promise

Oregon's Promise

An Interpretive History

David Peterson del Mar

Oregon State University Press
Corvallis

For my mother and father,
my mother's mother,
and all my Oregon ancestors and kin

భర్ భర్

Photographs on front cover courtesy of Lloyd Treichel (top), Historic Photograph Collections, Salem (Oregon) Public Library (below)

The paper in this book meets the guidelines for permanence and durability of the Committee on Production Guidelines for Book Longevity of the Council on Library Resources and the minimum requirements of the American National Standard for Permanence of Paper for Printed Library Materials Z39.48-1984.

Library of Congress Cataloging-in-Publication Data
Peterson del Mar, David, 1957-
 Oregon's promise : an interpretive history / David Peterson del Mar.—1st ed.
    p. cm.
Includes bibliographical references and index.
Contents: Natives and newcomers—Taking Oregon—Resettling Oregon—The industrialization of Oregon—Political and urban transformations—Oregon becomes modern—Oregon and the world in depression and war—Prosperity and its problems—A polarized state.
 ISBN 0-87071-558-5 (alk. paper)
 1. Oregon--History. I. Title.
F876.3 .P48 2003
979.5--dc21
                        2003007845

Oregon State University Press
101 Waldo Hall
Corvallis OR 97331-6407
OREGON STATE 541-737-3166 • fax 541-737-3170
UNIVERSITY http://oregonstate.edu/dept/press

Table of Contents

Acknowledgments

In this book, the first in which I have relied largely upon the works of other scholars, I found myself continually humbled by and thankful for the prodigious labor that historians of Oregon have accomplished. My notes and bibliography are but a faint suggestion of my debt to them, and I hope that readers will use these references to read more deeply about Oregon. I am especially grateful to Dorothy Johansen and Gordon Dodds for their fine and detailed treatments of the state's history that I repeatedly opened and reopened.

I am also indebted to those who read and made suggestions for improving this book: Carl Abbott, Katrine Barber, Richard Maxwell Brown, Wendy del Mar, Robert Johnston, Lee Nash, Kenn Oberrecht, Jeffrey Ostler, Brenda Peterson, Carlos Schwantes, Armand Smith, and Oregon State University Press's editorial board. Mary Braun and Jo Alexander at OSU Press have been exemplary acquisitions and text editors, respectively.

I was fortunate to have Richard Maxwell Brown as my mentor in Oregon and Pacific Northwest history, and many of his insights reside in this book's pages. I have learned a great deal from my students in courses on Oregon or Pacific Northwest history at Oregon State University, Portland State University, and the University of Oregon.

I am most grateful to Wendy and Peter, who are largely responsible for both bringing me back to Oregon and filling my days with so much laughter and love.

Introduction

The Golden Man

"The winner got to go to Oregon."
Murl Peterson to author.

T he four massive paintings above you barely cover a half century. We begin with Robert Gray at the Columbia River's mouth in 1792 and move to Lewis and Clark and the missionaries before closing with the wagon trains of 1843.

Walk through the massive doors and down the broad steps. Turn and consider two sets of sculpted figures. To your left ride Lewis and Clark. Sacagawea is motioning them into Eden, her head bent submissively. The explorers ride by as if she were not there, eyes forward. On your right is another trio of figures. A pioneer mother bends to hold her son, who turns from her, straining to join his father, a rigid man who is also, like the explorers, peering outward, away from his wife and child.

Above, standing atop the dome you just left, is the final figure. He, too, is a pioneer. He is coated with gold—a perfect, golden man. He holds an ax. He is utterly alone, looking northward, over the land that he and his kind tamed, where a new and different set of pioneers from Mexico now pick berries and thin Christmas trees.

Most of you—at least most Oregonians—will by now have surmised that the figures just described are from Oregon's state capitol building in Salem.

These images are among the most powerful and persuasive set of historical texts in the state. They are massive. They are compellingly rendered. They guard Oregon's seat of political power, the place where its future is contested, its laws passed. Created when the capitol was rebuilt in the 1930s, they say a lot. They assert that Oregon's history was brief. It began in 1792, when the first white man crossed the Columbia River bar. It ended in the 1840s when large contingents of overlanders arrived. Then, presumably, the die was cast, the trajectory of Oregon's future fixed.

The images also suggest that the exploration and settlement of Oregon was bloodless and noble. Indigenous peoples such as

Sacagawea recognized the white men's superiority. The golden man used his will and his energy to tame this promised land for his progeny, generations of Oregonians who have plucked the fruits of his sacrifice.

The golden man does not stand alone. His message is amplified and elaborated by accreted visits to historical museums and parks, roadside markers, fond memories of grade-school history courses. There are, to be sure, competing stories, versions of Oregon's past rendered by Native Americans, other minorities, and miscellaneous naysayers—public, academic, and amateur historians. Indeed, almost any serious student of Oregon's past would grant that the historical representations at the state capitol convey an oversimplified version of the state's history. But the story of the noble and courageous founders is difficult to unhorse. Visit university courses on Oregon history and observe how readily eyes glisten at the mere mention of Lewis and Clark and the pioneers, how eager and willing well-educated Oregonians are to mouth yet again the platitudes enshrined at our state capitol.

When I ask these students to tell me what the words "Oregon history" suggest, the word "pioneers" inevitably trips off their tongues. The word, like the golden man, is larded with historical assumptions, with stories and virtues so often repeated and lovingly invoked that they constitute a deeply felt common history.

When I say, then, that my ancestors came across the Oregon Trail, most Oregonians will immediately begin filling in the blanks: They arrived in the mid-nineteenth century. They were neither rich nor poor. They came seeking a better life in the Edenic Willamette Valley that they had heard so much about. The journey was very difficult. Maybe a child or two died. But after many travails they reached and claimed their piece of paradise. The first year or two of farming was trying, but soon enough they became successful, if not wealthy. Their children and their children's children also prospered, some staying on the land that their forebears had tamed.

The truth is more complicated—and, at first glance, less flattering. Martin and Elizabeth Ripley, my mother's maternal grandparents, came from Nebraska in 1889, long after the Oregon Trail's heyday. Most immigrants then came by rail, which took a few days rather than a few months. But the Ripley family couldn't afford such extravagance. Their sandhill farm had not yielded much in the way of crops, and Martin tended to drink up what little money they had. A change of scenery might offer both better financial prospects and fewer temptations.

Martin accomplished one of these two goals. He quit drinking. Oregon improved neither his health nor his ambition. He hoped to farm but was many years too late to claim fertile land. The family eventually settled on eighty hilly and wooded acres well up the Miami River in Tillamook County, on the western slope of Oregon's coastal mountains. They planted root crops such as turnips and potatoes and harvested fruit and wild berries. One winter they were reduced to a diet of milk and potatoes. Martin occasionally earned a few dollars working on road crews or doing chores for a nearby farmer. Lizzie bore and tended eleven children. Her health, too, was poor.

Annie was one of the older girls, and her childhood ended early. She made it through only the fourth reader at school. Family tradition has it that Martin and Lizzie couldn't afford to buy her the next one. There were, in any event, babies to care for, housework to do, money to be made. Martin soon enough discovered that his ten daughters represented, if not a gold mine, at least a way to keep body and soul together without having to bestir himself. He sent them out to work in other people's homes and collected their wages. Annie secretly reserved a small portion for herself. She was not going to live this way forever. In 1907, while working at Netarts, she met a young man named Hugh Barber at a croquet game. They married a year later, in Tillamook's Methodist Episcopal Church.

Hugh was a lot like Annie. His family, too, had hoped that Oregon's rain would somehow dry out an alcoholic father. One of his most vivid childhood memories was of waiting outside Wisconsin saloons for his father to become so drunk that his companions would carry him out and load him in the wagon for the journey home to his careworn wife. Hugh's father kept right on drinking in Tillamook County, and Hugh left school long before he had wanted to so that he could support the family. Like Annie, Hugh was determined that his adulthood would be much different from his blighted childhood.

The earnest and reserved young couple succeeded where their parents had not. Hugh was a hard-working cheese maker, who arose even before Annie to build a fire and receive the milk of neighboring farmers. Annie kept house, which included raising chickens as well as four children. She and Hugh were dedicated and pious church members, respectable and industrious people not much given to mirth and frivolity. But their second child, my mother, recalls afternoon drives in the Model T and countless picnics. They subscribed to magazines and took a strong interest in their children's education. Indeed, my mother graduated from high school, went to college, and became a teacher. Annie and Hugh accomplished what

*Annie Ripley Barber
around the time of her
wedding*

every good parent yearns for: their children enjoyed a far better childhood than they had had.

But Annie never truly escaped her blighted beginnings. Her want of formal education continually embarrassed her. There were other reminders of poverty. One day, when tasting scalloped potatoes for the first time, she inexplicably burst into tears. If only her mother had known how to cook potatoes that way, she explained to a perplexed daughter, Annie's childhood might have been a bit less impoverished, her mother a bit less beleaguered.

Annie Ripley Barber died at age 47 of Bright's Disease. Her youngest son was yet a boy. She would never see most of her grandchildren.[1]

Yet this woman profoundly influenced the lives of descendants who never knew her. Her obsession with education, which her husband shared, certainly took root. Their twelve grandchildren include teachers, social workers, and ministers. She also contributed to my mother's, my siblings', and my own cautiousness, to our collective sense that things could certainly and easily become a lot worse than they are—especially if we start to think otherwise. We are temperate people well schooled at deferring gratification.

Like all parents, Annie shaped the personalities and proclivities of her children and her children's children, by accident and design. She has also, as I've studied her life, taught me about the nature of Oregon history, that beneath the mythic, golden veneer of flawless pioneers teem lives that are far more messy and compelling and even, I would argue, more noble.

Growing up on the banks of the Lewis and Clark River, just a mile and a half from Fort Clatsop, as I did, ought to have been sufficient to forever obscure that insight, that gift from the grandmother who died a quarter century before her second daughter birthed me. The Astoria area was and is still suffused with references to heroic seekers: the peerless explorers who had wintered so close to my home, of course, but also Captain Robert Gray, credited with discovering the Columbia River, and the Astorians, who established the settlement that bore their name in 1811, long before even the Whitmans came to the Oregon Country. I was raised in a land of mythic giants.

But these giants made but little impression on the daily warp and woof of my life. Their names, to be sure, were everywhere. But none of these restless men left much of a mark on the land. The Fort Clatsop replica's artifice was all too patent: it looked exactly as if it had been fashioned in an airport hangar by some people who had a lot of time and power tools at their disposal. I could not and cannot discern in it the hands of sodden, exhausted men desperate to get out of the rain, men who must have sworn and spat and yelled like my father did when he was out of sorts. The Lewis and Clark Expedition didn't stay here long enough to much occupy even an archaeologist. They were, in a sense, tourists—which is why, I suppose, Seaside is so determined to establish itself as the end of the Lewis and Clark Trail.

Replica of Fort Clatsop, south of Astoria. The Lewis and Clark Expedition wintered near this spot in 1805-06 in a less polished set of buildings. Photo from the Historic Photograph Collections, Salem (Oregon) Public Library

But if the explorers' tracks were ephemeral, the same could not be said for those who had come before and after. My friend Brent Seppa, who lived a mile or so upriver, found arrowheads and other stone tools left behind by Native peoples who had lived for millennia upon the land his family now farmed. Many years later I ran across an archaeological report of a dig just a few feet away from where I used to beach my rowboat when I crossed the river to play baseball or football at his house. Countless long bus rides to and from Lewis and Clark Consolidated School took me every day past artifacts that were more manifest and recent: a tar-encrusted water tower that had once fed logging trains; rusting farm equipment that never moved on fields that had gone to seed; a rotting footbridge high above the Lewis and Clark River that could barely support its own weight; low, metallic mink ranches that sat empty. The green, wet valley was suffused by history, though not the sort that anyone wrote about or celebrated.

Mythic history oversimplifies and obscures the past. My maternal great-grandfathers were pioneers of sorts, but not particularly heroic ones. They evidently spent more time with a bottle or a pipe in their hands than an ax. Lewis and Clark, to be sure, were noble and hard working. But did they really determine the course of Oregon's history? My childhood bus rides suggested that the Lewis and Clark Valley had been more profoundly shaped by shifts in technology and global markets than by the people whose names it bore.

There is, of course, enough room in this book for people both obscure and famous, for the history of transportation, logging, and agriculture *and* the history of exploration. Indeed, most of its short biographies are of prominent Oregonians. But this book, more than most state histories, is concerned with the events and especially the processes that most profoundly affected the everyday lives of ordinary people.

Historians of a particular place—be it a town, a state, a province, or a region—are understandably tempted to emphasize the historical developments that made and make that place distinctive. This is a temptation that I have generally tried to resist. In the first place, these developments almost always turn out to be much less peculiar than one had thought. Some residents of the Pacific Northwest, for example, tout salmon as the region's defining characteristic. Historian John Findlay points out that the same species makes itself at home in much of Russia, surely a very different place from Washington and Oregon.[2] A second and even more important reason for not emphasizing the purported uniqueness of a given place is that one is apt then to overlook the many ways in which it has been shaped by national or global forces. Should we ignore the impact of the automobile in Oregon because it also spread across the rest of the U.S.? Of course not. Automobility constituted one of the most influential developments in Oregon history, and we can't hope to explain even the broad outlines of the state's history without examining it.

This is not to say that the history of Oregon is simply the same as the history of any other place. But we cannot hope to understand much of the state's past if we are only interested in its purported peculiarities.

We must also acknowledge that "Oregon" is something of a fiction. For millennia Native peoples managed just fine without it. Indeed, many peoples, such as the Nez Perce, straddled what would one day become the boundaries between two or three states. Such complexities did not disappear with the arrival of non-Indians. "Oregon" at first referred to a vast, ill-defined extent of land west of the Rockies, north of Spanish America, and south of Russian America. Hence Chapters One and Two of this book sometimes refer to events that occurred in the "Oregon Country," but outside of what is now Oregon. After the boundary settlement with England in 1846, "Oregon" included what is now Idaho and Washington. By the close of the 1850s the state had assumed its current configuration. But its boundaries obscured significant climatic, economic, social, cultural, and political divisions. Those living east of the Cascades, west of the Coast Range, or south of Eugene have often pointed out that both popular and scholarly interpretations of the state have centered on the Willamette Valley and Portland. Life elsewhere has been, as we shall see, quite a bit different. Residents of southern Oregon (technically southwestern Oregon) have gone so far as to ponder seceding from the state altogether to work out their destiny in common with a region with which they feel much more affinity: northern California.

Why, then, even bother to attempt a history of a particular place when the boundaries seem so permeable and contrived, its development so conditioned by external forces?

For two reasons: because all history has to start somewhere and because place still matters. One cannot simply study national, let alone global, trends. The examples one uses are inevitably plucked from particular locales. Yes, a history of Oregon may tell us as much about the history of transportation as about the history of Oregon. But that is a strength, not a weakness. Indeed, one of the great benefits of local or state history is that people's intense interest in that place can connect them to larger historical developments. When reading about the career of Oregon's leading senator, Charles McNary, for example, I found myself learning diplomatic history—not a topic that I often choose to explore. Why are most Oregonians more interested in the career of McNary than of, say, Henry Cabot Lodge? Because McNary was one of ours, because the boundaries that humans so arbitrarily impose on the landscape have weight, have power.

Many Oregonians have made the state a key part of our identity. Having grown up in the extreme northwest corner of Oregon from the late 1950s to the mid-1970s, I have some firsthand knowledge of Oregon chauvinism. My parents took me to Washington about as often as they took me to the moon, even after the bridge replaced the ferry. But we traveled far and wide to the south and east. I recall deer hunting in south-central and northeastern Oregon. I remember trips to Oregon Caves, near (but not over!) the California border, Crater Lake, and Crescent Lake and backpacking near Mt. Jefferson and in the Strawberry Mountains south of John Day. I don't recall ever going to Ilwaco, Washington, a drive that would have taken about half an hour. Going to the beach always meant going to an Oregon beach. It wasn't that my parents had anything against Washington. But they were Oregonians. My father occasionally shared his memories of a cold childhood in North Dakota, where his family lived until shortly after the influenza pandemic of 1919 killed a younger sister. "Every spring they had a big poker game," he'd recall. "The winner got to go to Oregon."

Did the Dakotans of my father's childhood really favor Oregon over all other states? Was and is Oregon really much different from Washington? Does the state have a singular identity that definitively sets it apart from other places? Of course not. But many Oregonians— my father among them—have tried to believe or pretend otherwise. And that belief has, in fact, helped to make Oregon more distinctive than it would otherwise be.

I share my father's prejudices. I have tried several times to leave the state. Academics and other professionals are routinely told that place doesn't matter, that income, vocation, or the life of the mind is everything. But I've returned to Oregon six times now. I, of course, know that Oregon is not really superior to other places. But it seems so to me. It is a place where my child can grow up knowing his grandparents and aunts and uncles and cousins, a place where I can regularly see my gentle mother. Being close to kin is profoundly important. But Oregon is a place, too. The ground on one side of the "Welcome to Oregon" signs seems different from and more familiar than the ground on the other side.

Ultimately, then, the history of Oregon matters to Oregonians not because the state is much better than or even much different from other states, other places. It matters because we believe that it matters, because Oregonians care about where we live. Oregon is our home—either because we were born here and chose to stay or return, or because we decided to come here.

A great temptation, seldom resisted, when studying the history of a place and a people dear to one's heart is to celebrate them. To criticize the history of one's home, after all, is to imply a criticism of oneself. Such criticism also robs us of our desire to imagine or construct a past in which times were simpler, people nobler. Oregonians are particularly prone to romanticize our past, I think, because the leading protagonists, "the pioneers," were rather ordinary people whom we like to assume were therefore virtuous.

But mythic, uncritical history impoverishes and distorts both our past and our present. Learning that my grandfather beat my father so badly that my grandmother feared for his life has given me a much better understanding of and respect for my father than I would otherwise possess. Such events ought to sadden, not disable, us. History and experience alike reveal that people are deeply flawed. Pretending otherwise only makes matters worse, and history provides a venue in which to understand our contemporary lives, not to lament or escape them. True patriots are therefore more interested in improving their society or nation than in celebrating them. To care about a place entails building on its strengths and identifying and remedying its weaknesses. I hope that this history of the state that I love will help us to make it a better place to live.

Before plunging ahead I would remind the reader that what follows is in no way a definitive history of this state. The historical record is irrevocably fragmented and incomplete. At the same time, those fragments are so numberless that a historian working for a lifetime in even so small a place as Oregon could not hope to capture but a small fraction of them. That capturing, moreover, must and should entail interpretation, the imposition of some sort of order on a welter of facts and events and processes that would otherwise amount to a procession of tiresome and disconnected minutiae.

My interpretation of Oregon history—the analytical thread that will, I hope, order the succession of topics that you are about to read—entails returning once more to the golden pioneer.

The man with the ax obscures at least as much as he reveals about Oregon history. He does not suggest much about the experiences of people of color, women, children, or settlers who were not especially industrious. He is very much dated. He knows nothing of railroads and automobiles, let alone lattes and microchips.

But the state's dominant historical image speaks to Oregon's possibilities as well as its limitations. We celebrate the pioneers in part because they represent a democratic urge. The golden figure atop the state capitol is not, after all, a king, a general, a governor. He has no name. He is just a man—one of thousands of men who came to Oregon determined to make a better life for themselves and their families. They did so, more often than not, without benefit of slaves or indentured servants. Their only tools were the crude ones they carried in their hands—the axe, the gun, the plow. Their story still resonates so richly not simply because we are nostalgic for simpler times, but because we hope that those times have not passed us by, that ordinary people can still, through honest hard work, fashion a good life in this good state.

This is of course a variation on the promise of the West, which is a variation on the promise of America. The American dream is ultimately about freedom, about opportunity. The American West represents that dream squared: fresh starts in an open, pristine landscape and few constraints from government or the heavy hand of tradition.

But Oregon's version of the western or American dream has been relatively restrained. Here growth has been less explosive, people less apt to come and go. We have been less ambitious, less relentless than residents of Washington, let alone California. In a region and nation prone to extremes, Oregon has represented a more moderate vision of what constitutes success.

As the state capitol's monumental art suggests, that vision has excluded many people and peoples. Oregon hardly seemed very promising to Native Americans forced onto reservations, African-Americans excluded by law, nineteenth-century women's rights advocates, Asian-Americans run out of their homes, Latinos denied decent living conditions, or gays and lesbians. Yet many of these "outsiders" have, like Abigail Scott Duniway or William Naito, insisted on making themselves at home here, have persevered in enriching the lives of all Oregonians.

This treatment of the state's past will, of course, consider many people and developments, not all of them very closely related to each other. But at the heart of this book is an examination of Oregon's promise and the extent to which its residents have succeeded in realizing it.

Chapter One

Natives and Newcomers

To the early 1840s

"What kind of food are we going to have?"
Kamukamts to Gopher

The indigenous peoples depicted in the public art at Oregon's state capitol are backdrops. This commonly held view of Native Americans implies a sort of timelessness, as if Oregon history did not begin until pink-skinned people arrived. One is left with the impression that those who had been living here for thousands of years had been marking time, waiting patiently, generation after generation, for Gray, Lewis and Clark, and the Whitmans to show up so that they could at last watch something interesting happen.

Scholars have perpetuated this view. Many draw a thick, impermeable line between the history of people who wrote things down and people who committed them to memory. Historians have studied the former, anthropologists the latter. Historians tend to emphasize progress: change and dynamism. Anthropologists tend to stress continuity, and for many decades they followed Franz Boas in attempting to capture before it was too late the essence of cultures thought to have been static. Indeed, we often refer to the vast period of time before contact in the Americas as "prehistory," a term that connotes a sort of timeless emptiness.

Much is lost when we treat the indigenous and Euro-American peoples of what is now Oregon as if they were separate species. Written records or no, a great deal transpired in the many millennia between Native and Caucasian discoveries of the land now known as Oregon. To be sure, the great majority of this history is unrecoverable (as is most of any people's lives). But archeology and oral tradition have much to tell us about these societies. Documentary historical evidence also reveals that they neither disappeared nor crumbled upon contact, that they maintained political, social, and cultural autonomy for many decades after the first explorers arrived. Contact with ambitious explorers and traders neither began nor ended the history of Native peoples in the Oregon Country.

11

First Peoples

Water covered everything when Kamukamts's canoe came to rest on the roof of Pocket Gopher's lodge. Kamukamts went down into the house and conferred with Gopher. "You had better be thinking of what is the best thing to do," he remarked. "What kind of food are we going to have?" Gopher opened his mouth, and fish, roots, and berries poured out.

Later that night, while Kamukamts slept, Gopher burrowed into the lake bottom and created hills and mountains that broke the lake's surface. The next day Kamukamts decided that elk, deer, bears, and mountain lions would live in the mountains, and that several peoples would live among them. He created singular objects for each: tules for the Klamath, obsidian for the Paiute, marble for the Shasta.

Then Kamukamts saw smoke, smoke from the fires of the humans Kamukamts had created. The two listened. They heard talking and laughter and the sounds of children playing. The people were here.[1]

This is an abbreviated Klamath Indian creation account. Like many other stories from across North America it depicts people coming out of the earth itself.

The Cascade Mountains have constituted the key geographic and cultural divide in Oregon for thousands of years. Map by A. Jon Kimerling from Atlas of the Pacific Northwest, published by Oregon State University Press

Archaeologists offer an account that is less evocative, more global and scientific. Here is their creation story.

Hominids in Africa began fashioning stone tools roughly two million years ago. *Homo sapiens*—creatures with the same physiology as modern-day humans—appeared about a hundred thousand years ago. They spread across much of the "Old World" in the coming millennia, to what we know as the Middle East, Europe, and Asia. Some thirty to forty thousand years ago hunter-gatherers moved north onto the Arctic plains of Siberia, where they found an abundance of big game animals such as mammoths and musk oxen.

Then, about twenty-five thousand years ago, the world's climate changed—with profound consequences for a vast extent of unpopulated land that would one day be known as the Americas. Sea levels fell as more and more of the earth's water was bound up in massive ice sheets. The receding oceans exposed land that had been underwater, including Beringia, a vast stretch of ground that connected what is now eastern Siberia and western Alaska. The hunter-gatherers followed the large animals they hunted into a New World.

Some eleven thousand years after the seas had fallen, they rose, and Beringia again slipped beneath the sea about fourteen thousand years ago. The hunter-gatherers who had entered the New World were now cut off from their counterparts in Asia, Europe, and Africa.

This isolation brought certain advantages. The people were hardy; they had survived long journeys through a harsh, arctic environment. They encountered few diseases in their new home and soon fanned out across the two continents.

Isolation also brought disadvantages. These peoples were isolated from technological developments in Asia, Europe, and Africa. Europeans would adapt navigation and military technology from the Chinese. The Coos and the Klamath could not. They were also handicapped by the relatively narrow range of fauna of their continents. Peoples of the Old World domesticated oxen and horses, with profound ramifications for agriculture and warfare. Peoples of the New World had no cattle or horses at hand: they domesticated a much smaller and less useful animal: the dog.

Even Native peoples' relative freedom from infectious diseases would prove disastrous. They escaped the horrible plagues that Europeans suffered through during the Middle Ages. But these horrors were only deferred and magnified when Europeans carrying smallpox, measles, and other diseases began spreading them in the late fifteenth century. Europeans were by then more resistant to these afflictions;

Native peoples were not. For them, the cruelties of conquest and colonization would be inextricably bound up with the still more horrible visitations of deadly enemies that they could neither see nor fight.

But all of this lay many generations in the future when the first people walked or paddled into what would one day be known as Oregon. It is impossible to date their arrival with any precision. Earthquakes and tsunamis would wash away coastal villages, and debris borne by immense floods cover the early archeological record of the temperate Willamette Valley. Certainly by 11,500 years ago people were in much of Oregon. Clovis points—named after the New Mexican town near which many were found—date from around that period, and Clovis points have been found across the state.

Clovis points suggest much about the lives of the big-game hunters, the Paleo-Indians who crafted and wielded them. The carefully wrought projectile points were roughly nine centimeters (three inches) long and fashioned from fine-grained, rare rocks such as chalcedony or obsidian and then hafted onto wooden spears. These peoples lived in small, mobile groups and derived much of their sustenance from roving herds of mammoths, giant bison, and other large mammals. That these animals were common across the Americas meant that the first peoples of what would become Oregon lived in much the same way as did their counterparts in what would become Delaware or northern British Columbia or the Yucatan Peninsula. But this would soon change.

Large mammals became extinct about eleven thousand years ago, evidently due to some combination of overhunting and climate change. The disappearance of these huge, relatively accessible packages of proteins, fats, and amino acids meant that peoples had to pay much greater attention to the remaining fauna and flora of their particular locale. It no longer made sense to roam so widely and boldly, for a group's well-being now depended on a finely detailed knowledge of the specific fish, mammals, berries, roots, and other plants with whom they shared their home. A deep sense and knowledge of place took root among the many peoples who spread across the diverse landscape of what would many generations later constitute the state of Oregon. On this point the indigenous and scientific creation stories converge: Native peoples were deeply rooted to particular places.

Diverse Societies

The diverse environment of what would one day be Oregon profoundly shaped the nature of its new societies. This was nowhere more obvious than in the arid Great Basin that covered the southeastern quarter of what would become Oregon, as well as Nevada, Utah, and parts of several other western states.

This was not a lush landscape, and the climate was harsh, the temperatures extreme. Food of any sort was scarce, its appearance often unpredictable. The Great Basin demanded that its residents practice flexibility, that they utilize many foods. Well-worn millstones used to break open and process seeds testify to the importance of that source. Wada seeds were especially useful. The people also gathered and stored blue camas and several varieties of roots and berries. Crickets constituted a high-protein, easily preserved food. Elk, deer, antelope, and smaller game such as water fowl and rabbits were available, and fish. Human scat from thousands of years ago found at the Dirty Shame Rockshelter near the state's southeast corner exhibit an extraordinarily diverse menu: crayfish, molluscs, fish, small rodents, antelope, sunflower and goosefoot seeds, wild rose, cherry, prickly pear, sego lily, and wild onion. One could ill afford to count on just a few foodstuffs in such a demanding and capricious environment.

Finding food demanded travel. Winters were typically spent at a single spot, consuming the fruits of last season's labors while hunting for available game. Spring brought the onset of a long round of visits to various gathering, hunting, and fishing camps. Archeologists have reconstructed the movements of some bands from several thousand years ago. They wintered in the vicinity of present-day Burns. In April they walked east, to a root camp in the Harney Valley, near Stinkingwater Pass. Then men and later women went to the Malheur River's headwaters to catch and dry salmon. In late spring the blue camas near Malheur Lake was ready. Summer brought dispersal as people fanned out to gather and process crickets, hunt game, and pick berries. In late August they harvested the wada seeds of Malheur Lake. The fall brought more organized hunts for deer, antelope, and rabbit. This was also the time to collect pine seeds. It would soon be the lean part of the year again, time to return to winter camp, This seasonal round might be accompanied by less predictable moves: to lakes laden with fish during relatively moist years and to higher, plant-rich elevations during more arid periods.

This flexibility created a particular sort of society. Population density was, by necessity, low; the land simply could not support many people. The premium placed on adaptability encouraged small groups. Though women and men here, as elsewhere, performed different tasks, Great Basin society featured few if any social distinctions. No one could amass much wealth or command the labor of others.

The peoples of the lower Columbia River and the Pacific coast were very different from their counterparts in the Great Basin. They were part of an unusual culture that stretched from Yakutat Bay in what is now Alaska to northern California. Northwest Coast peoples maintained densely populated societies without benefit of agriculture. They enjoyed a variety of advantages: a mild climate, great stands of cedar that could be fashioned into massive canoes, and an assortment of fish, shellfish, other marine life, plants, and mammals. But the most important resource by far was salmon.

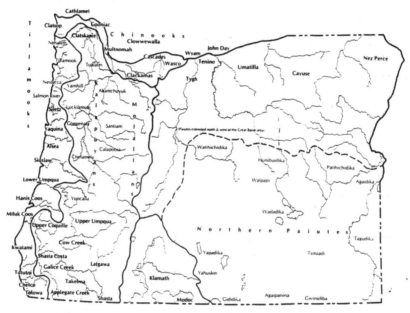

The land that would become Oregon hosted a variety of indigenous nations and cultures. Reprinted from Jeff Zucker, Kay Hummel, and Bob Hogfoss, Oregon Indians: Culture, History, and Current Affairs (Portland: Oregon Historical Society Press, 1983), p. 9. © 1983, Western Imprints, The Press of the Oregon Historical Society. Reprinted with permission.

These Indian artifacts were found near Fairfield in Marion County. Native peoples utilized many types of stone to acquire and process their food. Photo from Historic Photograph Collections, Salem (Oregon) Public Library

Salmon runs were predictable and rich, particularly on the lower Columbia River. Every year countless salmon left the ocean for their riverine spawning grounds, and every year Natives set up camps at strategic locations where the huge fish were apt to tarry, such as waterfalls and rapids. The fish were not hard to find. Some streams were choked with them. Scholars estimate that the average resident of the lower Columbia or coast ate about 365 pounds of salmon a year, a pound a day.

The relative ease with which these people could feed themselves shaped their culture. Like their counterparts to the southeast, they had a seasonal round, but it seldom took them far from their villages. The resources of the estuaries on which they lived were so bountiful and diverse that they did not need to travel far to eat. The ease with which food could be procured allowed more time for ritual and trade. It also created social distinctions. A wealthy man might have several wives, even some slaves. Natives of the Northwest Coast were by far the most status-conscious residents on the north Pacific slope.

Natives who lived on the upper Columbia and its tributaries, on the plateau, created societies that in many respects stood between those of the Northwest Coast and the Great Basin. This culture group stretched from Klamath Lake to the south well up into what would be British Columbia to the north.

Salmon was a key food source. Work groups fanned out from villages of pithouses to fish along the region's many streams. But salmon were not nearly so plentiful two or three hundred miles up the Columbia River as they were near its mouth. Residents of the plateau therefore had to rely on a broader range of foodstuffs, particularly roots and game, in a landscape that was varied but often harsh. They did not achieve the high population densities of their counterparts on the lower Columbia.

Plateau society tended to be egalitarian. It lacked the status gradations and consciousness of the Northwest Coast. Prominent people might hold slaves, but slavery was rare and comparatively mild.

The Great Basin, Northwest Coast, and Columbia Plateau peoples were part of extensive culture groups that covered much of what would become western North America. They happened to meet in what would one day be known as Oregon. In the interstices of these three large, well-defined groups resided two smaller and less-distinct ones.

The peoples of the Willamette Valley are often included as part of the Northwest Coast. They lived between the Coast and Cascade mountain ranges and enjoyed a mild climate. But the high falls near the Willamette River's mouth, where Oregon City would one day stand, kept salmon out of the valley. Its people nevertheless enjoyed a plentiful range of foodstuffs, particularly deer, elk, camas, and nuts. They encouraged the growth of these species and others through burning. Fire opened up the valley's understory and eased hunting and the gathering of acorns and tarweed seeds.

Yet the Willamette Valley's population densities did not approach those of the lower Columbia River's. Its peoples instead resembled that of the Columbia Plateau. Social relations were relatively egalitarian, slavery uncommon.

Much the same can be said of those who lived in the mountains of what would become southwestern Oregon. They relied more heavily on both salmon and acorns than did their neighbors to the north, in the Willamette Valley. But the valley bottoms were narrow, and population numbers therefore modest. These people, too, moved around a great deal, to and from the rivers to the mountains to oak groves. They, too, used fire to drive and attract game. They also maintained relatively egalitarian societies.

This panoramic overview of these five culture areas suggests that these peoples' lives were historically static. They were not.

We have already addressed perhaps the most important change: from an economy based largely on large mammals to one based on a much wider range of less-mobile foodstuffs. This shift led to more cultural and social diversity between various peoples. Most became more sedentary and socially stratified.

We also know that the peoples in what would become Oregon suffered several catastrophic disasters. The most dramatic of these was a series of floods that thundered down the Columbia River late in the ice age. The warming climate caused ice and snow to melt high in the Rocky Mountains. These meltwaters backed up behind and eventually burst immense ice dams. The floods scoured out the scablands of what is now eastern Washington before rushing down the Columbia River Gorge. The waters were deep enough to cover Crown Point, approximately five hundred feet above the river's normal level today, just east of the Sandy River's mouth, and to wash large boulders up the Willamette River nearly a hundred miles. The last of these floods occurred about thirteen thousand years ago. Any people living in the Columbia or Willamette valleys surely perished.

Global warming also affected peoples living on the Pacific coast. The sea level rose three to four hundred feet in the several thousand years after the ice age ended. The Oregon coast did not reach its present appearance until about four thousand years ago. Most of the changes occurred gradually, giving coastal residents ample time to move their villages inland. But several offshore earthquakes and accompanying tidal waves suddenly submerged portions of the coast, sweeping away villagers and their villages, burying rich ecosystems under the ocean's waves or tons of sand.

Deposit of ash from the eruption of Mount Mazama. Photo courtesy Oregon Historical Society, OrHi 80006.

East of the Cascades, the eruption of Mount Mazama (creating what we know as Crater Lake) some seventy-six hundred years ago brought extensive change to what is now central Oregon. Six inches of ash and pumice fell, fouling streams and lakes and choking fish and plants. Toxic fumes and acid rain poisoned the environment. Flora and fauna eventually recovered, of course, but to this day the region's plant life is less diverse than it was before the mountain exploded.

Most ecological changes have been more gradual—but no less profound. The world's climate continued to warm after the ice age ended. Some massive bodies of water vanished entirely. Today the trained eye can discern the shorelines of ancient lakes hundreds of feet above the floor of the Great Basin. Then, four to five thousand years ago, the climate again cooled, though not as dramatically as in the ice age.

Native peoples could not change the weather. But they could adapt to it. The area around Mount Mazama was less rich after the mountain exploded, and people therefore used it less intensively. The cooler climate that arrived in what is now southern Oregon some four thousand years ago encouraged the advance of conifers at the expense of more varied forests composed of grasslands, oak, and pine, an ecosystem that was rich in plant and animal life. Natives may have used fire to encourage the survival of oak and pines (which were fire resistant) and to stave off the arrival of the more sterile Douglas and white fir forests that otherwise would have advanced with the cooler climates.

People east and west of the Cascades alike created technologies that helped them to more successfully manipulate their environments. The bow and arrow appeared two to three thousand years ago and supplanted the atlatl, a modified spear. The new tool improved both velocity and accuracy and could accommodate smaller projective points used to hunt birds and other small game. Coastal peoples learned how to utilize a broader range of foods and to preserve some more effectively, changes that permitted population growth.

Salmon preservation began at least twenty-five hundred years ago. Natives around The Dalles became particularly proficient at drying salmon on massive racks. Salmon pemmican, packed into baskets, might last for several years and offered an extremely high nutrition-to-weight ratio. This technology rendered the succulent and nutritious fish many times more durable and portable. Salmon pemmican helped make The Dalles the greatest trade center of the north Pacific slope. From roughly fifteen hundred years ago until well into the nineteenth century, people from much of North America came to trade hides, various foodstuffs, obsidian, hemp, slaves, a variety of luxury items, and much, much more for salmon and other products of the mid-Columbia River.

The political histories of these peoples are much more difficult to trace than their dietary and trade patterns. We can of course identify the groups that existed at the time of contact with Euro-Americans: the northern Paiute of the Great Basin; the Umatilla, Cayuse, Nez Perce, and Klamath of the Columbia Plateau; some two dozen peoples on the lower Columbia and coast, including the Wasco, Clatsop, Tillamook, and Coos; various Kalapuyan peoples in the Willamette Valley, such as the Tualatin and Santiam; and the Takelma, Shasta, and others in the mountainous country of what would become southwestern Oregon. People living in what would become Oregon spoke nearly two dozen languages by the time of contact with whites.

But these labels suggest a fixed or common history often at odds with how Native people actually lived. Most Native peoples thought of themselves as members of particular villages and lineages, not "tribes." The political and economic units were small—seldom more than a few hundred people and often far less. Intermarriage softened the boundaries between various peoples, and the geographic boundaries between groups were of course subject to changes wrought by war and ill or good fortune.

The reader will by now, I hope, have gained some appreciation for the diversity of societies and cultures which for thousands of years flourished in what now is Oregon. Those societies changed over time as the flora and fauna that surrounded them changed and their technologies improved. Settlements on the Columbia Plateau, for example, became more dense and stratified as people learned how to more effectively harvest camas and preserve salmon. They also differed by place. Peoples living in the Great Basin at the time of the American Revolution lived in tiny willow-frame houses, enjoyed egalitarian social relations, and foraged across great, arid expanses for a wide variety of foodstuffs. Their counterparts along the lower Columbia resided in elaborate, cedar-plank houses that might stretch more than a hundred feet. Their societies were much more stratified, and they traveled not to eat, but to conduct trade and war.

Yet these peoples also shared much in common. Like all peoples, they depended utterly on the landscape to feed, clothe, and shelter them. More so than the Caucasians that they would soon encounter, they realized and dwelled upon that dependence.

Approaching the Environment

Native peoples did not imagine that they enjoyed control or dominion over the rest of creation. Indeed, the lines between human, animal, and noncorporeal spirits were often vague and permeable. A Wasco story, for example, tells of how a boy who was mending a canoe with his father slipped away and joined a group of seals. His people managed to retrieve him, and his parents slowly succeeded in getting him to eat foods other than raw fish and to talk again. He said that the seals were just like humans, that "they moved from place to place, camped at night." Indeed, the seals had not forgotten him and came near him when they could. His parents tried to keep him from seeing his old companions, but one day he threw off the cover they had put over his head, called the seals by name, and leaped from the canoe. He resurfaced far away, assuring his mother and father that "I have a home down in the water."[2]

By the same token, animals and other entities could assume human form. A Klamath story recounts how a monster devoured a woman's child and then "substituted himself in the cradle board." The mother suspected the trick only when the monster battened onto her breast when she suckled it and would not let go.[3]

A world in which one's nursing child might be an insatiable monster was neither safe nor predictable. Everything had power, had agency: monsters, deceased ancestors, animals, rocks and trees, places. Many of these potent entities were indifferent or hostile to a human's plight. Survival—let alone success—depended on one's ability to propitiate and manipulate an extraordinarily complex maze of beings. Shamans were men and often women skilled at negotiating with and within this unseen world, at driving away disease or other misfortunes. But everyone needed to pay close attention to the spirit world. A common rite of passage for youths was to spend several days or more in isolated fasting, seeking a spiritual sponsor who would protect him or her during adulthood.

Seeking and respecting the spirit world was an ongoing process and profoundly shaped how Native peoples approached their environment. A Tututni story recounts how the creator instructed the first man "not to cut down more trees or kill more animals than he needed."[4] Horrible, tragic results visited people who ignored this commandment. An elk promised to be the "guardian spirit" of a Wasco boy and "help you in every necessity" if the boy would "serve me," act humbly, and not kill more than he needed. The young man soon became a fine hunter. But his father scolded him for not doing better. The hunter responded by killing five herds of elk—far more than his people required. Then the guardian-spirit elk, angry at the father and son, went into a lake and feigned death. The young hunter, not knowing who this elk was, tried to pull him out and instead sank with him to the bottom of the lake. There he saw innumerable bear, deer, and elk, all of them in human form. Those whom he had killed were groaning. His master "the great Elk," scolded him for inflicting "many needless wounds on our people" and told him that he would no longer be his guardian spirit.

The young man went home. He asked his two wives to fix his bed. He lay in it for five days and five nights. Then he told the people what had happened. "The spirit has left me," he concluded, "and I die."[5] It was, as folklorist Jarold Ramsey observes: "A terrible fate, indeed, to be rejected by the very source of one's accustomed psychic vitality, … analogues in Christian terms to loss of the soul and in psychological terms to loss of ego."[6]

Native peoples required the flesh of deer, salmon, and many other powerful creatures whom they could not afford to offend. A Modoc prayer to a slain animal described the deceased as "our friend" and asked its relations to also offer up their lives to humans.[7] Animals were not apt to make such offerings unless the people who hunted them followed prescribed rituals. A northern Paiute recalled how his father walked him through these observances after he had killed a deer. They hung the carcass carefully. The son then removed his clothes and beads before carefully stepping in and out of a wooden ring. His father continued moving the ring over his body, calling "all kinds of game—goose, swan, mountain sheep, bear, elk, and otter."[8] The ritual would make the boy successful in hunting, the father explained. The boy was by now eager to eat the meat from the deer. But his father said that he must wait another day.

Rituals were especially complex around the taking of salmon. Such an extraordinary gift demanded great respect and care. A Coos story described how the salmon sent a tidal wave to a village in which some boys had dishonored a fish by using it to play a trick on a younger boy. A story from the Columbia River's mouth recounted how even Coyote labored to master the complex fishing rituals at Neacoxie Creek, that the first annual silver-side salmon at that spot must be split and roasted, not cut and steamed, that a certain number of spits had to be employed and the gills burned, that all the fish that one caught must be roasted before one could sleep. The laborious lesson had to be repeated many times. Each species and place demanded particular rituals, and a myriad of customs also stipulated when one could fish, who could fish and eat, and how the non-edible remains were to be disposed of.

Modern-day preservationists often celebrate North American Native peoples as the original nature lovers. This well-intentioned compliment is somewhat off the mark. "Fear played as strong a role as reverence," points out Joseph Taylor in his fine history of salmon fishing.[9] These peoples' approach to the nonhuman environment reflected not simply a deep affinity for animals and plants. It expressed a realization that the animals and plants were essential and therefore dangerous entities that both sustained and threatened life. Traditional indigenous understandings of nature offer little succor to the more sentimental strains of environmentalism. They instead support approaches to the environment that begin with the realization that we are utterly reliant upon it, that appreciating nature ought to mean appreciating that our well-being is entirely bound up in its well-being.

Society

Native people's social relations also emphasized dependency. Kin relations were dense. Ties of birth, marriage, and ceremony placed each individual in a complex web of mutual obligations.

The individual therefore counted for little. It is very difficult for those of us raised in modern western societies to fathom these peoples' perspectives. We are prone to ask questions such as how much individual autonomy Native people enjoyed, or whether Native women were equal to Native men. Native peoples were in some respects highly autonomous. Parents rarely punished their children, and western legal sanctions such as jails did not exist. Individuals had considerable discretion in how they might act. But these acts occurred within a context of intense social scrutiny, and individuals who acted without considering the welfare of the group as a whole risked ostracism, a sort of death when one's physical and social survival depended on the group to which one belonged.

This orientation toward the group certainly shaped gender relations. Scholars disagree sharply on the nature of these relations. On the one hand, men generally filled leadership positions and expressed considerable fear that menstruating women might offend some potent spirit. Husbands were more apt to beat their wives than vice versa, and gender roles did not much overlap. On the other hand, formal leadership positions did not count for much when leaders enjoyed little authority, masculine fears of menstruation might simply have expressed men's recognition of women's power, and husbands' rights to hit wives were generally constrained to situations in which the wife was suspected of jeopardizing the group's lineage by committing adultery. Specialized gender roles did not necessarily mean that women's work was less important than men's. Indeed, some scholars have argued that women's control over many aspects of food gathering and production lent them considerable power. Some Native peoples reckoned descent through fathers (patrilineal), but others reckoned it through the mother (matrilineal). Women in some societies, including the Clatsop and the Klamath, moved to their husbands' group upon marriage (patrilocal) and lived among strangers, but in others, such as the northern Paiute, it was the young men who had to leave home upon marrying.

In sum, gender roles varied considerably among Native peoples, and that it would be misleading to label their societies as either matriarchal or patriarchal. Modern-day concepts of equality and opportunity were foreign to people who were much more concerned about the welfare of the group than the freedom of the individual.

This is not to say that Native people were without social distinctions. Leading Clatsop men along the lower Columbia, in particular, were apt to have more than one wife and to enjoy substantial prestige and property, including slaves and rights to particular fishing sites. But custom dictated that much of this wealth be distributed to others. Indeed, the rituals surrounding young people's first gatherings or killings often required that they give the food away. Individual and corporate welfare could not be easily separated. The presence of slaves did not contradict this emphasis on the common good, for slaves, by definition, were outsiders, people captured from and often by other peoples.

Oral tradition underscores and illustrates this group orientation. "Little Racoon and His Grandmother," a Wasco account, describes the plight of a spoiled boy. One day young racoon refused to eat anything that his grandmother offered: wapato, jerky, dried fish eyes. The exasperated woman ordered him to find his own dinner—and to stay out of the acorns that she had stored for the winter. The grandson of course found himself at the pits where the acorns were stored and proceeded to eat all of them, replacing them with his dung. His grandmother discovered the trick and whipped him. Little raccoon sought refuge in nearby villages but was met with jeers for having cheated his grandmother. Who would want to live with such a child! Meanwhile, the indulgent grandmother's heart had softened, and she sought the ostracized boy. But her grandson had grown resentful, and when his famished grandmother found him he fed her twigs instead of serviceberries. She cried out for water, but he poked holes in the hat he carried the water in until she at last turned into a scolding blue jay. "Little Raccoon just sat down and cried; it was all his fault."[10] He was utterly alone. This was what came of not obeying your elders and of thinking of yourself first.

Not many modern-day Oregonians would feel much at home or at ease in these profoundly conservative societies, among people who placed the good of the group above that of the individual and who were more concerned with maintaining social harmony and ecological balance than in seeking wealth. But these peoples met their goals. Particular political or even cultural groups no doubt expired or transformed into others. But the people themselves persisted, generation after generation, for hundreds of generations and more than ten thousand years, through floods and eruptions and famines and other events large and small. They still persist today. But events in other parts of the eighteenth-century world were about to usher in a series of catastrophes from which Oregon's Native peoples are still recovering.

Premonitions and First Encounters

Non-indigenous peoples began influencing the lives of the Nez Perce, the Clatsop, and other peoples long before the arrival of Captain Gray and Lewis and Clark. Columbus's landing on Hispaniola in 1492 unleashed a series of biological changes that swept across North American in the vanguard of the Caucasian newcomers. Those changes were particularly sweeping on the Columbia River Plateau.

Horses came to Mesoamerica with the Spanish conquistadores and accompanied them northward. The Pueblo Revolt of 1680 in New Mexico abetted their dispersal. They appeared on the Columbia Plateau a couple of decades later, around 1700.

The Nez Perce, Cayuse, and others quickly made use of this amazing animal. Some men owned hundreds of them. Horses facilitated travel, trade, and hunting. By the 1750s many Plateau peoples had incorporated buffalo hunting east of the Rocky Mountains, on the western Great Plains, into their subsistence rounds. Horses allowed their hunters to get across the mountains more quickly, to hunt the massive animals more effectively, and to carry home far heavier loads of meat and hides.

Horses were much less consequential in the densely forested country west of the Cascades. As the next chapter will show, they did not become important in the Great Basin until well after contact. But they brought considerable prosperity to the Nez Perce, Cayuse, and Umatilla for a century before whites arrived.

This prosperity was not evenly distributed. Unlike most other sources of wealth, horses were possessed by individuals, a fact that must have at least challenged these people's strong group orientation. Women were particularly vulnerable. Men owned the great majority of horses, and horses aided men's economic activities more than women's.

Horses certainly led to more conflict with other groups. The Cayuse were able to dominate the nearby Walla Walla and raid peoples to the west and south. But horses also made it possible for groups that had once seemed distant—such as the Blackfeet to the east and the Shoshone to the south—to conduct raids onto the plateau for horses and slaves. Some of those same peoples reacted violently when buffalo-hunting parties from the plateau crossed the Rocky Mountains.

Vulnerability to attack altered internal political relations. Residents of small villages became increasingly reliant on more powerful groups and war chiefs. Like their counterparts on the Great Plains, young men on the plateau had long used warfare as a means to exhibit their bravery and gain status. But now such men were gaining power at the expense of other people. Horses erected divisions inside and outside Plateau society.

So did the fur trade. It certainly strengthened the Plateau peoples' enemies. By the 1790s the Blackfeet were exchanging furs for guns, giving them an advantage over their more isolated counterparts on the Rocky Mountains' west slope. By the late eighteenth century, then, the Nez Perce, Cayuse, and Umatilla had become both more wealthy and more beleaguered.

Then, in the late eighteenth century, a horrible calamity visited the Columbia Plateau: an epidemic killed from one quarter to one half of the region's people. Anthropologists believe that smallpox originating with Caucasians but carried by Natives arrived from the east in the late 1770s or early 1780s and swept down the upper and lower Columbia River. (Small pox or some other infectious disease may have arrived in the land that would become Oregon in the sixteenth century. Archeologists are not yet agreed on this.)

One can hardly imagine the impact of this disease. The practical implications alone of a people losing approximately one-third of its population within a few years were dramatic. The loss rendered villages less prosperous, less strong. It disrupted families and lines of succession, for the aged and the young were especially susceptible. These tangible tragedies were compounded by psychological ones. Smallpox, in the words of Alfred Crosby, quickly reduced a healthy person "into a pustuled, oozing horror."[11]

Like most eighteenth-century people, the residents of the Columbia Plateau did not attribute such a horrible event to the vagaries of chance or science. The disease clearly demonstrated to them that something was out of balance in the cosmos, in the spirit world that controlled the sensate world. This fear was reinforced when a deep layer of ash from a volcanic eruption covered the area around the turn of the century. This "dry snow" suggested that the old circle of life was about to rupture, that unprecedented events had begun to unfold.

Indeed, the first in a long series of prophets appeared on the plateau in the late eighteenth century to announce that the world was about to end. This ending would mark the beginning of a much better era. A supernatural "chief" told the prophets that the end of time, the apocalypse, would usher in a new world in which all the people, dead and alive, would live together happily and harmoniously. Some of the prophets predicted that this transformation could not begin until the appearance of new, strange peoples.

An unidentified man holding beeswax found near Nehalem in 1955. The beeswax was in a Spanish galleon that sank in 1679. Photo from the Historic Photograph Collections, Salem (Oregon) Public Library

The Plateau peoples were therefore much excited by the arrival of the Lewis and Clark Expedition in 1805. They wondered if these were the peoples their prophets referred to—and they were cheered by the captains' promises of closer trade and the prospects of acquiring firearms.

First contacts with European organisms, tools, and people were not as dramatic in the rest of the Oregon Country. As noted, smallpox devastated Native peoples along the lower Columbia River around 1780 before moving north, to the peoples of Puget Sound. But the horrible disease apparently did not provoke the same crisis of confidence that it did farther up the Columbia, perhaps because the horse had not transformed and disturbed social and political relations along the lower Columbia. Groups living on the coast to the south of the Columbia River, in the Willamette Valley, or near the California border were evidently untouched by this first epidemic. Nor were they much disturbed by other premonitions of sustained contact. Wrecked Spanish galleons may have occasionally found their way onto Oregon beaches. Large blocks of beeswax and candles have been found near Tillamook, from those ships or from ill-fated Portuguese or Japanese vessels. But such articles hardly affected the Tillamook in the way that the horse affected the Plateau peoples.

The peoples of the coast and lower Columbia were, on the whole, pleased to encounter early explorers. The Clatsop and Chinooks at the Columbia River's mouth were especially eager to trade, as this had long been one of their primary occupations. Spanish ships landed briefly along the coast in the 1770s. Robert Gray's entry into the Columbia River in 1792 inaugurated a period of sustained and intense exchange at that place. By the time the Lewis and Clark Expedition arrived thirteen years later the Clatsop and Chinook had bartered with dozens of traders from the United States and Europe. Some could even swear in English.

Contacts in southwestern and southeastern Oregon were more fleeting and strained. Natives of the southwest interior generally treated fur traders with suspicion, if not outright hostility. Thomas McKay was turned back by Native people along the Umpqua River in 1820, the first of many clashes between whites and Natives in that area. Explorers and fur traders largely ignored Oregon's arid Great Basin.

The initial impact of European animals, diseases, and people varied dramatically. It affected some peoples hardly at all, others profoundly. But in no instance did the white newcomers simply overwhelm their hosts.

The Fur Trade

Land-based fur traders replaced maritime traders early in the nineteenth century, and in the coming decades they would shape the lives of Natives across the region.

The British North West Company in 1807 established Kutenai house on the border of what is now British Columbia and Montana. Fort Astoria, the Pacific Fur Company's ill-fated venture at the Columbia River's mouth, followed in 1811 and was soon supplanted by the North West Company, which changed the post's name to Fort George and added several smaller ones in the interior. Another British concern, the Hudson's Bay Company, took over the system in 1821.

The peoples of the lower Columbia River had been very active in the maritime trade, and they eagerly and skillfully traded at these new posts. Indeed, the Astorians and Nor'westers were often frustrated at the prices these Natives demanded—and by their success at establishing themselves as intermediaries between the whites and more distant Native groups.

The Hudson's Bay Company successfully integrated many Native groups into its trade. In 1825 it moved its headquarters upriver, to Fort Vancouver, a more central and fertile location than Fort George had provided. From there it maintained a series of smaller posts and sent out far-ranging fur brigades. The company also extended credit so that acquisitive Native people would become permanently attached to their enterprise. But many of the Oregon Country's people were not particularly acquisitive. Plateau peoples, as we have seen, desired the same access to weaponry that their enemies enjoyed. But this requirement was soon met. George Simpson, in charge of the Hudson's Bay Company's operations in North America, lamented that these Natives "are very independent of us requiring but few of our supplies." "It is not until absolutely in need of an essential article of finery such as Guns & Beads that they will take the trouble of hunting" furs, he concluded.[12] The company established several small posts in the southwestern interior and conducted several fur-gathering forays through it. Some of the region's peoples traded with these expeditions. But others attacked them.

The Hudson's Bay Company lacked the wherewithal to control the region's indigenous peoples. John McLoughlin, Fort Vancouver's Chief Factor, could order his charges to attack villages that he suspected of wrongdoing, and he could try to track down and punish particular Natives. His men killed four Clatsop and burned their village when the Natives refused to return goods they had scavenged from a shipwreck. He punished a Native who had eloped with the wife of an employee by having one of his ears cut off. But the posts of the Hudson's Bay Company were small islands of European governance in a sea of autonomous Native peoples. Hence when David Douglas, the celebrated British naturalist, resolved to beat his guide in 1826, the Native man simply ran away. McLoughlin and other whites could occasionally punish particular individuals or even groups. But they could not hope to rule them.

Nor did they need to. The Hudson's Bay Company, like the North West Company, the Pacific Fur Company, and maritime traders before them, required neither Native people's souls nor lands. Yet they deeply affected Native societies.

Perhaps the most obvious impact was environmental. People of European descent came to the north Pacific slope for one reason in the late eighteenth and early nineteenth centuries: to get furs. The sea otter expired first. Its rich, luxurious pelt had inaugurated the prolific maritime trade on the Northwest coast in the 1780s, and it was nearly extinct a quarter century later. The fur traders then moved inland, reducing the number of beaver and other fur-bearing animals across the Oregon Country, particularly in the Willamette and Snake River drainages, which the Hudson's Bay Company transformed into a "fur desert" in the 1820s to forestall the arrival of American fur traders.

Native peoples both profited and suffered from intensive trapping. Many availed themselves of the new products the trade offered and devoted much of their time to it. Along the lower Columbia River, where the trade began, the Chinook and Clatsop gained wealth, status, and power by acquiring prestigious and useful objects of European manufacture. Women's status suffered in some respects. Native men trapped the fur-bearing animals, and the tools, utensils, and clothing they traded for often replaced items that their wives had once produced. Of course females and males suffered alike from the ecological imbalance that intensive trapping brought. Every animal provided a particular bundle of provisions, and some of those provisions were becoming more scarce. More difficult to assess is the psychological or spiritual impact of an economic activity that violated traditional norms by encouraging Native people to trap as many animals as they could, rather than as many as they needed.

White traders were much less successful at convincing indigenous people to change their approach to harvesting salmon. Taylor observes that Natives "implored whites to observe rules for cutting, cooking, and eating salmon, and when they balked, Indians would intervene to preserve good standing with the fish."[13] For example, Natives traded only small amounts of salmon at any given time, a method calculated to ensure that the newcomers would not insult the fish by waiting until the following day to eat it. Some traditional practices were too sacred and crucial to be negotiated or breached.

The fur trade quickened the slave trade. Many white traders transported this lucrative human cargo up and down the coast, to people with newfound wealth to spend. Northwest Coast society had long been more stratified and status-conscious than other societies of the north Pacific slope; the fur trade made it much more so. The Modoc of south-central Oregon began trafficking in slaves in the mid-1830s, after several of them traveled to The Dalles and resolved to acquire horses. The Modoc's country was not rich in furs, so they instead acquired human beings to trade by raiding to the west and the south, by capturing Takelma, northern Paiute, and various California peoples. Like the arrival of the horse on the Columbia Plateau, the slave trade transformed relations outside and inside of Modoc society. It increased friction and warfare with other peoples, and it enhanced the status of young, aggressive males. "The younger men who had always deferred to their elders were the ones who visited The Dales, learned the Chinook jargon, and brought home new styles in clothing," observes historian Keith Murray.[14]

The fur trade spread disease along with slavery. Smallpox returned to the lower Columbia and the Plateau in 1801 and apparently in the mid-1820s. The most virulent epidemic of all erupted in the summer of 1830, when malaria appeared near Fort Vancouver, the trading post that brought people and diseases from distant places. By 1841, on the eve of extensive U.S. settlement, the Willamette Valley's number of Native people had plummeted by about 90 percent in just one decade.

Native people by now knew where such diseases came from. Indeed, the Clackamas and Kalapuya of the lower Willamette River identified two ships that had wintered in the vicinity of Fort Vancouver as the sources of the malaria epidemic of 1830. But this knowledge did not explain the deeper reasons for this horrible disease, a sickness that seldom killed the people who brought it. The epidemics spawned social disorganization and cultural malaise along with corpses.

Yet even the demographic catastrophe of epidemic diseases did not render Native peoples helpless during the fur trade. They played an active role in the creation of new societies. Fort Vancouver was the most prominent of these. Present-day visitors to the historic site are exposed largely to the lives of a handful of leading English and Scottish men who resided within the fort. Most of the post's several hundred residents lived outside its gates, in an extensive tent village that housed not only Caucasian laborers but Hawaiians, Iroquois and other Natives from eastern North America, a variety of local Natives, and a panoply of mixed-blood peoples. Intermarriage had begun in 1813, at Fort Astoria. Many marriages followed, at first to Nor'wester leaders and clerks, then to the rank and file. Soon the daughters of prominent lower Columbia Natives were more apt to marry non-Natives than Natives.

Intermarriage was not a radical departure from Native tradition. Such unions were a time-tested means of cementing relations between two groups. The daughters of prominent Chinook and Clatsop women had for many generations left home upon marriage, moving up or down the coast or inland to marry prominent men of other groups. Intermarriages with white fur traders served the same purpose: it ingratiated the bride's parents with her husband's people.

The extent to which such intermarriages benefited the Native women who participated in them is more difficult to discern. Very little historical documentation records the nature of these unions. They were apparently apt to suffer abuse from their white husbands, who could desert them if they chose to—though McLoughlin required his employees to continue supporting them. Yet it is clear that these women were not simply passive victims of their husbands' violence or indifference. Some of the traders took these unions seriously. McLoughlin himself enjoyed a long and evidently satisfying marriage to Marguerite, a Métis (half Native) from central Canada. Native women wedded to less-responsive men were not without recourse. Simpson complained that they made too many demands of their white husbands, and the husbands complained that their wives might leave them. Native women, in other words, continued to exercise their traditional prerogatives: they believed that marriage obligated wives and husbands alike and that women had a right to leave indifferent husbands.

❧ ❧

The behavior of intermarried Native women was something of a metaphor for Native societies more generally, for the fur trade did not render Native peoples dependent. To be sure, the trade and the pathogens and animals that preceded and accompanied it ushered in dramatic and in many ways devastating demographic, ecological, economic, social, and cultural changes, particularly for the peoples of the Willamette Valley, lower Columbia, and Columbia Plateau.

Native populations were much reduced. Some groups and individuals, to be sure, became much more wealthy and powerful, but often at the expense of less fortunate or ambitious peoples and people.

Yet, with the exception of the lower Willamette Valley, Native peoples remained autonomous and powerful in the early 1840s. The fur trade had dramatically increased the tempo of change after over ten thousand years of gradual transitions. But Native people were active and potent participants in the fur trade, not over-matched pawns at the mercy of such men as Simpson and McLoughlin. They continued to draw upon traditional ecological and social beliefs in making their way through this thicket of unprecedented challenges and choices.

But their task would soon become more difficult. The balance of power on the north Pacific slope was about to shift dramatically.

Biographies

The Ancient One/Kennewick Man

The two names attached to this person suggest something of the controversy that has surrounded him for the past several years.

"Kennewick Man" is a collection of several hundred bones found near Kennewick, Washington, in 1996. These fragments constitute about 80 percent of a man's skeleton. Kennewick man died in his mid-forties—perhaps from a projectile point embedded in his pelvis, though that wound may have been inflicted many years before. He lived more than nine thousand years ago. His skeleton is one of the oldest discovered in the Americas.

One of the most surprising aspects of Kennewick Man is that his cranium does not resemble those of modern-day Native peoples. Indeed, it at first appeared to some that the skeleton might have been that of a white settler. More careful investigation revealed resemblances to Polynesian and Japanese peoples. Kennewick Man has drawn the interest of so many archeologists in part because his skull suggests that not all early settlers of North America came from Siberia, over the land bridge.

But such debates have angered and saddened many of the region's Native peoples. Some of them believe that they have always lived in North America. They claim "The Ancient One" as one of their own, as an ancestor whose spiritual beliefs require that his bones be reburied, not analyzed. Picking apart his remains to discern where he came from constitutes, for them, a racist and disrespectful act.

In 2000 the Department of the Interior ruled in favor of the five Northwest tribes who had asked for the bones. Archeologists, having established, at least in their own minds, that Kennewick Man bears little resemblance to Cayuse or other Plateau peoples, appealed the decision in court, and in 2002 they won the right to research his remains, though that decision was also appealed.

The Ancient One, then, has revealed several crucial and contested questions in modern North America. First, his remains suggest that the original settling of the continent may have been much more complex and varied than archeologists have traditionally thought. But some Native peoples reject the entire notion of settlement, arguing that this account violates their religious beliefs. Important political and economic questions are also at stake: do theories of migration to the Americas weaken the claims of tribes who assert that their ancestors established stable, geographically rooted societies that persisted from time immemorial until white conquest? This question in turn bears upon a final and more practical one: who owns the bones of people who died in North America many thousands of years ago, Native peoples or scientists? Who are the Ancient One's heirs?

The People of Fort Rock Cave

Fort Rock Cave is one of the most important and earliest archaeological sites in the Pacific Northwest. Excavated during the 1930s by the University of Oregon's Luther Cressman, it is near the northern boundary of the Great Basin, some sixty miles southeast of present-day Bend.

Carbon-14 dating indicates that humans inhabited the cave at least ten thousand years ago, when it bordered on a lake that has long since disappeared. This cave—like many others in the arid Great Basin—offered shelter from sun and rain.

Many of the cave's artifacts lay beneath a layer of ash deposited by the explosion of Mount Mazama (which created Crater Lake) more than seven thousand years ago. These included a piece of basketry, a piece of a fire drill, two bone awls, a flaking tool (used for working stone) made from a deer's antler, four mano or grinding stones, and many stone projectile points and scrapers. These artifacts suggest some of the activities of the people who lived in the Great Basin long ago.

Sagebrush bark sandals from Fort Rock Cave, dated 9,300 to 10,500 years old. The sandals were discovered under a layer of Mount Mazama ash in 1938 by archaeologist Luther Cressman. University of Oregon Museum of Natural History

The cave's most evocative artifacts were—and are—several dozen sandals. Such personal articles of apparel seldom survive for decades, let alone millennia. Constructed of shredded sagebrush bark, many of the sandals were deeply worn. The volcanic rock of the region must have put a premium on reliable footwear for people who had to walk long distances to find sustenance. More than any other artifact, these sandals have given modern-day Oregonians a sense of connection to the distant past.

Cressman's academic reports on the Fort Rock excavations were dry and factual. But the sandals that he found there fired his imagination, too. His popular survey of Oregon archaeology, published in 1962, is entitled *The Sandal and the Cave.*

Watkuweis

The Nez Perce had several reasons for welcoming the tattered members of the Lewis and Clark Expedition who appeared along the Clearwater River in 1805. The descendants of those Native people recall that an old woman named Watkuweis provided one of them.

Like many Nez Perce, Watkuweis had been captured by the Blackfeet or Atsinas late in the eighteenth century, while she was part of a buffalo-hunting party. They traded her to a group farther east. She was eventually traded to a man who was at least half white, and she lived among his people for some time. They treated her kindly and healed her trachoma, a disease of the eye that could have blinded her.

Watkuweis and her child eventually escaped. The child died, but the mother, aided by some Salish, finally made her way back to her people. She was the only one to have seen a Soyappo (white person), and her stories about the white people spread among the Nez Perce villages. They began calling her Watkuweis, meaning "returned from a faraway country."[15]

Many years later she heard that strange, light-skinned people had arrived. She assured the people in her village that they had nothing to fear from them. "These are the people who helped me," she said.[16] Clark was of course not privy to these conversations. He simply noted that one of the camp's women had been captured by the Atsinas and had seen whites. He did not realize that the Nez Perce received the worn-out explorers so warmly in part because of an old woman's memories of her husband's people.

The Nez Perce helped Lewis and Clark in many ways. They advised their canoe-building operation and provided guides for their travels. They wintered their horses and hosted the thirty-three expedition members when they returned in the spring and waited for the mountain passes to clear.

The U.S. did not bring the trade and peace to the plateau that Lewis and Clark had promised. But not until 1877 would a portion of the Nez Perce take up arms against the people that Watkuweis had convinced them to trust.

Comcomly

Contact and trade with whites brought death, slavery, and other misfortunes to many Native peoples. But it brought unprecedented riches and power to some. Comcomly used the fur trade more adroitly than any of his peers, rising from a position of modest leadership among the Chinooks to head the lower Columbia River's most powerful group.

Comcomly was a well-established leader by the time the maritime fur trade began at the Columbia River's mouth. Charles Bishop, one of the earliest captains, frequently dealt with him. Lewis and Clark presented him with a peace medal while wintering at Fort Clatsop in 1805-1806. But the explorers did not much interest Comcomly, for their store of trade goods was by now much reduced.

The pace of trade quickened when the Astorians arrived in 1811. Comcomly's people rescued two of the enterprise's partners,

Alexander McKay and Robert Stuart, from the Columbia River, and Comcomly frequently visited the fort that they erected.

But the Astorians were soon cursing the canny Chinook leader. He tried to monopolize the trade by frightening away other Native peoples, and he and his people were ruthless bargainers.

The Astorians were disgusted to learn that Comcomly thought no more of them than they did of him. Late in 1813 he rushed to Fort Astoria to report that a "King George" ship had appeared off Cape Disappointment and to assure the Americans, "our friends and allies," that the Chinook would drive off the interlopers. Duncan McDougall rewarded Comcomly's loyalty with a suit of clothing and assured him that there was no need for fighting. He need not have worried. Comcomly was soon on board the *Raccoon*, telling its captain that he was delighted to again see a British ship on the river. He departed with a British flag, coat, hat, and sword. The Chinook leader wore this new regalia to Fort Astoria the following day, and became, as a disgusted Astorian put it, "as staunch a Briton as ever he had previously been an American partisan."[17]

Indeed, Comcomly was soon very tight with the leaders of Fort George. McDougall stayed behind to work for the North West Company, and he had already married one of the Chinook leader's daughters. Other daughters followed suit, establishing liaisons that gave Comcomly even more influence.

The mid-1820s brought much misfortune to Comcomly. He wept upon learning that the Hudson's Bay Company was moving its headquarters far up the river. Within a two-year period eight of his immediate family died, including some of his sons. Comcomly died a decade later, one of many Chinooks who perished in the epidemic that raged along the lower Willamette and Columbia rivers in the 1830s.

The fur trade by this time no longer centered at the Columbia River's mouth. But for some three decades Comcomly had made the Chinook the wealthiest people of the Oregon Country.

Chapter Two

Taking Oregon

1492-1877

"Never sell the bones of your father and your mother."
Hin-mah-too-yah-lat-kekht (Chief Joseph, the
younger) recalling his father's last words

Here is the entire text of Chapter Three of the *Union
Centennial Album,* a book published in 1978: "Before the
days Union became a town Indians camped on the site.
When the white man moved in, the Indians moved out." The chapter
is entitled "Before White Men."[1]

That chapter neatly divides the history of northeastern Oregon's
Native peoples into two sentences. One sums up the history of the
area's Native peoples before contact. The other asserts or at least
implies that they simply and quietly disappeared when people of
European descent arrived. The settling of Oregon, by this account,
was neither violent nor contentious.

Taking the Pacific Northwest in fact brought less bloodshed than
in the Southwest. There was no counterpart to the Mexican-American
War here. The United States and England settled the boundary
peaceably, and the balance in the U.S.'s favor was tipped as much by
the appearance of homesteaders as by the sabre rattling of politicians
and journalists.

Yet Oregon was formed in strife's crucible. Several European nations
contended for control of its rich resources—and ultimately for the
territory itself. The United States joined this contest late in the game
and eventually won when thousands of its citizens made themselves
at home here in the mid-1840s. The 1846 treaty with Great Britain
established that the territory south of the 49th parallel belonged to
the U.S. (The 49th parallel is now the border between Washington
State and Canada.)

But the 1846 treaty did not settle questions of sovereignty for the
region's many Indian nations. Settlers had already pushed aside the
beleaguered Native peoples of the Willamette Valley, and many

subsequent newcomers to other parts of the territory and state would try the same combination of coercion and intimidation. The federal government tried to reduce friction and conflict by concluding a series of treaties that it hoped would make Native peoples' lands available for settlement by removing them to isolated reservations. But the process was patently unfair and coercive, and many Natives fought and died rather than submit. The resettlement of Oregon was therefore accompanied by considerable international and interracial strife, a process in which the U.S. government and U.S. citizens wrested away claims from European and land from indigenous nations.

Spain's Losing Battle

European exploration of what would become Oregon was rooted in a larger, complex process of economic, technological, political, and social transformation. At the close of the Middle Ages, in the fifteenth century, many European economies began to quicken, led by merchants and manufacturers. Their efforts were encouraged by several nation states that had begun to both consolidate and expand. These developments prompted exploration and trade: Asia, Africa, and eventually the Americas offered new products and markets. Technological innovations, such as tools that enabled mariners to navigate far from shore, facilitated what soon became a global competition for products and colonies.

Spain enjoyed a big jump on its European rivals in the Americas by virtue of Columbus's voyages in the 1490s. The Spanish immediately set about plundering and exploring this New World, looking both for riches and a convenient passage through it, so that they could get to Asia more easily than by sailing around Cape Horn. They reached the Baja Peninsula in 1533 and a decade later may have sailed along what is now the southern Oregon coast. They of course found no Northwest Passage, a water route across the continent. Spanish explorers on foot and horseback ranged over much of North America's interior, though not into what would centuries later become the state of Oregon. In 1598 the Spanish established what for many years would be their northernmost colony in New Mexico, among the Pueblo.

Other European nations soon challenged Spain's massive American empire. England's Francis Drake entered the Pacific in 1577 and began looting its Spanish ports. He may have sailed as far north as the Oregon coast but was put off by "vile, thicke and stinking fogges" and the absence of booty.[2] He soon discovered what Spain had been keeping secret for half a century: that galleons laden with treasures annually crossed between Spanish America and China. Drake also challenged Spain's title to all of North America. Somewhere along the coast, probably just north of San Francisco Bay, he claimed for his queen "New Albion," which England took to mean all of western North America that Spain did not actually occupy. Drake's successes emboldened English colonizers on the Atlantic—first at Roanoke— and English privateers in the Pacific.

Spain took defensive measures. Its leaders hoped that a more thorough knowledge of the north coast would facilitate Spanish colonization or at least help their galleons elude English privateers. Their expeditions bequeathed some Spanish place names to the southern Oregon coast: Cape Blanco (which at times appears white) and Cape Sebastian (after a saint). But the coast above Baja California did not appear to possess much wealth, and Spain lacked the resources to establish new colonies on such unpromising ground. Its leaders also feared that discovering a passage through the continent would inevitably draw other nations into the Pacific. Spain therefore suspended its northern explorations and focused on the south Pacific. England, France, and other European powers also turned their attentions to other parts of the globe during the seventeenth century. In an age of expansion and colonization, the north Pacific slope was forgotten. Then, well over a century later, a series of events pulled the region into European politics.

The first interloper was an unlikely one. Russian traders had expanded into Siberia in the mid-seventeenth century, drawn by its furs. This profitable eastward expansion prompted maritime expeditions by Vitus Bering and others that eventually brought the Russians to present-day Alaska. By the mid-eighteenth century they were harvesting great numbers of furs in the Aleutian Islands and probing farther south, along the coast.

Another, more familiar, threat to Spanish interests soon appeared. Great Britain was again pushing into North America. Its 1763 victory in the Seven Years' War (known in North America as the French and Indian War) won it France's Canadian colonies. Spain was well aware that aggressive English settlers were likely to continue their westward expansion, toward Spanish America's northern frontiers. The Spanish were now more worried about English than Russian expansion in the north Pacific. In 1769 they began planting a series of settlements in upper California that reached as far north as San Francisco. A few years later Spain began sending Juan Perez and other captains north to explore and claim the land that they had for so long ignored. Perez ranged far, reaching the Queen Charlotte Islands in 1774. A year later Bruno de Hezeta became the first documented European to see the Columbia River, though he did not risk crossing its treacherous bar.

In 1745 the British Parliament had offered a prize of twenty thousand pounds (the equivalent of at least several hundred thousand dollars today) to the man who found a water passage across the vast continent. This drew the attention of James Cook, a distinguished explorer. He sailed from England in 1776, just a few days after the American patriots had declared their independence from Britain. Cook's interests were manifold. He had been instructed to claim for Great Britain land not possessed by other European powers. Expedition members also made scientific observations. Nor were economic opportunities neglected. The Spanish feared that Cook and other British captains would, at the very least, open up markets that they had worked so hard to keep closed.

Cook was killed in Hawaii, after finding no trace of the Northwest Passage. But his voyage nevertheless created a sensation. In 1780 his crew arrived in Canton—a Chinese port closed to Russian traders—and found that the Chinese were willing to pay very handsomely for sea otter pelts that they had purchased for a pittance on the northwest coast. The news finally gave merchants a reason to scour the anchorages of what are now British Columbia, Washington, and Oregon. Within a decade, traders from several nations were engaged in procuring and transporting sea otter pelts. The most popular trading spots were north of the Columbia River, and the most active and numerous traders were British.

This profitable business in furs sounded the death knell for Spanish pretensions of sovereignty on the north coast. The showdown came at Nootka Sound, on Vancouver Island, in 1789-1790, when they seized three British ships and reasserted a right to exclusive control over the west coast of the Americas, up to the Russian settlements. But in the face of British truculence and naval superiority, Spain at last backed down. It agreed that territory that it had claimed for centuries but not occupied was now open to all comers.

This was a great victory for Great Britain. The ascendant British could not match Spain's discoveries in the Americas. But now, by Spain's admission, trade could trump discovery, and no nation seemed better positioned to trade than Great Britain.

What had these various voyages and international rivalries meant for the place that would eventually become the state of Oregon? In some respects, very little. Some early Spanish explorers viewed and even named parts of its coast, but they did not land there. A Spanish galleon wrecked near Nehalem Bay, probably around 1707. Other ships and even sailors may have washed ashore elsewhere. Later in the eighteenth century Cook, the explorer, named several coastal features, including Capes Foulweather and Perpetua. But he did not land. The great international confrontation between two global empires occurred not on the banks of the Columbia River but farther north, at Nootka Sound.

Yet Cook's voyage and the Nootka Convention of 1790 would prove very consequential indeed to Oregon history. The first event, the discovery of a lucrative market for sea otter pelts, meant that many traders would soon be making their way into the Columbia River. The second established that participation in this trade would be based not on ancient expeditions and proclamations but rather on the capacity of a nation and its people to undertake and prosecute profitable but risky business ventures. This opened the door for Great Britain. But it also drew the attention of a still more pugnacious nation.

The Victory of Manifest Destiny

The British did not dominate the maritime trade for long. American ships easily outnumbered their European competitors on the northwest coast by the turn of the nineteenth century. British traders had to work around the monopolistic South Sea and British East India Companies and, from 1789 to 1815, wars with France. U.S. traders suffered from no such restrictions. Some seventy-two ships traveled from the U.S. to the northwest coast from 1787 to 1806, the great majority from Boston.

Captains John Kendrick and Robert Gray inaugurated the U.S. trade when they set out from Boston in the fall of 1787. Gray began trading at Tillamook Bay the following summer, but quickly left when Marcus Lopius, his Black servant, was killed when attempting to retrieve a cutlass. Gray returned to the Oregon coast in 1792, and on May 11 he and his crew became the first whites in recorded history to enter the Columbia River. The traders gathered only about 150 sea otter skins in the estuary, together with a few hundred other, less valued, pelts. Yet the lower Columbia became a popular destination. Some captains wintered there, and the area's Natives produced clamons (thick elk-hide armor) that were much in demand elsewhere on the coast.

As sea otter populations plummeted, a land-based trade in other furs supplanted the maritime trade. Alexander Mackenzie, one of the North West Company's founders, made his way along the Peace and

Fraser rivers and then overland to the shores of the Pacific Ocean in 1793, in what would become British Columbia.

To the south and east, the United States continued to expand. After the Revolution thousands of pioneers poured across the Appalachians, into the eastern half of the rich Mississippi River basin. Then, in 1803, France unexpectedly sold the other part of the vast watershed to the U.S. At the stroke of a pen, the young nation had more than doubled its size.

Spain was worried. France had promised Spain that it would not sell Louisiana, a vast territory that ran up to Spanish America's doorstep. It had opposed an overland expedition that President Thomas Jefferson had been planning even when it seemed unlikely that France would part with such a large chunk of North America. Jefferson assured Spain that the expedition's goals were purely literary and scientific. Spain doubted it.

Indeed, Jefferson's instructions to Meriwether Lewis, the expedition's co-leader, made it clear that he hoped the enterprise would stimulate the nation's economic and political fortunes. His principal goal was as old as it was wrongheaded. He hoped that the explorers could, by traveling up the Missouri River, find a stream that would flow to the Pacific Ocean, thus establishing a "direct & practicable water communication across this continent for the purposes of commerce." Likewise, the expedition members were to take pains to treat the Native peoples they met "in the most friendly & conciliatory manner which their own conduct will admit," to "make them acquainted with the position, extent, character, peaceable & commercial dispositions of the U.S."[3] Even the expedition's scientific observations were often calculated to serve the nation's material interests. Clark, for example, noted that the Willamette Valley appeared to have excellent agricultural potential.

The Lewis and Clark Expedition was a remarkable adventure, and its journals make for good reading to this day. But the expedition members' heroism and accomplishments should not obscure the enterprise's larger historical significance: it constituted a bold attempt to extend the economic and political influence of the United States across the North American continent.

The expedition was succeeded by a still more daring venture. John Jacob Astor, perhaps the young nation's wealthiest man, began finalizing his ambitious plans for the Pacific basin shortly after its return. The Pacific Fur Company's operations would center at the Columbia River's mouth, near where Lewis and Clark had spent the winter of 1805-1806. Employees would fan out to gather furs up and down the coast and far into the interior before shipping them to China. There was more. Astor negotiated a pact making him the sole supplier of goods to isolated Russian America, and he hoped to tap that region's furs, too. His employees, who included a number of Canadians and Hawaiians, arrived on the lower Columbia River early in 1811 and soon set about implementing his dream.

That eight of the Astorians died crossing the Columbia River bar was not a good omen. More deaths soon followed, when the crew of the *Tonquin* died in a quarrel with Natives to the north. The enterprise's overland party arrived late, after suffering great hardship along the Snake River. The Astorians gathered thousands of furs and traveled far up the Columbia River. But morale at the fort was low, relations with nearby Natives often strained, and supply ships from the U.S. unreliable.

The War of 1812 between the U.S. and Great Britain made a bad situation worse. Astor used his considerable influence to lobby government officials to protect his post, even arguing that Thomas Jefferson, now out of office, had asked him to undertake the endeavor. But it was to no avail. Most of the post's disappointed leaders were prepared to sell the operation to the North West Company even before a British warship arrived late in 1813. Fort Astoria became Fort George. For a couple of decades the U.S. had dominated trade in the region, first with its independent maritime fleet and then, briefly, with the Astorians. Now the British were back in the saddle.

The North West Company was more durable than Astor's enterprise had been. It had begun setting up posts in what is now British Columbia around the turn of the seventeenth century. One employee, David Thompson, had arrived at the Columbia River's mouth only months after the Astorians. Now, with the Pacific Fur Company out of the way, the Nor'westers expanded their operations southward. Employees transported furs gathered at posts scattered throughout the Columbia River's watershed to Fort George, where they were packed for shipment to China.

The trade's tempo quickened after the Hudson's Bay Company, a joint-stock venture, absorbed the North West Company in 1821. George Simpson, one of the company's leading men, soon determined that the Columbia River's fur trade "has been neglected, shamefully mismanaged and a scene of the most wasteful extravagance and the most unfortunate dissention."[4] He moved the company's headquarters upriver, from Fort George to Fort Vancouver, where its employees could more easily feed themselves. To the east, in the Snake River country, he ordered his charges to trap everything they could find so that the aggressive American traders would turn back upon reaching this "fur desert." Along the coast, in areas that seemed more secure, he favored a more sustainable trade in which the company relied largely on Native trappers. Indeed, the Hudson's Bay Company created a credit system that served to tie Indians more closely to the company through debt. In sum, Simpson made the Oregon Country's fur trade more centralized and profitable—for the Hudson's Bay Company.

Did these sundry fur-trading businesses serve mammon or country? Both. Some traders, such as Robert Gray, were more interested in furs than in nation building. Upon entering the grand Columbia River, for example, it did not occur to him to take possession of the land it drained on behalf of his country. Astor was more patriotic—at least when it suited his purposes. During the War of 1812 he implored President Madison's administration to intervene at Fort Astoria for the good of the country. Likewise, Simpson hoped to repel both American traders, who would provide unwelcome economic competition, and American settlers, who would stimulate U.S. claims of sovereignty. The Hudson's Bay Company served the interests of its shareholders and Great Britain alike.

But its position deteriorated in the 1840s. The two nations had agreed with the Convention of 1818 had established that they both had rights to the vast Oregon Country that stretched west of the Rocky Mountains, between Spanish and Russian America. The British, as we have seen, were far more active here than the Americans. But the Americans were quickly moving west, and as they did so they became increasingly convinced that it was the nation's "manifest destiny" to spread from sea to sea. The British doubted that God and nature had set aside the Oregon Country for the exclusive enjoyment of the United States. But they were unwilling to spend blood and money contesting the truculent upstart's conceit. The Oregon Treaty of 1846 set the 49th parallel as the boundary between the U.S. and Canada, a settlement that Great Britain had heretofore rejected.

Why was Great Britain willing to give up land that its citizens had occupied for the past three decades? Negotiations turned partly on matters of discovery and exploration, and Gray, Lewis and Clark, and Astor gave the U.S. some leverage here. But practical concerns also weighed heavily. The fur trade was declining in what would become Oregon and Washington, and crossing the Columbia River bar was dangerous. The U.S. ultimately prevailed on the strength of ordinary citizens who were voting with their feet. Nearly nine hundred overlanders arrived in 1843. Two years later that number had nearly tripled. The Hudson's Bay Company offered land and employment to British citizens—but on terms less than generous. It could not hope to match American settlement.

A long-standing diplomatic issue had been resolved without recourse to arms. But the Oregon Country was no empty garden waiting to be filled.

Colonization and Disease: The Northwest

Northwestern Oregon was the only quadrant of the state in which Native peoples did not take up arms against the white settlers. This was partly a matter of choice. The peoples of the lower Columbia River had welcomed and eagerly participated in the fur trade. There were, to be sure, disagreements and confrontations, particularly early in the nineteenth century with the Wasco and Wishram who lived along the river's portages. But trade with Europeans and Americans served to enhance the status of influential groups and individuals.

Trade also spread disease. This was particularly true around the lower Willamette Valley, where malaria epidemics in the 1830s killed the great majority of Kalapuyans. The whites multiplied as quickly as the Kalapuyans died. An 1837 census showed more than one hundred people at French Prairie, north of present-day Salem, where a number of retired Hudson's Bay Company employees and their families had taken up farming. These families were interracial, but they were soon followed by ones that were not. A small contingent of Methodists arrived in 1834, and six years later fifty more came. The missionaries, unlike the fur traders, were deeply interested in transforming Native religious beliefs and cultural practices. Jason Lee, the mission's head, quickly established a school so that he could "acculturate" Kalapuya children. But when he left, less than a decade later, "there were more Indian children in the mission grave yard … than alive … in the manual labor school."[5] Concentrating Native people with whites quickened the spread of diseases that had already been spreading very quickly.

When Lee gave up and went home in 1843 the first big wave of overland settlers was about to arrive. These people were drawn by the prospect of free, fertile farms. They hungered after Natives' land, not their souls. It was obvious enough to them that the valley's riches were wasted upon a people who hunted and gathered rather than farmed. Certainly God did not intend for such rich soil to be wasted. The settlers therefore quickly set about marking off their claims and raising their cabins. The valley's Natives were by now in no position to resist such encroachments. They constituted a shrinking and demoralized minority of the populace. The newcomers viewed them as, at best, a cheap source of labor.

The boundary settlement changed little. The federal government asserted that Native title should be extinguished before settlement proceeded. But thousands of American citizens had already established homes in the Willamette Valley by 1846. They were not about to vacate their farms and wait until the federal government clarified matters. Anson Dart, the Superintendent of Indian Affairs in Oregon, negotiated a series of treaties in 1851 by which the valley's bands surrendered the vast majority of their territory in return for small reservations on their traditional homelands and the right to fish, hunt, and move about freely. But settlers protested that these terms were too liberal, and the treaties were never ratified. A few years later most of the valley's surviving Natives were sent west, to the Siletz Reservation on the Oregon coast, to land the settlers considered of little value.

The same sort of process occurred at the Columbia River's mouth. The Clatsop, like the Kalapuya and Clackamas of the Willamette Valley, had a long history of sustained contact with fur traders. Fort George's

Philip Sheridan, who became famous during the Civil War, lived with Indian women while stationed at Fort Yamhill in the 1850s. He reportedly purchased this woman, Harriet, for $300. Photo from the Historic Photograph Collections, Salem (Oregon) Public Library

population had declined precipitously after 1825, and the Clatsop remained more isolated and autonomous than their counterparts along the lower Willamette River. The Methodists established a mission station in 1840, but the Natives paid them little heed. A white settler who arrived a few years later said that the Clatsop, who then numbered about two hundred, "looked down on us very much." But this quickly changed. The settlers kept coming and taking up land that the Clatsop depended on. They killed game, the sawdust of their mills fouled streams, and their livestock rooted up plants needed for food. Sailors spread liquor and venereal disease, which brought further demoralization and death. By 1853 the few Clatsop who survived believed that they would "soon be dead and leave their country in the possession of the whites."[6] That prediction was more right than not.

The Natives of northwestern Oregon did not take up arms against the settlers for several reasons. They had a long legacy of closely associating with whites, in trade and intermarriage. These associations, though increasing the wealth of many individuals, accelerated the spread of deadly diseases and thereby weakened their capacity for warfare. This weakness was not critical during the fur trade, when whites numbered only a few hundred and did not covet Native land. But when thousands of homesteaders arrived in the 1840s and 1850s they quickly overwhelmed and shunted aside the Native peoples who had survived.

The Rogue River Wars

Native-settler relations were much different in southwestern Oregon. The Takelma, Tututni, and other groups had remained relatively isolated from the fur trade, partly by choice. Indeed, whites had taken to referring to these peoples as the "Rogues," a not-so-subtle indication of how they viewed these indigenous peoples. It would be interesting to know what the "Rogues" called the whites, but they obviously developed a dislike for them too. In 1828 a band of Kalawatsets killed fourteen of the eighteen members of the Jedediah Smith party as they camped on the Umpqua River. Members of the famous mountain man's expedition had evidently been molesting Native women shortly before the attack.

This pattern would persist for several more years. In 1834, for example, Ewing Young and Hall Jackson Kelly made their way north from California with fourteen men and some one hundred head of livestock, intent on establishing a colony in Oregon. They murdered several Natives along the way, including two on the Rogue River. The region's Native peoples responded in kind, and the Oregon-California trail became soaked by the blood of whites and Natives alike. Conflicts increased in 1846, when several Willamette Valley settlers established the Applegate Trail, a wagon route through southern Oregon for overlanders. Natives routinely attacked these trains, both out of resentment and to capture livestock.

Two years later, in 1848, the discovery of gold at Sutter's Mill greatly increased traffic through the Rogue River country, as hundreds of Oregonians headed for the California gold fields. In 1850 the Natives drove a party returning from California out of their camp and then took the gold dust they had left behind. The miners demanded that the territorial governor, Joseph Lane, an experienced Indian fighter, do something.

Lane, accompanied by some fifteen settlers and Quatley, a Klickitat Indian leader from just north of the Columbia River, met with more than 150 Latwagas and Takelmas. Lane insisted that the Natives return all the property they had stolen since 1846 and promised protection and gifts in return. The Natives seemed unpersuaded until Quatley seized their leader by the throat and Lane took him captive. Some of the stolen property reappeared over the next two days. Lane declared the meeting a success and then, like so many before him, headed for the gold fields.

But southern Oregon exploded in violence a year later. Gold had been discovered on the Shasta River in northern California. The strike drew thousands of miners into the region, men who often, in the words of historian Stephen Dow Beckham, attacked Natives "at the slightest provocation."[7] The Natives retaliated violently. The resulting wars drew a small party of federal troops into the area, as well as a company of Oregon volunteers led by Lane, who was no longer governor. Clashes also erupted to the west, where gold seekers sifted coastal sands. Conflict abated somewhat over the next two years, as federal agents and soldiers tried to negotiate treaties and maintain peace. But miners continued to scour the region, settlers staked out homesteads, and the town of Jacksonville soon appeared.

War returned in 1853. Miners near the Applegate River's mouth lynched several Natives whom they suspected of murder. Natives retaliated for this act of cruelty and others by killing isolated travelers, miners, and settlers. These acts in turn incited the miners. A Jacksonville mob hanged two Shasta men and a seven-year-old boy. These killings were soon followed by organized military campaigns.

In September roughly half of southern Oregon's Natives surrendered and agreed to live on the small Table Rock Reservation.

But the worst still lay ahead. Natives across the region found that settlers and miners were consuming the food that they had relied upon for generations: hunters killed game, mining debris fouled streams, and hogs and plows dug up camas and other plants. Violence increased. Miners massacred or raped Native women. An epidemic erupted on the reservation. Tipsey's Shasta band, which opposed treaty making, killed Tyee Jim, a Native who had tried to accommodate the whites. A party of Natives murdered a dozen miners. Tipsey's band attacked a wagon train in the Siskiyous, and a Shasta man killed a prospector who had taken his wife. Enraged volunteers took to the mountains to hunt Indians. One Jacksonville party massacred some twenty-eight natives, most of them children and women. Natives retaliated by murdering a reservation employee and several others, including some women and a girl. These killings aroused the whites still further, and five hundred volunteers had soon enlisted in Jacksonville. The natives defeated two white offensives before winter shut down further campaigns. Self-professed exterminators had to settle for venting their frustration on a band they had promised not to attack, killing nineteen men and leaving the survivors, women and children, to starve and freeze.

The following year hostilities moved westward. Early in 1856 a group of Tututni warriors ambushed a camp at Gold Beach and eventually killed twenty-three. This success prompted the volunteers and federal government to redouble their efforts, however, and by the end of June they had finally conquered the Natives they called the "Rogues."

Soldiers took two thousand survivors north to the Siletz Reservation, about one fifth as many as had lived in southern Oregon at the turn of the century. Many more had died. Whites hunted down the handful who remained, capturing a few, killing more.

To the north, in the Willamette Valley, Natives' capacity to resist had been worn down by a half century of disease and extensive trade by the time overlanders took their land. The peoples of southern Oregon remained very strong and autonomous when miners and farmers arrived in the early 1850s. But the newcomers were exceedingly numerous and violent, and they speedily killed or drove away the Rogue River's peoples.

The Wars of the Great Basin

Settlement came much later east of the Cascades, in Oregon's arid Great Basin. The northern Paiute, the basin's most numerous residents, therefore remained free longer than their counterparts to the west. The Paiute, as we have seen, had not been much concerned about warfare. They were geographically and politically dispersed, and making a living in an arid, unforgiving landscape consumed most of their energies. Early settlers often referred to them contemptuously as "diggers," people who resorted to roots or even insects to feed themselves.

But these settlers unwittingly abetted the Oregon Paiute's military capabilities. Large overland parties began disrupting the Paiute's subsistence patterns in the mid-1840s. The pioneers cut down prized stands of nut-producing pines for firewood. Their livestock consumed grain-bearing grasses. But the newcomers also brought large numbers of cattle, horses, and other forms of wealth. The opening of the Warm Springs Reservation, to the north of the Paiute, also helped. The Paiute began raiding both white travelers and the nearby reservation for horses and other booty. For millennia peoples of the Great Basin had supported themselves through a painstaking round of hunting and particularly gathering activities. Now they were mounted raiders plundering far and wide.

Paiute Indian encampment near Burns. Photo from the Ben Maxwell Photography Collection, Salem (Oregon) Public Library

The new economy transformed Paiute society and politics. Paiute bands became larger. They also became less egalitarian, as men in general and warriors in particular gained status. Organized warfare exacerbated these trends, as chiefs like Paulina became powerful leaders in battles and negotiations with white soldiers.

By the time of the Civil War, the Paiute constituted a potent military force. They raided prospectors along the Malheur River and elsewhere. These raids increased in 1862 as overland migration to Oregon grew and mining booms erupted in and around Canyon City and Auburn, to the north. White stockmen arrived to feed the miners, moving onto grasslands that had nourished the Paiutes and their horses. Far-ranging bands of warriors attacked miners, ranchers, farmers, stagecoaches, and freight wagons across much of eastern Oregon during the Civil War—both to defend their territory and to attain horses, cattle, grain, guns, blankets, and other goods.

These raids prompted offensives by volunteers and federal troops. Indians at Warm Springs—frustrated by repeated raids—served as scouts. These parties met with little success until the close of the Civil War, when the U.S. Army could again focus its resources on fighting indigenous peoples. In 1866 Colonel George Crook began a system of dogged pursuit and forced the Paiute into dozens of skirmishes that eventually wore them down. The conflict ended in 1868, when most of the survivors surrendered. They agreed to cease raiding and to settle near Camp Harney. The government agreed to give them rations. A few years later many moved to the newly opened Malheur Reservation. Some moved west, to the Klamath Reservation.

But the Paiute's power was not spent. Growing numbers were disgusted by poor conditions on the reservation and refused to live there. Then, in the spring of 1878, the Bannock of southern Idaho, angered that settlers' hogs were ruining their camas grounds, asked the Paiute to join them. The Bannock War, fought largely in Oregon's southeast corner, ended quickly and, for the Paiute and Bannock, badly. The government punished them by closing the short-lived Malheur Reservation. Paiute prisoners were sent away from their homeland, to the Yakima Reservation in Washington. Some also went to Warm Springs, to live among Native peoples they had once raided and who had helped to defeat them.

The Modoc reacted in much the same way as the Paiute. They lived to the west of the Paiute, on the eastern slope of the Cascades in southern Oregon, where Plateau, Great Basin, and California culture groups converged. They had switched to a raiding economy a decade or so before the Paiute, capturing slaves to fund their acquisition of

War chief Umapine with four Umatilla and Warm Springs Indians, allies of U.S. troops during the Bannock-Paiute War. Photo courtesy Oregon Historical Society, OrHi 9526

horses. The Applegate Trail that appeared in 1846 represented both a threat and an opportunity: the settlers' wagon trains drove away game but included scores of horses and cattle. A smallpox epidemic in 1847 slowed their raids. But in 1849 the Modoc were again attacking immigrant trains. The arrival of thousands of gold seekers in 1851 multiplied interracial conflicts. Intermittent attacks and counter-attacks by both sides continued for several years, including an instance in which the notorious Indian fighter Benjamin Wright led a party of Yreka residents who massacred and mutilated some forty Modoc.

Hostilities abated with the close of the Rogue River War in 1857. Unlike their defeated counterparts west of the mountains, the Modoc stayed on their lands and tried to survive on the margins of the white economy. The Yreka miners who had once slaughtered them now used Modoc women as prostitutes and Modoc boys as servants. Settlers at last moved into Modoc territory during the Civil War, and in 1864 the Modoc yielded to pressure and agreed to go onto the newly created Klamath Reservation.

The arrangement did not last long. The reservation was situated on Klamath, not Modoc, land, and the Klamath treated the Modoc as interlopers. Like Warm Springs, this reservation was vulnerable to raids

Graves of four Modoc traders executed at Fort Klamath in 1873: Schonchin, Captain Jack (Kintpuash), Black Jim, and Boston Charley. Photo courtesy of Oregon State Library

by the Paiute. Conditions were poor. Promised supplies did not materialize. White officers at Fort Klamath seized Native women as concubines. Agency employees smuggled whiskey. These difficulties were compounded by a split within the Modoc between Schonchin, who tended to cooperate with reservation authorities, and Kintpuash—also known as Captain Jack—who did not. Kintpuash and his followers left the reservation just one year after they had arrived and returned to their traditional territory along the California border. For several years they lived independently, combining traditional subsistence activities with visits to Yreka.

But the federal government eventually resolved to humble the independent Modoc. Responding to complaints by the growing numbers of settlers near Tule Lake, a detachment of cavalry set out from Fort Klamath late in 1872. Kintpuash and about fifty warriors escaped to some lava beds to the south where for some six months they held off a force of over one thousand soldiers equipped with howitzers and mortars. The battle turned when Kintpuash, goaded by some of his fellow fighters, shot down General Edward Canby at a peace parley. This act silenced Modoc sympathizers and prompted the army to redouble its efforts. The Modoc scattered, and the army picked them off one by one. One group of captives, led by Hooker Jim, volunteered to hunt down Kintpuash in exchange for amnesty. Kintpuash and the three warriors who had remained with him were put on trial, hanged, and buried. Hooker Jim and the rest of the survivors were sent east, to Indian Territory in Oklahoma.

Kintpuash went east, too. Some enterprising whites dug up his corpse and displayed it in eastern carnivals. Kintpuash had fought a long, losing battle to remain free. Now, even in death, his bones were far from home, in the hands of the people who had defeated and killed him.

Accommodation and Resistance: The Columbia Plateau

The extent and nature of Native resistance to colonization varied across Oregon's regions. It also varied within regions. This was nowhere more true than on the Columbia Plateau, among the Cayuse and Nez Perce.

These Plateau peoples had evidently desired the arrival of whites. The previous chapter traces how a prophetic movement in the late-eighteenth century promised that the arrival of new, strange people bearing a book would usher in a golden age in which the dead so recently struck down by disease would return to the earth and all hardships and strife would cease. The Lewis and Clark Expedition had failed to fulfill this prophecy, but a band of Iroquois who had been instructed in Catholicism arrived among the Flathead of what is now Idaho and western Montana in around 1820 and added a more explicitly Christian component to the prophecy. Some Plateau groups began saying daily prayers and observing the Sabbath. Old Ignace, the leader of the Iroquois band, said that they needed some black robes—some priests—to more fully understand the new religion and its book. The Hudson's Bay Company had no trouble getting Plateau leaders to send two of their sons east for religious instruction. Spokan Garry and Kutenai Pelly returned from the Red River mission school in 1829. In 1831 the Nez Perce and Flathead, frustrated by the slow pace of religious instruction from the Hudson's Bay Company, resolved to seek out guns and missionaries from U.S. fur traders. Several of these Natives soon turned up in St. Louis.

The news that distant Indians were seeking the Bible electrified pious Protestants across the United States. "The story has scarcely a parallel in history," enthused a writer in the a Methodist newspaper early in 1833. "Let the Church awake from her slumbers and go forth to the salvation of these wandering sons of our native forests."[8]

Those wandering sons did not have to wait long. The Methodists settled in the Willamette Valley in 1834, and two years later a party of Presbyterians headed by Marcus Whitman headed for the plateau. They were enthusiastically received by the Cayuse and Nez Perce and set up a mission among each of them.

The Natives and the Presbyterians were soon disappointed in one another. The Cayuse and Nez Perce were interested in Christian ritual and acquiring new technologies. They were not prepared to abandon traditional practices and were offended that the missionaries expected them to set aside polygamy and hunting, for example. They were also put off by Christianity's hostility toward pleasure. One told Narcissa Whitman that "it was good when they know nothing but to hunt, eat, drink and sleep; now it was bad."[9] The Cayuse and Nez Perce were also puzzled by the newcomers' bad manners. They beat children. They gave gifts only in exchange for work. They appropriated Cayuse land for their garden and then, when the natives harvested part of that crop, tainted the melons. Nor did they welcome the Cayuse into their homes. That Catholic priests, who began proselytizing in the late 1830s, were more flexible about native beliefs and practices only exacerbated Natives' frustrations with the Protestants.

The missionaries, for their part, asserted that the Cayuse and Nez Perce were lazy, dirty, and proud. They respected neither the missionaries' sensibilities nor privacy. A strong conviction that God was calling her to save the lost souls of pathetic savages had drawn Narcissa into marriage and across the continent. Now she was gradually realizing that she did not much care for the people she had gone to serve. Indeed, the Whitmans failed to convert even a single Cayuse in a decade's work at the Waiilatpu mission.

Relations between the Cayuse and the Whitmans deteriorated in the mid-1840s as growing numbers of immigrants passed through the mission station. The travelers consumed precious resources: game, wood, and grass. Anyone could see that the missionaries were becoming more prosperous, that they were increasingly devoted to serving the thousands of white newcomers who were flocking to Oregon rather than the Native people whose land they lived upon and cultivated. Tom Hill, a Native man of Delaware ancestry, warned the Cayuse of what the future would bring: more and more and more white men.

Then, in 1847, a measles epidemic spread among the Cayuse. Up to thirty who lived near the mission died within two months. Only one white died. Marcus, a doctor, was evidently unable or unwilling to protect Native people. Many of the Cayuse suspected him of sorcery. The Plateau Natives had sought religious instruction in the hope of ushering in a utopian, millennial world in which the dead would return. The exact opposite was happening. It was the living who were joining the dead.

The Cayuse deliberated over what to do. The younger, more angry men eventually prevailed. More whites were passing through and staying at the mission each year. They had tried and failed to force the Whitmans to leave. Now Marcus was evidently killing them. Shamans guilty of such acts were put to death. It was time to act.

Late in 1847, without warning, a party of Cayuse attacked the missionaries. They killed twelve and took some fifty captive. Narcissa was the only woman whom they murdered, a choice that the Cayuse underscored by mutilating her body.

This attack provoked a swift if somewhat ineffectual reaction. The Cayuse handed the prisoners over to the Hudson's Bay Company. They offered to forget the killing of a Native who had been murdered by whites while traveling in California if the Americans would forgive these killings and agree to stop traveling through their lands. The enraged Americans would not. Willamette Valley settlers formed a volunteer militia and marched east. They soon attacked, but with more vigor than discretion. Cornelius Gilliam, who headed the militia, was accidentally killed by his own gun. Their indiscriminate killings drew into the conflict Natives who had not been hostile. The Cayuse eventually prevailed upon five of the killers to turn themselves in two years later. They were hanged in Oregon City, after accepting Catholic rites. Tilokaikt, one of the few Cayuse who had taken much interest in Christianity, reportedly remarked that the five, like Christ, died "to save our people."[10]

Indeed, the executions bought the Cayuse some time—but not much. Part of their land was opened for settlement. They allied with the Sahaptin peoples in the mid-1850s in an attempt to drive out gold seekers, but were defeated. Most of the survivors went onto the Umatilla Indian Reservation in 1860.

The Nez Perce were much more reluctant to take up arms against the white invaders. Several had converted by the time of the Whitman Massacre, and many more had begun farming. The mission closed in 1847, but the split that the missionaries had initiated persisted. The Presbyterian Nez Perce continued to meet daily for prayer. Some kept raising crops and keeping livestock, endeavors that increased their wealth and influence. More conservative Nez Perce stuck to their traditional religious practices and subsistence rounds, which included raiding.

The division became more explicit with the 1855 treaty, part of an ambitious federal policy to open eastern Washington and northeastern Oregon to settlement by confining Native peoples to reservations. Most of the Plateau peoples, including the Cayuse, objected, and several years of conflict—the Yakima War—ensued. But some Nez Perce agreed to the treaty—in part because the proposed reservation would be located on their land and their leaders would receive special compensation. Indeed, white treaty makers identified Hallalhotsoot, whom the whites called the Lawyer, because of his negotiating skills, as the head of all the Nez Perce. Traditionalist Nez Perce such as Apash Syakaikt (the older Looking Glass), reacted angrily: "My people, what have you done? While I was gone, you have sold my country."[11]

Yet Nez Perce traditionalists and accommodationists alike managed to stay out of the Yakima and Coeur d'Alene Wars that reduced many of their neighbors from 1855 to 1858—though Apash Syakaikt was sorely tempted to vent his anger toward the whites. Part of this was luck: miners had not yet discovered gold on Nez Perce land, and the Wallowa Mountains were not especially inviting to homesteaders. This noninterventionist strategy enabled the traditional Nez Perce to remain autonomous and powerful long after the Umatilla and Walla Walla had been subjugated. But they would now stand alone, shorn of allies or potential allies.

The Nez Perce remained divided. Roughly two thirds, or nearly three thousand, cast their fortunes with Hallalhotsoot and lived on the reservation to pursue "peace, plows, and schools." But the government for several years failed to deliver on its promises. In the meantime, miners discovered gold along the Clearwater in 1861. The resulting rush brought money, alcohol, and violence to the reservation Nez Perce. It also reduced their lands. An 1863 treaty stipulated that each family would get but twenty acres.

Hallalhotsoot's people continued to struggle. In 1866 an agent fled with forty-six thousand dollars earmarked for the reservation Nez Perce. But a few years later three of their leaders took their case to Washington, D.C. The 1863 treaty was finally ratified, monies began to arrive more regularly, and schools opened. Whites continued to discriminate against even the most pious, acculturation-minded Nez Perce. But it seemed that they at last had a future.

The traditionalists, meanwhile, clung to their independence. They at times traded and associated with the growing number of whites in the region. But they spurned the annuities and gifts offered on the reservation and continued the mobile subsistence round that had characterized their lives for centuries. Many followed the teachings of Smohalla, a prophet from the mid-Columbia who assured Native peoples that reverence for traditional ways would usher in a return of their ancestors and the disappearance of the whites. By now no Indian imagined that the whites were harbingers of paradise. Even if Smohalla were mistaken, one could hope that the whites would leave the people alone, that these Natives could remain in the Wallowa Valley.

But white settlers were not about to let that happen. By 1871 several overcame their fears and moved into Nez Perce territory. The federal government at first wavered, recognizing that the Wallowa Nez Perce had not signed the 1863 treaty surrendering their homeland. But settlers who voted were enraged by this, and federal agents were soon insisting that these Nez Perce go to the reservation on the Clearwater. Hin-mah-too-yal-lat-kekht, known to whites as Chief Joseph, was one of several leaders who argued eloquently that this was a great injustice, that the accommodationists had bargained away land that was not theirs to give. It was as if a white man had purchased his horses through a neighbor, without his permission. Hin-mah-too-yal-lat-kekht did not wish to sell his horses; he and his people did not wish to leave their land.

General Oliver Howard became impatient with the Nez Perce arguments and entreaties: "Twenty times over you repeat that the earth is your mother, and about chieftainship from the earth. Let us hear no more, but come to business at once."[12]

It appeared as if the Nez Perce leadership was about to capitulate. In 1876 white settlers killed one of their number, and the government seemed ready to force their removal. They threw Toohoolhoolzote, one of the most persuasive traditionalists, in jail. Then, in 1877, a young Nez Perce, stung by the taunts of a friend, killed several white settlers who had treated his people cruelly. Now there was no turning back. The Nez Perce would certainly be punished harshly for this act. They resolved to flee.

The Nez Perce began a remarkable fighting retreat in which seven hundred people, defended by only one hundred fifty warriors, traveled hundreds of miles and held off several hundred cavalrymen. They were finally stopped in northern Montana, some thirty miles short of the Canadian border. Only half of the party remained. Those who survived were without food or blankets. Children were freezing to death. Hin-mah-too-yal-lat-kekht's stirring surrender speech detailed all of this and more—and stimulated considerable national sympathy.

He and his people hoped to return to their beloved Wallowas. The officers that Hin-mah-too-yal-lat-kekht surrendered to assured him that they would. Like many whites, they admired the Nez Perce for fighting so courageously and effectively. General Tecumseh Sherman—no stranger to ruthless warfare—commended them for not attacking noncombatants or scalping.

But Sherman and other national leaders refused to let the Nez Perce go home. The residents of northeastern Oregon were dead set against it. An article in the La Grande newspaper published a year after the Nez Perce's departure captured white settlers' attitudes. The piece remarked on a pair of "splendid Indians" who, "unlike any others of their race" were "calm, quiet and considerate," who "even refused whiskey though offered to them." What was the secret of their exemplary manners and habits? They had, for "many days," been hanging from "a tree with a rope around their necks."[13]

The defeated Nez Perce went east instead of west. After seven years on the southern plains, 268 survivors returned to the Pacific Northwest—but not to the Wallowas. Some at last joined their more acculturation-minded counterparts at the Lapwai reservation. Most—including Hin-mah-too-yal-lat-kekht—went to the Colville Reservation in eastern Washington. In 1899 the aging leader visited his old home, some twenty-two years after he had fled. But local citizens refused to consider a return of the Nez Perce. He died five years later, far from the land that he had promised his dying father to defend.

❧❧ ❧❧

The Nez Perce, perhaps more than any other group, reveal the diverse ways in which Native peoples responded to the juggernaut of colonization, to missionaries, settlers, armies, and the federal government. Some, such as the Kalapuya of the lower Willamette Valley, were simply and quickly overrun by these forces. Others, like some of the Modoc, both mingled with the newcomers and insisted on living where and as they pleased. These differences were shaped by variables that lay beyond Native people's control, particularly patterns of disease and settlement. But Native people's reactions to colonization were the product of preference as well as circumstance. One part of the Nez Perce chose farming and Christianity while another fought tenaciously to maintain its cultural traditions and political independence.

These varying reactions should not obscure a harrowing and horrible common denominator: colonization brought unprecedented suffering and dispossession to all Native peoples. Some groups, to be sure, had more choices than others. But none of the choices was good. By the late 1870s all of Oregon's surviving Native peoples were despised, dependent, and impoverished, regardless of whether they had fought to the last warrior or agreed to settle on a reservation at their first treaty meeting.

The Indians depicted at the state capitol seem willing enough to step aside so that a new race of people, the golden pioneer, can occupy the land that its first inhabitants knew and cherished so intimately. But bitter military and political battles waged both by distant diplomats and local soldiers and warriors preceded and accompanied settlement. The Spanish, the Russians, and the British eventually relinquished their claims. But that surrender cost them little: except for some scruffy fur traders, Oregon had never constituted home. It was but one small colony among many.

Not so for Oregon's indigenous peoples. They occupied the land, depended upon the products of its earth and waters. White settlement therefore required, as Cole Harris puts it, "resettlement," a process in which non-Natives effected "the transfer of land from one people to another."[14]

It was a transfer, a conquest, that Oregonians have yet to come to terms with.

Biographies

Joseph Whitehouse

We know very little about most of the men who visited the Pacific Northwest in the late eighteenth and early nineteenth centuries. Ships' logs and travel diaries were usually kept by and describe the lives of captains, officers, or clerks, people who were not much concerned with those who were setting the sails or paddling the canoes.

The Lewis and Clark Expedition was exceptional in this regard. The two captains kept detailed journals, of course. But so did several of the sergeants and privates. The most obscure author was Joseph Whitehouse.

Whitehouse was born in Virginia in about 1773. His family moved to Kentucky in 1784, and he enlisted in the Army in 1798. He later recalled being interested in the possibilities of traversing the continent and was evidently pleased to be selected for the expedition.

But Whitehouse was not a particularly impressive explorer. He is rarely mentioned in the expedition's other journals, in part because he was an indifferent woodsman. The captains seldom selected him to go hunting or trading or to undertake any other special assignments. During 1805 he got a bad case of frostbite, lost a pipe tomahawk, and nearly broke his leg. Whitehouse had been a skin dresser before joining the Army. He stitched and repaired much of the expedition's clothing and sewed together the hides that covered Lewis's collapsible, iron-framed boat. But the covering was not watertight, and the craft sank.

Nor did Whitehouse much distinguish himself after the expedition's return. He was arrested for debt, reenlisted in the Army, and fought in the War of 1812. He deserted a few years later and faded from the historical record. Captain Lewis had named a creek after him in Montana. It no longer bears his name.

Whitehouse took great pains to keep his journal, and he would no doubt be pleased to know that it survived him. His entries convey a strong sense of what the expedition was like for an enlisted man. The private spent his precious time and ink on practical matters: whether the wind blew or the rain fell, the strength of a river's current, the game that the hunters brought to camp.

Whitehouse's journal reminds us that the epic accomplishments of Lewis, Clark, Cook, and Grey depended on the hard labors of ordinary, undistinguished working men who excited little interest then or later.

John McLoughlin

John McLoughlin's remarkable life spanned three eras in the Oregon Country: the fur trade, the missionaries and Indian wars, and American settlement.

He was born in 1784 in Canada, where he studied medicine before joining the North West Company. He eventually became a partner and was sent to the isolated Columbia Department after that concern's merger with the Hudson's Bay Company, where he became Chief Factor, the monarch of Fort Vancouver. McLoughlin was ideally suited for this role. He was very much at home in the Oregon Country. His wife, Marguerite, was half Native, half Swiss. Their sons were fur traders. Simpson, his superior, described him as "such a figure as I should not like to meet in a dark Night in one of the bye lanes in the neighborhood of London." The massive man's clothes were "covered with a thousand patches of different Colors," and "his beard would do honor to the chin of a Grizzly bear."[15]

Yet the chief factor could be a charming and magnanimous host. He welcomed a long succession of visitors from across the world to Fort Vancouver's fine dining room. Adventurers, scientists, missionaries, and settlers enjoyed his legendary hospitality.

Native peoples and employees saw McLoughlin's other side. His monumental temper was easily aroused, and he endeavored—though not always successfully—to avenge swiftly and ruthlessly attacks upon the company's employees or property. McLoughlin was no democrat. He exercised complete authority over his employees and did not hesitate to beat those who offended him. He was amused when Simpson professed concern over such violence, finding it peculiar that his dictatorial superior had "become all at once very sensitive about striking the men."[16]

McLoughlin increasingly clashed with the Hudson's Bay Company's leaders as the fur trade waned and U.S. settlement waxed. He was angry over Simpson's refusal to more fully investigate the apparent murder of his son on the British Columbia coast in 1842. Simpson and other company leaders, for their part, were critical of the chief factor for regularly loaning food and supplies to impoverished overlanders who threatened the long-term interests of the Hudson's Bay Company and Great Britain.

McLoughlin felt ill-paid for this generosity when many of the American settlers contested his land claim at Oregon City. Yet he stayed in Oregon after the boundary settlement and became an American citizen. History was kinder to him than his contemporaries had been. In 1957, a century after his death, the Oregon Legislature bestowed upon him the title "Father of Oregon."

Celiast Smith

This Clatsop woman was born shortly after the turn of the nineteenth century, a couple of years before her father, Coboway, regularly visited members of the Lewis and Clark Expedition at Fort Clatsop.

Like her sisters before her, Celiast married young, to an employee of nearby Fort George. Her husband, Basile Poirier, was a baker for the North West Company. Several years later, in 1825, she went with him some one hundred miles upriver to Fort Vancouver, the new center of trade for the Hudson's Bay Company, which had absorbed its long-time rival. Celiast was evidently unhappy with Basile. Her son from a second marriage would later describe the French-Canadian as an abusive alcoholic. But McLoughlin, the dictatorial head trader at Fort Vancouver, would not hear of her eloping with a voyageur who had become attracted to her.

Then, in 1832, a New Englander named Solomon Smith turned up at Fort Vancouver. He had come west with would-be entrepreneur Nathaniel Wyeth, and he settled at Fort Vancouver where McLoughlin employed him as a school teacher. It is not clear why or how he came to know Celiast. He was several years younger than her, and she was a married woman of little status. But the two of them nevertheless concluded to join their unpromising fortunes. In 1833 or 1834 Celiast, leaving behind her husband and three sons, went with Solomon to French Prairie, where her two sisters lived with their white husbands who had retired from the fur trade to take up farming.

Here Celiast began a new family with Solomon. One day, while her Protestant husband was away, a priest came and baptized their children into the Catholic faith.

Then, in 1840, Celiast became a Methodist. She, Solomon, and their children joined some missionaries on Clatsop Plains, where she had grown up. Native peoples remained strong and autonomous around the Columbia River's mouth at that date, and Celiast's high status among her people safeguarded Solomon. But the tables quickly turned. A few years later the Clatsop had become a small and beleaguered minority, and Celiast found herself relying on the loyalty of her prominent husband and, as they matured, her half-white, half-Native children.

Solomon remained with Celiast until he died. She lived near or with her daughter Charlotte, a midwife who divorced three husbands, and her son, an attorney and prominent member of the Oregon Historical Society.

Celiast lived well into her eighties, and after Solomon died she returned to the language and practices of her childhood. That Celiast managed to survive and even prosper when so many Native people did not certainly owed something to luck. She benefited from being the daughter of a prominent Clatsop leader and was fortunate to survive a series of potent epidemics. But Celiast also relied on her own quick wits and sound judgements in making a place for herself and her children in a society hostile to Native people and mixed-race families.

John Adams

Adams, a Native American, was born around 1850, when gold seekers began probing the valleys of southern Oregon. Many years later, in 1912, he sat down with Edward Curtis, the famous ethnographer and photographer, and recounted his life.

"Awful hard time when I'm baby," he recalled. Soldiers came, driving his people to the hills. His father died and his mother, too. As the soldiers closed in his uncle urged the child's grandmother to hide him. They could return once the soldiers had gone. But his weeping grandmother refused, saying "I old, I not afraid die." The pair somehow survived the winter, caring for one another until the uncle returned and found them.

Soon the soldiers were back. This time Adams's grandmother was too old to walk and had to stay behind. "Maybe she die right there, maybe soldiers kill her." Adams would never know. Then his uncle died, and "I'm 'lone."

Adams was taken in by a succession of Native people before going to the Siletz Reservation several years later. Here his troubles continued, for the reservation included many peoples, some of whom did not get along with each other. One group said that he had "bad blood," that his people had started the Rogue River War. They threw rocks at him and knocked out his front teeth. On another occasion a soldier with a gun threatened to "fix me."

But Adams made it clear to Curtis that he was not simply a victim. When his rock-throwing tormenters cornered him he fended them off with a fence rail and some stones. He confronted the armed soldier with his ax, threatening to "fix him first plenty."[17]

To survive the Rogue Indian War and the Siletz Indian Reservation required luck, the support of kin, and no small amount of courage.

Chapter Three

Resettling Oregon

1811-1860

They "were very independent."
Observer describing Willamette Valley settlers in 1850

The story of Oregon's resettlement in some respects was an old one, following a script laid out in New Mexico and other parts of the Southwest, the Chesapeake, Massachusetts Bay, New York and Pennsylvania, the Ohio River Valley, the deep South, and other parts of the vast territory drained by the Mississippi River. People of European descent had been planting new societies in what would become the United States for well over two centuries when an annual succession of wagon trains began rolling over the Oregon Trail in 1843. They faced the same sort of challenges: long journeys, wresting control of the land from Native peoples, learning how to wring a living from new soils, creating or recreating social and political institutions. It was all part of what historians used to call the "frontier," the process by which peoples from Spain, France, England, Russia, the American colonies, and especially the United States settled North America.

But such terms as "frontier," "settlement," or even "westward expansion" lend a false sense of coherence and uniformity to this process. The life of an *encomendero* in New Mexico differed dramatically from that of a Puritan in New England in the early seventeenth century, and two centuries later the young plantations of southern Mississippi did not much resemble the rough homesteads of northern Illinois.

Mining dominated the settlement of North America's western slope. The discovery of gold at Sutter's Mill in 1848 touched off the largest migration. It was followed up by booms in British Columbia, Idaho, Nevada, and Montana. These findings drew the same sort of people: young, generally unattached men who seldom stayed more than a few months. Most of the communities these people formed were long on style but short on substance. They often dried up as quickly as they had appeared. Where mining persisted it soon passed into the hands of a few large companies, and the miners became wage earners.

Oregon had a few mining enthusiasms: in the southwest corner of the state in the early 1850s and a decade later along the John Day and Powder Rivers of eastern Oregon. But the great majority of people who came to Oregon in the 1840s and 1850s came to mine its soils, not its minerals. These men and women were drawn not by the promise of quick riches but by the prospect of establishing expansive farms that would shelter their progeny for generations to come. It was this conservatism, this desire for stability and continuity, that made Oregon something of an anomaly in the otherwise unbridled far West of the mid-nineteenth century.

Going to Oregon

Non-Native peoples began settling in Oregon in 1811, when a collection of people from the United States, Canada, and Hawai'i founded John Jacob Astor's ill-starred venture at the Columbia River's mouth. These fur traders were soon followed by employees of the North West Company and the Hudson's Bay Company. Many of these men stayed for only a few years. But in 1829 some French-Canadian retirees settled with their Native wives at French Prairie, north of what would become Salem. Others soon followed them, and by the early 1840s some sixty families farmed there.

An eclectic collection of settlers from the United States was also filtering into the Willamette Valley. Some were fur traders who had resolved to set down some roots with their Native wives in western Oregon's temperate climes, men such as Ewing Young, Caleb Young, Joe Meek, and Robert Newell. They established "Rocky Mountain Retreat," a small farming community near what would one day be Hillsboro. More pious immigrants soon followed. Methodist missionaries led by Jason Lee came in 1834 and settled just south of French Prairie. Despite indifferent success, others soon arrived, including fifty in 1840. By then the Methodists had a station at The Dalles, up the Columbia River, and they soon added a small outpost on Clatsop Plains, near the river's mouth.

Oregon was also attracting attention from visionaries with more patriotic and entrepreneurial visions. Stirred by Lewis and Clark's journals and conversations with other explorers, Boston's Hall Jackson Kelley asserted in the 1820s that "active sons of American freedom" ought to make their way to Oregon.[1] Nathaniel Wyeth, young and ambitious, was determined to put legs on Kelley's dream. His Pacific Trading Company aspired to run the Hudson's Bay Company out of business. His party straggled into Fort Vancouver, in 1832, embarrassingly short on men (twelve) and trading goods (none). But Wyeth was nothing if not determined. He returned to Boston, hatched the Columbia River Company, and was back in Oregon in 1834. This time Wyeth stayed longer, but with poor results. His British rivals quickly ran him out of the fur business, and his plans to ship salmon to the eastern United States foundered. He gave up and went home in 1836, though some of his employees remained.

Wyeth and the Methodists failed miserably at their respective goals of making a fortune and converting Natives. But they did a fine job of publicizing the virtues of Oregon—real and imagined.

Tales of rich soils and mild winters drew the attentions of many midwestern farmers. Here the impact of the Panic of 1837 still lingered, for the ensuing depression had made it impossible for many to pay their farm mortgages. These financial difficulties were compounded by destructive floods and sicknesses along the bottoms of the Missouri, Iowa, and Illinois rivers, particularly malaria, the dreaded "fever and ague." The Willamette Valley held out the prospect of land fertile and free. These were the children and grandchildren of men and women who had been moving west for generations, away from the tidewater then, after the American Revolution, over the Appalachians to the continent's heartland. Now, seeking a bountiful landed legacy for their children's children, they were prepared to pull up stakes again and move some two thousand miles to the latest promised land.

The nature of the trip encouraged some and deterred others. Not every family could purchase the necessary equipment, including oxen, their running gear, and a strong wagon. Farm families were accustomed to eating what they raised, but undertaking a six-month journey put a premium on lightweight, often store-bought foodstuffs. Some financed the trip by selling their land and most of their possessions. Others, especially single men, signed on as hired help, essentially trading their labor for board and room, food and passage. Many couples also made the journey, especially newlyweds. Like other recently opened areas before and after, Oregon represented a chance at a fresh start.

The journey itself was more tedious than harrowing. They travelled along the Missouri River and then along the Platte and Sweetwater rivers to the gentle South Pass and then north to Fort Hall, in what is now southeastern Idaho. From there they toiled northwestward along the Snake River plain and over the Blue Mountains. Most proceeded along the Columbia River and ended their passage with a perilous raft ride at The Dalles or, starting in 1846, hauled their wagons around

Mt. Hood on the precipitous Barlow Toll Road. Diarists complained of dust, heat, and sore feet. "This day has been insupportable!" exclaimed one woman in Wyoming. "Oh, the dust and excessive heat is scarcely to be endured. I try to be brave but in times like these my spirit falters."[2]

Dangers accompanied these discomforts. Few of the wagon trains were confronted by hostile Native peoples, especially before the mid-1850s. Attacks were most common on the Applegate Cut-off through eastern Oregon, though some of the raids attributed to Indians were in fact carried out by white desperadoes. Drowning brought about as many deaths as Native Americans did. Firearms and heavy wagons caused not a few maimings and killings. But the biggest killer by far was disease, accounting for roughly 90 percent of deaths on the trail. Cholera, mountain fever, and scurvy were the most potent killers.

Few early emigrants undertook the journey alone. The great majority traveled in wagon trains during the 1840s. They congregated at jump-off points such as Independence or St. Joseph, Missouri. Here they formed companies, the male household heads electing a set of officers who assigned various duties. The families were expected to feed and care for themselves. But some leaders attempted to impose their wills on others, such as requiring that every man was "to carry with him a Bible and other religious books, as we hope not to degenerate into a state of barbarism."[3] Such strictures soon bumped up against American individualism, particularly once fears of being attacked by Indians wore off. Disagreements erupted over the extent of officers' authority, how quickly the train should move, and whether or not it ought to travel on Sundays. Like contentious Protestant denominations, the companies often fractured into smaller collections of like-minded individuals as they moved west. This is not to say that the overlanders were incapable of cooperation. Men routinely pitched in to help each other at river crossings and watched each others' stock. Women commonly shared cooking. But the core social unit of these overlanders remained the family, broadly defined. This family orientation distinguished the Oregon immigrants from other collections of western migrants: miners headed for California, soldiers on patrol, or traders headed for Santa Fe or other parts of the Southwest.

Until 1842 migration to Oregon had been sporadic. That year over one hundred came over the Oregon Trail, and for the first time women and children combined to outnumber men. In 1843 nearly nine hundred people came to Oregon, and two years later some twenty-five hundred did. The Willamette Valley was starting to fill up.

Community

These newcomers formed societies that resembled the ones they had left behind. Unlike emerging communities in California, British Columbia, and other parts of the western slope, the Willamette Valley of the mid-nineteenth century would be overwhelmingly agrarian, family oriented, and homogeneous.

Like other parts of the far West, Oregon's population grew quickly. In early 1845 at least two thousand Caucasian people lived there, and that number was more than doubled by that year's complement of overlanders. Five years later Oregon's non-Native population exceeded twelve thousand, and ten years later, in 1860, it had increased more than fourfold, to over fifty-two thousand.

Yet this growth, impressive enough by contemporary standards, was relatively modest for that day. San Francisco, to take a particularly explosive example, grew from one thousand to fifty thousand people between 1848 and 1856. When Oregon became a state in 1859, then, it had far fewer residents than California's leading city.

Oregon was also much more family oriented than other parts of the West. By 1860 there were 1.5 white males for every white female in the state. The ratio was much more skewed for people in their twenties

First log cabins in Scottsburg, 1850. Sketch by Captain A. Lyman. Courtesy of the Douglas County Museum

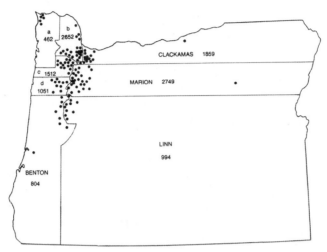

Oregon population and counties in 1850. Each dot represents 100 persons. Reprinted from Samuel N. Dicken and Emily F. Dicken, The Making of Oregon: A Study in Historical Geography *(Portland: Oregon Historical Society, 1979), p. 79. © 1979, The Oregon Historical Society. Reprinted with permission*

or thirties, but not nearly as uneven as in most newly settled areas. A census taker in British Columbia's Cariboo mining region counted just twenty-five women among more than fifty-five hundred residents in 1863. Oregon's women were fecund as well as numerous. In Washington County, which included the fertile Tualatin Valley, most women married before turning eighteen, and those with at least two children gave birth about every twenty-four months. This made for a young population. In 1860 more than twenty-two thousand of Oregon's fifty-two thousand whites were under the age of fifteen.

Oregon drew and contained a much more homogeneous population than did other parts of the far West. Some Chinese Americans had been drawn to southern Oregon by the mining booms of the 1850s, but the state's census recorded only 425 in 1860. African Americans were still more scarce: just 128 lived here. Only one out of ten Oregonians had been born overseas in 1860, with most hailing from locales familiar to native-born Americans: Ireland, Germany, the British Islands, England, or Canada. These people were much more apt than their American-born counterparts to be single men and to live outside the Willamette Valley.

Portland in 1857. Photo courtesy of the Historic Photograph Collections, Salem (Oregon) Public Library

Oregon most resembled the rest of the far West not in the Willamette Valley, but in Portland, its only city, and in the unpolished settlements that lay to the valley's south, east, and west.

By 1860 Portland had grown to nearly three thousand. It included about 6 percent of the state's population but 25 percent of its foreign born and a large portion of its merchants. Many of its commercial leaders were from Germany, including several prominent Jews. More still hailed from the northeastern U.S. The little city boasted some fifty manufacturing concerns, but they employed just 167 men, about three per establishment. Commerce loomed larger than industry. Standing just a few miles south of where the Willamette River met the Columbia, it was the "city that gravity built," the place where the valley's agricultural bounty was funnelled downstream and loaded into ships bound for San Francisco and more distant ports. It would soon extend its reach eastward, to supply the Idaho gold fields. By 1859 Portland's newspapers advertised the services of bankers, attorneys, notaries, physicians, druggists, advertising agents, insurance agents, surveyors, architects, singing and dance instructors, and a wide range of craftspeople: dressmakers, milliners, carpenters, masons, painters, blacksmiths, gunsmiths, tanners, bakers, barbers, and jewellers. Portland was as close as Oregon came to being cosmopolitan.

Southern Oregon enjoyed robust growth in the 1850s and by the decade's close contained 16 percent of the state's population. It featured a mixed economy. Farmers scattered across its many small valleys. A pair of gold mines in Josephine County occupied about 140 workers in 1860, and determined Chinese miners examined the tailings that their less patient white counterparts had discarded. Jacksonville and Roseburg were the major towns, each with nearly a thousand residents.

Settlements were much more scattered west of the Coast Range. Much of the Oregon coast was still dominated by Native peoples, though many were perishing under the horrible conditions at the Siletz and Grand Ronde reservations. Most of the white population—many of them bachelors—were trying to make a living raising stock or crops on coastal plains or in narrow river valleys. The salmon and timber booms still lay in the future.

White settlement was more sparse still in eastern Oregon, much of which was still controlled by Native peoples in 1860. That year's census counted about two thousand whites east of the Cascades, most of whom lived in The Dalles or elsewhere along the Columbia River. Eastern Oregon's Wasco County covered about half the state but included barely 3 percent of its non-Indian population.

The Willamette Valley drew the great majority of immigrants because there was fine land for the taking. In 1843 Oregon's provisional government established that settlers could claim 640 acres. In 1850, four years after the boundary dispute had been settled, Congress passed the Donation Land Law, which granted 320 acres to resident white male adults and another 320 to their wives. Couples who went to Oregon after the law's passage got half as much. These generous provisions prompted much immigration to and marriage in Oregon, and within a few years little first-rate land remained unclaimed in the valley, a development that would help spur settlement in eastern Oregon beginning in the 1860s.

Most of the people who took up claims in the 1840s and the 1850s hailed not from the eastern seaboard, where most of the nation's people lived, but from more recently settled states: Missouri, Illinois, Ohio, Kentucky, and Indiana. Many traced their ancestry to Kentucky or other parts of the Upper South. The newcomers soon overwhelmed the missionaries and mountain men who had preceded them. The more prosperous and educated Yankees often referred to the newcomers as "hoosiers." The term was not meant to be complimentary. "A hoosier family to visit me, and certainly I am glad they are gone," sniffed Margaret Jewett Bailey in 1849. The "lady" had mussed her carpet, the "gentleman" spat upon her floors, and the children made kindling of her rocking chair. "Such are," she concluded, "some of the best from Western America, and our improved state of society."[4]

The great majority of these settlers had emigrated as part of a large family and kin group, and once in Oregon they maintained and strengthened those ties. The valley's large farms separated people's homesteads. But these homesteads were teeming with people. Emigrants from the Midwest had more children than other Oregonians, and they were also more apt to include in their households members of their extended family, such as parents, than lodgers or hired help. Not many members of these farm families traveled much, and parents often played a large role in choosing whom a daughter wed. Most marriages were therefore between people who lived in the same area, a practice that bound their communities still more tightly.

It was the Willamette Valley's many "hoosier" families that made Oregon such a peculiar western society in the 1840s and 1850s. In a region and a nation so often devoted to quick money, mercurial growth, and evanescent social relations, they established communities that looked backward rather than forward: stable, family-oriented homesteads and neighborhoods that would, they hoped, sustain their progeny for generations to come.

The Economics of Subsistence

Conservatism and geography conspired to hinder Oregon's early economy.

Before the advent of railroads, it cost as much to move goods a few miles in a wagon as it did to transport them across oceans. The Columbia River offered a broad artery into the heart of the Oregon Country. But its bar was notoriously treacherous. The fertile Willamette Valley was well watered by the Willamette River and its numerous tributaries. But the falls at Oregon City, just fifteen miles from the river's mouth, interrupted boat traffic, and upstream the river was a braided network of channels and marshes. The depth of smaller streams, such as the Tualatin and the Santiam, varied considerably by season and locale. In any event, early settlers, remembering the floods and diseases of the Midwest, homesteaded on higher ground when they could. Getting goods to market was therefore expensive and time consuming.

That is not to say that people did not try. Steam-powered vessels offered unprecedented speed and reliability in the early nineteenth century, and they soon appeared in Oregon. Portland enjoyed regular steamship links with San Francisco from 1850, and that year the steamboat *Columbia* began service between Astoria and the Cascade Rapids, which lay some 150 miles upriver. A year later the *James P. Flint* began toiling above the rapids, and the *Multnomah* began the challenging work of negotiating the shallow Willamette River's waters. Many others soon joined them. But steamboats foundered on the smaller streams which served the majority of the Willamette Valley's residents. Not until after the Civil War—more than two decades after settlement had begun—did a steamboat manage to push itself up the Tualatin River to Forest Grove. Roads were the obvious solution. Washington County's government devoted a great deal of attention to their construction in the late 1850s. It required men aged twenty-one to fifty to donate two days each year to laboring on them. But more ambitious projects required substantial private capital. The Portland and Valley Plank Road Company sank $15,000 into a road from Hillsboro to Portland before giving up in 1852. Four years later the task was finally completed, though one sufferer referred to it as "one of the hardest roads ... that ever a man travelled in his life."[5] Bridges were expensive, too, and apt to wash away.

In sum, getting around in mid-nineteenth-century Oregon was difficult, especially during the long rainy season. Moving people was bad enough. The stage between Portland and Salem, a distance of about fifty miles, consumed a day. Getting a wagonload of grain or lumber to a steamboat landing could take much longer.

Nor were Oregon farmers capable of producing much grain. To be sure, the land was bountiful, and controlled fires set by Native peoples had cleared much of it from trees and brush. But plowing, planting, cultivating, harvesting, and processing crops required long, tedious hours of hard work by humans and other animals. Threshing, for example, the laborious process of separating grain from chaff, entailed spreading shocks of wheat out on a hard surface and leading oxen or horses over them. Creating a bushel of wheat that sold for a dollar was a backbreaking, labor-intensive endeavor, and the Willamette Valley did not have much labor to spare.

Oregon's early economy was slowed by attitudes as well as geography and technology. The Willamette Valley's settlers hoped, as historian David Johnson sums up, "to remake a kin-based, mixed subsistence-market agriculture on better terms than they had known in their midwestern homes."[6] Many—remembering the depression of the late 1830s—were wary of speculation. They were not, to be sure, opposed to prosperity, but they distrusted distant markets and were not willing to risk the long-term viability of their ample homesteads on its vagaries. They instead grew, processed, and stored most of what they ate and relied on kin and neighbors as much as possible for everything else—credit, temporary shelter, or labor. Constructing a large barn, for example, began with some six months labor by a builder and an assistant or two before being completed or raised in a single day by twenty to thirty men. Land for these people constituted and represented security, not real estate. Property that could have been sold to newcomers eager to cultivate its soils therefore lay idle for many years. An educated New Englander in 1850 characterized the Willamette Valley's farmers as more honest than hard working, as people who "cared little about luxuries" and "were very independent."[7]

This is not to say that Oregonians of the 1840s and 1850s were indifferent to money. Their first big break came in the summer of 1848, when news of the discovery of gold at Sutter's Mill spread. Oregon quickly lost a large fraction of its men. An Oregon poet lamented the exodus in lines more heartfelt than graceful:

> *That glittering gold is dearly won,*
> *That disunites congenial minds,*
> *Our fathers, husbands, friends and sons,*
> *Have fled to California's mines.*[8]

Indeed, the first meeting of the Territorial Legislature was postponed because so many of the legislators had gone south. Peter Burnett, an early leader who had arrived in 1843, left never to return and was soon governor of California. But many "web foots" returned, and, since they had been able to get there ahead of just about everyone else, not a few of them came back with pockets bulging. Oregonians mined some $5 million of California gold. More important, California's booming economy provided Oregon with a growing and nearby market for lumber, wheat, and beef. Ships rarely visited the lower Willamette River in the mid-1840s. But in 1849 at least fifty docked there, bearing captains eager to purchase any grain and timber they could lay their hands on. The discovery of gold in southern Oregon a year later helped sustain the boom. The gold rush quickened Oregon's nascent economy. Gold dust provided a widely accepted medium of exchange and lubricated economic transactions. Profit-minded farmers clambered for transportation improvements and began to purchase machinery that helped them to plant, cultivate, and harvest more acres. Wheat—the quintessential cash crop—dominated many of the fields in the northern Willamette Valley, where farmers tended to be more market oriented. Portland emerged as an important mercantile center.

Yet the gold rush amended rather than transformed Oregon's economy. Substantial technological and even ideological gaps separated the majority of the Willamette Valley's farmers from the ships plying between Portland and San Francisco. Nor did Oregon's manufactures develop very much. Timber had been the state's principal export even before the California boom. Like the Hudson's Bay Company before them, early U.S. entrepreneurs sent many of their exports to Hawai'i—though California and Russian America were also important. Five export mills quickly arose to serve the California market: two in or near Astoria and three in the Portland area. In the coming decade Oregon timber also found its way to China and Australia. By 1860 Oregon had 127 sawmills—four times as many as Washington. But Washington's mills employed nearly twice as many people and produced much more lumber. Geography favored the Puget Sound, where ships could easily come and go and innumerable islands and inlets provided easy access to forests. There outside

Salem Flouring Mill, 1865. Top photo shows wood frame construction and workers roofing the structure. Lower photo shows completed building. Photo courtesy of the Historic Photograph Collections, Salem (Oregon) Public Library

investors established large, steam-driven mills. The great majority of Oregon mills were small, water-powered affairs that turned out modest amounts of lumber for local markets. Much the same could be said of its other industries. With an exception or two, such as the woolen mills in Salem, Oregon's flour mills, leather workers, furniture factories, and wagon makers employed at most a few people. All told, its 309 manufacturers engaged less than one thousand workers—this out of a population of over fifty thousand.

Aspiring manufacturers were hamstrung by laws that made borrowing money difficult. The 1857 constitution stipulated that banks could not incorporate, that they had to be financed by one or two owners who would be "held directly accountable to their creditors."[9] Nor could these banks issue notes that would circulate as currency. Oregonians did not much trust bankers, and the first bank, Ladd and Tilton, did not appear until 1859.

By the eve of the Civil War, technological, industrial, and economic changes had transformed much of the northeastern United States. California, to the south, was rapidly becoming integrated into the nation's emerging economy. But, by accident and design, Oregon's tradition-minded farmers remained insulated from those sweeping changes.

Gender and Race

Industrialization reworked social relations in much of the northeastern U.S. in the decades before the Civil War. Well-to-do women, freed from the labors of subsistence household economies, began exercising more control of their homes and their communities. More and more women and men reformers argued that slavery was an inhumane and anachronistic institution that had no place in modern America.

Such movements made little headway in conservative Oregon. The great majority of Oregon's settlers had no use for slavery, but most of them hated people of color even more. Nor were the heads of many Oregon households the least bit sympathetic to the movement for women's rights. Male settlers routinely assumed and asserted superiority over their wives.

The very decision to go to Oregon often underscored husbands' authority. Many Midwestern women would have stayed put if they could. Such farm women found meaning in the context of kin and community ties and domestic responsibilities. Leaving home disrupted both. It meant separating from grandparents, parents, siblings, other relations, and friends. It meant giving up a house and farm, first for a cramped covered wagon, then for a rude cabin. Yet women married to men determined to go West had little recourse: it was pretty hard to support oneself and one's children without a man, and, in the eyes of the courts, a wife who refused to follow her husband had deserted him. Wives were supposed to go when and where their husbands commanded.

The overland trail exacerbated marital inequalities. Most men regarded the trip as the adventure of a lifetime—their chance to "see the elephant," to break out of life's routines and enjoy strange sights, maybe even fight Indians. They headed up the trains, decided where and when to camp, drove the wagons, minded the stock, and hunted. Women spent much of their days riding or walking and trying to keep young children from being maimed or killed by oxen and wagons. They worked late into the night and rose early in the morning to unpack, gather fuel, prepare meals, clean up, make the beds, and repack, all the while watching their children.

Arriving in Oregon brought only partial respite. It took years to restore a sense of domesticity. The typical family lived for several years in a log home with one or two rooms and a loft. Permanent barns usually preceded permanent houses. The settlers' large homesteads left many women isolated from each other. This was especially true in lightly settled areas: on the edges of the Willamette Valley and in coastal and eastern Oregon. Men were more apt to leave homesteads than women were, to attend political meetings, conduct business at a courthouse or store, or take crops to market. Men did most of the field work, but women worked very hard inside and outside the house. Abigail Scott Duniway later recalled that she had "milked milk enough with my two hands to float" a steamboat and "made butter enough for market with the propelling power of my hands at an old-fashioned churn … to grease the axles of creation."[10] Wives also kept gardens and chickens, helped with harvesting other crops, put up preserves, cooked, cleaned, spun wool, made and mended clothes, nursed and cared for children, among other tasks.

Oregon's skewed sex ratios and the provisions of the Donation Land Law of 1850 meant that many women married men twice or more their age. Men in their twenties and thirties greatly outnumbered their women counterparts, and marriage could double the amount of property that a man could farm. This sometimes meant that young women had their choice of several men. But their parents' wishes often trumped their own, and the matches were made at a young age. "What could a girl of 14 do to protect herself from a man of 44," wondered a woman whose husband "used to beat me until I thought I couldn't stand it."[11]

Nor did women's scarcity bring them many economic advantages outside of marriage. Women launderers and bakers might become rich in the California or Nevada gold fields. But few Oregon men had money to spend on such luxuries. Portland was a magnet for independent-minded women. Some 11 percent (65 out of 475) of its adult females were employed outside the home in 1860, a much higher proportion than in the state as a whole. But 60 percent of those women were in one of three marginal occupations: domestic service, miscellaneous semi- or unskilled work, and prostitution.

Women who aspired to prominence courted censure. Margaret Jewett Bailey's *Grains*, an autobiographical critique of several leading Methodist men disguised as a novel, appeared in 1854. It drew ready and critical attention from Portland's leading newspaper, the *Oregonian*: "We seldom read books of feminine production, believing *their* (the females) province to be darning stockings, pap and gruel, children, cookstoves, and the sundry little affairs that make life comparatively comfortable and makes them, what Providence designed them 'Helpmates.'"[12] Four years later, Asahel Bush—no friend, as we shall see, of the *Oregonian*—reacted similarly when social reformer Ada Weed lectured in Salem on women's rights. "The true sphere of woman is in the domestic circle," he asserted, for "there she is the chief ornament and attraction, and there she excites the holiest and purest emotions of which the heart of man is capable."[13] A woman's place was in the home.

The ideal Oregon couple featured an energetic housewife who deferred to her hard-working husband. Husbands expected their wives to obey them, to recognize and respect their authority. Indeed, some husbands struck recalcitrant wives with a stick or switch, as if they were disciplining a willful child. Oregonians expected husbands to be industrious and responsible. A Portland man who gambled away the family's last cow admitted "that he was not 'fit' to have a wife," that he "would rather be around among the boys."[14]

Many Oregon women and men accepted and met these expectations. Frictions and difficulties ensued when one or both parties did not. Assertive wives were censured inside and outside their homes. Abusive men were less vulnerable to criticism. Divorces were much easier to come by in Oregon than in most of the United States.

But divorces were expensive and humiliating. Many Oregonians shunned divorced women on principle. Unhappy couples therefore tended to stay together.

Gender constituted a profound social marker in mid-nineteenth-century Oregon. Men wielded authority outside and inside the family and enjoyed many prerogatives that women did not. Yet race was a still more telling divider. Indeed, angry husbands commonly included racial slurs in their invectives, such as "lower than a Chinese whore," to imply that a woman could sink so low that she was no longer white.[15]

Oregon was much whiter than most of the United States. Native Americans were by far its largest minority population, and the great majority of them lived away from other Oregonians, on reservations or in their homelands. Hawaiians, Blacks, and interracial peoples had worked on the north Pacific slope as fur traders. But Oregon contained only a few dozen African Americans in 1850. The mining excitements in southern Oregon drew more people of color in the ensuing decade, but in 1860 the census counted just 553 people of Chinese and African descent—about 1 percent of the young state's population. This was no doubt an undercount. Census takers were apt to ignore or miss marginal peoples. At least a few Mexicans and other Latin Americans lived in or passed through the state. Even so, Oregon was overwhelmingly white.

White Oregonians wanted a white state. Some feared that African Americans might ally with Native Americans. Most associated slavery with class privilege. A man who came to Oregon in 1844 remarked, "I'm going to Oregon, where there'll be no slaves, and we'll all start even." But only white males were to get the chance to "start even." Such men, as Jesse Applegate pointed out, "hated *free negroes* worse even than slaves."[16] One of the first acts of the provisional government in 1844 was to exclude Blacks—slave or free—from Oregon. This policy was reaffirmed in 1849 and 1859, after Oregon became part of the United States and achieved statehood, respectively. These laws were enforced only once, against Jacob Vanderpool, a West Indian businessman living in Oregon City in 1851. But they served as a potent deterrent. People of African descent were much more likely to live north of the Columbia River, in sparsely settled Washington Territory, than in Oregon.

Oregon's white majority created a thicket of other discriminatory laws. People of color could neither vote nor own land. Samuel Thurston, Oregon's congressional delegate, made sure that the Donation Land Act of 1850 excluded African Americans and

Hawaiians. The young state's constitution stipulated that neither African Americans nor Chinese Americans could vote.

Oregon billed itself as a place where privilege counted for little, where a person who worked hard could become prosperous. But these opportunities were in fact hedged with exceptions. Women were supposed to enjoy them through their husbands, not independently, and people of color were discouraged and forbidden from enjoying the good life in Oregon under any circumstances.

Organizing Oregon

The good life in Oregon did not come easily to anyone. The settlers who trekked here in the early 1840s realized all too well that they had entered a contested place. The Hudson's Bay Company still dominated the area, and there were no guarantees that Oregon would become part of the United States. The newcomers worried over their futures, and for nearly a decade they labored to erect political solutions to this uncertainty.

There were two major political forces in the Willamette Valley by 1840: the Hudson's Bay Company and the Methodists. The former, whose initials suggested to some the sobriquet "Here Before Christ," had flourishing lumber and grist mills and farms in addition to its extensive fur trade. Fort Vancouver dominated the region's economy. Early settlers went there to beg, borrow, or purchase seed and livestock, to buy and sell, even to sharpen their tools. Moreover, Chief Factor John McLoughlin and the company had considerable influence over the sixty or so retirees who had settled on French Prairie.

The Methodists constituted a much different society from the heterogenous settlements at Fort Vancouver and French Prairie. The missionaries were highly educated emigrants from the northeast United States who came to save souls, not make money. But Jason Lee and his subordinates, confronting a dying and indifferent Native population, soon turned their considerable energies to more secular affairs. By 1841 they were cultivating two hundred acres and caring for growing herds of livestock. Fort Vancouver still dwarfed these enterprises, but the Hudson's Bay Company leaders could readily discern that Americans were growing stronger in the valley by the year.

The Americans' first occasion to organize arose early in 1841, when Ewing Young died. The retired fur trader had brought large numbers of cattle to Oregon and possessed a substantial estate. Jason Lee urged the attendees of Young's funeral to create some sort of mechanism to dispose of Young's belongings and, more generally, to help preserve "peace and good order."[17] The ambitious Lee proposed a full set of officials: a governor, judge, three road commissioners, even two overseers of the poor. Most of the settlers, a mixed collection of French Canadians and sundry Americans, were more circumspect and chose to elect only a sheriff, three constables, and a probate judge. Father Blanchet, a Catholic priest with ties to the Hudson's Bay Company, headed a committee charged with drafting a civil code. The probate judge saw to it that Young's property was auctioned off and sent the proceeds to his heirs in New York. But the committee charged with creating the civil code never met, perhaps because Blanchet hoped to forestall the mission party's plans.

But the Americans were persistent. They were energized by the arrival in 1842 of many overlanders, including Elijah White, who had just been appointed Indian agent of Oregon Territory. The United States, of course, did not yet possess said territory, but White's party brought news that growing numbers of Americans were determined that it soon would, and that still more settlers would arrive the next summer.

Growth fostered division within the Americans' ranks. Many found White officious and ambitious. He had once worked for Lee, and the two resented each other. The settlers' differences were ideological as well as personal. How could they ensure that future immigrants would not seize their land? What would they do if the Indians attacked? Some favored following Texas's lead and establishing a separate republic. Others wished for the United States to take possession of the Oregon Country as soon as possible, but disagreed over whether or not to cooperate with the Hudson's Bay Company until then. In the meantime, British citizens were growing alarmed by the growing numbers of American settlers.

The stalemate was broken by subterfuge in the spring of 1843, when a group of settlers called for a general meeting—ostensibly on how to keep wolves and other predators from attacking their livestock. The settlers agreed to set up a mechanism to pay wolf bounties, including a method of taxation, and they elected officers to administer it. Then someone broached the larger question: a broader system of government. The attendees appointed a dozen men to explore that possibility. A few weeks later the committee reported its recommendations to 102 voters, nearly one half of the valley's white men. These men decided by a narrow margin to create a government. Most—though not all—of the French Canadians then withdrew in protest. The remainder elected a nine-person committee to draft a code of laws. Two months later, on July 5th, the settlers met again to hear and approve the code. The provisional government's laws were patterned after Iowa's. But the committee made some singular provisions with special appeal to Oregonians. All law-abiding men could claim 640 acres, and taxes would be paid on a voluntary basis.

The overlanders who arrived later, in 1843 and in 1844, were not much impressed by Oregon's half-formed government, and they were numerous enough to do something about it. They soon established compulsory taxes, pared the Methodist mission's land claim, replaced the three-person executive committee with a governor and the legislative committee with a thirteen-member legislature, and organized counties. George Abernethy, a merchant who had overseen the Methodists' business affairs, was elected governor in 1845.

Oregonians learned late in 1846 that the boundary with England had finally been settled and that it lay far to the north. But the Oregon Treaty left many issues unresolved, and Congress seemed in no hurry to clarify them. Longtime settlers wondered if the federal government would recognize their extensive claims. The newcomers pouring into the Willamette Valley hoped that they would not. It seemed un-American and unjust to find the cream of the land skimmed off by the Hudson's Bay Company, the mission party, and early settlers and merchants, including Governor Abernethy himself. Charles Pickett— who, like many other recent arrivals, settled on land that was already claimed—called the old guard a "vulgar, tin-peddling, shaving, picayune, upstart Yankee and Cockney canaille."[18] Considerable conflict and hard feelings accompanied the carving up of Eden.

The Whitman killings late in 1847 at last prompted Congress to act. It narrowly passed a bill organizing the Oregon Territory in 1848, and President Polk signed it. Oregon would now enjoy the protections and expenditures of the federal government. Two years later, in 1850, the Donation Land Law affirmed that Oregon's early settlers would be able to keep their land. Their calculation had paid off. Their title was at last secure.

Less than ten years before a few score settlers had organized themselves into a government, this in a land whose title was disputed and under the nose of a powerful British monopoly. Now they were part of the United States.

Territorial Politics

Oregon's provisional government had been riven by local divisions: the Hudson's Bay Company and the mission party; recent versus earlier arrivals. In the 1850s these rivalries faded. The Hudson's Bay Company moved its headquarters to Vancouver Island, and the Methodists dispersed. Federal legislation and the work of surveyors brought clarity to land tenure. Yet the 1850s would be a decade of acrimonious political debate and division, though the divisions would increasingly arise from national rather than local issues. Democrats stood on one side of the political divide, a fractured opposition on the other: Whigs, anti-immigrant Know-Nothings, and, eventually, Republicans.

The great majority of Oregon's voters were enthusiastic Jacksonian Democrats. Most of the territory's settlers hailed from the Midwest, where the party was strong. They favored individual enterprise and liberty and distrusted merchants, banks, manufacturers, urbanization, and reformers. They tended to be less educated than average and, with the exception of Baptists, unchurched. Indeed, Oregon's Democratic Party constituted a social as well as political vehicle, a place where the white men of Oregon could affirm their solidarity in a round of political meetings, celebrations, and elections.

Asahel Bush became the editor and publisher of the Oregon Statesman *newspaper in 1851 and was for many years the mastermind of Oregon's Democratic machine. Photo courtesy of the Historic Photograph Collections, Salem (Oregon) Public Library*

Oregon's Democratic Party of the 1850s was dominated by Joe Lane, the territory's first governor. President Polk could hardly have selected a more fitting man. Born in 1801 in North Carolina and raised in Kentucky, Lane had become an Indiana legislator by age twenty-one and distinguished himself in the Mexican-American War. He was also a splendid backwoods politician: unpolished but hard working and charismatic; ambitious but, by the standards of the day, principled. Lane was swept out of office after the Whigs captured the presidency. But in 1851 Samuel Thurston, Oregon's congressional delegate, passed away, and Lane was elected to succeed him.

If Lane constituted the public face of Oregon's "Democracy," Asahel Bush was its guts. Bush had come to Oregon on Thurston's invitation, to start a newspaper boosting the congressman's political fortunes. He soon settled his press in Salem and established, through the *Oregon Statesman* and unstinting correspondence, what one historian terms an "elaborate political-intelligence network."[19] Other members of the inner circle included southern Oregon's Matthew Deady, the territory's leading jurist, and James Nesmith, who had served in the provisional government. Oregon's Democratic Party, then, had two very different sides: a small cadre of leaders who funnelled federal oppointments and monies to themselves and their friends and a broad base of voters devoted to Joe Lane.

Their opponents enjoyed few successes. Oregon's Whigs were always a small minority, though their economic and public influence outstripped their numbers. The territory's Democratic farmers seldom contemplated any other occupation. They were determined to stay on the land. Whigs tended to view farming as just one of many ways to make a living, and they therefore kept their eyes open for other business opportunities. Whigs were also more apt to interest themselves in religion and reform. They believed that government could play an active and salutary role in society—by passing and enforcing laws that punished drunkards and Sabbath-breakers or by enhancing large manufacturers, for example. The short-lived Know-Nothings or American Party advocated immigration restriction, particularly of Catholics.

Oregon's minority parties were too small and fractious to mount a successful challenge to their Democratic opponents, but their stinging criticisms helped divide the majority party. The Whig *Oregonian*, a Portland newspaper, coined the term "clique" (pronounced "clee'-cue") to describe the machinations of "Ass-a-hell" Bush, whom it castigated for "unholy, ungodly and pusillanimous, semi-official and understrapper attacks."[20] Bush gave as good as he got, and Oregon's pioneering journalists were without peer at hurling invective. But resentments arose within as well as between the parties. Democrats in the northern Willamette Valley, castigated as "softs" by Bush, were more interested in national than territorial politics and chafed at the clique's control of the party. Lane, who remained Oregon's lone congressional delegate until the decade's close, was much more tolerant of these softs than Bush and enraged the clique by giving some government positions to them. For years the two parts of the party had served each other effectively: Lane was a popular and electable leader who funnelled patronage to the Oregon leadership; that leadership amplified his accomplishments through its newspapers and got the Democratic vote out when he was up for election. But by 1858 the alliance was fraying.

Controversy over slavery constituted the most daunting challenge to the Oregon Democracy, just as it did for the national party. The territory's Democrats were united in their opposition to African Americans, and the great majority believed that slavery did not belong in Oregon. But where did it belong? Stephen Douglas of Illinois argued for popular sovereignty, that states and territories alike ought to be able to exclude or choose slavery. President Buchanan expressed the southern Democratic view, that slavery could exist everywhere that states had not forbidden it. Under his plan, then, Oregon would be opened up to slave labor at least until it became a state. This pro-slavery argument violated a central tenet of the Democratic Party: the right of self-determination—in this case Oregon Territory's right to exclude slavery. But the southern point of view also resonated with many Oregon Democrats, for it was sensitive to the property rights of individual slaveholders. Centrists tried to convince the Democratic combatants that the point of contention was moot: Oregon was not suited for plantation agriculture, so slavery would not take root here whether or not the law countenanced it. But strongly felt Democratic principles—self-determination and property rights—were at stake, and the pursuit of them pulled Oregon's Democrats apart.

The slavery crisis did serve at least one politically constructive purpose in Oregon: statehood. Oregonians had narrowly voted it down three times. Advocates argued that it would bring telling political advantages: a pair of senators and a voting member of the House of Representatives. Naysayers worried about additional taxes. Democratic and Whig partisans waxed hot and cold on the issue, depending on which controlled the presidency. Then, in 1857, the Supreme Court's Dred Scott decision asserted that only a state had the right to outlaw slavery. Southern congressmen, as we have seen, were asserting the same thing. Oregon's electorate did not want these sorts of decisions taken out of their hands, and in 1857 it voted for statehood by a margin of more than three to one. A divided Congress narrowly approved the bill early in 1859.

Statehood did not save Oregon's Democratic Party. It ran aground on the shoals of the 1860 presidential race. Bush and most of the Salem clique backed Douglas, the nominee of the northern Democrats. Lane, after seeking the presidential nomination, became John Breckinridge's running mate on the renegade southern Democratic ticket. The two Democratic nominees combined to poll over nine thousand votes in Oregon's 1860 presidential nomination, but they divided those votes so evenly that neither had enough to overcome Lincoln's 5,343. Oregon, a Democratic stronghold, helped elect the nation's first Republican president.

Fort Sumter put Oregon's Democrats out of their misery. Few Oregonians outside of Jacksonville and pockets of the southern Willamette Valley were prepared to support the Confederacy once it fired on federal troops. Lane retreated, amidst much calumny, to his farm outside Roseburg. A year later, in 1862, Oregon's Douglas Democrats combined forces with its increasingly powerful Republicans to sweep the elections.

Oregon's map bears witness to the political transformation that had occurred. Many of its early counties bore the names of prominent Democrats, particularly in the southern two-thirds of the state: Jackson, Douglas, Marion, Polk, Linn, Benton, and of course Lane, named after the most popular Oregon politician of the 1850s. Counties created after the Civil War paid homage to Republican war heroes: Lincoln, Grant, Sherman, and Baker, an Oregon senator who died in an early battle. A small county in northeastern Oregon illustrated the trend still more explicitly: Union.

❧ ❧

The Civil War constitutes a thick dividing line in U.S. history. It freed the slaves, abetted the rise of the Republican Party, and encouraged improvements in transportation and industry. The war's impact in Oregon was less dramatic. Differences of opinion provoked some hard feelings and fist fights, but no battles. The war hardly affected the young state's race relations. There were few slaves to free, and even Oregon's Republican press assured its readers that Lincoln was no abolitionist. The war, as we have seen, strengthened Oregon's Republican Party. But Oregon Republicans were much less progressive than some of their counterparts in the urban northeast. They were occupied with the preservation of the union, not the liberation of slaves.

Oregon had filled up considerably in the two decades between the first big wagon train of 1843 and the Civil War. But it remained an isolated backwater dominated by conservative Willamette Valley farmers. Soon, though, in the closing decades of the nineteenth century, technological and industrial revolutions that had already reshaped much of the nation would make their way here.

Biographies

Joe Meek

Joe Meek may not, as is popularly believed, have drawn a line in the ground at Champoeg in 1843 and urged his fellow Oregonians to join him on one side of it in voting to form a government. But he was one of Oregon's most colorful and influential citizens.

Born in 1810 to a well-connected Virginia family, he soon headed west. By 1829 he was trapping for William Sublette in the Rocky Mountains and would range as far west as California. In 1840, as

Joseph Meek, 1810-75, trapper and trader, cultivated a romantic image. Photo courtesy of the Historic Photograph Collections, Salem (Oregon) Public Library

the fur trade declined, Meek and his indigenous wife joined some other fur-trade families in a trek to the Willamette Valley. They soon found congenial company at the aptly named Rocky Mountain Retreat, near present-day Hillsboro, where they farmed.

Meek took an interest in Oregon politics. In 1843 he was elected sheriff of the new government he had helped to create, which proved to be a thankless job. Collecting taxes and arresting law-breakers was anything but easy in a place so full of independent-minded and contentious settlers.

Respectability did not much cramp Meek's style. Eyebrows were raised when he spoke out for temperance and, as historian Robert Utley notes, "there were those who doubted the depth of his conviction" when a Methodist baptism moved him to declare "that Joseph Meek, that old Rocky Mountain sinner, has turned to the Lord."[21]

The Whitman Massacre of 1847 catapulted Meek onto a larger stage. The Oregon legislature reacted to it by seeking assistance from and admission to the U.S. and selected Meek to carry the petition. Meek's small party made it to St. Louis in just two months. Once in Washington, D.C., he purportedly announced himself as "Envoy Extraordinary and Minister Plenipotentiary from the Republic of Oregon to the Court of the United States" and demanded to see the president.[22] Meek was better at telling stories than the truth, but his presence in the nation's capital evidently helped speed Oregon's territorial bill through Congress at a time when sectional tensions made its passage difficult. That Meek was related to both President Polk's wife and private secretary could not have hurt.

Polk appointed Meek federal marshal of the brand-new Oregon territory. Meek swung through Indiana to pick up Joseph Lane, whom Polk had made Oregon's governor, and by March of the following year, 1849, Meek and Lane were in Oregon.

Meek's political independence dimmed his political star. He lost his federal position in 1853, though he remained an active citizen until his death twenty-two years later. He was by then much renowned. Frances Fuller Victor, for many years the state's leading historian, met him shortly after she arrived in 1865 and relied heavily on his memory and stories in writing her history of Oregon for Hubert Bancroft. She also produced a biography of Meek, *River of the West*. Meek, who traveled from Seattle to Klamath Falls boosting the book, offered a title that better suggested his life's cultural breadth: "From the Wigwam to the White House."[23]

Jesse Applegate

Jesse Applegate was one of Oregon's most prominent and peculiar pioneers.

Applegate had first learned of Oregon from some very distinguished people. While working as a teacher and then surveyor in St. Louis he rubbed shoulders with Wilson Price Hunt, Jedediah Smith, and other old fur traders. Then, in the early 1830s, he turned to farming. His education and anti-slavery Whig politics sharply contrasted with the views of most of his neighbors. In 1843, discouraged by hard times, he and two brothers and their families headed for Oregon.

Applegate quickly became a leader—on the trail and afterward. He played an important role in the provisional legislature of 1845 and a year later, with his brother, Lindsay, established the Applegate Trail, which offered overlanders a southern option from Fort Hall, Idaho, to the Willamette Valley. He prospered after moving to the Umpqua River Valley in 1849, where he established an impressive library and lived into his late seventies. His education and accomplishments eventually led Oregonians to dub him the "sage of Yoncalla."

But Applegate felt dogged by misfortune. His eldest son and a nephew perished in the Columbia River, near the end of the Oregon Trail. Oregon politics often disgusted him and prompted him to resign from office. His sympathies for Native and African Americans won him few friends in southern Oregon, and when one of his daughters eloped with a Jacksonville man with southern sympathies he excised her name from the family Bible. He began losing money in the 1860s and in an 1868 letter lamented that his constant struggles to wring a living from his farm left him little time to read or think. "I am no longer fit companion for those engaged in intellectual pursuits," he concluded, and "no longer complain of neglect for there is nothing about me to inspire love or retain friendship."[24]

In a territory overflowing with brash, practical men, Applegate's restless desire to improve both his society and his own character and intellect set him apart.

William T'Vault

This Tennessee-born attorney was one of early Oregon's most contentious and peripatetic politicians. T'Vault became active in Oregon politics soon after his arrival. In 1846 he was elected to the legislature and quickly became Oregon's postmaster general.

His tenure as the territory's first newspaper editor, with Oregon City's *Spectator*, was brief—perhaps because of his poor spelling and certainly because he expressed opinions at odds with the newspaper's backers, a group he characterized as a "class of mungralls [mongrels]."[25] Like many newcomers, he believed that "the present aristocracy" had unfairly monopolized the best land in Oregon.[26]

T'Vault found southern Oregon more congenial to his beliefs and prospects. In 1851 he led a small party into the interior. Most were ambushed at a Coquille village. T'Vault escaped and, thanks to some sympathetic coastal Indians, survived. Jacksonville's gold rush began shortly after this, and T'Vault made his way there. In 1855 he began the *Table Rock Sentinel*.

Unlike most members of the Salem clique, T'Vault was a staunch southern Democrat who defended states' rights and slavery. Jackson County elected him to the legislature in 1858, where he became Speaker of the House. He stuck by Joe Lane when more moderate Democrats did not. Indeed, he presented to the legislature petitions arguing that Oregon ought to defend the rights of its citizens to own slaves—this despite the fact that Oregon voters had just rejected slavery by an overwhelming margin. He persisted in these views after the war broke out and castigated President Lincoln for prosecuting a "tyrannical and unconstitutional war."[27]

T'Vault suffered for his ideological consistency; his political star sank with the Confederacy's. He died in a Jacksonville smallpox epidemic three years after Appomattox, in 1868.

Ada Weed

Dr. Ada M. Weed was way ahead of her time when she and her husband came to Salem in 1858.

Born in Illinois in 1837, she moved from Iowa to New York City to study hydropathy, the use of water in lieu of drugs to promote health. Like many reformers, she also championed women's rights. She married a like-minded classmate, Gideon Allen Weed, and they set sail for the West.

Salem's doctors and opinion makers did not welcome them. Established physicians were put off by the claims that they made for the "water cure." According to the Weeds, "Old School" doctors went so far as to accuse them of "losing patients that we never had, and who were already dead when we arrived in the Territory!" Ada Weed's public insistence that women enjoy more opportunities in education and "a broader field of labor" for which they would "receive a just remuneration therefor" moved Asahel Bush, Salem's leading editor, to criticism and ridicule.[28]

But Weed persisted. She delivered more lectures in Salem—this time to women only—and she and her husband practiced their form of medicine and spoke across the heart of Oregon, from Eugene to The Dalles. The Weeds expounded on many sorts of reforms, from the importance of regular bathing to the evils of tobacco and greasy foods to the way to marital harmony. Ada Weed's lectures to women likely advised them to exercise, dress comfortably, and to limit sexual intercourse.

Not a few Oregon men and women found such teaching unorthodox and objectionable. Gideon Weed reported that residents of one town libeled them as "Free Lovers" and asserted that his wife's lectures were obscene.

Oregon's economic depression also hampered the Weeds. Many of those who sought their services could not pay for them. They left for California in 1860, and eventually settled in Seattle, where Gideon pursued a more conventional and remunerative medical practice and was elected mayor. Ada became a mother and society woman. She continued working for social reforms, though more cautiously than before.

Her influence back in Oregon is difficult to trace. She lived here less than two years, and created no women's rights organizations. But scores of Oregon women who heard her speak began to contemplate, at least quietly and privately, a world in which women enjoyed far more choices and possibilities.

Chapter Four

The Industrialization of Oregon

1860-1900

I "would not have the world altogether cut up into cabbage patches."

John Waldo

Market capitalism had already spread its wings in much of the northeastern U.S. when thousands of overlanders went to Oregon in the 1840s. Railways joined canals to speed the movement of goods, large factories turned out textiles, furniture, boots, plows, firearms, and a host of other products more quickly and cheaply than ever before, and farmers increasingly approached farming as a business, using new horse-drawn implements to plant, cultivate, and harvest crops that railroads whisked to remote markets. The outcome of the Civil War— the defeat of the South and the abolition of slavery—served to underscore the virtues of unrestrained capitalism, a dynamo that soon touched Oregon's shores and valleys.

Oregon was no Pennsylvania, and Portland was no Pittsburgh. Manufacturing would remain a relatively minor part of the state's economy. But a series of advances culminating in the intercontinental rail link of 1883 made its products available to factories and consumers far outside its borders. There were many ambitious entrepreneurs in Oregon in the 1840s and especially the 1850s. But few of them had been able to amass much wealth; Oregon's society, economy, and politics were dominated by militantly independent, small-scale farmers. Technological improvements in the subsequent decades bequeathed to ambitious men the wherewithal to change this.

Yet the very forces that powered Oregon's economic boom fostered trends that undercut the new order. Farmers noticed that the fruits of progress were distributed unevenly, that railroad owners, merchants, and other nonproducers seemed to be making more off farmers' labor than the farmers themselves. Economic prosperity freed Oregon women from much of the household labor and isolation that they had suffered from during the settlement era, and thousands of them began criticizing and reforming the political and cultural institutions that their fathers, husbands, and brothers had created. Railroads and industry made Oregon more socially diverse as well as more wealthy. They drew thousands of Chinese to the state and created a working class whose interests often clashed with those who owned the railroads and sawmills and canneries.

Industrialization brought division along with prosperity and growth.

Oregon's Age of Industry

In Oregon, as in most of the rest of the United States, the greatest barrier to economic growth was the difficulty of moving goods to market. In the late 1840s a determined resident of the southern Willamette Valley built himself a dugout canoe to carry some two thousand pounds of bacon to what was then the head of navigation: Oregon City. But such measures were at best time consuming and at worst senseless. The expansion of steamboats on the Columbia and Willamette Rivers in the 1850s helped, as did subsequent aids to navigation such as dredging and locks. But ambitious Oregonians were already anticipating the arrival of railroads, technological marvels that would provide cheap, reliable, year-round transportation of all manner of goods.

Celilo portage railroad at The Dalles. This short line was built in 1863. Photo courtesy of Oregon State Library

The Oregon Steam Navigation Company built the state's first railroads in 1863: a pair of short portage lines to move goods around the rapids at the Cascades and Celilo Falls.

The flamboyant Ben Holladay began building a railway up the Willamette Valley in 1868. As its name implied, the Oregon and California Railroad was supposed to link Oregon to the transcontinental railway that was about to reach California. The project took much longer than Holladay had promised: until 1887. But it began tapping the bounty of Willamette Valley farms long before then. Rails reached Eugene in 1871, and smaller lines soon joined it in linking the Willamette Valley to Portland's seaport. But a transcontinental rail link was still many years away. This is not to say that people were not trying! Congress approved construction of the Northern Pacific Railway to the Pacific Northwest in 1864. But progress was slow. By the 1873 financial panic the railroad reached only as far west as North Dakota. It would take another decade, and the bold, determined leadership of Henry Villard, to link the Pacific Northwest with the East.

Railroads were widely sought and celebrated, but they benefited some places at the expense of others. Portland's economic elite discovered this later in the 1880s when Jim Hill's Great Northern reached western Washington, redirecting much of the grain and other products of the Pacific Northwest's interior to the Puget Sound rather

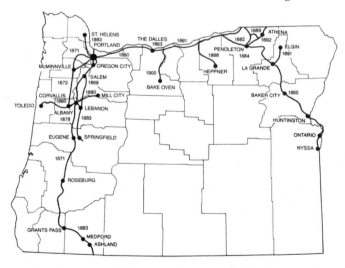

Railroads in Oregon in 1900, showing the principal cities served and the dates of construction. Image reproduced from Preliminary Atlas of Oregon *by William Loy courtesy of the University of Oregon Press.*
© 1972 University of Oregon Press

than to Portland. Towns without any rail service were of course in still more of a bind. Jacksonville had been at the heart of southern Oregon's mining boom in the early 1850s. But three decades later the O&C bypassed it for Medford and Ashland, a decision that prompted an economic decline. The crowning indignity came some years later, when Ashland wrested away the county seat.

Nor did the presence of a railroad guarantee its prosperity. The Oregon Pacific aspired to put Corvallis in the middle of a railroad stretching from Yaquina Bay to points well east of Oregon's border. The eastern road never made it over the Cascades, and the section linking Corvallis to the coast was not completed until 1885. Larger concerns discriminated against the little railway that threatened to tap Willamette Valley products formerly funneled to Portland, and the road, soon known as "the frustration route," was rickety and unreliable.[1]

Railroads also seemed to exacerbate economic inequalities within towns. In 1866 the richest 10 percent of Roseburg residents owned 44 percent of its wealth. In 1880, eight years after the O&C's arrival, they had captured 63 percent of its wealth, and a growing proportion of townspeople were landless.

There is no disputing that railroads brought growth and prosperity to Oregon. The state's population came close to doubling every decade from 1860 to 1890, when the great majority of the lines had been completed. Emigrating by rail was of course much easier than the overland or oceanic journeys had been, and Villard drew many settlers to the lands along the Northern Pacific by advertising the region's economic possibilities. More important, the railroads provided a reliable and less costly link to distant products and markets. They carried in bulky equipment: horse-drawn seeders and cultivators and steam-powered threshers that made it possible to multiply the number of acres a family could farm. They carried out tons of wheat and other crops. In the southern Willamette Valley's Linn County, for example, wheat production soared 250 percent in the seven years after the railroad's arrival in 1870. Farm families who in the 1840s and 1850s had reserved the vast majority of their ample homesteads for subsequent generations started planting every acre that they could, often selling the rest for a tidy profit that financed the purchase of the new and expensive farm machinery. Their goals "shifted from perpetuation of the family on the land to acquisition of wealth," as historian Dean May puts it.[2] Farmers became more specialized, more interested in making the greatest possible profit and less concerned with feeding and clothing themselves. Bread and cloth, after all, could

now be purchased at reasonable prices, and many farmers had money
to spend.

Industrialization and agricultural mechanization drew and drove
increasing numbers of workers to towns and cities. Portland, as we
shall see in the next chapter, was the leading example. But smaller
places also grew substantially. By the 1870s the little southern
Willamette Valley town of Brownsville was home to engineers,
photographers, coopers, wagon makers, justices of the peace,
telegraphers, gardeners, and woolen-mill workers. Wage workers still
constituted just a little over 5 percent of the state's population by the
century's end. But the number of Oregonians engaged in manufacturing had grown dramatically: by 383 percent in the 1880s alone.

Oregon's manufacturers diversified as they expanded. Railway
repair shops, woolen factories, fish canneries, print shops, and flour
mills followed lumber as the leading industrial employers. Even small
towns were apt to have a brick factory or a sash-and-door mill for
local builders, as well as blacksmiths, wheelwrights, furniture makers,
and printers. Most of these industries served local markets. Lumber,

*Steamboats were central to the economy, linking towns to
market. This photograph shows Joel Palmer's grist mill,
Captain Exon's warehouse, and Iler's sawmill in the town of
Dayton. The steamers are the "A.A. McCully" and the
"America." Photo courtesy of the Historic Photograph
Collections, Salem (Oregon) Public Library*

salmon, and wool constituted Oregon's only significant processed exports.

Timber remained the leading industry and, like farming, it was becoming much more mechanized. Steam locomotives traveled narrow-gauge tracks into western and even parts of eastern Oregon, dramatically increasing the amount of land that could be profitably logged. Steam donkeys hauled or yarded logs from stump to railway. Steam technology supplanted water-powered mills. It ran huge, multiple band saws that could cut all day and year long. The logging and milling of timber became fixed occupations for owners and workers alike, not a seasonal break from farming or other activities. Only corporations or wealthy individuals could afford the expensive new equipment and large work forces that the industry now required.

Here, too, the railways played a crucial role. The building of them, their ties and trestles, consumed a vast amount of lumber. The completed roads cut into ocean-going transport. By the 1890s Portland was sending a large fraction of its timber exports east, along the Northern Pacific, rather than west, by steamship. This shift to rails undercut one of the Puget Sound's chief advantages and helped boost Oregon's timber economy at the turn of the nineteenth century. It also jump-started eastern Oregon's timber industry. Mills west of La Grande, for example, were sending lumber east late in the century.

East of Eden

Boom times east of the Cascade Mountains began well before the railroad's arrival. The vast region held a tiny proportion of the state's population in 1860. But a year later prospectors located gold in the John Day and Powder River valleys. Business people followed the miners and so did ranchers, drawn by markets and pushed by an increasingly crowded Willamette Valley. Many of these people persisted long after most of the gold had been mined, and in the 1870s northeastern Oregon was on its way to supplanting western Oregon as the state's leading wheat producer.

The discovery of gold in the Blue Mountains near Baker in 1861 drew tens of thousands of people to eastern Oregon. Auburn, which no longer exists, and Canyon City, now a sleepy town just south of John Day, each had five thousand residents or more for a year or two. Many more fanned out to ferret out or exploit smaller bounties. Early mining focused on placer or surface finds that could be washed out of the gravel in streambeds. But as gold became more scarce it required more capital and equipment to unearth, and the lone prospector became an anomaly. Like those in southern Oregon before them, the mining districts of eastern Oregon were soon dominated by large concerns.

Towns that served the miners also spurted. The Dalles was transformed into a trading and transit center replete with ample stores, hotels, and restaurants. By 1864 it boasted a flour mill and about twenty-five hundred residents. Its transient population, the number of people just passing through, at times numbered ten thousand. Umatilla Landing, another hundred miles up the Columbia River, provided similar amenities. By 1865 it offered some twenty-two saloons and gambling houses. Transit companies also flourished. The Oregon Steam Navigation Company, which quickly bought out its competitors, carried nearly twenty-five thousand steamboat passengers in 1862 alone. It also bore many tons of freight: the flour, bacon, coffee, whiskey, overalls, and innumerable tools that miners required. At The Dalles, Umatilla Landing, or smaller depots, that freight was transferred to smaller operators: mule and then wagon trains that hauled the goods over trails and roads to the mining districts. Way stations appeared in the arid interior, near or in what would become Mitchell, Antelope, and Clarno.

Mining had slumped by the 1870s, but many of the enterprises that had sprung up to support it persisted. Ranchers and farmers who had settled in the valleys of the Blue Mountains near such towns as La Grande discovered that the area was much more hospitable and productive than they had expected. Settlers began moving into the lands south of The Dalles in the early 1850s. In 1864 a group of ranchers and merchants from Linn County, in the southern Willamette Valley, punched a rough road across the Cascades, over the Santiam Pass, and within five years eighteen ranching families had settled in the Ochocos. One Francis B. Prine of Scio moved his blacksmith tools to what would soon become Prineville, long the area's major trading center. That same year, in 1869, John Devine laid out Whitehorse Ranch far to the southeast. Several other big cattlemen followed him and staked out extensive empires in Oregon's most remote and arid corner.

These big ranchers did well in eastern Oregon. As the first white settlers they were able, through means fair and foul, to control thousands of acres of land, much of which was, at least for the time being, well suited for grazing. Their proximity to mining centers

An early combine harvester in Sherman County. Photo courtesy of Oregon State Library

provided them with early and profitable markets. Once these markets declined, moreover, they could drive their cattle hundreds of miles overland to railheads at relatively little expense.

Eastern Oregon's early farmers were more vulnerable. Wheat could not walk, and eastern Oregon contained precious few navigable rivers. Once nearby mines played out in the late 1860s and 1870s, those who lived more than twenty miles or so from the Columbia River found it difficult and expensive to get their crops to market. The farmers' fortunes rebounded in the late 1870s, as both rails and the realization that the Columbia Plateau was ideal for growing wheat began to spread. Rails cut through the heart of Umatilla County in 1883, followed by several branch lines. By 1893 that county alone had more than two hundred miles of rail. By 1900 rails connected Moro, Grass Valley, and Shaniko in Sherman County's interior to the Columbia River railroads and steamboats. The little county trailed only Umatilla in wheat production.

These wheat concerns were not cheap to run. The large, flat farms of the Columbia Plateau were ideally suited for new and expensive agricultural machines. In the 1890s most of their wheat was threshed by commercial operators who hauled their steam-driven contraptions from farm to farm. These machines were in turn eliminated by elaborate combines drawn by up to forty head of horses.

Towns reflected and drew on the farmers' prosperity. Places like Moro gained railway employees, grain warehouses, brick works, and various stores and services catering to the needs of well-heeled farm families. But much of eastern Oregon's population was transient. This had been especially true during the 1860s, when tens of thousands of miners had come and gone. The cowboys and laborers who worked on the region's large ranches and farms also consisted of largely young, unattached men who moved seasonally. These miners, cowboys, and farmhands often made things lively when they came to town. "There was more life in The Dalles in a day than there was in Portland in a month," observed a man who had moved there in 1864. Some three decades later a young man described some fellows who lived near Prineville "in a state of somewhat pugnacious exuberance."[3] Much the same could be said for Shaniko, where a roving population of teamsters and ranchers enjoyed its saloons and brothels.

The legal system was less organized east of the Cascades than west of them. The residents of Auburn hastily captured and lynched "Spanish Tom" in the 1860s after he evidently killed one of the men who would not let him join a card game. Anglos might also run afoul of extra-legal justice. In the 1880s a group of Prineville vigilantes executed several men accused of stealing livestock. Friction between cattle and sheep ranchers and farmers lay behind other disputes. Sheep moved into eastern Oregon in the early 1880s. Tensions between sheep and cattle ranchers in central Oregon increased in the 1890s, as grazing land became more scarce, with the latter claiming that sheep cropped the grass so short that they ruined rangeland for cattle. Some cattle ranchers made a habit of shooting sheep on sight, and the conflict was not resolved until the federal government began to regulate access to public lands shortly after the turn of the century.

Ranchers faced off with farmers in Oregon's Great Basin. This was a region of jarring social contrasts. By 1890 just three ranchers owned 61 percent of Harney County's cattle. Their employees were wage-working cowboys, including some *vaqueros* of Mexican descent. The northern part of the county was populated by smaller ranchers and farmers. Here was the county's largest town: Burns, with its newspapers, lodges, schools, professionals, and the great majority of its women. The two sides quarreled over the county's real estate. Many of the recent arrivals tried to settle on land already claimed by the cattle barons. To the settlers, the big ranchers were monopolists who had manipulated the law to gain control over more than any person had a right to. To the ranchers, the settlers were Johnny-come-latelies who lacked the good sense to realize that this place was suited for big ranches and not much else. The resulting lawsuits made lightly populated Harney County a lawyers' heaven. It had eleven near the century's end: one for every twenty-five citizens.

The quarrel came to head in 1897 when a homesteader named Edward Oliver shot and killed unarmed Peter French, one of the county's big three ranchers, and a man who had not disguised his scorn for "jug bellies" (farmers).[4] A jury composed of fellow settlers wasted little time in finding Oliver not guilty.

Eastern Oregon was reworked by the same economic forces that shaped the rest of the state in the decades following the Civil War. But its economy and society remained distinct, giving it more in common with the rest of the arid West than with the Willamette Valley.

Environmental Changes

From the arrival of fur traders in the late eighteen century, Oregon had not wanted for men who aspired to wrest from its soils and waters as much money as they could. Now, a century later, such people could more fully impose their will on the landscape.

Early settlers had wrought significant, if localized, changes. By 1850 the ten thousand whites in the Willamette Valley owned some forty thousand head of cattle, thirty thousand hogs, fourteen thousand sheep, and eight thousand horses. These grazers competed with deer, elk, and other indigenous animals, animals that also declined because settlers shot and ate them. Predators such as wolves, bears, and cougars were hunted for a different reason: they preyed on the settlers' livestock. Indeed, the settlers' first political meeting was for the ostensible purpose of establishing a system for paying bounties on such animals.

The settlers also transformed the valley's flora. Their livestock cropped its grasses so closely that exotics quickly spread—including such plants as dandelions and thistles that the settlers tried to root out. But the newcomers made a conscious effort to encourage the growth of other imported plants: wheat, potatoes, barley, and fruit and nut trees. Fields filled with a single species replaced the more complex and varied ecosystems that had flourished in the Willamette Valley since the retreat of the glaciers thousands of years before. Settlement and agricultural production increased severalfold during the 1850s, as the California gold fields provided the first big market for the valley's farms. Oregonians had put about nine hundred thousand acres of land into production by 1860. Two decades of white settlement had transformed much of the Willamette Valley.

These changes became more extensive and intensive in the next four decades. Farming expanded. The valley's wheat production soared from less than seven hundred thousand bushels in 1860 to more than 5.3 million in 1880. Settlers moved down from the foothills to take up the fertile land near the valley's rivers and streams, draining swamplands and confining waterways behind dikes. Enterprising business people facilitated navigation of the Willamette River by deepening its bed and blasting out snags, stumps, and trees. The meandering network of swamps and channels had become a sharply defined, swiftly moving river. Wetlands and the birds and other animals that depended on them were reduced, and sediments that had once blessed the valley's floor were carried far down river. But these losses elicited little concern in what historian William Robbins describes as "a society filled with confidence and engaged in building an agrarian paradise."[5]

The same could be said for the environmental changes occurring east of the Cascade Mountains. A growing proportion of Oregon's wheat and livestock production began shifting to this more arid region in the 1870s. The ecological consequences were especially profound in the Great Basin of the southeast, where ambitious entrepreneurs established huge herds of cattle and sheep in Malheur and Harney counties. These animals quickly transformed the landscape of sagebrush and grasses that had sustained the Northern Paiute into the desert of today. They were especially hard on the region's scarce streams, trampling stream banks and compacting soil, which sped erosion and dried up marshes and meadows.

Hydraulic mining washed tons of sediment away. Photo courtesy Oregon Historical Society, OrHi 102209

Grazing and agriculture constituted the most extensive ecological changes in Oregon. Mining was the most intensive. The industry directly affected only a small portion of the state: pockets of southern and eastern Oregon. But even small-scale gold mining was environmentally disruptive, as it entailed churning through streambeds in an attempt to extract minute particles of gold from everything else. Areas that showed promise were quickly subjected to much more concentrated attention. Hydraulic mining was the most efficient means for processing large amounts of gold-bearing gravels. Troughs or pipes carried water from streams to the mining site many miles away. There the water was pumped into high-pressure hoses that washed entire hillsides into long sluice boxes, where a series of wooden slats or riffles caught a portion of the gold particles. Hard-rock gold mining required going underground to extract large amounts of gold-bearing ore or quartz. Massive machines, called stamp mills, crushed the ore, which was then smelted to capture the gold.

Gold mining made many men's fortunes, but it was an ecological disaster. Even relatively small operations entailed turning streams and streambeds inside out. Large hydraulic operations devoured entire hillsides, washing away tons of sediment. The waters of streams that bore no gold might be diverted to watersheds that did. All of this devastated aquatic ecologies. Mining also released poisons. Quicksilver or mercury attracted gold, and the miners routinely applied it to their sluice boxes. Much of the valuable mercury escaped and poisoned streams for many years to come. Hard-rock mining exposed to air and water minerals that had been bound up deep in the earth, setting off noxious chemical reactions. Miners also caused substantial collateral damage. Their homes, sluice boxes, viaducts, and shafts required much wood, and the denuded hillsides near mining camps led to rapid run-offs that washed tons of debris downstream. Mining directly affected only a small proportion of Oregon, but it left a deep and lasting scar on the lands it touched.

Timber was much more important than mining to Oregon's economy, and it had a much broader ecological impact. Oregon's earliest settlers had of course logged, both to clear land and to provide materials for their cabins and fuel for their fires. They also cut down trees for Oregon's growing number of sawmills. But crude technology limited their impact. Loggers toiled with single-bit axes to fell trees, and bull teams dragged or skidded them to water. Most mills were small and powered by water. Their modest saws could not handle the largest trees in western Oregon's extensive forests. Not surprisingly, then, Oregon's old-growth forests remained almost entirely intact. The high cost of moving logs made it uneconomical to log more than a couple miles from large bodies of water. Even the small proportion of forests that were logged retained much of their canopy and diversity.

The application of steam to logging in the late nineteenth century changed this. Huge steam-powered mills replaced the small water-driven ones. They could handle many more and much larger logs. Railroads were infinitely more efficient at moving huge logs than were bull teams, so logging railroads and logging spread across much of western Oregon. Steam-driven donkey engines moved logs from stump to railhead. Even felling trees became easier, as loggers switched from axes to cross-cut saws.

The new system was economically efficient and ecologically harmful. Loggers now cut down all large trees, and the few that they left standing were knocked over and smashed in the process of yarding or dragging the logs out. When the loggers moved on to a new site they left behind a clear-cut, with no trees left to spread their seed and no overstory to slow the erosive work of water and wind. The waste or "slash" often burned, creating extremely hot fires that consumed most of the remaining biomass.

Logging and mining created much of what a euphemist might call collateral damage, especially to salmon. Sawdust and bark from mills fouled waterways and suffocated fish. Clear-cutting warmed streams by removing shade and increased their sediment load by abetting erosion. But the most spectacular destruction of streams occurred where loggers utilized splash dams to float their logs out of the forest. These barriers were created by blocking small streams until a substantial reservoir for storing logs had been created. The dam was then breached, so that the pent-up water could shoot its burden of timber to a larger river. Splash dams devastated salmon. They blocked access to spawning grounds, and the logs released when the dams burst gouged and scoured the streambeds, sweeping away salmon, their eggs, and their habitat.

Mining had much the same effect. It churned up streambeds and rerouted and poisoned their waters. It created an extraordinary amount of erosion, dumping tons of gravels and other sediments into creeks and rivers, smothering spawning beds.

Salmon also suffered from overfishing by the late nineteenth century. Their habit of spending several years in the ocean before returning to spawn allowed Oregonians to take all the salmon that they could get their hands on for some time before reaping the consequences. The salmon catch grew quickly in the late 1860s and steadily thereafter, until the mid-1880s, when it fell sharply. The industry rebounded, but only temporarily. Pacific Northwest salmon were already headed toward our contemporary crisis.

The decline in salmon was so obvious—and economically damaging—that it prompted concern and even action. Many placed their faith in technology. The first salmon hatchery appeared in 1877. But hopes that hatcheries would supply unlimited numbers of salmon proved to be unfounded. Proposals to restrict fishing met concerted and effective resistance from many interests. The times were not propitious for any measures restricting people's access to Oregon's bountiful and profitable natural resources.

People of Color

Most western frontiers were racially and ethnically diverse. Not mid-nineteenth-century Oregon. The great majority of its Native peoples either died or were shunted to isolated reservations before the Civil War. They were replaced by thousands of whites from the U.S. seeking free and fertile land, and both law and custom made it very difficult for people of African or Asian or Mexican descent to claim pieces of the verdant Willamette Valley. Portland and the mining region around Jacksonville attracted some people of color and foreign born in the 1850s. But farming dominated Oregon's economy before the Civil War, and farming was dominated by Native-born whites.

This started to change in the early 1860s, with the discovery of gold in the John Day and Powder river basins. Like gold rushes elsewhere, these excitements drew a diverse range of hopefuls, including hundreds of men from China who had been laboring in California. The rushes played out in a few years, but many Chinese Americans stayed to pick over ground that no else thought was worth troubling with. Whites had routinely excluded the Chinese from mining areas that whites thought might be profitable. The 1870 census counted more than sixteen hundred Chinese in Grant and Baker counties combined. Nearly one half of Oregon's Chinese lived in counties that contained less than 6 percent of the state's total population.

People of Chinese descent soon shifted from mining to other work. They constituted a large proportion of those who built Oregon's railroads. Wa Kee and Company of Portland, one of several powerful labor contractors, provided a crew of some one thousand in the late 1860s. Large numbers were by then working in the lower Columbia River's salmon canneries. By the 1880s mining, railroad construction, and cannery work were declining, and many of Oregon's Chinese made their way to Portland, which housed about three quarters of the state's total by 1900. Here they worked on the city's economic margins, running small businesses, gardening, and toiling as domestic servants.

The Chinese were drawn to the United States and Oregon by the prospect of prosperity. They came from Kwangtun and other regions of southern China, driven by banditry, political instability, and grinding poverty, problems exacerbated by the penetration of western products. Nearly all of these emigrants were young men. In North America they could make ten times more money than in China and might in a decade or so save enough to ensure a prosperous life for their families back in China. Few arrivals in Oregon were as desperate or determined as these sojourners.

All of these men faced great difficulties. Most were impoverished when they left China and had to labor for several years to pay the cost of their passage to America. Most found work, but not the sort of work that one could count on. Mining was notoriously streaky, and if they were fortunate enough to come across a rich vein local whites were apt to run them off it. Work on railroads and canneries was more predictable but subject to interruption, and Chinese contractors or labor bosses commanded a large proportion of their workers' wages. Like early white miners, they were subject to attacks by Native Americans. Some ninety died at the hands of Northern Paiute in Baker County in 1866. Chinese Americans were more commonly attacked by whites. One of the state's most violent and little-known events transpired on the Snake River northeast of Enterprise in 1887, when a gang of whites robbed, tortured, and murdered thirty-one Chinese American miners. "I guess if they had killed 31 white men, something would have been done about it," an observer later recalled, "but none of the jury knew the Chinamen or cared much about it, so they turned the men loose."[6] Anti-Chinese violence peaked in the mid-1880s, when hard times and racism combined to spawn a well-organized movement against Chinese labor. Rioters drove Chinese Americans out of Oregon City, East Portland, Salem, and Yamhill. Most Chinese faced violence that was less dramatic but still humiliating: eastern Oregon cowboys who cut off the men's queues (long braids) or Portland school children who hurled rocks at gardeners during recess. Southern Oregon's Chinese-American miners, observed a white man, moved "from mining locality to mining locality, fleeing from the kicks of one to the cuffs of the other."[7]

Legal discrimination compounded these cruelties. Oregon's Constitution excluded Chinese Americans from citizenship, and its

Chinese children were rare in Oregon and were prized by Chinese-American adults in their attempt to maintain their distinctive culture. This photo shows a group of children in front of the Marion County Courthouse in about 1900. Photo courtesy of the Historic Photograph Collections, Salem (Oregon) Public Library

courts viewed their testimony with great suspicion. State and local law imposed special taxes on Chinese miners and merchants. This discrimination came to a head in 1882, when Congress, under considerable pressure from western states, passed the Chinese Exclusion Act. Chinese continued to immigrate to Oregon, often via the porous Canadian border. But the legislation had an impact. The number of Chinese Americans in Oregon and the United States, around the turn of the century, began a long decline.

Oregon's Chinese Americans constituted a highly distinctive community. The overwhelming majority were young men. As time passed and immigration slowed to a trickle this community of course aged. The men lived in highly segregated communities, in mining camps, cannery bunkhouses, or the cramped Chinatowns that sprang up in several Oregon towns and cities, especially Portland. Most of the few women who arrived at least began as prostitutes, an occupation that did not carry nearly as much stigma in China as in western countries. Many of these women married high-status Chinese men and formed a handful of Chinese-American families. Yet most of the unattached men had strong familial connections in China: they sent money home to their parents or wives and tried to play the role of the good son or husband. This is not to say that many did not stumble along the way. Whites were fascinated by what they regarded as the exotic criminality of the Chinese community and seemed not to notice that many Chinese Americans neither gambled nor took drugs. Yet there is no denying that many laborers took refuge in these practices. Opium offered a temporary escape from one's troubles, and gambling offered the opportunity to cast off self-restraint and modesty and to win a fortune in a place where making money was much more difficult than the sojourners had expected.

The Chinese-American community was not of one piece. Class and wealth constituted the most obvious divider. Immigrants who picked up English quickly and who could negotiate skillfully with both Chinese and whites established themselves as labor contractors for railroads, canneries, sawmills, and other businesses. These were the men who used the unaccustomed freedoms of the American marketplace to wrest for themselves a fortune in this new world. The men who labored for these contractors often resented them and occasionally struck for higher wages or better working conditions. But for recent emigrants, especially, finding employment was much easier with a contractor than without. Associations or *tongs* also divided Oregon's Chinese-American communities. These groups were an extension of large family associations in China. In this new, unfamiliar land they provided opportunities for Buddhist worship along with credit and other forms of mutual aid. The *tongs* often jockeyed for economic supremacy, and these battles sometimes turned violent— though not nearly as often as many whites liked to think.

Chinese Americans were Oregon's largest minority group by far from the 1860s to the 1880s. They made up 5 percent of the state's population according to the 1880 census, which certainly under-counted them.

Oregon's mining booms attracted other peoples of color. Mexican packers dominated the mule trains that provided the most reliable transportation in much of the Pacific Northwest. Many of them passed through The Dalles, a key supply point for Idaho and eastern Oregon camps. In 1858, for example, Mexican pack trains carried supplies for some three hundred miners embarking from The Dalles to British Columbia's Fraser River mines.

Like the Chinese, many of Oregon's African Americans came in search of gold and, over time, gravitated to Portland. The virulence of small-town racism played a role in this migration. Pendleton's public school refused to let two African-American children attend in 1871.

Liberty, a misnamed town outside of Salem, expelled an African American in 1893, and some residents of Marshfield, on Coos Bay, lynched another a decade later. The Northern Pacific's arrival in 1883 brought more Blacks to Portland: porters, waiters, and others who worked for the railroad. So did the Portland Hotel, which opened in 1890 and recruited many African Americans from the South. Several Black churches formed. But the number of African Americans in Oregon remained small: just over a thousand by 1900.

Oregon's Chinese, Mexican, and African Americans were drawn by the state's economic growth in the last four decades of the nineteenth century, though they all faced daunting economic, political, and social barriers.

The state's Native Americans were becoming less numerous and powerful with each passing year. The state's Indian reservations bred poverty and often death. Their boundaries began to shrink almost immediately after their creation. The federal government began opening the Siletz Reservation to white settlement in 1865, and by the turn of the century western Oregon's Native people owned but a small fraction of the land that had been set aside for them in the 1850s. "I want the whites to stop troubling us about our land and removing us," asserted Native leader George Harney in 1873. "What have we done?"[8] Indians on the Warm Springs and Umatilla reservations of central and eastern Oregon fared better, though the allotment policies of the late nineteenth century whittled away at their holdings, too. Indian agents increasingly controlled indigenous peoples. Boarding schools at the coast began in 1877, and three years later the Bureau of Indian Affairs opened an ambitious Indian Training School in the Willamette Valley that soon became Chemawa, north of Salem. These were simply the most overt expressions of a determined effort to acculturate Oregon's Native Americans. Records kept early in the twentieth century reveal that up to seventy students ran away from Chemawa a year. Other Native peoples sought autonomy by living off reservations at least temporarily, picking crops in the Willamette Valley, selling horses, maybe trapping.

Oregon's people of color, then, shared much in common. They regularly confronted racist laws, practices, and attitudes. They were consigned to the margins of the state's economy. But the very nature of that economy required laborers who were willing to work hard and long hours for low pay building railroads, harvesting crops, canning fish, and running mule trains. Yet few white Oregonians expressed much concern for people of color, and a great many wanted them run out of the state.

Women and Change

The prosperity that drew people of color to Oregon reworked the lives of its white women.

Oregon's settler women had not enjoyed much freedom. The hard, tedious work of subsistence agriculture consumed most of their days and hours. Few belonged to any organizations save their church. To address a gathering larger than one's family was to court notoriety. Law and custom placed married women firmly under their husbands' authority.

Women were more active outside their families by the turn of the twentieth century. The 1900 census counted more than eighteen thousand female employees. More than half of them worked in the old standbys: domestic and personal service, dressmaking, or millinery (hat making). But growing numbers were procuring jobs in fields that Oregon men had dominated in the 1850s: teaching, office work, and sales. Most of these working women were single, in part because Oregon women were getting married much later than their mothers or grandmothers had. Indeed, more women were single than not among those aged twenty to twenty-four in 1900. Marriageable men had greatly outnumbered marriageable women in Oregon before

Teachers and children outside their schoolhouse in Drew, Douglas County, about 1900. Courtesy of the Douglas County Museum

Woman's Christian Temperance Union in Albany, 1895.
The WCTU offered middle-class women the opportunity to
reform Oregon society. Photo courtesy of the Historic
Photograph Collections, Salem (Oregon) Public Library

the Civil War. By 1900 sex ratios were approaching parity, so women tended to marry later—or not at all.

Economic changes freed married and single women alike. The arrival of cheap mass-produced materials meant that families could purchase goods that settler women had fabricated, from bread to trousers. Wives' social and cultural roles expanded as their economic ones shrank. Women now had more time to devote to their children— even as they had fewer of them. They also had more opportunity to help and visit each other. Much of this socializing occurred at church or informally, with relatives and friends. But women's associations were becoming more structured and political.

Thousands across the state joined the Woman's Christian Temperance Union in the 1880s and 1890s. As its name suggests, the WCTU was principally concerned with drunkenness, but it addressed many other reforms. Others joined the General Federation of Women's Clubs, associations that began by stressing self-improvement but, like the WCTU, often shifted to broader concerns, such as building libraries, caring for orphans, or urging reforms in how the state treated the insane. Women's roles increased even in male political groups. The Oregon Grange was a social and political organization for farmers, and when Lydia Ann Buckman Carter attended her first meeting in the late 1860s she found that women "were supposed to cook the meals and to be seen and not heard." But a decade later she was elected head of her grange.[9] More women were concerning themselves with public and political issues, with closing saloons and lobbying legislators. Many of these middle-class women eventually concluded that Oregon and the nation would realize their potential only when women received the vote, and they waged a number of determined if unsuccessful campaigns for it in the 1880s and 1890s.

Legal changes accompanied these social shifts. Oregon women had some important economic prerogatives even during the settlement period. The Donation Land Act of 1850 enabled a wife to hold 320 acres "in her own right," and delegates to Oregon's Constitutional Convention of 1857 decided married women could hold property separately.[10] Legislation for women quickened during the rest of the century. They gradually gained effective control of their own property and the right to bring lawsuits. By 1880 they enjoyed the same parental rights as their husbands. Indeed, judges in divorce suits became likely to grant custody of children to wives. Marriages were more easily dissolved, and Oregon's divorce rate was among the highest in the nation.

Women were gaining power and influence inside as well as outside the home during the late nineteenth century. Witnesses in divorce suits were much less likely to emphasize wives' submissiveness and obedience. Ida Brown of eastern Oregon complained in the 1890s that her husband "believed that women were only made for men's convenience," that he was "an ignorant, uneducated man" unfit for a wife like her, a woman "accustomed to being treated as man's equal, and not as a slave."[11] Men, for their part, were more reluctant both to hit or to defend hitting their wives. They described wife beating as a momentary and regrettable loss of self-control, not as part of their rights and responsibilities as the family head.

These changes should not be exaggerated. Oregon's political and economic life remained firmly in the hands of men at the end of the nineteenth century. Only a few hundred of the state's women made enough money to enjoy a comfortable living, and many wives remained very much subordinate to their husbands. Women's advances were partial and qualified. In gaining more time for child rearing and social activities, for example, housewives moved to the periphery of household production, of their families' economic lives. In establishing the right to advocate publicly for the rights of others, such as their children, women became so associated with selflessness that they often found it difficult to stand up for their own rights. Yet Oregon's women had made important inroads in what had been an overwhelmingly masculine society. Their efforts would bear important fruits early in the twentieth century, with reforms that would reshape the political and social lives of both women and the state as a whole.

Gilded Age Politics

Oregon's politics, like the nation's, were generally conservative and corrupt during the closing decades of the nineteenth century. Politics usually followed money in Gilded Age Oregon. R. D. Hume's biographer remarks that the Gold Beach businessman's tenure in the legislature constituted "neither service to the state nor desire for personal glory, but a business expense requiring the careful investment of time and money."[12] Hume rose only to the Oregon House of Representatives. Oregon's congressmen hitched their political and economic fortunes to more consequential business people. John H. Mitchell, a four-term U.S. senator, faithfully served the Oregon and California Railroad and the Northern Pacific. Such links bore fruit. Holladay extracted nearly four million acres of public land from the state legislature in 1868 for a railroad that he never completed. These giveaways angered many Oregonians. But legislators bought by Holladay and other railway owners headed off Oregonians' attempts to reform freight rates or other regulatory measures. They also provided cover for cattle kings, timber barons, and ruthless speculators who took for their own lands that Congress had intended for the use of ordinary Americans. Their manipulation of "swamp lands" was especially notorious. Intended to promote the reclamation of agriculturally unproductive areas, the Swamp Land Act became a cover for well-heeled people inside and outside of the state government to acquire thousands of acres of valuable real estate. The legislature compounded matters by spending the anticipated revenues of swamp-land sales on grants to road companies that seldom completed their projects.

The race for public lands revealed how the nature of Oregon politics had shifted. Mid-nineteenth-century leaders had been concerned primarily with patronage, with obtaining and distributing federal jobs and monies. Oregon's growing prosperity meant that land had become the federal and state governments' most coveted prize.

Reform made some inroads in mainstream Oregon politics. The Civil War had reversed the Democrats' fortunes; the Republicans won every presidential election in the state from 1872 to 1908, and they controlled the state legislature from 1880 forward. But the Republicans were often divided, and Democrats occasionally won the governorship. Democrat Sylvester Pennoyer, a Portland attorney, businessman, and editor, was drawn into state politics on behalf of the anti-Chinese movement of the 1880s. He was elected governor in 1886 and advocated some reforms that made him unpopular with conservatives: a state income tax, the regulation of railroads, higher tariffs, and an expanded currency. Pennoyer also criticized a practice that would soon make Oregon notorious: land grabs. He went over to the Populists in 1892.

The politics of privilege drew especially sharp protests from rural Oregonians. Progressive Willamette Valley farmers had begun forming societies and organizing fairs in the 1850s. Here they shared tips for more efficiently producing crops and livestock and awarded each other prizes for the best products. The first state fair was held in 1861. But these meetings soon turned from discussions of how to produce the most bushels of wheat per acre to lamentations over the transportation monopolies of the Columbia and Willamette rivers,

Crowfoot Grange Hall, Linn County. Many grange halls still stand across rural Oregon. Photo courtesy of the Historic Photograph Collections, Salem (Oregon) Public Library

companies whose high freight rates eroded farmers' profits and raised the cost of their machinery. Rates on Holladay's recently completed line between Portland and Roseburg were so high that farmers felt that they had been deceived. Part of the problem was structural. Rail links made faraway markets accessible to Oregon farmers, but they also made local markets accessible to faraway farmers. Like factory owners, agriculturalists found themselves competing in a national or even global economy. But Oregon farmers suspected that the railroads were putting them at a competitive disadvantage, charging three times as much or more to carry the same freight as their Midwestern counterparts had to pay. Local farmers' clubs began to discuss how to avoid the monopolies. In 1873 some sixty-five delegates from these Oregon clubs met and resolved to build their own warehouses and riverboats.

A national organization known as the Patrons of Husbandry, or Grange, arrived in Oregon at about this time and began leading rural reform efforts. The Grange was a peculiar institution whose functions were fraternal as well as economic and political. Some farmers were put off by its secrecy. Day-long meetings at grange halls, many of which still stand, afforded isolated families opportunities to socialize as leaders tried to shape them into a potent political force that would convince the legislature to end monopolies, regulate freight rates, and create an income tax. The Grange played a key role in organizing the Oregon Agricultural College in Corvallis. On its own, without benefit of new government commissions or laws, it constructed a parallel set of cooperative businesses run by and for farmers. They built warehouses along the Willamette River, stores, and fire insurance companies. But the Grange did not accomplish its most ambitious goals. It simply lacked the economic resources to defeat or replace the monopolistic companies that it railed against.

The state's early labor unions also lost more struggles than they won. Oregon's first labor organization appeared in 1853, when some printers met in Portland to discuss working conditions. Portland's longshoremen organized a twenty-five-man union in 1868, and a year later workers who had been replaced by Chinese immigrants at the Oregon City Woolen Manufacturing Company formed the White Laborers' Association in a fruitless attempt to reclaim their jobs.

Labor organizations blossomed during the expansive 1880s. The Knights of Labor was a national organization with an ambitious and broad agenda. It advocated temperance and proposed worker cooperatives such as the Harrisburg chapter's broom factory as an alternative to unfettered capitalism. Like the Grange, it aimed to educate its members on a broad range of issues and offered women as well as men the chance to speak and lead. In 1880 a Portland mass meeting drew four thousand. By 1886 it had about two thousand members in at least thirty-two assemblies stretching from the south coast to the northeastern mountains. But the Knights fractured over whether or not to back socialism, and they spent much of their energy opposing Chinese immigration. Such measures served the Knights well when sentiment against Chinese Americans was high, but its membership fell later in the decade as nativism subsided with renewed prosperity.

The Knights were supplanted by unions with less ambitious goals. Samuel Gompers, the national leader of "bread and butter" unionism, brought the American Federation of Labor (AFL) to Portland in 1887. This revived the moribund Federated Trades Assembly (FTA), which by 1889 had a membership of two thousand. The FTA focused on skilled labor, and it tried to resolve disagreements between workers and employers without recourse to strikes or boycotts. Those who did strike seldom won. In 1890, for example, Portland's largest union, the carpenters, struck for the eight-hour day. They succeeded, but at the same hourly rate, meaning that they were both working and earning less.

Unions' prospects dimmed during the mid-1890s, as a sharp depression undercut their bargaining power. Some unemployed men joined Jacob Coxey's "Industrial Army" to demand that the federal government do something. Portland rallies enlisted several hundred members, some of whom stole a train in Troutdale to speed their trip

Oregon State Penitentiary in Salem in the 1880s. State institutions grew in the late nineteenth century. Photo courtesy of the Historic Photograph Collections, Salem (Oregon) Public Library

to Washington, D.C. But the riders got only to Pendleton before being arrested.

The Populist (People's) Party constituted the most successful reform movement of the late nineteenth century, in Oregon as elsewhere in the United States. Previous reformers had hesitated to constitute a third party. Grangers had been willing to vote for the Republican or Democrat who seemed most sympathetic to their interests. But in 1889 a coalition of reformers—Grangers, the Knights of Labor, and the Prohibition Party—met in Salem and formed the Union Party. Three years later members of various Farmers' Alliances, a reform group that had maintained a low profile in the Pacific Northwest, created the Populist, or People's, Party in Omaha, Nebraska. The new party articulated a clear and detailed political program. They wanted government ownership of railroads and utilities, a more liberal monetary policy to counteract the deflation that harmed farmers encumbered with mortgages, and the nullification of liberal land grants to railroads. They anticipated the Oregon System by calling for the initiative and referendum and the direct election of United States senators. Populist leaders, determined to create a national party, fanned out across the nation.

They found some very sympathetic ears in Oregon. In southern Oregon's Jackson County, for example, farmers who condemned low prices, monopolistic railroads and flour mills, and corrupt local governments flocked to the Populist standard, awarding Populist presidential candidate James Weaver 50 percent of the county's vote in a three-way race in 1892. That same year Oregonians elected five Populists to the state legislature. In 1894, fusing in many counties with the state's beleaguered Democrats, they doubled that number. In 1896 they had eighteen legislators.

But joining forces with the Democrats helped to splinter the Populists as an independent and radical political force. The party also suffered from the relative prosperity of Oregon farmers, who were much more apt to own their property outright and less likely to rent than their counterparts in most of the rest of the nation. Indeed, it was Jackson County's more isolated, marginal farmers who tended to stick with the party. The men they elected often served poorly. Historian Jeff LaLande concludes that Jackson County's Populists were swept from office in 1898 because so many of them were "opportunistic demagogues who also appealed to nativism and fears of conspiracy to build support."[13]

The Populists and other reform groups of the late nineteenth century found it very difficult to change the face of Oregon politics.

One of their central goals, the regulation of freight rates, provides a telling example. The state legislature moved toward regulating rates in the 1880s. But it could never quite bring itself to create a law establishing specific rates. Instead in 1887 it created a commission that could recommend, but not require, rate changes. The 1891 legislature strengthened the commission, but the body was never very effective, and, under fire from reformers and conservatives alike, it disbanded in 1898.

By the close of the century, the People's Party constituted the latest example of a reform movement that had begun with much promise before crumbling, leaving Oregon's political landscape little changed. But the hope that the Populists had aroused and the abuses they had identified outlived the party's demise. As one leading Republican put it: "I have a lot of Pops in my district and I have to do something to keep them happy."[14] To a large extent, that "something" would be the Oregon System, to be treated in the next chapter.

❦ ❦

The history of Oregon between the Civil War and the turn of the century consisted of several seemingly unrelated, even contradictory, developments. This was a time of profound economic growth. The state's population grew substantially. The application of steam in logging, factories, and, especially, on railroads multiplied the pace of production and transportation, processing and exporting grain, lumber, wool, and fish at a much quicker rate and bringing to Oregon's burgeoning population a stream of manufactured goods like cultivators and reapers that in turn sped production still further. Oregon's politics generally followed its economy, smoothing the way for powerful business people to control unprecedented amounts of land and capital.

But Oregon's industrialization had less-anticipated consequences. It attracted thousands of Chinese Americans willing and able to mine unpromising tailings, gouge railway beds out of the hard earth, and perform a myriad of other tedious jobs. Oregon's economic transformation also created growing numbers of middle-class women even as it freed them from much of the drudgery that had dominated the lives of their counterparts of the 1840s and 1850s. Women, like men, used their growing leisure time in many ways: nurturing their children, socializing, and vacationing. But growing numbers were following the lead of Oregon's founding woman's rights advocate, Abigail Scott Duniway, in demanding both a greater political role and specific political reforms.

Many farmers and workers who felt cheated by the new order also expressed dissatisfaction with it. The efforts of farm, labor, and other reform groups culminated with the emergence of the Populists as a potent, if short-lived, political force in the 1890s.

Oregon had modernized its economy. But meaningful political reform lay ahead.

Biographies

Abigail Scott Duniway

Abigail Scott Duniway was arguably the most determined and distinguished reformer in Oregon history. Few observers would have predicted this during the first decades of her life.

She was born in an Illinois log cabin in 1834 and crossed the Oregon Trail as a child. She soon married, began having children, and spent several years on 320 unpromising acres south of Oregon City, helping her husband grind out a living and serving a seemingly endless train of his friends who stopped by to visit, eat, or even have their clothes washed.

All this began to change when Ben Duniway lost his farm and then his health. The family moved to Lafayette in 1862, where Abigail taught school. Three years later she opened a new school in Albany and soon began a millinery shop. Selling women's hats brought her in touch with many local women and their legal and economic vulnerability to abusive and irresponsible husbands. In 1871 she moved the family to Portland and began the *New Northwest*, a newspaper that would for the next sixteen years advocate woman's suffrage, expose and prescribe solutions for the many disadvantages that women labored under, and boost the economic prospects of the growing Pacific Northwest.

Duniway crisscrossed the region to sell her paper and her cause. At the end of 1886 she recounted 181 lectures and three thousand miles. She was not always well received. Male detractors argued that women belonged at home and that women's rights would lead to the neglect of children and husbands while promoting divorce. Malicious gossips said that Duniway "drinks, and smokes and swears like a man" and charged her with "indulging in Bacchanalian revelries with men." But Duniway could take it—and dish it out. She described an opponent's "fishy eyes … surmounted by a forehead quite pointed in the region of the organ of obstinacy, bare at the summit, and embellished at the sides with scraggy fetlocks."[15]   Or she might simply point out that too many Oregon men cared more about the health of their livestock than the well-being of their wives. She was often at odds with Harvey Scott, her celebrated and conservative little brother who, as the editor of the *Oregonian*, the Pacific Northwest's leading newspaper, sometimes opposed her efforts.

Strong-willed and more than a little egocentric, she could be just as hard on fellow reformers. She came to despise temperance advocates and warmly resented woman's rights advocates outside or inside the state who opposed her leadership or strategies, especially as the ranks of suffrage advocates swelled in the late nineteenth and early twentieth centuries.

But Duniway's persistent insistence that Oregon's women deserved the same rights as Oregon men bore fruit in 1912, when Oregon voters at last approved woman suffrage. Two years later, just before her death, Duniway at last cast her ballot.

Henry Villard

Henry Villard acted on stages much larger than Oregon's, but his efforts brought many economic and educational benefits to the state. He was born Ferdinand Heinrich Gustav Hilgard in Bavaria, where he received a strong education. He emigrated to the United States at eighteen, studied law, and was a prominent newspaper writer. He married Fanny, a daughter of abolitionist leader William Lloyd Garrison, in 1866, and became something of a scholar.

He became a powerful financier in the 1870s, upon being asked by a group of Germans to look after their investment in Ben Holladay's Oregon and California Railroad. Villard soon took over the O & C along with some other transportation companies to create the Oregon Railway and Navigation Company and began building rails up the Columbia River. When the Northern Pacific balked at cooperating he used a blind pool (eliciting investments for an unspecified venture) to raise $8 million that he quietly used to gain control of that concern. Villard then pressed ahead, and Oregon got its long-anticipated transcontinental link in 1883. In celebrations in Portland, note historians Dorothy Johansen and Charles Gates, "the city fathers, business firms, and private citizens vied with one another in lavish decoration, pageants and parades."[16]

But Villard had overreached himself. Finishing the line had cost a fortune, and in 1884 he had to resign as the Northern Pacific's head. He regained his place some years later only to see the company bankrupted in the depression of the 1890s. He died in 1900.

Villard changed the face of Oregon. He was a philanthropist as well as a businessman, and his contributions to the University of Oregon, where a building bears his name, saw the state's leading liberal arts college through some difficult times. But his impact on Oregon's economy and society were far more profound. The year 1883 will always constitute a watershed in the state's history. Ever since then goods have flowed to and from Oregon much more easily.

Bill Hanley

In contrast to the staid and densely settled Willamette Valley, eastern Oregon has attracted more than its share of large land owners and flamboyant characters. Bill Hanley qualified on both scores. Born in 1861 and raised on a southern Oregon ranch, Hanley helped his father to drive grain and livestock across the Cascade Range to Fort Klamath and the Klamath Indian Agency. At age sixteen or seventeen, he joined some others in taking cattle east, "hunting grass and water in a new country not claimed yet." His father accompanied him to the peak of the pass and before returning home advised young Bill to "Go till you find a big country" since "you will never get any bigger than the country you are in." A few cattle barons, including Pete French, had preceded Hanley. But much of Oregon's Great Basin had not yet been appropriated by whites.

Hanley settled in what would become Harney County and set to work. He drove and traded cattle, mowed hay, and started buying out his neighbors, who headed back to the damp side of the mountains. By age twenty he had $7,000, an awful lot of money in the early 1880s. Hanley was just getting started. He eventually owned nearly twenty-five thousand acres.

Hanley maintained a high profile. His propensity for story telling and (unsuccessful) bids for the governorship earned him the title "Sage of Harney County" or "Oregon's Sagebrush Philosopher." He burnished this reputation by hiring a fine writer, Anne Shannon Monroe, to help with his autobiography, *Feelin' Fine! Bill Hanley's Book!*, which was published in 1930, five years before his death.

Hanley was an extroverted ruminator and a self-professed nature lover. But he was also a shrewd businessman and a tireless booster of Harney County. It irked him that western Oregonians viewed his side of the Cascade Mountains as "a worthless waste" and saw no good reason to spend money getting a railroad there. Hanley worked hard for that railroad, and when leaders of the Great Northern Railway Company took an interest in 1910, Hanley gave them a tour during which, a Portland newspaper noted, he lost "no opportunity for showing the noted travelers the country's great resources with its magnificent prospects of being a populous and fruitful empire."[17] A year later, when James J. Hill drove the last spike connecting Bend to the rest of the country, Bill Hanley was there, and he made a speech before the laying of the new station's cornerstone.

John Waldo

The year 1889 was not a propitious time to introduce legislation to "set aside and forever reserve" thousands of square miles of Oregon forest. But that is precisely what freshman representative John Waldo asked his peers to do for the high Cascades. Waldo was a man ahead of his time, one of Oregon's earliest and most articulate nature lovers.

Waldo's pioneer credentials were impeccable. His parents, Daniel and Malinda, had arrived in the storied wagon train of 1843, the year before John's birth, and created one of the earliest and most prosperous farms near Salem, not far from Waldo Hills. John was graduated from Willamette in 1866 and joined the state bar four years later. He became an active Republican and Granger and ascended to Oregon's Supreme Court in 1880.

Waldo paired an affinity for such nature writers as Wordsworth and Thoreau with a love for the outdoors. He was a life-long hunter, which was commonplace enough, but also a devoted observer of nature who mounted many expeditions into the Cascades. More than anyone, he publicized the Santiam Pass. But his months in the woods were not simply devoted to utility and progress. Waldo enjoyed wilderness. In 1888, on the shores of the lake that bears his name, he wrote: "The Lake looks beautiful lying embossomed in the evergreen forests—dark timbered peninsulas jutting into it, with the broad snow fields of Diamond Peak, and bluemountains looking down upon it. Fire has not troubled its shores, and everywhere about it extends the green aromatic forest."

Some months later Waldo was trying to convince his peers that the high Cascades' "wildness, game, fish, water and other fowl, its scenery, the beauty of its flora, the purity of its atmosphere, and healthfulness" made essential its preservation. Livestock interests stalled Waldo's proposal. He responded by taking his case to the federal government, which created a 4.5-million-acre Cascade Range Forest Reserve in 1893. A variety of economic interests in Oregon decried this designation, and early in the next century the reserve became part of the newly established Forest Service, which emphasized conservation—the judicious use of forests—rather than their preservation, as Waldo had advocated. Not until much later would a substantial portion of Oregon be set aside for those, who like Waldo, "would not have the world altogether cut up into cabbage patches."[18]

Chapter Five

Political and Urban Transformations

1900-1919

Once "the lawmaking power" was in "the hands of the people, we could get anything we wanted."
William U'Ren

Oregon has seldom attracted much national attention. The early years of the twentieth century were one of those exceptional times that it did. The obscure, lightly populated state on the Pacific Coast remade itself into the workshop of democracy. In a nation concerned over public corruption, the Oregon System of distributing political power to ordinary citizens through the use of the initiative and referendum offered a compelling model for many progressives. In Oregon itself, the initiative and referendum became tools for at last accomplishing several reforms: woman suffrage, prohibition, improved working conditions, and closer regulation of corporations.

But to tout the accomplishments of "direct democracy" is to leave much unsaid. The most determined advocates of the initiative and referendum system were disappointed by its application. Like their more radical counterparts, they hoped to remake, not simply revise, Oregon politics.

Reformers were most numerous in Portland. Oregon's only city was growing even more quickly than the state as a whole, and staid residents were disturbed to find that many of the newcomers were immigrants, laborers, working women, and radicals. Respectable Portlanders, especially women, spent much of their energy trying to protect and reshape their city's most vulnerable residents.

In Oregon generally and Portland particularly, Progressive Era reform assumed many guises, from liberal to radical, political to social, ameliorative to apocalyptic. The diverse range of hopes and programs reflected the growth of the state and its leading city.

The Oregon System

The Oregon System won overwhelming support from Oregon voters, who immediately put it to good and frequent use. But the series of legislative reforms that made up the core of the system were proposed because of the dogged persistence of a few people.

The initiative and referendum lay at the heart of the Oregon System. The former enabled citizens who gathered a sufficient number of signatures to put proposals on the ballot. The latter enabled citizens to vote on whether to approve bills passed by the legislature. The measures were often referred to as "direct legislation," since they enabled voters to express their political will on specific measures by voting on them, rather than indirectly, through the election of state representatives and senators.

Reformers began advocating for the initiative and referendum in the 1880s, for reasons that to them were as plain as day. In 1883 the *Oregon Vidette and Antimonopolist,* a newspaper for the "producing and industrial classes," proposed legislation that would "defend a citizen's rights against injustice by powerful corporations."[1] The authors believed, with ample reason, that Oregon politics were controlled by implacable monied interests who bribed and otherwise influenced state legislators. This secret and corrupt form of governance made Oregon politics well-nigh impervious to the popular will. Direct democracy, reformers believed, would change all that. Once "the lawmaking power" was in "the hands of the people," asserted William U'Ren, its most devoted advocate, "we could get anything we wanted."[2] As we shall see, U'Ren wanted a great deal.

The initiative and referendum gained momentum in Oregon with the growth of Populism. An 1892 Farmer's Alliance meeting in Milwaukie, just south of Portland, invited members of the Grange, Portland Federated Trades, Knights of Labor, and even the Portland Chamber of Commerce to form a joint committee to push for direct legislation. The chamber, a pro-business organization, declined the favor. The reformers who attended created a coalition that continuously put the measures before Oregon's voters and legislators.

Of course the reformers ran up against the very arrangement that the initiative and referendum were intended to remedy. The Oregon establishment was not eager to reform a system that had served its interests well, especially when the agitators were a collection of third-party enthusiasts.

A frustrated U'Ren concluded that one had to play by the rules in order to change them. He took advantage of division within Oregon's powerful Republican Party in 1897 and offered to throw the Populists' thirteen votes in the legislature behind William Mitchell's election to the U.S. Senate if Mitchell would tell his backers in the state legislature to vote for direct democracy. "I am going to get the Initiative and Referendum in Oregon if it costs me my soul," he proclaimed.[3] But Mitchell, a more practiced soul seller than U'Ren, concluded that he did not need the Populists and reneged on his promise. U'Ren adjusted. He made common cause with Mitchell's enemies, and the unlikely coalition managed to keep the legislature from meeting, thus making impossible Mitchell's election to the Senate, since senators were, at the time, still elected by the legislature not the voting public.

The tactic proved decisive. Many Oregonians, including not a few reformers, were put off by it. But blocking Mitchell's election served to deliver additional legislative votes to the initiative and referendum. U'Ren followed up this accomplishment by inviting powerful interests into the movement. The Direct Legislation League was replaced by the Non-Partisan Direct Legislation League, and its leaders included influential members of the establishment such as banker W. M. Ladd and *Oregonian* editor Harvey Scott. Direct democracy had become mainstream.

Why this sudden shift? Both sides moved toward the center. Conservatives realized that Oregonians were becoming increasingly alarmed over reports of bribery, land fraud, and other sundry corruptions. They could not afford to be the target of a mass movement of indignant voters. U'Ren, for his part, stopped talking about the radical promise of direct democracy. He strove, as historian Robert Johnston puts it, "to disarm the fears of the conservative elements," even suggesting that the initiative and referendum constituted "ample insurance against any revolutionary laws, the very sort of laws he hoped to pass."[4]

This rapprochement would eventually break down. Oregon's conservatives would soon be lamenting the initiative and referendum, and its radicals would be using it to propose all manner of ambitious reforms. But for several years around the turn of the twentieth century, the truce held.

It did not need to hold for long; victory was quick and decisive. Oregon's Constitution was difficult to amend. Indeed, it had never been done before. Bills had to pass two successive legislatures before being approved by the voters. But the legislature approved the initiative and referendum in 1899 and 1901, and in 1902 Oregon's voters backed the amendment by a margin of more than ten to one.

The implementation of the initiative and referendum facilitated the adoption of other elements of direct democracy. The Direct Primary Law passed easily in 1904, meaning that voters, not party leaders, would now choose who would run for election to the U.S. Senate. But legislators did not have to select the candidate who won the most votes in the general election and therefore remained susceptible to the machinations of powerful lobbyists—or at least party discipline. U'Ren came up with an ingenious plan to ensure that the nominee with the most votes in the general election would win. He drafted a piece of legislation requiring candidates for the state legislature to indicate whether or not they would vote for the senatorial aspirant who had received the most popular votes. It worked. Oregon's legislature, frightened of potential backlash from an electorate that had voted for Jonathan Bourne in 1907, made him the first popularly elected senator in the nation. Two years later, in a stiffer contest between the popular will and party ties, the Republican-dominated legislature joined the state's voters in choosing Democrat George Chamberlain for the U.S. Senate—the first non-Republican from Oregon elected to that body since 1879. Indeed, from 1902 to 1914 Oregon Democrats won three of five senatorial races, a remarkable record in a state that remained overwhelmingly Republican.

Voters used the initiative and referendum to gain additional power. In 1906 they made it easier for the legislature to refer constitutional measures to them. A two-thirds vote had been required in both houses. Now only one half of the legislators in the state senate and house needed to approve them. In 1908 voters rounded out the Oregon System by approving initiatives that provided for regulation of elections (the Corrupt Practices Act) and the recall of public officials. These measures—the initiative and referendum, the direct election of senators, and the recall—removed barriers that had stood between voters' will and Oregon law. Now, at last, the people would decide their own political destinies. But, with political power at last in their hands, what would they do with it?

The Oregon System in Practice

Oregon was not the first state to pass the initiative and referendum. North Dakota and Utah had preceded it. But, just as U'Ren had hoped, Oregonians would become the first Americans to use these mechanisms regularly, though with results that often disappointed him and other radicals.

Oregon voters began availing themselves of the initiative and referendum shortly after approving them in 1902. Three ballot measures appeared in 1904, including two key ones that passed: the direct primary and a local option law (for prohibition). The number of measures quickly increased, to eleven in 1906, nineteen in 1908, thirty-two in 1910, and thirty-seven in 1912, the peak year. Most of these proposed amendments or measures were submitted by initiative petition rather than by the legislature.

Oregonians approved many pieces of legislation, large and small. Woman suffrage and prohibition were arguably the most important. But there were many others. The voters decided to tax express, telephone, and telegraph companies and to regulate some aspects of public utilities. They made it illegal for public officials to accept passes from railroad companies. They passed laws limiting the number of hours for women factory workers and established a minimum wage, workers' compensation, and an eight-hour day for people laboring on public works projects. They even, in 1914, did away with the death penalty, though they changed their minds just six years later.

Yet more and more Oregonians expressed reservations over what they had wrought. Support for direct democracy began to dwindle soon after it appeared. Many voters were put off or confused by the growing number of decisions they were asked to make. The 1910 ballot confronted them with some thirty-two measures and prompted complaints that Oregonians were being asked to vote "by the square yard."[5] Indeed, two years later, Portlanders faced a ballot measuring 4.5 square feet. Nor were voters necessarily sure what they were voting on. Ballot titles could contain no more than twenty-five words. Explanations had to be kept under one hundred. Complicated legislation could not be explained that concisely. A sort of voter fatigue or backlash set in, with many Oregonians voting against all initiatives on principle. Only four of twenty-nine measures passed in 1914.

Direct democracy was undercut by ideological cleavages as well as apathy. U'Ren and his fellow radicals discarded their moderate disguises once the initiative and referendum became law and founded the People's Power League, an organization whose title suggested its ambitious progressive agenda. With the tools of direct legislation finally in place, now was the time to begin transforming Oregon law. Some of the league's proposals won voter approval, such as the recall and closer regulation of utilities. But others struck most Oregonians as extreme. In 1912 and 1914, for example, the People's Power League presented a measure that would abolish the state senate (which it described as "lobby-ridden, expensive, interfering, [and] utterly useless") in favor of an unicameral legislature based wholly on proportional representation. This proportion, moreover, would be based on occupation, not place of residence. If housewives and laborers outnumbered lawyers in the general populace, they would also outnumber them in the legislature. This was a bold democratic reform, one that would have gone much further than the initiative and referendum in opening up Oregon politics. But it was too radical for most Oregonians. The *Oregonian*, which by now had returned to opposing Oregon's leading reformer, dubbed it "strictly U'Renic," and the voters decisively rejected it.[6]

Oregonians also spurned the economic heart of reform: the single tax. Popularized by Henry George's *Progress and Poverty*, the single tax promised a more just and equitable distribution of wealth by taxing only income that accrued to idle speculators and financiers. The details of the system were complicated, but the intent was clear enough. "I intend to help make such laws in Oregon that no man can get a dollar without working for it and no man shall produce a dollar of value without getting it," summarized U'Ren, who believed that the single tax constituted the linchpin of progressive economic and social reform.[7] For people like U'Ren, the initiative and referendum and other elements of the vaunted Oregon System were largely a means to an end, and the end was the single tax.

But Oregonians resolutely voted down even mild versions of the single tax. Wealthy business people, many of whom had made their fortunes in real estate, were of course dead set against it. The owners and managers of railroad companies that owned vast swaths of Oregon land that they hoped eventually to sell for handsome profits recognized that the reform targeted them and waged a vigorous and well-financed campaign against any proposal that would raise their taxes. But small landowners, especially farmers, worried that all real estate might be heavily taxed. Oregon's single taxers assured these "producers" that their ballot measures would affect the pocketbooks of only a small group of wealthy people, that everyone else would benefit from legislation taxing land-grabbing monopolists and thereby releasing millions of acres for hard-working Oregonians determined to create productive and profitable farms. But it was no use. Single-tax measures were resoundingly defeated, and by growing margins.

A number of other radical measures also failed decisively. Oregon had a small Socialist Party. Unlike the People's Power League, which sought to make capitalism more humane and fair, Socialists wanted to do away with it altogether. In 1914 they sponsored a right-to-work measure that would have been funded by a tax on inheritances of more than $50,000. It failed.

In sum, direct democracy revealed the limits as well as the accomplishments of Oregon reform. Oregonians wanted less-corrupt political practices. Though often frustrated by the number of ballot measures they confronted, they could not agree with conservative Republicans and other critics who wanted to scrap what Salem's *Oregon Statesman* sneeringly referred to as the "iniquitive and disputandum."[8] They did not want a return to a system in which party leaders largely controlled the legislative process. They were also willing to back a number of social reforms: suffrage and prohibition, most notably, but also moderate steps toward regulating working conditions.

But Oregonians were much more reluctant to pass measures that cost much money or threatened to overturn the socioeconomic status quo. A significant minority of the state consisted of radicals who wanted to do just that. But the majority of their fellow citizens were unwilling to follow them. In 1916, discouraged after the single tax had won the approval of just 16 percent of the state's voters, long-time reformer A. D. Cridge vented his spleen against "the boneheaded, retroactive, standpat, and mossback Oregonian."[9]

The Oregon System was proposed and implemented by Oregonians who were well left of center, men and women who hoped that direct democracy would provide the wherewithal to implement an ambitious program of social and political democracy. But, once in place, the Oregon System was the tool of moderate, not radical, reform.

Oregon's Metropolis

Most late-nineteenth-century reformers had been rural. The Populists constituted the most obvious example. But the most active reformers of the early twentieth century lived in or near cities. There was a reason for this: the nation's cities were bursting at the seams. This growth generated optimism and anxiety: optimism because nothing was more American than getting bigger, anxiety because change is stressful and urban traditionalists were alarmed that their cities were increasing in diversity as well as size.

Portland was no exception. It has often been described as the city that gravity built, a place whose leaders were content to reap relatively modest economic returns while more ambitious competitors—

Horsecar No. 22 on its last day of operation in about 1895.
A new electric trolley can be seen in the background. Photo
courtesy Oregon Historical Society, CN 023679

Seattle, that brash upstart to the north, comes to mind—passed them by. But Portland was one of the fastest-growing cities in the United States around the turn of the twentieth century, outstripped only by Los Angeles and Seattle, and its leading citizens worked hard to make it so.

Portland's population boomed from 1890 to 1910, from 46,000 to 207,000. Part of this increase was a function of incorporation. The towns east of the Willamette River, a collection of semi-rural communities and small farms, became part of the city in the 1890s. Technological change facilitated residential expansion. The Morrison Street Bridge spanned the river in 1887, and a horsecar line began running on the east side. Commuter steam trains soon connected Oswego, St. Johns, and east Portland communities to downtown. In 1887 cable cars succeeded in surmounting the steep grade up Portland Heights to the west, opening another section of the city to homes.

But the great majority of expansion was to the east, across an undulating plain broken by occasional crests or hills. Electric trolleys provided reliable and cheap transportation to the growing city's fringes by the turn of the century. A rectangular grid of lines radiated outward from downtown. Portland ran more trolley cars per capita than any other city in the nation. Families in dozens of comfortable residential neighborhoods or suburbs took the trolleys or interurbans to work or shop downtown.

This expansion made rich Portland families richer still. Real-estate speculation had long been a leading source of wealth here. But these people were not content to just take what came to them. They aspired to put Portland on the nation's map. The Lewis and Clark Exposition would be their most ambitious vehicle for doing so. The Lewis and Clark Expedition had helped to publicize the Pacific Northwest a century before. Portland's leading citizens hoped that the celebration of the expedition's centennial would lead to an economic boom in their own time.

The fair's central purpose was to attract people and capital to Portland, and not just for a week or a day. It offered, to be sure, a broad array of amusements, from bands to "Professor Barnes' Educated Horse and Diving Elk" that jumped forty feet into a tank of water. But the fair's exhibits were central. Many of them underscored the region's economic accomplishments, such as the forestry building, the world's largest log cabin. Promoters also touted the possibilities of the Pacific Rim, for Portland was as well positioned as any other port city to reap its trade. Indeed, the event's full title was the "Lewis and Clark Centennial Exposition and Oriental Fair," and Japan contributed a large set of displays. The fair would bring more immediate business for Portland hotels, restaurants, transportation companies, and retailers.

The fair's organizers went to great lengths to publicize it. Twenty-nine Portland businessmen, led by Henry Corbett, pledged about $150,000 to jump-start the endeavor. They published and distributed three hundred thousand copies of a book on Oregon. Advertisements and promoters blanketed the nation. The work paid off. By the spring of 1905, a few weeks before the fair began, organizers were receiving five hundred letters of inquiry a day. The fair itself drew 1.6 million visits, about a quarter of them from people outside the Pacific Northwest. It even turned a tidy profit. Most importantly, it appeared to accelerate what had already been a very rapid pace of growth in Portland.

The city was not just large. It was also diverse. In 1890, some 37 percent of its residents had been born outside of the U.S., a higher figure than for any other major western city except San Francisco. Many of these immigrants blended easily into the city's Anglo-dominated fabric. More than a quarter were from the British Isles or Canada. But at least one in six were from China. The city's Chinese population would fall in ensuing decades, but more Japanese, Russian Jews, Italians, and Scandinavians chose Portland. Each group carved out economic and spacial enclaves within their city. The Italians, most of whom were single men and laborers, concentrated south of downtown, in Johns Landing. Many of them moved in and out of

Portland seasonally, as work opportunities in rural sawmills appeared and disappeared. Others settled in Parkrose or Milwaukee, where they ran truck farms, or, like many area residents, made a bit of money from small vegetable gardens. Jewish immigrants from eastern Europe were more apt to come as part of a family, though they were less prosperous than their German-American counterparts who had arrived earlier. Norwegians also tended to settle down and form families. Many of the young women toiled as domestic servants, but many of their male counterparts knew a trade: carpentry, tailoring, or shoemaking. Though not as distinctive as Portland's immigrants from Asia, southern, or eastern Europe, they tended to marry each other, and they formed several ethnic organizations. Immigrants made up a declining proportion of Portland's population after 1890, and many married, bought homes, and became part of its middle class, broadly defined. But Portland remained a place of many cultures and languages in the early twentieth century.

Many of these immigrants belonged to Portland's growing working class. The city had never been a manufacturing center. Most of its early business had focused on shipping, and grain exporting remained very important at the end of the century. But the city contained many sawmills, as well as print shops, bakeries, and textile factories. The Northern Pacific's arrival created hundreds of jobs for men who maintained tracks and kept locomotives running. The city's rapid expansion of course generated a great deal of employment for laborers: men who graded its streets and built its transit and water lines. Carpenters and other craftspeople found employment fashioning its new homes.

Many working people labored in the city's service industry. Domestic service employed thousands of women, especially immigrants and African Americans. Most native-born Portland women had more options. Increasing numbers worked as waitresses, or as saleswomen or stenographers in Portland's flourishing department stores and offices. Most of these women workers were single, widowed, or divorced. Fewer than one in eight was married in 1900.

Portland was in a sense two cities. Those who were relatively well off worked at dependable, well-paying jobs and resided in spacious homes west of downtown or across the river, along the curvilinear streets of Laurelhurst, Eastmoreland, and Alameda Park. They cultivated fine gardens, filled up the city's leading (largely Protestant) churches and synagogues, and supported its art museums and charities. The "other" Portland crammed itself into boarding houses, hotels, and apartment houses in and just north, south, and east of Portland's downtown. They made less money—and at jobs that were less stable. They were apt to be "ethnic," single, and mobile. There were of course many exceptions to these generalizations. Skilled workers, in particular, could aspire to and succeed at owning their own home in one of east Portland's working-class neighborhoods. Many immigrants, such as Simon Benson, from Sweden, did very well indeed in Portland. But status and ethnicity generally correlated with each other. John Reed, the future Bolshevik, learned this firsthand when his family fell on hard times in the 1890s and left a mansion in the west hills for a rough-and-tumble neighborhood where the unfettered Irish boys of Goose Hollow made life interesting for the frail and sensitive newcomer.

Reed eventually made himself at home among these children of the immigrant working class, but most respectable Portlanders did not. Indeed, they expressed a considerable amount of anxiety over people unlike themselves. The *Oregonian* in 1904 fretted that Portland had become the destination of "a steadily increasing number of foreign laboring people, particularly from Southern Europe."[10] A headline in the *Oregon Daily Journal* referred to a group of Russian immigrants as "FOREIGN THUGS."[11] Such fears shaped Portland's legal system. Its judges sentenced just three men to be whipped for beating their wives from 1905 to 1911: an Irishman and two immigrants from eastern Europe. Portland's legal establishment was especially concerned over its tiny complement of African-American residents. Those fined for committing assaults paid an average of $62.88 from 1900 to 1910, more than twice as much as their white, native-born counterparts. Traditional Portland expressed in word and deed its anxiety over the city's diversity.

Leading Portlanders were less critical and more protective of its growing numbers of working women. They feared that young, unattached women might be easily taken advantage of, seduced, even coerced into prostitution in the city's department stores, factories, offices, and restaurants—not to mention its theaters, movie houses, shooting galleries, and other places of amusement. Police woman Lola Baldwin asserted that dance halls, where young women cavorted with men of all ages, were "an unmitigated evil, the threshold to the wineroom and the brothel."[12]

In sum, respectable Portlanders were both proud of and concerned over their expanding city. They congratulated themselves over the splendors of the Lewis and Clark Exposition and worried that it drew a class of footloose and immoral visitors to Portland. They celebrated the city's burgeoning population and industry and noted that this expansion had attracted many people unlike themselves: non-English foreigners, Catholics, laborers, all manner of unattached men and women.

These anxieties would shape the direction of Portland reform.

Portland Reform

A number of historians have pointed out that the Oregon System was not driven by middle-class anxieties over immigration and other perceived urban/industrial ills. Fair enough. But the initiative and referendum were not the alpha and omega of Portland's Progressive Era.

Portland was home to a diverse group of reformers in the early twentieth century. Some, like their counterparts on the state level, wanted to clean up the city's politics, to make the system more honest, open, and efficient. Others wished to clean up the city itself. Their proposals ranged from the practical (collecting and disposing of garbage) to the ethereal (instituting an ambitious city plan that would transform the city's ambience). Others focused on perceived social problems, such as child neglect. But many of the objects of these proposals, the poor and the immigrants, were busy promoting their own political agenda: radical shifts in Portland's political and economic structure that would create opportunities for all.

Portland's government provided plenty of grist for reformers. Many of its leading business people routinely avoided paying taxes. Certain businesses could count on being awarded city contracts. And the city, though more inhibited than Seattle, was not exactly chaste. A visitor in 1898 described "blocks on blocks given up to prostitution, gambling, saloons and every variety of dive the world holds. ... It is as wide open as the sun is at noon, and no one tries to disturb it."[13] Indeed, police countenanced these many vices—collecting bribes from business owners and placating powerful city leaders who owned many of the buildings in which said businesses were being carried out.

That politics tended to follow money was hardly unique to Portland. But the rose city's elite was unusually wealthy and coherent. Ensconced in spacious homes in the west hills, many of these fifty or so leaders traced their Portland fortunes back to the 1850s. Their children intermarried, they belonged to the same clubs and causes, and they assumed that running the city was, as historian Carl Abbott puts it, "their privilege and responsibility."[14]

Portland's elite could not win elections by themselves. Much of their support came, ironically, from Portland's marginal men. As in many cities, Portland's politics were run by a machine, in this case Republican. Party operatives bought working men's votes through direct payment and by fending off prohibition and other moralistic crusades that threatened such men's pastimes.

This arrangement fell victim to rising indignation and an expanding east-side middle class in the 1905 election. Harry Lane, grandson of Oregon's first territorial governor, beat perennial machine-candidate George Williams. Though hamstrung by a city council dominated by entrenched interests that regularly overrode his vetoes, Lane attacked the Portland establishment early and often. He personally inspected and tore apart recently constructed sidewalks and curbs to expose the shoddy work of corrupt contractors. He railed against the council for giving public property away to private companies. He insisted that the police raid gambling and prostitution houses. Arrests for soliciting prostitution rose from 31 in 1901 to 92 in 1903 and 180 in 1905, the year of the Lewis and Clark Exposition. Lane was reelected in 1907 but declined to run in 1909, worn out by the obdurate opposition of the Portland establishment. He was replaced by Joseph Simon, a long-standing member of the city's elite.

But urban reform continued. In 1909, Portland voters used the initiative to approve a cluster of measures that more closely regulated public utilities. In 1912 Governor Oswald West, a reform-minded Democrat, announced his determination to clean up Portland.[15] A vice commission investigated for nine months before reporting that Portland contained some 431 establishments devoted to prostitution, and the council agreed that the public had a right to know who owned the buildings that housed the prostitutes. In 1913 the Democratic *Oregon Journal* publicized another report, this one revealing chronic waste and inefficiency in nine of ten city departments. By this time many Portland citizens and organizations had become outspoken critics of the city's large monopoly, the Portland Railway Light & Power Company, arguing that its leaders had been much more attentive to making a profit than to expanding service to the city's growing populace.

Ambitious reforms and reformers did well under such conditions. Portland voters were more receptive than their counterparts in the rest of the state to single-tax initiatives, and in 1917 single-taxer and anti-monopolist Will Daly came close to being elected mayor.

But, as in the state as a whole, less radical reforms and reformers won the day. In 1913 the city's electorate narrowly approved replacing the city council with a commission form of government. Middle-class reformers tended to back the measure, hoping that a body consisting of four full-time commissioners elected on a city-wide rather than ward basis would be less partisan and more professional and efficient than fifteen councilmen elected by particular wards had been. But the new system was less, not more, democratic. The first council included two managers, an insurance executive, a civil engineer, and an attorney. These men were not, remark historians Dennis Hoffman and Vincent Webb in a nice piece of understatement, "as accessible to the influence of members of the working class as were the councilmen they replaced."[16]

Moderate reformers also turned their attentions to Portland's physical environment. Much less crowded than eastern cities, Portland had been a relatively salubrious place. The city had established a board of health in 1873, and a flurry of ordinances passed in 1881 regulated the disposal of excrement and garbage and the condition of stables and food. A pest house, to isolate people infected with noxious and communicable diseases, also opened that year. But by the 1890s Portland still suffered from several glaring health problems. Much of the garbage carted to Guild's Lake, just northwest of the city, sat and festered. Sewage ran into the Willamette River and wells, from which the city drew its drinking water. Food, too, might be tainted. In 1905 an investigator described markets selling rotting poultry, fish, and other meat, "all this surrounded by disease breathing garbage, fetid rubbish, floors soaked with corruption."[17] Reformers were especially concerned over reports of unsanitary dairies. Some critics estimated that three to four hundred babies a year died of typhoid from drinking impure milk.

These critics demanded and instituted changes. The city constructed a new and larger garbage crematory. Sewers were built. The Bull Run reservoir, east of the city, supplied pure water. The city passed new ordinances and enforced old ones to improve sanitation. Dairies received particular attention, with more active inspection programs and the spread of pasteurization. The death rate of Portland children plummeted.

Advocates for a cleaner Portland were concerned with much more than disease and life expectancy. Pure drinking water and sanitary markets were part of a larger program to beautify the city. Reformers asserted that the physical environment profoundly shaped people's lives. Playgrounds and gardens would occupy and morally elevate children. Wide, tree-lined boulevards would encourage pleasurable drives. Verdant parks would draw Portlanders out of their homes and into the salving balm of nature. Other proponents' motives were more narrow. They hoped that a more beautiful city would, like the Lewis and Clark Exposition, draw more investment and business.

This coalition of reformers and boosters started strong. In 1903 the city's park board invited John C. Olmsted, nephew and business partner of the renowned Frederick Law Olmsted, to Portland. The eastern consultant readily reported that the city ought to create a system of "park squares, play-grounds, small or neighborhood parks, large or suburban parks, scenic reservations, boulevards, and parkways." The result would both increase the value of property and "improve public taste."[18] Some years later, in 1909, a group of wealthy Portlanders formed the Civic Improvement League, which quickly raised $20,000 and hired English architect Edward Bennett to create a detailed plan for the city.

The plan's scope was breathtaking. There would of course be many more parks, large and small, for the "daily refreshment of the people."[19] But other aspects of the city's built environment would also be reworked. The river channel must be deepened and the harbor rebuilt to accommodate more shipping. New, wider streets stretching as far as twenty miles from downtown would be constructed, along with bridges and tunnels. A civic center would contain a cluster of new buildings: a courthouse, city hall, and library. There would be a new art gallery and civic auditorium.

The plan did not get very far. Portland voters approved it by more than a two-to-one margin, but then proved stingy when it came time to allocate money. Farmers, east-side residents, and labor unions objected to their tax monies paying for pretty vistas when many parts of the city and its environs still lacked adequate roads and water and sewer service. Some business people worried that reconfiguring Portland's streets and buildings might well harm their livelihoods. The economic doldrums that arrived in 1914 further dampened the plan's prospects.

City-planning advocates were not left empty-handed. City (now Washington), Maclean, Mt. Tabor, Columbia, Sellwood, Peninsula, and Laurelhurst parks were created. So were some playgrounds and playing fields. The city even managed to create a curvilinear, tree-lined boulevard replete with pleasant vistas: Terwilliger. But the Bennett Plan simply called for more extensive spending and change than most Portlanders were willing to make.

Portland's moderate reformers accomplished a great deal. By 1920 the city's residents enjoyed more parks and playgrounds, better drinking water, and more sanitary milk and meat than they had a generation before. Garbage and sewage were disposed of more efficiently, with less chance of causing disease. But Portland had been improved, not remade.

Other Portlanders were more concerned about their city's social environment, particularly the plight of poor or neglected children. Many couples of little means succeeded in providing loving and stable homes for their children. But they faced substantial handicaps: poverty itself, of course, but also associated ills—overcrowding, proximity to vice, and marital dissolution following death, chronic unemployment, or desertion. Many middle-class reformers suspected all impoverished parents, especially immigrants. The head of one child-saving institution declared that "the manner in which foreigners, especially those of Russia, Italy and other European countries have raised their children is not permissable in this country, as we do not allow them to cruelly beat or punish their children."[20] Well-to-do reformers who concerned themselves with the plight of marginal children were therefore inspired by two very different motives: a recognition that hundreds if not thousands of Portland children lacked sufficient food, shelter, and nurture and an assumption that race, ethnicity, or economic status rendered some adults incapable of raising their children.

These twin concerns generated many child-saving institutions. The Oregon Boys and Girls Aid Society was among the earliest and largest. Founded in the 1880s by a collection of prosperous Portlanders, the society supervised and cared for hundreds of children each year. Some children had been brought there by court order. Other beleaguered mothers and fathers left their children in the society's care until they could provide a stable home. Many of these children returned to their parents after a few months or years. Others did not and found a home, or a succession of homes, elsewhere. Infants were the easiest to place for adoption. Older children more often went to foster homes, where they received room, board, schooling, and, hopefully, at least a modicum of affection. The aid society was joined by many other institutions. The Baby Home and Children's Home cared for destitute children. The Florence Crittenton Home, House of the Good Shepherd, and Salvation Army Rescue Home served older and often "wayward" children. Some of the institutions were run and funded by churches. The Ladies Relief Society had charge of the Children's Home. All of these reformers aspired to supply their charges with more than food and shelter. They hoped to provide structure and discipline, to replace what they imagined to be the vagaries and weaknesses of impoverished families with an environment calculated to teach the virtues of temperance, industry, and honesty.

Indeed, some of the state's most determined reformers favored the sterilization of people deemed unfit to have children. "Degenerates and the feeble-minded should not be allowed to reproduce their kind," asserted Governor Oswald West, a progressive-minded Democrat, in 1913. The state's sterilization law was less ambitious. It included only "habitual criminals, moral degenerates and sexual perverts."[21]

Portland's mainstream reformers, then, were neither as disinterested nor as humane as they seemed. They rescued children from poverty, neglect, and abuse, but sometimes harmed poor families and people in the process. Prosperous Portlanders boosted a plan calculated to both improve the physical environment of the city and to increase their own prosperity. They created a new form of city government that may have been more efficient, but that was certainly less democratic, less susceptible to ordinary citizens' influence.

Radical Reform

Not all of Portland's reformers were moderate.

The city housed the state's only major concentration of working-class people, and sheer numbers alone ensured that they would exercise considerable political influence. These men, as noted above, often frustrated reformers. Most of them opposed prohibition and, fearing that women would vote Oregon dry, they tended to vote down suffrage, too. Multnomah County ranked twenty-ninth out of thirty-three counties in backing measures such as prohibition that would promote social conformity. In other respects, though, Portland voters favored progressive measures. The county stood sixth in supporting the political reforms that created the Oregon System. Its voters strongly backed legislation calculated to reform economic relations, such as workers' compensation and shorter work weeks.

But many Portland workers wanted much more than these reforms. They advocated overthrowing or replacing capitalism altogether.

Only a minority of Portland workers lived in poverty. A large proportion of the city's residents owned their own homes, including many who worked with their hands. Most of Portland's unionized workers were in the AFL, the "bread and butter" union that concentrated on improving the pay and working conditions of skilled workers, not overturning capitalism. These unionized workers constituted less than 10 percent of Portland's employees. They occasionally made common cause with those who were less well off and more radical. For example, Portland's AFL leaders sometimes cooperated with and supported the Industrial Workers of the World, or Wobblies, a decentralized collection of highly marginal and mobile laborers who preached the necessity of class struggle on street corners and logging camps across the western United States.

The Socialist Party enjoyed a broader, more varied membership than the Wobblies, though it, too, aspired to do away with capitalism. Many regarded measures such as the single tax, let alone the Oregon System, as merely tinkering with an oppressive economic arrangement that must be replaced by one promoting cooperation and equality. Oregon's Socialist Party was less powerful than those of other western states, though nearly 10 percent of the state's voters backed their perennial presidential candidate, Eugene Debs, in the 1912 election.

Oregon's working-class radicals were more devoted to organizing than to voting. In 1913, for example, between fifty and one hundred members of the Oregon Packing Company's all-women workforce walked off the job to protest their wages and working conditions. Portland's legal establishment ordered them to quit speaking and picketing. The strike's leaders did not back down: "Bring on your injunction, bring on your patrol wagon, and take us to jail," the women replied.[22] The police obliged by trying to intimidate the picketers and arresting three socialist women. Mayor Albee then banned non-religious speeches on the street. A collection of strikers, Socialists, and Wobblies challenged the measure and were clubbed and arrested for their trouble. When some members of the AFL protested, the mayor relented.

Later that year the Portland Wobblies organized about three thousand workers into an unemployment league that demanded food, shelter, and jobs. Portland's leaders reacted decisively. Early in 1914 the police targeted the league. Arrests for vagrancy, a time-tested way of jailing radicals real or suspected, rose.

Persecution of radicals accelerated when the U.S. entered World War I. In 1917, as the Wobblies planned a tremendous timber strike, Portland police arrested suspected members, raided their offices and halls, and seized papers. A Portland pacifist who refused to buy war bonds was hounded into resigning from her job with the county library. An editorial asserted that she did not belong "among Americans who love their native land."[23]

Attacks on civil liberties persisted after the war. In 1919 the Criminal Syndicalism Law banned advocating crime or violence to accomplish industrial or political goals, and Portland police used it to arrest dozens of suspected Wobblies. Even sleepy Tillamook joined the fray when

American Legion members and businessmen formed a vigilance committee and detained twenty men with IWW cards. Oregon's radicals would never again be nearly as strong as they were in the early years of the twentieth century.

More moderate reformers enjoyed many more successes and invited much less violence and calumny. But Portland's Wobblies and Socialists succeeded in raising a question that most reformers skirted: was industrial capitalism in fact capable of being much improved, or did the entire system need to be rooted out and replaced by economic and social structures that were more humane?

Women and Reform

Gender of course cut across class lines, and Oregon women participated in all of the Progressive Era's diverse reform movements. They also constituted a growing proportion of Oregon workers and strikers. But their contributions and efforts deserve separate treatment because of the peculiar barriers that they faced and the centrality of the woman suffrage campaign.

As we saw in the previous chapter, Oregon women began expanding the boundaries of the home and their sphere in the last decades of the nineteenth century, arguing that protecting their children required doing battle with any number of public menaces.

No issue galvanized nineteenth-century women as readily as drunkenness, a habit that caused, as one group of women put it, "desolated homes, blasted hopes, ruined lives and widowed hearts."[24] Such fears lay behind the first large public demonstrations by Oregon women. In 1874 a group of church women formed the Woman's Temperance Prayer League and began visiting Portland saloons, where they attracted notice by singing hymns and praying among the city's tipplers. Several of them were even arrested and served a few hours' jail time. This was a radical step. Reformer and historian Frances Fuller Victor observed that "very few of these women had ever prayed aloud in their own churches." Only one had ever before "spoken in public."[25] Their efforts bore fruit. Portland saloons kept serving liquor, but in just four days around two thousand Portland residents pledged to stop drinking it.

Temperance agitation grew as the years passed. Oregonians passed a local option in 1904, which gave counties and towns the choice of voting themselves dry. The state passed prohibition in 1914, the first election in which women were permitted to participate.

Sargent Bar, Portland, about 1910. Such places constituted a social center for many working-class men and alarmed many middle-class residents, especially women. Photo courtesy Oregon Historical Society, CN 015533

But by this time many women reformers had moved on to other concerns. The Woman's Christian Temperance Union was a prime example. It was a national organization; the first local Oregon chapter appeared in 1881, and a decade later the state boasted seventy-one chapters. As its name implied, its members were also concerned with reforming men's drinking habits. Members in the tiny northeastern town of Elgin, for example, reported in 1891 that they were petitioning to stop a new saloon from getting its license and had persuaded a church to stop using fermented wine in communion. But members interested themselves in a great many other reforms, too. By 1908 Oregon's W.C.T.U. had thirty-five departments, including labor, penal and reformatory, Sabbath observance, and physical culture. If some aspect of Oregon society needed reforming, chances were that the W.C.T.U. was doing something about it.

Members of the Oregon Federation of Women's Clubs underwent a still more dramatic conversion. A number of women's clubs began meeting in the 1890s. In 1899 eleven of them formed the federation, including chapters from La Grande, Pendleton, Silverton, and Astoria. The first meetings seemed innocuous enough, with members and guests presenting papers on history and culture. Eugene's club, which began in 1893, at first had trouble finding a member willing to serve as president, for few women were accustomed to taking positions of leadership. But this club's members became increasingly active. In 1895 they started a library, an endeavor that led to the founding of Eugene's city library thirteen years later. They funded housing for women students at the University of Oregon (Gerlinger Hall). By 1909 a group who had visited the state convention returned to announce that "self-culture is out," that club women had turned their attentions from Greek art and Shelley to "altruistic and philanthropic work and civic education."[26] Indeed, the 1910 president's report advocated investigations into conditions at the jail and juvenile court, among many other concerns.

Portland club members underwent a similar metamorphosis. They formed in 1895 over a game of whist and resolved to leave matters of politics and religion outside their discussions. But within a decade they supported woman suffrage, and by 1915 they were lobbying lawmakers on a host of issues, from forestry to public health.

Oregon's African-American clubs were not accepted into the state federation and created their own federation in 1914. They, too, pursued a wide range of concerns, including a study of how Oregon law treated minorities. As their refusal to join with African-American women suggests, Oregon's white women reformers seldom tackled the most divisive issues of their day. Few of them were radical. The great majority were prosperous, middle-class wives and mothers who were interested in improving social and political systems, not replacing or transforming them.

One can certainly discern the hand of social control in many of these endeavors. Immigrant and working men feared that women reformers were especially concerned with reforming their habits, particularly their right to enjoy a good drink or two with friends after a hard day's labor. Young women who ventured to Portland in search of excitement and autonomy along with decent wages were also wary. A "working woman" explained that she and her friends preferred living on their own rather than within the more protected and regulated confines of the Portland Women's Union because "the very fact of having to live under restrictions makes it appear as if we are in need of surveillance and incapable of taking care of ourselves, and no girl likes to admit that."[27] Like other reformers before and since, these well-to-do women were vulnerable to the charge that they were simply trying to force on others their values and habits.

But middle- and upper-class women reformers were also trying hard to help people less fortunate and more vulnerable than themselves. In advocating that Portland department stores close by

6:00 p.m., for example, they argued that saleswomen ought to be allowed to return home while the city's streets were relatively safe and that they ought not to be compelled to work at night. The same could be said of protective legislation for women workers, legislation (upheld by the U.S. Supreme Court in *Muller v. Oregon*) that both restricted women's employment opportunities and shielded them from overwork. The Consumer's League of Oregon, another reform movement dominated by women, urged its members to only purchase goods produced under humane working conditions.

Many reformers, furthermore, were concerned not simply with protecting women, but with expanding their rights. Full suffrage, the right to vote in all elections, became the lodestone of women's reform. In the first place, they argued, refusing women the franchise constituted a bald and forceful denial of citizenship and strongly implied that they could not be trusted. Not having the vote also hampered women's efforts to improve society. Just imagine how much good could be accomplished if women did not have to beg and plead and reason with male legislators and voters and could instead march right to the polls to make their voices heard—or aspire to political office themselves. The franchise for women was like the initiative and referendum for U'Ren: the key to unlocking all doors.

But many men, afraid of the very reforms that suffrage augured, resisted. Sustained suffrage agitation began in 1871, when the renowned Susan B. Anthony toured the Pacific Northwest with Abigail Scott Duniway, who had just started the *New Northwest*, her woman's-rights newspaper. She was not well received by the region's men. A Salem editor blamed her, implausibly, for "a raging fire of divorces."[28] But the suffrage movement forged ahead. Two years later, in 1873, the Multnomah County Woman Suffrage Association appeared, followed in another two years by the Oregon Woman Suffrage Association. They succeeded in getting suffrage on the ballot in 1884, but 72 percent of the electorate rejected it. This resounding loss and division among suffrage advocates stalled the movement.

Suffrage resurfaced in the 1890s, fuelled by growing numbers of women reformers. Duniway helped found the Oregon State Equal Suffrage Association in 1894 and edited a new suffrage newspaper, the *Pacific Empire*. The state legislature passed the measure at two separate sessions, meaning that if passed by the voters in 1900 it would become law. They did not, though the margin was narrow: a little over two thousand votes out of more than fifty-four thousand cast.

The movement then faltered. Duniway blamed the temperance movement. She branded its leaders as impractical elitists who had "sat in the sanctuary singing, 'Where Is My Wandering Boy Tonight,' when the little hoodlum was kicking up a rumpus at my suffrage meetings."[29] Most of these temperance advocates backed woman suffrage, but Duniway feared that their efforts did the cause more harm than good, confirming to working men that women would vote Oregon dry as soon as they got the chance to. The strong-willed Duniway therefore insisted that the movement use a "still hunt" approach to winning the vote. She and other leaders would work discreetly, behind the scenes, with influential legislators and civic leaders. The liquor interests, suppliers and purveyors of alcohol, would be lulled into a state of lassitude and would not bother to mobilize the thousands of laborers whose votes could turn the election. The strategy did not work. Suffrage lost by very large margins, winning just 39 percent of the vote in 1908 and 36 percent in 1910.

Even so, Oregon's suffrage proponents stuck to the high ground. Unlike many of their counterparts elsewhere, they seldom played on nativist fears by arguing that respectable men needed the votes of respectable women to counteract the influence of voters from southern or central Europe. Indeed, they more often charged their opponents with being part of the status quo: "the saloons, the brothels, the trusts, the railroads, the machine politicians, and the society women of Portland."[30] They argued that women deserved and needed the vote, that they were just as entitled to full citizenship as their husbands and brothers, and that the franchise would allow them to more fully defend their rights.

In 1912 women's rights advocates returned to a more public campaign, and the tide finally turned. Suffrage won a narrow victory. Perhaps the recent death of Duniway's conservative brother, Harvey Scott, an influential foe of suffrage, tipped the balance. A more plausible explanation is that women had become such a fixture of Oregon's public and political life that most men concluded that they might as well vote, too.

≈≈≈

Contrary to many women's hopes and expectations, suffrage did not lead to wholesale political change in Oregon. Women helped vote the state dry in 1914. But very few women were elected to office, and Oregon women apparently did not vote much differently from Oregon men. The woman suffrage movement was something of a metaphor for Oregon reform more generally. Though pursued with high hopes of political and social transformation, it amended rather than overturned the status quo.

Oregon's Progressive Era created state and local governments that were more efficient and less corrupt. It spawned healthier physical and more humane social environments. The Oregon System of direct democracy gave voters more control over the laws that they lived under.

Many Oregonians had wished for more: a legislature in which housewives outnumbered attorneys, laws that would take land out of the hands of powerful corporations and distribute them to hard-working people, even an economic system characterized by cooperation and harmony rather than competition and strife. At no time in Oregon's history would calls for radical reform be so powerful and compelling. But the majority of Oregon's electorate was not quite willing to venture into waters so uncharted. They chose instead to improve existing economic and social systems, to reduce capitalism's abuses rather than rooting it out.

Then, in the mid-1910s, even moderate reform waned. Teddy Roosevelt's Progressive Party made a decent showing in Oregon in 1912 before withering. The number of initiative ballot measures declined dramatically after 1914. The Republican Party regained its momentum and dominance as its leaders resolved their differences and learned to live with the direct primary and other elements of direct democracy. Oregon was about to enter a more conservative period. But it would do so with new political and social structures that would shield its citizens from the worst abuses of the Gilded Age.

Biographies

Charles Erskine Scott (C.E.S.) Wood

Soldier, attorney, reformer, man of letters, artist, and radical gadfly, Charles Erskine Scott Wood was one of Oregon's most notable and flamboyant residents for much of his long life.

The son of a highly literate naval surgeon, Wood grew up in the East and was graduated from West Point Military Academy in 1874, at age twenty-two. The Nez Perce and Bannnock Wars brought him to Oregon a few years later, and he recorded (and tweaked) Chief Joseph's well-known surrender speech. He married Nannie Moale Smith in 1879. Impatient with military hierarchy, he resigned from the U.S. Army. Having recently earned a bachelor of law degree from Columbia University, he moved his family to Portland and in 1884 began practicing there.

Photo courtesy Oregon Historical Society, OrHi 23607

Urbane and charming, Wood was soon on good terms personally and professionally with Portland's elite. He played a key role in creating Skidmore Fountain, directed the city's library association, and helped establish the Portland Art Association. Never one to stint on the finer things of life, Wood struggled to live within his means. He relieved his overextended finances by successfully defending a speculator's claim to nearly eight hundred thousand acres that Wood then helped to sell.

Wood's private and political lives were less conventional. He had a string of extra-marital affairs. He criticized President McKinley's expansive foreign policy and the nation's "lust of power or love of wealth and luxury." He wrote articles supporting woman suffrage and lamenting the very land grabs that he defended in court. He welcomed Emma Goldman, the prominent and much-hated anarchist, to Portland and defended the rights of radical labor activists to free speech. In *The Poet of the Desert*, inspired by a vacation on Bill Hanley's Harney County ranch, Wood associates freedom with nature and laments that civilized man has bound himself.

All of this made Wood vulnerable to criticism. His knack for drawing the affections of women who were married or later committed suicide invited censure. Members of the Portland establishment who read Wood's defense of anarchists and anarchy could not but wonder about their old friend. Radicals, on the other hand, wondered about Wood's consistency and sincerity. His dearest love, Sara Bard Field, found him narcissistic and asked if Wood wasn't "sorry you can't be in love with yourself and get your own letters?"[31]

In 1919, denied a divorce by Nannie, he at last made an explicit break with respectability by moving to San Franciso and living openly with Sara. Their home quickly became a gathering point for the city's artists, bohemians, and radicals. In 1927 Vanguard Press published Wood's *Heavenly Discourse*, a biting criticism of political and social conformity which sold seventy-five thousand copies in just eighteen months. He died in 1944, laboring over his autobiography.

Beatrice Morrow Cannady

This woman was one of the most active and least recognized Oregon reformers during the 1910s and 1920s.

Morrow moved to Portland in 1910, at age twenty, after graduating from college in Texas. Two years later she married Edward Daniel Cannady, a waiter. They soon had two sons. She graduated from Northwestern College of Law and became the first Black woman to practice law in Oregon in 1922.   ·

Cannady was a reforming whirlwind. In 1912 she became assistant editor of the *Advocate*, Portland's leading African-American newspaper. She was among the founders of the Portland National Association for the Advancement of Colored People (NAACP) chapter in 1914. Two years later she spearheaded a successful attempt to ban in Portland the showing of *The Birth of a Nation*, a highly racist and popular film. She waged a tireless campaign to win equal access to public accommodations—in restaurants, theaters, and hotels—both through her newspaper and by drafting legislation. In 1925 she succeeded in convincing Oregon voters to repeal, by a convincing margin, the state's so-called "black laws." These notorious measures had been overturned by the Fourteenth and Fifteenth Amendments of the federal Constitution but had remained in the state's constitution to remind Blacks that white Oregonians did not welcome them.

She did more. Cannady and the NAACP led successful campaigns against school segregation in Vernonia and Longview. She wrote and lectured widely on race issues. She even maintained her own lending library on African-American history and culture and filled requests from as far away as Prineville and Bend. She worked for prison reform and international peace, reforms calculated to improve the lives of people across the nation and world.

Cannady believed that interracial association and friendship held the key to unlocking racism. "When people do not know one another, they are suspicious and distrustful of one another," she asserted. "Only by contact of the races will ever an understanding be reached."[32]

Beatrice Morrow Cannady left for Los Angeles in 1934, after a quarter-century's work here.

Laura Rogers Pinkstaff (these names are pseudonyms)

We know very little about the lives of most early twentieth-century Oregonians. We would know almost nothing of Laura Rogers Pinkstaff if her guardian had not intercepted the letters that passed between her and her eventual husband.

Laura claimed that she had been orphaned at a young age. The Boys and Girls Aid Society, whose ward she became, noted that they took charge of her upon discovering that her mother was trying to give her away. Her first set of foster parents quickly returned the five-year-old, though she had been asking "if this is'ent her home now." A well-to-do Portland family kept her for less than two months, requesting a younger child and lamenting her "sharp temper." Laura eventually settled in with a Portland woman and her grown daughter. Unlike many abandoned children, she had found a stable, if not nurturing, home.

Then, when Laura turned sixteen, a working man and socialist named Lawrence Pinkstaff asked for her hand. William Gardner, the superintendent of the aid society, remained Laura's legal guardian and asked Pinkstaff to wait a year, and to stay away from Laura in the meantime. The two lovers then began a covert correspondence that did not always assuage their loneliness and doubts. Laura felt wounded when Lawrence took her to task for not writing more frequently. Her foster family was working her from 7:30 a.m. to 2:00 a.m., and she was without "a cent to my name" for stamps. But she reassured him of her devotion: "I've no one to go to with my troubles, no one to drop a kiss to when my blood is boiling with love, but never mind wait till I am with you, you won't have a minute's peace when I'm around."

Superintendent Gardner was not pleased by these words and others when he read them, and he called Laura to account. She admitted that she had allowed two other men to be sexually intimate with her. Gardner blamed Pinkstaff for turning a virtuous girl into "a delinquent" and had him prosecuted. Laura went to a new, much more prosperous, home where the lady of the house treated her gently and taught her to use a sewing machine. The two lovers were again separated.

But their love persevered. Pinkstaff now obeyed Gardner's commands; he and Laura waited for each other. Shortly after her seventeenth birthday they married. Pinkstaff promised Gardner "to lead the noblest life of which I am capable, and to be ever true to Laura." He pledged "to try to be the best son-in-law the Aid Society has, which is no doubt setting the mark high." Gardner accepted this olive branch: "Let us hope that yours will be the most happy of weddings and that you may enjoy a long and prosperous married life."[33]

The couple lived in Portland for nine years, then disappeared from its city directories. The letters they left behind testify to their devotion to each other. They also speak to the many pitfalls that abandoned children like Laura navigated around the century's turn and the determination of reformers like Gardner to protect and control them.

Will Daly

That Will Daly nearly became mayor of Portland in 1917 indicates how radical the city once was.

Daly grew up in Missouri, the child of a southern mother and an Irish immigrant, a shoemaker who died during Will's childhood. Will started earning money a few years later, at age ten. He worked in the printing business, married Daisy Flannery in 1892, then moved to Oregon a decade later.

Daly soon became prominent in Portland. He worked at his craft for the *Oregonian* and then the Portland Linotype Company before establishing his own business, the Portland Monotype Company, which earned him up to $4,500 annually. He became president of the Portland printers' local and the Oregon State Federation of Labor in 1908. Two years later he headed the powerful Portland Central Labor Council.

Portland's leading union leader won election to the city council in 1911. Conservatives took notice. By 1915 the *Oregonian* was complaining that Daly entertained "socialistic plans and rosy dreams," that he planned "to make of Portland a rainbowed haven of little work and abundant ease." Daly was undermining the powerful Portland Railway Light & Power Company by appraising its property more accurately and by defending jitneys, privately owned automobiles that, in functioning as taxis, cut into streetcar ridership. The Portland establishment, noted the *Labor Press*, opposed jitney operators for presuming to create "their own jobs" and unionizing. Daly backed other measures popular with Portland radicals. Like U'Ren, he favored the single tax, arguing that it would wrest land away from monopolists and make it available "to those who want to use it."[34]

Daly's decision to run for mayor in 1917 brought a hailstorm of charges upon his head. Portland's leading Republican papers accused him of supporting a general strike while the nation was at war. Then, just a few days before the election, burglars broke into Daly's home and rifled his files. A product of that raid appeared in Sunday's *Oregonian*: his 1910 application to join the Socialist Party. That was seven years before, and in 1912 Daly had rejoined the Republican Party. But with the election at hand, Daly had no time to mount an effective defense. He lost the election to establishment-friendly George Baker. Yet the margin was narrow: less than two thousand votes of more than forty-eight thousand cast. Portland had evidently been prepared to elect as its mayor a man highly sympathetic to unions and critical of monopoly. But it could not quite bring itself to vote for someone who seemed so sympathetic to socialism.

Like the rest of the nation, Daly became more private and conservative after his defeat. He died in 1924.

Chapter Six

Oregon Becomes Modern

1920-1929

"The three committees on roads were in session daily, and occasionally two and even three times a day."

The *Oregonian* on the 1929 legislature

I t may seem peculiar that a book devoting just nine chapters to more than two centuries sets aside one for a single decade. To be sure, the author has fudged a bit by including here some developments in rural and small-town Oregon that began around the turn of the century. Still, this chapter is devoted largely to events and processes that occurred between 1920 and 1929.

Students of U.S. history, particularly its twentieth century, often subscribe to the "pendulum" view of history. They argue that every age has an identity, an outlook, and that said outlook is formed largely in reaction to the previous era's. Hence the excesses of the Gilded Age produced the reformism of the Progressive Era which prompted the hedonism of the Jazz Age, and so on. From the vantage point of our new century, though, it looks as if the pendulum has been static since the early 1970s, when the nation shrugged off the idealism and indignation of the 1960s and embraced materialism, cynicism, political conservatism, and individualism.

But it was not the first time the nation had done so. The last three decades of the twentieth century were more than a little reminiscent of its third decade, the 1920s. After World War I, a strong economy, automobility, world weariness, and political reactionism combined to create cultural, social, and political patterns that would reemerge a half century later after the dust had cleared from a convulsive depression and war.

Oregon by no means led the way toward modernity in the 1920s. But it was carried along by its currents.

Economic Growth

With a few exceptions, including a sharp depression following World War I, the first three decades of the twentieth century brought substantial economic growth for most Oregonians. The state's population continued to expand much more rapidly than did that of the nation as a whole, swelling from 413,000 in 1900 to 953,000 in 1930. World War I provided particularly intense growth. The outbreak of the conflict increased European demand for Oregon crops, especially timber, and shipbuilding became a major industry in Portland, drawing thousands of workers to the city. After the war, Oregon's manufacturers, with the exception of the timber industry, remained limited. But the state nevertheless enjoyed an impressive amount of economic growth during the 1920s.

Wheat remained a major crop, and its production continued to shift eastward. By 1929 a tier of counties (Umatilla, Morrow, Gilliam, and Sherman) bordering the Columbia River grew much more wheat than did the Willamette Valley. Expanded rail service abetted this growth. In 1905, for example, trains linked Dufur to The Dalles, cutting transportation costs and therefore expanding wheat cultivation on the plateau's interior.

Mechanization accompanied growth. Farmers in the northeastern wheat belt switched to tractors in the 1920s, beginning a shift from horse, mule, and human to gasoline power that would be completed across Oregon three decades later. Those who could afford the new machines were able to plant, cultivate, and harvest land much more quickly than before. Fewer farm laborers had to be hired. Less land needed to be set aside for hay to feed the animals that the tractors were replacing. Large farms therefore became more productive. They also became larger, as smaller eastern Oregon farmers who could not afford the new equipment or lacked enough land to make efficient use of it sold out.

Most of eastern Oregon was still given over to the production of beef cattle and sheep. The latter were especially crucial to the rise of Shaniko, which housed many tons of wool waiting to be shipped. But the sheep range contracted early in the twentieth century, and Shaniko began its long decline. Cattle did better, especially on the wide ranges of southeastern Oregon, the most sparsely populated quarter of the state.

Other parts of southeastern and central Oregon went under the plow early in the twentieth century. The Enlarged Homestead Act of

Tractor-drawn harvester at work in pea fields, Umatilla County. Photo courtesy Oregon State Library

1909 opened more public land for settlement and eased the requirements. Settlers had only to cultivate 12.5 percent of their claim within three years. Boosters estimated that Harney County would soon enjoy a population of 350,000. Nowhere near that many people arrived, but the promise of prosperous farms touched off the West's final land rush. Some twelve hundred people—mostly from the Pacific Northwest and the Midwest, and some Europeans—came to the Fort Rock and Christmas Lake valleys southeast of Bend from 1905 to 1915. About one half of the claims were settled by families, one third by single men, and a few by single women.

These twentieth-century homesteaders struggled. The land had little timber, meaning that building materials had to be purchased, though juniper made serviceable fence posts. The ubiquitous sagebrush was cleared by digging and burning. Water was notoriously hard to come by. Arthur Donahue, a Christmas Lake Valley homesteader, recalled that in 1910 his family "hauled water on a hand cart 3/4 mil., over a road mostly filled with drifted sand. Such a task, my wife says, must be performed to be fully appreciated."[1]

The homesteaders scraped by for a few years. By 1915 about a quarter of the Fort Rock and Christmas Lake valleys had been plowed and planted, mostly in rye. Settlers also raised vegetables and fruit, kept hogs, cows, and chickens. In 1911 Fort Rock boasted two general stores, a hotel, a restaurant, a livery stable, a garage, a pool hall, a blacksmith and barber shop, even a newspaper. But these had been years of unusually high rainfall for this region, and when the drought

The town of Fort Rock had suffered two decades of decline by the time this photo was taken in 1936. Photo courtesy Oregon State Library

years returned, the homesteaders gave up. Most packed up in the 1910s. Others hung on until the 1920s. By 1940 the valley's population had declined to 10 percent of its 1912 total. A man who traversed the 135 miles between Bend and Burns in 1930 found only nineteen of seventy homes occupied.

Irrigation promised to change all this. Providing water for arid lands would work "magical effects on seemingly worthless land," as the *Oregonian* put it, peopling them "with prosperous farmers and orchardists."[2] Private enterprise funded most of the early efforts. But any but the most simple irrigation systems required a great deal of equipment and capital, much more than most companies could raise. The federal government became an active player in 1905, after the passage of the Newlands Act, though on a much smaller scale than later. It participated in two major Oregon projects, in Umatilla and Klamath counties. The former did not amount to much. By 1929 some eight thousand acres in west Umatilla County were withdrawn from the project. But the Klamath project irrigated nearly a quarter of a million acres and helped to prompt a population and economic boom in and around Klamath Falls. The county had about twenty-five hundred residents in 1890, well over thirty thousand just four decades later.

Agricultural development east of the Cascades, then, was uneven. Prosperous wheat farmers to the north and ranchers to the south did well, as did some farmers with access to irrigation around Klamath

Lake. Other areas developed slowly, and smaller operators, squeezed by mechanization and aridity, seldom succeeded anywhere.

Agriculture west of the Cascades followed a much different course in the twentieth century's first decades. Chapter Four recounts how large donation land claims began to fragment in the 1870s, as their owners sold off uncultivated land to purchase horse-drawn equipment. By the 1890s land companies were buying large tracts of prime land with good rail connections, planting them with fruit-bearing trees, and selling them in five- or ten-acre plots. The Salem Land Company, for example, started subdivisions named Fairview, Garden City, Hampden Park, and Auburn. Hundreds of farmers in Clackamas County, many of them from Japan or Italy, turned to truck gardening, harvesting vegetables, fruits, and berries for the booming Portland market. Other Willamette Valley farmers switched to ornamental crops. Marion County became a center for nurseries that produced thousands of fruit trees and berry bushes, and a wide variety of trees, shrubs, hedges, vines, and flowers that graced the region's proliferating streets and gardens. Dairying became an economic staple across most of the Willamette Valley and in selected parts of the coast, around Coos Bay and Tillamook. Hop growing also engaged a growing number of Willamette Valley farmers until prohibition in 1914. Traditional crops persisted, to be sure, such as oats for farmers' horses, since mechanization proceeded more slowly on western Oregon's small farms than on eastern Oregon's large ones. But the valley's agricultural products had become much more diverse than ever before.

Timber remained the only major rival to agriculture in Oregon. The switch from oxen to steam had greatly extended logging in the 1880s and had benefited larger operators at the expense of smaller ones. Technological advances slowed in the early twentieth century. But the industry continued to become both larger and more concentrated.

Large companies shifted their operations to the Pacific Northwest as timber production in the Great Lakes region slowed late in the nineteenth century. Frederick Weyerhaeuser of Minnesota led the way, buying up vast amounts of prime timber so that his huge mills would be guaranteed a steady supply of logs for decades to come. By 1913 the Weyerhaeuser Company and the Southern Pacific Railroad (which had received large bundles of public land for constructing its lines) owned some 22 percent of Oregon's privately held timber.

The Weyerhaeuser Company also led the way in innovative responses to problems of overproduction and price fluctuations. It was instrumental in forming the Oregon Lumber Manufacturers

Association in 1900 and the West Coast Lumbermen's Association in 1911. These groups by World War I controlled 90 percent of the Pacific Northwest's timber. They established uniform grading standards and set prices that members were not to undercut. Such measures did not eliminate competition, partly because the Pacific Northwest's lumbermen had little influence over what lumbermen located elsewhere in North America did. But they helped ensure relatively high and steady profits in an industry that tended to be volatile.

The early twentieth century saw Oregon's timber industry move east of the Cascades. Weyerhaeuser began buying prime pine forests around Klamath Falls in 1905 and eventually built a mill there. Rails finally reached Bend in 1911 and set off a timber boom dominated by two large Minnesota concerns: Shevlin-Hixon and Brooks-Scanlon. Prineville, a ranching center, suffered in relation to this upstart city to the west, but recouped some of its losses by building its own railway in 1918, which would help to draw mills there in the 1930s. Economic development inevitably favored some parts of the state more than others, and such towns as Prineville scrambled to keep up.

Growth brought environmental problems together with economic prosperity. The expansion of timber production to central Oregon spread the extent of clear-cutting and the disappearance of ancient forests. Dry weather that arrived in 1928 revealed that much of eastern Oregon's rangeland had been overstocked, causing loss of ground cover and accelerated soil erosion. Increasingly intense agriculture caused similar problems. The drawbacks of progress were perhaps most noticeable in irrigated areas. William and Irene Finley were saddened in 1925 to find that the Klamath irrigation project had left "a great desert waste of dry peat and alkali" where an extensive series of marshes harboring great flocks of waterfowl had once stood.[3] But few Oregonians joined them in expressing regret over the costs of progress. The 1920s was not a decade of regret.

Automobility

In Oregon and across the nation, the automobile symbolized the new century's expansive possibilities. It contributed mightily to economic growth. But the internal-combustion engine did far more than pull farm machinery and move goods. It moved people. Roads and cars spread like topsy in the 1910s and 1920s, making and breaking towns as the railroad once had and bringing even farm families to the doorstep of urban experiences and amenities.

As we saw in Chapter Three, Oregonians began advocating for good roads in the 1840s. But as steamboats and especially railroads replaced wagons, the impetus for road building waned. Indeed, by the close of the nineteenth century the leading boosters for good roads were not farmers, but bicyclists, young men and women who wanted smooth surfaces on which to ride their big-wheeled and expensive contraptions. Bicycles, together with all manner of other conveyances, were soon shouldered aside by gasoline-powered machines. By 1917 there was already one car or truck for every thirteen residents of Multnomah County. Just eight years later the ratio was down to one in five. By the time the Depression hit in 1929 one of every 3.7 Multnomah County residents—man, woman, and child—owned an automobile. By 1939, the Depression notwithstanding, a still larger proportion of Oregon families had a car.

This explosion in automobile ownership spawned new thoroughfares. In 1914, 86 percent of the state's thirty-seven thousand miles of road consisted of dirt and mud. Just twenty-five miles were paved, 232 miles planked. The state and federal governments changed this. Congress in 1916 voted to match state funding of roads dollar for dollar. The Oregon legislature had established a gasoline tax of one cent per gallon for road construction in 1919. The tax was doubled in 1921, then raised to three cents in 1923. The *Oregonian* reported of the 1929 legislature: "The three committees on roads were in session daily, and occasionally two and even three times a day."[4] Then, as now, Oregonians did not like to be taxed. But few complained when the funds built or improved roads. Even the Depression did not slow automobility. In 1940 Oregonians enjoyed more than two thousand miles of paved roads, and an extensive state-highway system linked its major population centers inside and outside the Willamette Valley.

Automobiles brought more than pavement to Oregon's landscape. Dealerships and repair shops pushed aside livery stables, harness shops, and blacksmiths. The changes did not occur instantaneously. Indeed, city streets were for many years choked by a chaotic mixture of wagons, streetcars, and automobiles, as three generations of transportation technology jockeyed for supremacy. No-parking zones and street lights appeared in the 1920s. But by that time the automobile was shifting people and businesses away from Oregon's downtowns. Commuting to work by car freed urbanites from needing to live on or near streetcar lines, and thousands of Portlanders filled in newly developed sections of Grant Park, Mount Tabor, Concordia, the West Hills, and elsewhere. Automobiles also decentralized shopping, since, unlike streetcars, they could readily convey their

A. C. Schaefer's blacksmith shop in Salem, 1911, a business that would soon be made obsolete by the automobile. Photo courtesy of the Historic Photograph Collections, Salem (Oregon) Public Library

owners to stores located outside of downtown. Indeed, suburban locales were in many ways preferable, their streets and parking spaces less congested. Portland's East 82nd Avenue and Sandy Boulevard were soon dominated by a string of gas stations, restaurants, and stores. Portland voters approved a simple zoning measure in 1924 that separated the city into residential, business, and industrial areas. Even factories moved away from their rail connections in or near city cores as trucks began to supplant boxcars. The center of Portland's economic and social life was spinning outward.

Small towns were affected still more profoundly. Some benefited from roads that brought urban and out-of-state tourists to popular destinations. By 1915, for example, the scenic and serpentine Columbia River Highway linked Troutdale, near Portland's eastern fringe, to Hood River and spawned a string of roadside lodging, camping, and eating establishments. By the 1920s paved roads circled Mount Hood and reached several resort towns on Oregon's coast. Bend's auto camps and motels could house more than two thousand tourists at a time by the summer of 1923.

Other towns were not so fortunate. Those within convenient driving range of larger centers withered. One-room schools began consolidating into larger districts. Farmers and even townspeople began doing their shopping in larger towns and cities, trading driving time, gas money, and local loyalties for lower prices and wider selections. The automobile was taking the heart out of big-city downtowns and small-town main streets.

Yet few people were counting the costs, for the automobile connoted a tremendous sense of possibility and freedom. Portland reformers had complained that the Portland Railway Light & Power Company constituted a corrupt and inefficient monopoly. The automobile made reforming public transit a moot issue: one simply drove a car instead of riding a streetcar. Farm families could take advantage of services that had once been out of reach: high schools, stores, and urban entertainments. Young people were especially drawn to automobiles. Cars offered unprecedented opportunities for independence and mobility. Young lovers left the watchful eyes of parents for the privacy of back roads: *From Front Porch to Back Seat*, as the title of a history of courtship puts it. Movies, dances, drinking parties—all of these entertainments and more were in the reach of any Oregonian with a will and a ride.

Prosperity plus automobility equalled a marked increase in leisure activities. The Jantzen Beach Amusement Park opened in north Portland in 1928. The Big Dipper, the largest roller coaster west of Chicago, was but one of many attractions. Other rides, the city's best

The automobile led to abandoned stores in rural areas—even stores that sold gas. This photo of a former gas station and store in Lincoln County was taken in the mid 1900s. Photo courtesy of the Historic Photograph Collections, Salem (Oregon) Public Library

swimming pools, a fine dance floor, picnic areas, and arcade games quickly made it a favorite of the area's young people. "The Wonder of the West" drew more than fifteen thousand on opening day.[5] Cars also carried pleasure seekers to more sylvan settings, including Oregon's growing number of parks. Visitors to Crater Lake grew fivefold in the 1920s. Trips to the ocean had once been reserved for the well-to-do, who had traveled by train and stayed for weeks at beach-side resorts and cabins in Seaside or Newport. Now working-class families could spend a weekend at "the coast."

Even mountain climbing, formerly dominated by urban professionals, was democratized. The pastime had been well-nigh monopolized by the Mazamas, a Portland organization which paired social distinction with highly regulated outdoor adventure. The Mazamas traveled en masse, by train, to mountains and then climbed together, documenting their achievements with flag plantings, summit registers, photographs, and written reports. But the automobile made mountain climbing available to a much broader range of people. In 1923 six teenagers from Bend became the first to climb Three Fingered Jack. A few years later a group of Bend climbers formed the Skyliners, an organization dominated by working-class immigrants. Its dues were $1.00 per year.

The automobile even fractured the Mazamas. If motor vehicles could carry outdoor enthusiasts to the base of Mt. Hood, reasoned some members, then why not run a tram to its summit? Why should the grandeur of Oregon's highest point be reserved only for those willing and able to scale its heights? The Mazamas split on this question, and the Forest Service turned the proposal down. "The gasoline motor has gotten possession of our souls," explained forester W. B. Greeley, in dealing unfettered mobility one of its few defeats.[6] People would still have to walk to enjoy this Oregon attraction.

The Pursuit of Pleasure

The automobile was one crucial part of a great cultural transformation at work in the United States by the 1920s. Historians have identified this decade as a critical watershed in a transition from self-restraint to self-realization, from deferred to immediate gratification. The transformation manifested itself in many ways. At the decade's outset most people paid cash for a car. By its close most bought on the installment plan, a development that even conservative bankers now touted. The shift toward pleasure also reworked gender roles, creating marriages in which husbands and wives often expected more of their spouses—but less of themselves.

The mass media of the day played a critical role in spreading the new ethos. Movies and radio had become commonplace by the 1920s and broadcast the new gospel of sex and pleasure to anyone with eyes and ears. Nard Jones, who later became a prominent Seattle journalist and writer, lived in Weston, near Pendleton, from 1919 to 1927, and drew from his experiences there in writing his first book, *Oregon Detour*. The novel, which resembles Sinclair Lewis's *Main Street*, describes how Hollywood images had become powerful even in remote corners of Oregon. The novel begins with the first day at Creston High School, with Etta Dant "dressed in the mode that Creston's girlhood had accepted as authentic from the photographic illustrations in 'True Confessions' ... from exaggerated cartoons of gilded youth in the newspapers, or an occasional collegiate motion picture showing at Memorial Hall." A few years later she knew the latest New York tunes as well "as any city girl," for "she heard them every night over the radio." She reflects that her young husband and his friends like to drink and dance not so much for the intrinsic pleasure of alcohol and rhythmic movement, but because such transgressions were "an imitation of something," a wan attempt to mimic "those light-hearted adulteresses, libertines, drug fiends, and drunkards" who populated the day's popular reading material.[7]

Ray Nelson, who moved to southeastern Oregon's Malheur County in 1922, told much the same story. "It was the days of the 'shiek' and the 'flapper,'" he recalled in 1976. Young men and women even in this remote corner of Oregon tried to look and act like the people they read about in popular stories or watched in movie houses. The boys arranged their hair into pompadours, and the girls put aside their corsets and long dresses for "low-necked, sleeveless blouses" and bobbed hair. "They painted their lips, rouged their cheeks, and penciled their eye-brows." They also joined the boys in smoking and drinking. Nelson, a self-admitted moonshiner, was engaging in more than a little hyperbole. Not every rural woman and cowboy was emulating "flappers" and "shieks." But many of them were.[8]

Such changes drew a firestorm of criticism, especially from parents and clergy. "You should have heard the howl the worry-warts made back in the twenties," recalls Nelson, who allowed that "maybe they had a reason to holler."[9] The worriers certainly thought so. A Portland minister fretted over the "orgy of materialism, hectic finance, pleasure seeking and ... sex freedom," that the pious mothers of his childhood were being replaced by "selfish cigarette-smoking, booze-drinking,

… pleasure-hunting, child-neglecting, home-destroying" women. A cleric who served both eastern Oregon and Portland perhaps best summed up the conservatives' worries, concluding that "the old time search for character" had given way to "the so called search for happiness."[10]

Concern was especially high among Oregon's (Old) Mennonites clustered around Hubbard, Albany, and other parts of the Willamette Valley who numbered nearly one thousand by the end of the 1920s. Like their Amish counterparts, they had relied on farming to keep them isolated from mainstream society and culture. But changes in agriculture were pushing many into working-class or professional occupations, often in urban settings. A growing proportion of Mennonite children were therefore growing up around non-Mennonites and staying in school longer than their parents had. Even those who lived on farms were able to move about a great deal more than before, thanks to the automobile. A 1922 speaker asserted that towns constituted "grave problems for our young people."[11] Other leaders worried about popular entertainments like movies and fairs. Even Mennonites were becoming increasingly exposed to these temptations.

Young men and women, single and married alike, spent more time with each other in the 1920s than they had before. Many more went to high school and college, and dating had become commonplace. The foundation of marriage shifted to "emotion work" as romance shouldered aside material considerations and as the average size of households shrank. Young couples referred to each other in much more intimate terms than their grandparents had. Letters between spouses and lovers were peppered with such endearments as "dearest Daddy," "sweet Daddie," "Sis," "papa," "kiddo," "sweetheart mine," Billie Boy mine," and "dear little baby."[12]

This shift was more than rhetorical. Husbands and especially wives wanted more from marriage and their spouses than their parents and grandparents had. Wives asserted their rights to pleasure and happiness in the semi-public forum of Bend's Deschutes County Circuit Court. "Just as soon as we got married he wouldn't pay any attention to my wishes at all," complained one woman of her husband. "I don't think we ever went to one picture show that was of my choosing."[13] Another admitted that she and her husband got along well "if I gave in to him in everything he wanted to do, but that gets kind of old." A third remarked that her husband initiated their quarrels, but that once the fight started "of course I didn't just sit and say nothing."[14] Some husbands adjusted to and accommodated women's increased desires for intimacy and equality. Many Oregon marriages became more romantically charged and mutually satisfying.

But the increasingly permissive climate of the 1920s could also undercut marriage and a regard for women's sensibilities. Oregon husbands demanded more sexual satisfaction than in the past and more commonly paired sex with violence. A Benton County woman complained that her husband handled her breasts "in a rough and cruel manner."[15] Increasing numbers of men pursued pleasure rather than observing traditional responsibilities. One husband who had deserted his wife sent her a photograph of himself with a "little jane" who had let him stay with her "three nights, Free of charge, love at first sight." More and more husbands and wives were violating their marriage vows, abandoning their spouses and beds for more exciting prospects elsewhere. "You are to old in your ways for me," wrote a Bend-area wife to the husband she was deserting in 1923. "All you do is stick around camp don't want to go no where." But women remained more economically vulnerable than their husbands, and they therefore had more to lose if a marriage dissolved. Despite or because of the growing sense of permissiveness, many women resolved to put aside their own desires and to instead focus on getting and keeping a good husband. Marian Miller, a Portland advice columnist, recommended that an intelligent but lonely young woman cultivate silence and "a baby stare" when in the company of an attractive man. "Bake them a good pie, make them talk about themselves and maybe they'll admire you," she counseled.[16]

But men's and women's increased desires for autonomy and pleasure played hob with traditional marital roles. Oregon's divorce rate continued to be among the nation's highest, and rising expectations for marital satisfaction, romance, and individual autonomy increased levels of spousal violence.

Strife between Oregon's parents and children also increased in the 1920s. Violence between parents and their biological children had been relatively rare during nineteenth century. Parents had asserted a widely supported right to strike disobedient children, but most children had respected the wishes of their parents. By the 1920s children, especially teenagers, were asserting and enjoying more autonomy than they had before. Parents therefore used violence more frequently. Young Tom McCall regularly defied his mother's authority on their ranch outside Prineville and received many whippings with a shot-filled riding quirt for his trouble. As norms of self-restraint eroded, such violence could become extreme, all out of proportion to children's transgressions. Killings of children aged one to twelve had been virtually unheard of in the nineteenth century. By the 1920s they constituted a growing, though still very small, proportion of Oregon homicides.

On the surface of things, life in Oregon during the 1920s was good. The times were prosperous, and the automobile and a host of other new inventions and entertainments bequeathed to the decade a patina of excitement and pleasure. But significant social strains were opening beneath this gay surface.

Oregon Literature

Oregon's literature reflected the decade's social norms and tensions.

The most popular Oregon novel by far had been Frederic Homer Balch's *Bridge of the Gods*, first published in 1890. Its protagonist is the pious Reverend Cecil Grey, who makes his way from New England to the Columbia River in the late seventeenth century to save benighted savages. Balch interviewed Native Americans along the Columbia River, and their myths color his popular novel. But the novel draws its readers' empathies to young Cecil, who meets a highly romantic and tragic end.

Oregon writers more commonly romanticized the pioneers of the mid-nineteenth century. Like the early pioneer and historical societies that formed late in the century, these books aimed at celebrating and immortalizing Oregon's early settlers. Eva Emery Dye started turning out popular historical novels in 1900, and her books are well populated with what one historian describes as "a crowd of heroes, a bevy of beauties, unnumbered cases of hardship and help, love galore and the carrying of the soul of American to the farthest reaches of the North American continent."[17]

This sort of literature by no means disappeared between the wars. *The Lariat*, a popular poetry journal edited by Salem's Colonel E. Hofer, aspired to provide "sweet, readable songs that leave a good taste in the mouth and sweet jingling in the hearts of readers."[18]

By the 1920s such art left increasing numbers of Oregonians and other Americans dissatisfied. World War I had contributed to a desire for prose and poetry that was more realistic. Many of the young men who went to war returned with altered sensibilities. Portland's Kirby Ross, for example, drank in French culture and wine. "Went to Folies Bergere, Casino de Paree, had some good drinks and dinners," he wrote. "Plenty of Mademoiselles. Some gay Paree." But America's soldiers also surrendered their innocence on much harsher ground.

He wrote of the "awful work" of identifying decomposing corpses, of bodies "going up" around him as he charged into battle, of the death of "my poor pal Sgt Fred T. Merrill." His diary could only suggest the effects of such carnage: "My, of all the bloodshed, bodies badly torn."[19] Many such men, like Ernest Hemingway, returned home exasperated with and weary of the pieties and sureties of American literature and culture.

American letters also shifted between the wars because of broad social and cultural changes. Younger, increasingly educated readers were impatient with the verities of their parents' generation and demanded literature that was more morally complex—or unconcerned altogether with moralism. Men, in particular, were less patient with self-restrained, Victorian protagonists and sought heroes who used violence readily and effectively. This demand for better and bloodier fiction made its mark in Oregon, as elsewhere.

The state's most distinguished writers mounted a frontal assault on the state's romantic and undistinguished literary tradition. The two leading critics were H. L. Davis and James Stevens. Both young men came from unpretentious backgrounds and grounded their writing in their experiences as working men in the early-twentieth-century West. One night in Davis's Eugene hotel room they began to chronicle the follies of Pacific Northwest literature and set about committing them to paper, on Davis's typewriter. *Status Rerum: A Manifesto, Upon the Present Condition of Northwestern Literature: Containing Several Near-Libelous Utterances, Upon Persons in the Public Eye*, was printed in 1927 and distributed by its authors. The region's publishers were not eager to associate themselves with such a vitriolic piece.

Davis and Stevens characterized the Pacific Northwest's literary tradition and output as "a vast quantity of bilge," a "seemingly interminable avalanche of tripe" produced by literati who "could not be trusted to manufacture rocking-chairs, to pile lumber, to operate donkey-engines, or combined harvesters; to shear sheep, or castrate calves." They were "posers, parasites, and pismires," and it was up to "young and yet unformed spirits," writers such as Davis and Stevens, "to cleanse the Augean stables which are poisoning the stream of Northwestern literature at the source."[20]

Davis and Stevens did more than criticize. They also created an impressive body of literature set in Oregon.

Stevens, born in Iowa in 1892, was already a well-established writer of the "new realism" school by the late 1920s. He had published several pieces in the *American Mercury*, H. L. Mencken's extremely influential journal, and a novel, *Brawnyman*. More was to come.

native-born Protestant could not qualify. This time the Klan's power centered outside the South, in the Midwest and on the West coast. Klan organizers did especially well in Oregon, where they had from twenty-five to forty-five thousand members. Residents of Portland and southern and coastal Oregon were particularly apt to join. Lightly populated Tillamook County, with less than ten thousand men, women, and children, had a klavern of eight hundred by 1923.

Oregon's Klan was headed by Grand Dragon Fred T. Gifford, who had been a Mason (member of a leading fraternal order), an electrical engineer, and an active unionist. Headquartered in Portland, Gifford became the leading Klansman on the Pacific coast.

The Oregon Klan's biggest triumph came in 1922, when Oregon voters approved, 115,506 to 103,685, a Compulsory School Bill that required all children to attend public schools. This measure was aimed at Oregon's growing number of Catholics, who by then constituted about 8 percent of the state's population. "These mongrel hordes must be Americanized," explained Gifford; "failing that, deportation is the only remedy."[26] The law was declared unconstitutional before it could be implemented, but it well expressed many Oregonians' fears that "aliens" were threatening to overwhelm the state. But it also echoed Progressive Era concerns over the elitism of private institutions. Public schools brought all Oregonians, all Americans, together.

A year later the Klan joined the American Legion in supporting an Alien Property Act that kept Japanese immigrants (Issei) from owning or leasing land. This law stood (similar ones had already been passed in California and Washington) although the Issei circumvented it by registering land under the names of their American-born (Nisei) children.

The Klan also wielded considerable clout in Oregon electoral politics. Members won election to the Eugene, Astoria, and Tillamook city councils and to the Multnomah Board of County Commissioners. Governor Ben Olcott publicly opposed the Klan in 1922, condemning them for "stirring up fanaticism, race hatred, religious prejudices and all of those evil influences which tend toward factional strife and civil terror."[27] He narrowly won the Republican primary, then lost decisively in the general election to Democrat Walter Pierce. Pierce was in many respects a liberal. But he won the Klan's support after pledging to support the compulsory school bill and also—so the Klan claimed—to send some patronage their way. Pierce did not openly support the Klan, and he later denied promising them government jobs in return for their votes. But in a state in which Republicans outnumbered Democrats two-to-one, the Klan could plausibly claim that they had elected Oregon's new governor and controlled the state legislature.

The Klan's successes alarmed moderate Oregon politicians. Senator Charles McNary, a Republican, reluctantly returned home from Washington, D.C. in 1922 to campaign for Olcott. In Astoria the local Klan interrupted his speech by setting off an alarm bell under the speaker's platform. An intimidated McNary withdrew from consideration for a federal appointment a loyal competent man whose only shortcoming was that his parents had been Catholic immigrants. "To think that a lot of darn cranks who ought to be put in confinement, can prevent an appointment of this character," concluded McNary, "makes me sick."[28]

Most Klan members devoted themselves to local concerns. Jackson County's were among the state's most active. In March of 1922 they kidnapped and threatened to hang a Medford piano salesman if he did not desist in his romances with two young women, cancel a debt owed him by a Klansman, and leave the county immediately. They also hoisted by the neck, without killing, an African-American man accused of bootlegging. Another resident, who may have been part-Mexican, was accused of being a chicken thief. When such acts elicited criticism, the Klan made highly publicized donations to a young Medford woman whose husband had deserted her and her children. Most klaverns were less violent than southern Oregon's. La Grande Klansmen, for example, often occupied themselves with exhorting each other to not patronize a popular Jewish-owned lunch spot.

The Oregon Klan's power dissipated quickly. Most of the bills it sponsored during the 1923 legislative session were defeated, including ones that would make sacramental wine illegal and require foreign-born business owners to post their nationality. By then the Klan had elicited some determined opposition: a few newspapers, some leading Protestant clergymen, and of course the people that it pilloried, including Roman Catholics and the Portland chapter of the National Association for the Advancement of Colored People. Oregon's American Federation of Labor condemned the Klan late in 1923.

By 1924 Oregon's Klan was in trouble. It had little apparent influence on that year's elections. Senator McNary, whom the Klan strongly opposed, easily won reelection. The Oregon Klan itself split, torn apart by regional and personal resentments. Some klaverns kept meeting into the 1930s. But they had little impact on Oregon politics and attracted little publicity.

Explaining the Oregon Klan's popularity is much more slippery than describing its rise and fall. It was clearly concerned with stamping out what it regarded as immorality: adultery, fornication, drinking, drugs, theft, and other crimes—especially if committed by non-whites.

Like Protestant clergymen, many of whom were Klan members or sympathizers, Klansmen feared that their communities were being engulfed by a flood of immorality. Residents deemed to be outsiders came in for the most criticism. Reverend Sawyer asserted to a Portland audience that "Jews" were "either bolshevists, undermining our government, or are shylocks in finance or commerce who gain control and command of Christians as borrowers or employees."[29] Catholics also impressed such men as exotic and dangerous interlopers, and Klan rallies sometimes featured women who claimed to have escaped from nunneries.

That an organization trumpeting papal and Jewish conspiracies could flourish in Oregon seems, on the face of things, absurd. This was a relatively homogeneous state in the 1920s: overwhelmingly white, native-born, and Protestant. Indeed, non-whites and people born overseas alike constituted a declining proportion of its population. But attacks on people considered exotic suggest a broader, more amorphous set of fears. The compulsory school bill seems, in retrospect, to constitute a dangerous piece of demagoguery, a bigoted assault on the civil liberties of non-Protestants. But to most Oregonians of the time, the school bill seemed like a balm, for in their minds the good old-fashioned American schoolhouse represented an economic and social melting pot, a place where the accidents of birth were subsumed under a veneer of patriotism and opportunity and virtue. Indeed, one of the Oregon Klan's primary publications was entitled *The Old Cedar School*, and its author described that building as "next in my heart to Mother's grave."[30]

The great majority of Ku Klux Klan members were middle class, especially lower-middle class: white-collar employees of modest means and skilled workers. Oregon's Ku Klux Klan promised to ease their communities' entry into modernity. Hence Tillamook's Klan flourished as the town became more prosperous and dependent on outside economic interests and processes. It helped local Protestants, as historian William Toll puts it, "to reconcile their commitment to change with their concurrent commitments to tradition."[31]

This is not to say that Oregon's Klan was innocuous. It played a major role in passing legislation that would have hamstrung Catholic schools. Some Catholics had trouble getting work in the early 1920s. Portland's African Americans had very good reason for alarm when fiery crosses lit up Mount Tabor. But the Klan's nativism and racism were part of a larger set of fears, an ambivalence over the quickening pace and very nature of modern life that somehow became the fault of Jews, Catholics, and Blacks.

Republicans Triumphant

The Ku Klux Klan's ambitious program disintegrated well before the end of the 1920s, supplanted by more moderate forms of conservatism. Two decades of political experimentation and reform were replaced, in Oregon as elsewhere, by policies that favored the status quo.

World War I was a watershed. Ballot measures, by initiative petition and referendum, peaked in 1914 and then declined dramatically. Senators George Chamberlain and Harry Lane, both progressive Democrats, had been replaced by a pair of Republicans by the end of 1920: McNary and Robert Stanfield.

Oregon's Republican Party, badly fractured and often on the defensive during the century's first decade and a half, recovered its preeminence. Oregon joined the nation in supporting Harding, Coolidge, and Hoover in the decade's three presidential elections—indeed, these presidents won every single Oregon county! The 1922 election, as we have seen, brought a Democrat, Walter Pierce, to the governor's chair. But in 1926 the voters turned him out in favor of Republican Isaac Patterson. As they had for decades, Republicans firmly controlled the Oregon legislature. In 1923, even with a Democrat in the statehouse, Republican legislators outnumbered their Democratic counterparts by a margin of more than six to one: eighty-five to thirteen.

Now it was Oregon's Democratic Party that found itself in disarray. One enduring problem was essentially structural: in a state that was overwhelmingly Republican, Democratic politicians could not afford to be very partisan. They spent as much or more time courting Republican voters than in rewarding faithful Democratic ones. "For the past 30 years there has been no Democratic party in Oregon," complained the Salem *Capital Journal* in 1928. "The few Democrats that have been elected owed their success to their personality ... and did nothing to build up organization."[32] Oregon's Democrats also suffered internal division. Some leaders quarreled, in part because of the decade's cultural divisions. Democrats who had been drawn to the Ku Klux Klan's program to restore traditional morality, for example, were put off by the party's 1928 nominee for the presidency: Alfred E. Smith, a wet (anti-prohibition) Catholic.

Taxation became a volatile political issue in Oregon in the 1920s. Some Oregonians, especially farmers, argued that the state should join the nation in assessing an income tax so that the burden of supporting state services could be shifted from the backs of landowners. But many others distrusted any sort of tax. Voters resoundingly defeated the state income tax that the legislature had passed. Yet these same voters expected increased state services. The problem was not resolved by the time the Depression hit in 1929, so the state entered the worst financial panic in the nation's history with a deficit.

A substantial portion of the state and the country was not yet ready for sustained government intervention in the private sector. This would soon change.

☙ ❧ ❧

The 1920s seemed like a peculiar decade. It paired political conservatism and reactionism with technological and cultural innovation. But this contrast was less paradoxical than it seemed; people in societies that are becoming more fluid often seek stability by blaming minority groups and embracing a politically conservative program. In this sense, prosperity, automobility, pleasure seeking, the Ku Klux Klan, and the waning of progressive politics and idealism were of a piece, with conservative political verities compensating for radical cultural shifts. Individualism constituted a common denominator that cut across and unified the decade's diverse trends.

The Great Depression of the 1930s capped by several years of war altered the trajectory of trends established during the 1920s. Hardship softened the pursuit of pleasure and political conservatism. But the modern forces that had dominated the 1920s never disappeared from the nation or from Oregon.

Biographies

Alice Day Pratt

Many homesteaders came and went from eastern Oregon in the twentieth century's first decades. Few were single women and fewer still left a lasting written impression of their challenging lives. Alice Day Pratt qualified on both counts.

Pratt was born in 1872 and spent her childhood in Minnesota and on a remote Dakota homestead. There she took an active interest in reading and botany. She never married and held several teaching jobs before deciding to leave North Carolina for a homestead in the West. She moved onto her 160 acres southeast of Prineville in 1911.

It was not easy. She at first lacked a horse and had to haul everything on her back, though the nearest store lay four miles away. Hawks ate her chickens. Rabbits devoured her garden. Most of Crook County's men did not much help her. Promised assistance seldom came, even if she had already paid for it. "The most melancholy theme of my homestead experience," she later recalled, "is the management of men." The neighboring farmers suspected single women homesteaders and educated people in general. She found their children "already somewhat bound and blinded by the prevailing bigotry," with the "habit of ridicule of all foreigners and foreign ways."

Pratt did not prosper materially at her new home. One winter, out of money and snowbound, she burned her chopping block and ladder for fuel. Her charitable and trusting nature also cost her. Pratt concluded that "a youth nourished largely upon Emerson and the poets, and a purely professional career possibly do not forewarn or forearm one quite adequately for practical business experience."

Yet Pratt enjoyed her land and its creatures, wild and domestic. Five years later, having "proved up," she cheerfully prepared to leave her home only to find that "tears were raining down my face."[33]

She moved often in the next few years, teaching both in the East and near her homestead. By the end of the 1920s she had about one hundred head of cattle. The drought and hard times of 1929 cost her that herd and drove her to Niagara Falls, where she lived with her mother and a sister. She would never return to Oregon and sold the hard-won homestead in 1950. She died thirteen years later, at ninety-one.

Pratt's memoir of homesteading, *A Homesteader's Portfolio,* had appeared in 1922, and has recently been republished, with a fine introduction from novelist Molly Gloss, so that a new generation of Oregonians can learn something of what it meant to be a woman and a homesteader in arid Oregon a century ago.

William L. Finley

Oregon gained a national reputation for conservation in the 1960s, while Tom McCall was governor. But many Oregonians were concerned about saving various parts of the nonhuman environment long before then. William Finley was perhaps the best known of them.

Born in California in 1876, Finley came to Portland as a child with his parents, where his father founded Finley Mortuary. As a child he collected eggs and bird skins. As a teenager he helped to begin the North-Western Ornithological Association.

Birds remained Finley's passion in adulthood. He began a long collaboration as a bird photographer with childhood-friend Herman Bohlman. Nellie Irene Barnhart married him in 1906 and shared his interest.

Wildlife photography in the early twentieth century was hard, strenuous work. Cameras and glass-plate negatives were heavy, and taking a good picture might require climbing trees or, near the ocean, rocky headlands. But Bohlman and Finley created thousands of photos of birds across Oregon.

Photography roused Finley to advocacy. He was aghast to learn that boatloads of tourists were shooting nesting sea birds near Tillamook for sport and opposed the trade in feathers for women's

William Finley and his colleague Herman Bohlman climbing a cliff at Three Arch Rocks on the north Oregon coast to photograph common murres. Photo courtesy Oregon Historical Society, Finley A2520

hats. He helped establish a chapter of the Audubon Society in Portland and prompted President Roosevelt to make Three Arch Rocks the West Coast's first bird refuge. He also helped to create the Klamath and Malheur refuges in southern Oregon and was disappointed when most of Lower Klamath Lake was drained for agriculture. "Man has a peculiar habit of building something with his hands and, at the same time, kicking it to pieces with his feet," he complained.[34]

Finley was for many years the state's leading environmental watchdog. He helped create Oregon's Fish and Game Commission in 1911 and soon became the state's head game warden. Like many conservationists at the time, Finley did not object to hunting and fishing. Indeed, he founded *Oregon Sportsman* magazine and wrote much of its content. He imported elk and used state hatcheries to increase Oregon's game fish.

He also wrote a great deal. His first book, *American Birds*, appeared in 1907. He and Nellie co-authored *Little Bird Blue* in 1915 and *Wild Animal Pets* in 1928, a book that sold well. They also made wildlife movies.

Finley put high stock in his opinions and could be difficult to work with. The Fish and Game Commission fired him in 1919, though he later returned to serve on that body.

Oregonians respected him as a knowledgeable and dedicated protector of the state's natural resources. He is memorialized by the William Finley National Wildlife Refuge south of Corvallis.

Ing Hay

Very few of the tens of thousands of Chinese who came to Oregon in the second half of the nineteenth century made much of an impression on the historical record. Most died, moved on, or returned to China. Those who stayed seldom kept diaries or wrote letters that would be deposited in Oregon archives. Ing Hay is one of the few early Chinese Americans whom we know much about, and he led a long, interesting life.

Like many young Chinese emigrants, Hay came to the U.S. with his father. The year was 1883, and he was then in his early twenties. In 1887 his father returned home, and Hay went to John Day. Though the mining boom had by then subsided, Hay found several hundred of his countrymen in John Day. He soon met and began a long, lucrative partnership with Lung On. They opened Kam Wah Chung and Company in 1888.

Their business provided many services to the Chinese-American community. On spoke fluent English and moved easily between the two cultures. He evidently provided false papers to Chinese entering the country after the Chinese Exclusion Act of 1882 made emigration much more difficult. The store served as a hiring hall, where whites looking for laborers, herders, and cooks could be supplied with Chinese-American workers. Hay, who began as a miner, began to practice Chinese medicine, which functioned much differently from its western counterpart. A devout man, he maintained a shrine where visitors could worship or divine the will of the supernatural.

The partners relied more heavily on the white community as people of Chinese ancestry became scarce in the region. Only a few dozen resided in all of Grant County by 1910. On invested in real estate and other ventures. Hay began treating more and more white patients, despite the opposition of white physicians. Indeed, he became known as "Doc Hay." The store began to fill up with the hundreds of herbs necessary to restore ill people to a state of balance and harmony. Recalled one observer: "The white doctors get ahold of 'em and they'd die, but this Chinaman would save them."

Hay's ties to China weakened as the years passed. He supported Sun Yatsen, the reformer who sought to overthrow the Manchu dynasty. But he seemed little interested in his parents or wife. His father took him to task in a 1903 letter: "Men go abroad so that they might make money for support of their families." But Hay had "sent neither money nor a letter." Such selfishness "is not suitable for a moral man."[35]

Hay was more generous to those who lived in his new home. He died in 1952 at age eighty-nine, with a few thousand dollars to his name and over twenty-three thousand dollars of uncashed checks from patients whom he had decided needed the money more than he did.

Pietro Belluschi

Oregon architecture, like its literature, remained undistinguished and derivative through the early twentieth century. Pietro Belluschi played a critical role in changing that.

Born to an Italian middle-class family in 1899, Belluschi served in World War I before earning a degree in civil engineering. After working as a housing inspector he emigrated to the United States where he studied at Cornell University, worked as an electrical engineer for an Idaho mining company, then, in 1925, settled in Portland, where he worked for Albert E. Doyle, who headed one of the city's leading architectural firms.

Blessed with charm and a strong work ethic, Belluschi quickly made his mark. He designed a mansion for the Corbetts, a remodeled lobby for the Benson Hotel, the Reed College library, and several office buildings. The Portland Art Museum's new building, finished in 1932, constituted his most celebrated accomplishment to date. The understated building reflected Belluschi's brand of modernism, in which function determined style rather than vice versa.

He was soon applying the same criterion to dozens of private homes. His sensitivity to context led to extensive use of wood. "A dominant industry always produces a corresponding architecture," he explained. He believed in creating homes that were "clean and simple" and "in harmony with the hills and Oregon." What did this look like? Belluschi homes had—and have—low profiles, broad roofs, clean lines, open floor plans, and lots of native, naturally finished woods. Together with John Yeon and Van Evera Bailey, Belluschi played a critical role in creating the northwest style of architecture.

Pietro Belluschi house on S.W. Beaverton Avenue in Portland, built in 1937. Photo courtesy Oregon Historical Society, OrHi 46679

Belluschi achieved national attention and acclaim. The American Institute of Architects selected two of his designs as among the top one hundred nationwide from 1920 to 1940. The Equitable Building of 1948, which featured an exterior of aluminum and green glass, elicited further praise. In 1951 he left Portland to become Dean of MIT's School of Architecture and Planning in Cambridge, Massachusetts. He had moved from the periphery to the center.

But difficult years ensued for the Belluschi family. Pietro continued his frenetic pace of design and was often away from his wife, Helen, who began drinking heavily and died in 1962. Their sons left home for a boarding school and did not return.

Belluschi struggled to keep in step with emerging styles. By the 1960s architects were turning to more self-conscious, less regional designs and arguing that they had a right to overrule their clients. Colleagues and students began to pillory Belluschi as dated and opportunistic. A man nearly as sensitive as he was ambitious, Belluschi came back to Portland in 1973. "Tired of being maligned," explains his biographer, "he was eager to return to the tranquillity of Portland where he was lionized, known as 'the venerable Pietro Belluschi' and 'the patriarch of American architecture' rather than a self-serving exploiter."[36]

Belluschi designed many more buildings inside and outside of Oregon and collected a succession of honors and awards. He died an old man, in 1994, and will long be survived by the hundreds of homes, churches, and office buildings that he designed.

Chapter Seven

Oregon and the World in Depression and War

1929-1945

" Undoubtedly our path in Oregon is going to be a great deal easier."

Minoru Yasui in 1940

Oregon had entered the nation's mainstream by the end of the 1920s. Life here had become increasingly indistinguishable from life in Wisconsin or even Florida. Regional characteristics faded as technological, economic, and cultural forces generated outside its boundaries reshaped people's lives. Two cataclysmic and global events would soon bind Oregon still more closely to the larger world: the most far-reaching depression and war in humankind's long history.

The former, the Great Depression, of course brought great hardship to Oregon. But it also prompted other, less pernicious changes. The war brought further difficulties and possibilities, depending on one's age, race, and locale. Young men and women left their homes to serve their country, and many never returned. Some places, such as Portland, boomed with activity. The war drew unprecedented numbers of African Americans and Mexican Americans to urban and rural Oregon, respectively. But the state's Japanese Americans were expelled from their homes.

By 1945 Oregonians had survived a decade and a half of dizzying difficulties and transformations. That Oregon was not unique in this regard, that other parts of the nation shared or even surpassed its rate of changes, did and does not diminish the enduring importance of this decade and a half.

Hard Times

The Great Depression that lasted from 1929 to about 1939 began when the stock market nose-dived in October. Other calamities across the nation and globe ensued: thousands of banks and businesses failed, millions of people lost their jobs, prices for farm products plummeted, and just about everyone's income fell, often dramatically. These disasters, then, were not confined to particular parts of the nation or the state. Americans could not simply pick up and move elsewhere to resume their normal lives.

The Depression touched every aspect of Oregon's economy. The timber industry, the state's only major manufacturing concern, was devastated. Employment dropped by some 60 percent from 1929 to 1933, wages by 77 percent. The W. A. Woodard Lumber Company of Cottage Grove shrank its payroll from 293 to 8 in four years. Garibaldi's mill hung on until 1935. The company homes were not empty for long, though. Families on relief moved in. Portland's economy was especially hard hit. Construction slowed to a snail's space. Two of every three small businesses were behind on their property taxes by 1933. The city's exports fell by more than one half. Exports declined so much because prices for farm products were so paltry. Oregon farmers got $1.11 per bushel for wheat in 1929, just 42¢ in 1932. The sufferings of farmers and stock ranchers east of the Cascades were multiplied by the same drought that forced so many farmers out of the "dust bowl" on the Great Plains.

Even so, the Depression did not hit as hard in Oregon as in most states. Oregonians were much more likely to farm than to work in manufacturing, and the great majority lived west of the Cascades, where the climate remained mild. Thousands of Oregonians left cities for the countryside during the Depression, enough to reverse, if only slightly, a longstanding trend toward urbanization. In 1930 48.7 percent lived in places of twenty-five hundred or less; in 1940 51.2 percent did. Many newcomers also arrived, mostly displaced families from the northern Great Plains who often settled on marginal land that had been logged. Wendell and Florence Harmon, for example, left Iowa for a 160-acre homestead outside Toledo on the central coast that cost them just $75.00. Here they raised vegetables, oats, and chickens to feed themselves. Willamette Valley farmers who owned their land outright were of course best situated to ride out the Depression. The valley's rich soils could grow a wide variety of crops, and most farmers there had already diversified and were therefore able to take advantage of market changes that made a particular type of crop profitable. Failing that, they could at least feed themselves. Even nonfarmers pursued a semi-subsistence lifestyle. People around Coos Bay, Bandon, and other parts of the coast survived by harvesting potatoes, fruit (wild and domestic), fish and other seafood, birds, deer, and elk—sometimes by poaching. Money could be made selling firewood and cascara bark, both free for the taking.

The Depression's hardships stimulated important but hardly revolutionary political changes. A little over a year into the Depression, by the end of 1930, Portland had put a larger fraction of its unemployed to work than any other city on the West Coast. Indeed, Multnomah County overspent its meager $100,000 relief budget in 1930 by some $15,000. Mayor George Baker, who had been in office since 1917, put himself at the forefront of this effort, urging administrators to pare their budgets to provide relief and to discover ways to put people to work. "I'll wreck the town if it will give employment," he announced.[1] Only family heads were eligible for relief work, and they had to rotate jobs so that scarce resources could be spread as far as possible. Lane County also multiplied its relief budget and paid jobless men to clean streets and improve roads. Its mobile canning plant enabled hungry

A hop picker's family near Independence, 1939. The family lived in a tent, and the cooking had to be done outside on a wood stove. Photo courtesy of the Historic Photograph Collections, Salem (Oregon) Public Library

These homeless men are in the facetiously named Hotel de Minto, named for Salem police chief John Minto, located on the top floor of Salem's city hall. Photo courtesy of the Historic Photograph Collections, Salem (Oregon) Public Library

families to preserve excess fruit gathered from orchards. Relief officials in southern Oregon traded canned fruit for canned salmon and mutton with their counterparts on the coast. Public employees donated one day's pay per month to relief.

But need overwhelmed these efforts. The Depression deepened in 1931. More and more people needed help, and fewer and fewer taxpayers were providing it. Tensions increased as people's desperation grew. Portland police arrested a man for taking a second slice of bread at a soup kitchen. A landlord killed a tenant for trying to avoid paying 80 cents in rent. By 1933 nearly 20 percent of the city's population was on relief.

Oregon's Democrats did much better under these sorts of conditions than they had during the prosperous 1920s. Oregon voters gave Franklin Roosevelt majorities in all four of his election bids. A whopping 68 percent backed him when he ran for a second term in 1936. In 1935 Oregonians elected a Democratic governor, Charles Henry Martin, and, for the first time in most people's memories, Democrats controlled the state's House of Representatives. Oregonians changed their voter registrations along with their votes. Republicans had outnumbered Democrats by more than two to one in the 1920s. Their majority nearly disappeared in the 1930s, when Democratic registrations accounted for 48 percent of the state's total.

Yet by World War II Republicans were again firmly in control of Oregon politics. How had the state's Democrats, blessed by a depression widely blamed on a Republican president and a recovery led by an immensely popular Democratic one, manage to squander this good fortune?

Much of the blame can be laid at the doorstep of Martin, the Democrat who won the state's governorship in 1934. Martin campaigned as a New Dealer. But the retired military officer soon repudiated most of Roosevelt's program, warning that western nations "have lost their moral force through pampering their people." Martin was willing to expend public money on "old folks," on people too feeble to work, "but I'll be damned if I'll feed the young ones." He referred to newcomers from the Great Plains as "alien paupers" and advised them to sell their "rattletrap automobiles" for food. The more Martin talked, and he seldom kept his thoughts to himself, the more he sounded like a cranky extremist. He noted that the state could save $300,000 by putting nine hundred of the residents of the state's home for the mentally ill "out of their misery."[2] Martin splintered Oregon's Democratic Party and allowed Republicans to oppose him by allying themselves with the popular New Deal. Martin could not even win the Democratic primary in 1938, and a moderate Republican, Charles Sprague, ascended to the governorship. The state's most prominent politician remained Senator McNary, a Republican who worked closely with Roosevelt.

Liberals and conservatives often debated public power during the 1930s. Electricity had come to the homes of most middle-class urban Oregonians by the 1920s. But the great majority of rural people, including two thirds of Oregon farmers, did not enjoy its advantages in 1930, for providing services to isolated houses was not cost efficient. Many farmers and the state Grange believed that electrical power held the key to economic prosperity, and they resented that monopolistic private companies were so reluctant to provide them with it. Urban residents, for their part, accused the private utility companies of overcharging them. Julius Meier, who ran and won as an independent candidate for governor in 1930, favored public power, as did Senator McNary. But such advocates were never able to overcome a combination of stumbling blocks: determined opposition from powerful utility companies, fractures within the Democratic Party, and voter reluctance to spend money on such projects. Oregonians would

Sisters, Oregon, 1930. Auto culture flourished even in the Depression. Photo courtesy of the Historic Photograph Collections, Salem (Oregon) Public Library

eventually get cheap, semi-public power. But not from their state government.

A lot of Oregonians wanted more than public power during the Depression. Here, as elsewhere, many formed Townsend Clubs that lobbied the federal government to provide generous pensions to the nation's elderly. More than fifteen thousand supporters gathered at Jantzen Beach Park in 1935. State labor leaders and revived Socialists tried to organize a Farmer-Labor movement in the mid-1930s to push for public ownership of utilities and other measures considerably to the left of the New Deal, though the movement never amounted to much. The Good Government Congress of Jackson County was more successful. Organized by newspapermen Llewellyn Banks and Earl Fehl, it mobilized a large fraction of the county's marginal farmers— what its prosperous critics referred to as "hillbillies" and "moonshiners from … way off the main runway."[3] The GGC drew on Populist roots in decrying concentrated wealth and power without consistently and explicitly attacking capitalism. It aspired to become a statewide and even national movement but fell apart when a theft of ballots went awry and Banks shot and killed a police officer.

Urban radicalism was more sustained during the Depression. There were, to be sure, many setbacks. Portland labor leaders' 1930 proposal of an ambitious public works program employing union carpenters was not enacted. Hard times made employees afraid to complain. "The competition for jobs was such, well, like honest-to-Christ, as a young married man some nights I couldn't do my homework," a droll longshoreman later recalled. "It was that bad."[4] But New Deal legislation that facilitated the organization of unions energized the labor movement after Roosevelt assumed office in 1933. In 1934 longshoremen all along the West Coast walked off the job, demanding a closed shop (union control over hiring) and more humane hours. The strikers, led by many former Wobblies or IWW members, divided into picketers and riot or flying squads, which, as their name implied, moved quickly along Portland's waterfront to protect picket lines and harass strikebreakers. Farmers supplied them with food.

Portland's business leaders were hurting and determined. The strike had shut down the port and sawmills that exported their products. The Citizens Emergency Committee (CEC), formed at the behest of the Portland Chamber of Commerce, employed special police to break the picket line. Four picketers were wounded in one exchange, but the line held.

The longshoremen's determination paid off. They routed a complement of special police living on the *Admiral Evans*, a ship docked under the Broadway Bridge. The Roosevelt administration refused to intervene in the strike. That one of the CEC's special police had fired on an inspection party sent by Secretary of Labor Wagner was, at the very least, poor public relations. The owners backed down after nearly three months and agreed to binding federal arbitration, which awarded the union what they had sought: better pay, shorter hours, and control over hiring.

This victory emboldened other workers. A year later, loggers and sawmill workers went on strike, though with little success. A strike by typographical workers shut down Portland's big three daily newspapers for five days in 1938. Strike leaders often ran considerable risks. Violence erupted during some disputes, and their employers might well discriminate against them after the strike was settled. A 1935 strike conducted by the AFL at the Woodard Lumber Company in Cottage Grove, for example, ended with little to show for the workers and with the labor leaders being laid off. Governor Martin used the state police and National Guard against strikers. But the Roosevelt administration's neutrality, a sharp departure from the attitude of previous administrations, made the 1930s an unprecedented era of union building in Oregon.

Many of the most violent battles were waged between unionists, as the new Congress of Industrial Organizations (CIO) vied with the well-established AFL for supremacy. An AFL leader was convicted of burning a Salem box factory whose employees had voted to affiliate with the CIO. But these battles were more jurisdictional than ideological. The Portland Police Department's Red Squad, which was devoted to identifying and combatting Communists, estimated that the city had less than two hundred in 1938, when the party's strength peaked. These members tended to be very active and influential members of their unions, and the Portland police took them seriously enough to arrest and harry them regularly. But the great majority of Portland and Oregon's working class were simply advocating for better wages and working conditions.

Much the same thing could be said of rural radicals. The desire for public power did not so much express a desire to end private enterprise as it articulated farmers' frustrations with the poor service that such companies were providing. The proportion of Oregon farmers who bought cooperatively shot up during the 1930s, from about 17 percent in 1929 to 31 percent a decade later. But celebrating the economic and moral virtues of cooperation was not the same thing as advocating for a truly socialistic system. Indeed, farmers rarely shared the equipment they needed to produce their crops, let alone their land; cooperation was reserved for marketing and purchasing.

In the Depression, as during the Progressive Era, most Oregonians wanted not to do away with capitalism, but for it to work more smoothly and fairly.

Conservation

President Roosevelt reformed capitalism and big business to save them. The same sort of pragmatism guided the federal government's approach to conservation during the Depression. Federal and state conservation efforts curbed some of the worst abuses of Oregon's environment during the 1930s, but their consequences were often mixed and bore most heavily on working people rather than large operators.

Conservationists urged the judicious use of natural resources. Preservationists lobbied for protecting some areas from logging, mining, and other intrusive forms of economic activity. Both groups had made substantial progress in Oregon by the Depression's onset.

Oregon's early settlers had remarked upon its natural beauty, and in 1902 the federal government had established Crater Lake National Park. Portlanders had created several parks around the same time, including two in the spectacular Columbia Gorge to the east: Multnomah Falls and Crown Point. The Columbia River Highway carried Portlanders to these sights and itself constituted a rural parkway. Not until the 1920s, however, did Oregonians begin preserving scenic land in a more systematic fashion.

Robert Sawyer, who bought the *Bend Bulletin* in 1917, was an early leader. He talked the Shevlin-Hixon Company, the enormous timber concern that played a crucial role in central Oregon's economic boom, into donating land for a park to the city of Bend, and timber owners agreed to preserve a scenic curtain of trees along the highway that stretched from The Dalles to California. Meanwhile, Governor Olcott, alarmed over logging along the Seaside-Cannon Beach road on the north Oregon coast, asserted in 1920 that it was the "patriotic and civic duty" of Oregonians "to preserve our wonderful natural surroundings."[5] The public generally supported the governor, agreeing that weekend drives through Oregon's countryside ought not to be spoiled by clear-cuts. Sawyer soon turned his attention from forested beauty curtains to parks, and his advocacy led to the creation of the Oregon State Parks Commission in 1929. Samuel Boardman became Oregon's first State Parks superintendent.

The Great Depression proved to be a propitious time to develop parks. To be sure, the state had very little money for purchasing land and administering parks. But much of Oregon's most scenic land wasn't yielding enough profit to cover its taxes, so many owners were happy to either give it away or exchange it for government land that was more productive. Boardman was especially intent on and successful at getting land along Oregon's seashore. The head of the National Conference on State Parks congratulated Oregonians after his 1936 tour of the coast: "Here then is a state which takes some 400 miles, leads its highway along the ocean, winds about through groves of marvelous trees and protects the surroundings from artificialities and desecration."[6]

Oregonians were concerned with conserving timberland for economic purposes, too. A series of dramatic and expensive forest fires early in the century had alarmed the owners and managers of large timber companies. They formed protective associations to snuff out fires and lobbied state and federal officials to devote public resources to the problem. They succeeded. In 1912 Oregon's state forester asserted that guarding "the present stands of timber until such time as they are cut or harvested" constituted the heart of forest practice.[7] A year later the legislature passed a ground-breaking compulsory fire-patrol law that required private timber owners to devote more attention to fire suppression. The state and federal governments were also helping to renew forests. The Department of

Agriculture reseeded thousands of acres of land that had been logged or burned, including approximately fifteen thousand acres consumed by the 1936 Bandon fire. Some state timber managers were by then arguing for a program of sustained yield to put Oregon's timber economy on a more stable footing. The timber industry, concerned that such measures would regulate and restrict their harvesting, evidently helped to shelve the proposal.

Forest conservation received a shot in the arm in August 1933, when a fire erupted in the Gales Creek watershed, northwest of Forest Grove. The ensuring Tillamook Burn ravaged what may have been the most extensive expanse of old-growth forest left in the lower forty-eight states, consuming nearly 250,000 acres. Three lesser fires followed, at six-year-intervals, over the next eighteen years. Although the precise causes of the first fire remain obscure, a widely accepted story blames the operators of the Elmer Lyda Company who, urged to stop logging under such dry conditions, decided to bring in one more log before shutting down—and that log touched off the conflagration.

This cautionary tale, this version of the Tillamook Burn, had a happy ending. If humans had caused the tragedy, they could also redeem it. Logging companies salvaged a great deal of charred timber, and then, starting in the 1940s, the state began an ambitious replanting program. New legislation required western Oregon's loggers to leave unscathed 5 percent of seed-bearing trees and loggers in eastern Oregon to cut only pines that were at least 16 inches in diameter. The legislation also facilitated replanting the burn. Prison inmates and volunteers, including school children, did much of the work. Today the Tillamook Burn is again covered by trees, and Oregonians have long pointed to this accomplishment as proof that they can create sustainable forests.

The federal, not state, government led efforts to conserve Oregon's rangelands. The Taylor Grazing Act of 1934 provided for much closer regulation of how livestock utilized the nation's public lands. The problem was clear enough: overgrazing had wreaked ecological havoc across the arid western United States, a problem exacerbated by the drought of the 1930s. Carl Ewing, Supervisor of the Umatilla National Forest in northeastern Oregon, observed in 1938 that parts of his domain "are so thinly covered with light soil that it is believed impossible to graze them intensively without excessive damage."[8] Restricting grazing and reducing herds also served to raise the price of beef and mutton, which, like other agricultural goods, had plummeted.

As with other New Deal agricultural programs, the burden of conservation fell largely on smaller operators. "Ultimately ranch property and range will need to gravitate into the hands of fewer owners and permittees," wrote Ewing.[9] More prosperous owners could more easily afford the costs of conservation, and it was easier for the government to work with a few big ranchers than with many small ones. Basque shepherds, whose ancestors had immigrated to southeastern Oregon from northern Spain, were especially vulnerable, for many of them had relied on federal land to graze their sheep.

Environmental and class issues had long been entangled with Oregon's salmon. State residents in the 1870s began hectoring each other not to repeat the catastrophes that had befallen Atlantic salmon. But by the 1880s several types of fishermen—sport, gillnetters, and big operators who ran fish traps, wheels, and seines—were blaming anyone but themselves for declining catches. The gillnetters, often immigrants, toiled long, hazardous hours in their small boats to make enough to live on. Fish wheels and traps required little labor but a great deal of capital. They were owned by wealthy business people. The sport fishermen, initially well-to-do Portlanders, proved to have the greatest political influence. Legislation banned fish traps, wheels, and seines in the 1920s and 1930s, moves that certainly slowed the rate of salmon's decline. But not all measures were so salutary. Sport fishermen successfully lobbied for importing exotic species that they enjoyed catching. Commercial fishermen countered that the imports

Aerial view of Bonneville Dam. Photo courtesy Oregon State Library

ate salmon eggs and fry. They were right, but they lacked the political clout to make the charge stick. People who fished for a living had less money than those who fished for fun, and their numbers declined as the sports fishermen multiplied. In 1927 Oregon voters closed the Nestucca River on the north coast to gillnetters.

Dams drew less censure than gillnetters, but they had a profound effect on Oregon's salmon. By 1937 there were scores of them along Oregon's waterways, each blocking a proportion of migrating salmon from their spawning grounds. Bonneville Dam was the greatest of them all, an immense concrete structure that both halted salmon and helped transform the free-flowing Columbia into a series of tepid lakes—not a friendly environment for salmon, this at a time when logging continued to degrade spawning habitat.

Yet few Oregonians grieved the passing of the wild Columbia River. The dam had employed thousands of people and promised to supply a seemingly infinite amount of cheap power to eager Oregon farmers and others. Like fire suppression and replanted forests, dams represented progress, a promise of a brighter future made possible by human's mastery and regulation of nature.

Oregonians enjoyed the outdoors and were proud of their growing number of parks. But a more sophisticated understanding of ecology lay well beyond the 1930s.

Big Government

We have already seen how the federal government affected many elements of Oregon life by the 1930s, from strikes to forest conservation. But these were just two of many ways in which decisions made in Washington, D.C., changed Oregon.

Settlers had established a modest government, including taxes and probate procedures, in the Oregon Country even before it had become part of the United States. These were soon followed by much more elaborate mechanisms on the local, county, territorial, and then statewide level. The state's insane asylum, for example, had over four hundred inmates by 1886. The federal government played a crucial role in distributing land, granting thousands of settlers their livelihood. Still, the average nineteenth-century Oregonian did not have much daily interaction with government.

Schools constituted the most ubiquitous public institution in early Oregon. But even their influence remained circumscribed for most of the nineteenth century. School terms generally lasted for about three months, until local districts ran out of money or parents needed their children at home, for work. During the 1884-85 school year, Tillamook County's fourteen schools enrolled just 272 pupils out of 633 eligible children. In other words, less than half of the county's school-aged children went to school, and many of those who did attended sporadically.

Matters changed early in the twentieth century. By 1914 Tillamook County's school terms lasted an average of seven and a half months a year, and teachers expected their charges to graduate from eighth grade, not just to go until they were needed at home. High schools appeared in Tillamook County and other rural parts of the state. Here students prepared for college or learned more practical skills, such as typing and shorthand, a variety of manual training, and home economics. Most one-room schoolhouses disappeared during the 1920s and 1930s as busses and paved roads carried children to town. The consolidated schools where students spent an increasing portion of their childhoods were more regulated than their dispersed predecessors had been, with the state overseeing curriculum, teacher training, and supervision.

The crisis of the Depression brought the state of Oregon into a wider range of activities. The legislature approved income and corporate taxes in 1929. In 1931 it started providing economic assistance to the elderly and the poor—activities that previously had been handled on the county level. It also began providing workers' compensation and unemployment insurance. The presence of federal dollars prompted Oregon to assist dependent children and the blind.

The federal government soon outstripped its state and local counterparts in intervening in people's lives. The most obvious example, at least in the early days of the New Deal, were the dozens of relief projects that sprouted across Oregon and the nation. Roosevelt was no radical, but he was eager to put unemployed people to work and willing to spend federal dollars to do so. The Civilian Conservation Corps (CCC) employed young, relatively unskilled working men, usually in isolated areas, such as the camp on Cape Perpetua, on Oregon's central coast. CCC workers built trails, planted trees, fought fires, and performed a variety of other jobs. The Civil Works Administration (CWA) lasted just four months but employed a large fraction of jobless Oregonians at about $1.00 an hour. Lane County's CWA workers repaired roads and schools, revamped Eugene's sewer system and airport, taught adults, and ran a nursery school. The CWA was followed by the most influential work program of all, the Works

Progress Administration (WPA), which created many roads, bridges, schools, airports, and Timberline Lodge. It also employed many types of professionals, women as well as men, from dancers to librarians. Many of the state's richest historical records were generated or organized by WPA workers.

The most ambitious federal project in Oregon was the Bonneville Dam. Though much smaller than its massive cousin to the north, the Grand Coulee Dam, Bonneville employed hundreds and, when completed in 1938, dramatically increased the region's electricity-generating capacity, though in the middle of the Depression that hardly seemed necessary. Bonneville was administered by the Bonneville Power Administration, a quasi-governmental agency.

The New Deal featured dozens of other programs. The National Recovery Act constituted the centerpiece of Roosevelt's early New Deal. But its attempt to bring government, industry, and labor representatives together to set production levels, market shares, and wages proved confusing and unworkable. A more modest program, the Rural Electrification Administration (REA) proved much more popular. The Nehalem Valley Cooperative Electric Association of Jewell built the first line financed by the REA, and it was soon joined by others. Hundreds and then thousands of rural Oregonians enjoyed the same amenities as people in the city: electric light bulbs, irons, radios, and more.

Oregon's indigenous peoples were especially affected by the New Deal. A federal investigation of Indian reservations across the nation had established that Native Americans constituted the nation's most impoverished and disenfranchised people. Visitors to the Klamath and Warm Springs reservations found that three quarters and one half, respectively, of tribal land had been leased to whites. Many Natives had lost their cattle for lack of land to graze them on.

The Roosevelt administration proposed an "Indian New Deal," the Indian Reorganization Act (IRA), to remedy these ills. Its more ambitious features, such as dramatically expanding Native land, did not make it through Congress. The heart of what did pass was an administrative shift. Indians now had the right to organize tribal governments to more fully control reservation life. Only two of Oregon's five reservations did so: the Grand Ronde and Warm Springs. Those living on the state's two largest reservations, the Klamath and Umatilla, chose not to, as did Native peoples at Siletz. Only four in ten of the more than thirty-two hundred Indians living on Oregon reservations chose the IRA program of self-government. Some

Klamath and Umatilla cited the government's lack of consultation to explain their opposition. Others, especially older Native peoples, simply distrusted any proposal that came from the federal government.

The New Deal programs were no panacea. Work-relief programs usually soaked up only a minority of the unemployed, and they discriminated against people of color and women. The New Deal's conservation measures harmed small producers. The much-trumpeted IRA made little impact on most of Oregon's indigenous peoples. But it is hard to argue that the New Deal did more harm than good in Oregon. Oregonians got more federal money than most people, ranking twelfth in per capita expenditures. That money both eased the Depression's sting and strengthened the state's infrastructure.

World War II

When the Kittredge family's radio brought news of the attack on Pearl Harbor their cook "went into hysterics," convinced "that the Japanese were coming at any moment."[10] The Japanese did not arrive in the remote Warner Valley or any other part of the state. A submarine lobbed a few shells harmlessly into sand dunes south of Fort Stevens, near the mouth of the Columbia River. A bomb that had been attached to a balloon exploded and killed three picnickers in southern Oregon. This would be the extent of the Japanese invasion. Yet the war would transform the state as much as or more than any twentieth-century event. It changed forever Oregon's demographics, the nature and distribution of its population. It also accelerated the state's reliance on the federal government.

If unemployment justified widespread governmental intervention, the prospect of Japanese invasion made it seem only more imperative. Dozens of training centers for the armed services soon dotted Oregon. Camp Adair, just outside of Corvallis, was by far the largest. The presence of these soldiers, as we shall see, had telling social consequences. They also goosed local economies by bringing an infusion of federal dollars to mills and contractors along with soldiers' spending money to restaurants, movie theaters, and other businesses.

Henry Kaiser quickly became Oregon's leading employer because of his ability to work with the federal government. He had already been awarded government contracts to construct several dams in the West, including Bonneville. He later explained his version of the

"Scrappo," a ten-ton, thirty-foot-high robot placed in the Marion County courthouse square to encourage scrap collection during World War II. Photo courtesy of the Historic Photograph Collections, Salem (Oregon) Public Library

private/public partnership: "We provided the organization, the major portion of the operating capital" and "the brains and the production. The Government provided the facilities."[11] The feds guaranteed companies such as Kaiser's a profit by awarding "cost plus" contracts. Kaiser ran three enormous shipyards in or near Portland, using recruiters and trains to lure and transport aspiring war workers to Portland from across the country.

These workers needed a place to live, and the Portland Housing Authority was not moving fast enough to suit Edgar Kaiser (Henry Kaiser's son), who oversaw the Portland operation. He won approval from a federal agency to build his own city, at government expense. Vanport, located on the floodplain north of Portland, was soon the second most populous place in Oregon. But it was a housing project, not an incorporated city. It had no homeowners, no mechanisms of self-government. It was built by a private company, funded by the federal government, and administered by the city of Portland. Its historian terms it "a huge quasi-business-governmental operation."[12] A resident offered a pithier definition: "a huge collection of crackerbox houses strung together fast and cheap."[13] The federal government, like the Kaisers, was more interested in efficient production than in building community.

The federal government also played a critical role in bringing Mexican labor to the United States. Oregon farmers who relied heavily on seasonal labor panicked once the war broke out. Demand for fruits and sugar beets was booming, but labor was very difficult to find. Workers lured from other parts of the United States soon found that they could make more money in the region's defense factories and quickly left.

The *bracero* program of 1942 was designed to avoid that eventuality. It stipulated that laborers from Mexico would be employed for a specific period of time and for a particular employer. Once the contract expired the workers would be transported back to Mexico, again with the federal government picking up the tab. In practice, as we shall see, Mexican workers both complained about and subverted this plan. But the *bracero* program constituted yet another way in which the federal government inserted itself into the private sector.

There were many other ways, too. Government propaganda urged Oregonians to volunteer for the armed services, work in a defense plant, buy war bonds, participate in scrap drives, and abide by rationing programs for gasoline, rubber, and many types of food. Posters cautioned soldiers and other citizens to not spread rumors or military information.

Oregon's schools changed their curriculum to aid the war. They organized their pupils into scrap collectors. Science instruction became more practical, emphasizing radio operation and aeronautics, for example. Physical education expanded. English classes taught military terms. Art classes focused on drafting. Home economics courses instructed young women on household conservation. In sum, students were being prepared to contribute to winning the war as soldiers, workers, and citizens.

Accelerated government spending also stimulated the nation's moribund economy, which at last pulled itself out of the Depression. All sorts of businesses boomed, as factories proliferated and farmers sold everything that they could harvest—and for good prices, too. Rich in natural resources and located on the Pacific Rim, Oregon became an important manufacturing and military staging area.

Many Oregonians entered military service. Thousands of men and not a few young women left homes across the state for far-flung training camps, the Pacific Ocean, and Europe. Many never returned. Those who did brought with them cosmopolitan and often terrifying experiences that helped to erode Oregon's insularity.

Few Oregonians opposed the war. Pearl Harbor gave the nation a sense of unity and purpose it had lacked in World War I. The great majority of pacifists, in Oregon and elsewhere, were pietistic, nonconfrontational Christians. One from the Harrisburg Mennonite Church later recalled being "more than willing to go out and work for nothing for my government."[14] The federal government enabled conscientious objectors to do just that by creating Civilian Public Service camps across the nation, where the "C.O.s" built trails and did other, largely menial, work. Waldport, Cascade Locks, and Elkton hosted C.P.S. camps.

The war touched all Oregonians, whether they were drafted or not. Ration stamps regulated the amount of sugar, meat, gasoline, and other staples that people could buy. Citizens across the state admonished each other to buy war bonds. Volunteers rolled bandages and collected scrap metal and other materials. Young Jimmy Hargis won a statewide contest by gathering two tons of scrap. People living in western Oregon prepared themselves to repulse an invasion by enforcing blackouts, scanning for enemy airplanes, and organizing themselves into volunteer military companies. Such fears seem hyperbolic in retrospect, but the shock of Pearl Harbor had ruptured the nation's sense of invincibility, especially on the West Coast.

The war brought many new people to Oregon. Thousands of well-paying manufacturing jobs appeared in the Portland area, especially in the Kaiser shipyards, but also in lumber and food processing. Smaller communities suffered, especially if there were no nearby military facilities. Their farmers and other business owners struggled to find the labor to keep up with the quickening economy.

Which is not to say that Portlanders, who had always been more ambivalent about unbridled growth than their counterparts in San Francisco, Seattle, and Los Angeles, were uniformly enthusiastic about the city's rapid expansion. "Portland neither likes nor knows how to accommodate its Virginia City atmosphere," noted a writer in *Fortune* magazine.[15] Workers from across the nation were pouring in, and Portland's leaders were not prepared to welcome them. By early 1943 some elementary schools in north Portland held nearly twice as many students as they had been designed for. Housing constituted the greatest challenge. The city provided some new housing, such as Columbia Villa, a set of four hundred apartments in north Portland. But new housing accommodated but a fraction of the newcomers. One pundit described the city as "one huge dormitory for shipyard workers," and the *Oregonian* advised people not involved in activities essential to the war effort to move east of the Cascades.[16] By the summer of 1942, less than a year after Pearl Harbor, federal officials estimated that the city would need thirty thousand housing units, far more than Portland's leaders were likely to construct.

Vanport was created to solve this problem, and in many ways it did. Most of its adult residents worked at one of the nearby shipyards, and by 1944 it had a population of over forty thousand. It was a self-contained community, with stores, schools, day-care centers, recreation halls, a theater, a hospital, and police and fire service. Hailed at first by an *Oregonian* headline writer as a "Masterpiece of Urban Planning," it soon became clear that Vanport was a dreary place in which to live.[17] The city was set in a bowl, and, in the words of historian Carl Abbott, "its dull gray buildings" were soon "awash in a sea of winter mud."[18] Residents came and went. The apartments were small and often infested with bedbugs, cockroaches, fleas, mice, and rats. Portland's leadership never really made its peace with Vanport, and living there soon carried a stigma.

Vanport was something of a metaphor for Oregon's experience during World War II. Its residents enjoyed both unprecedented prosperity and significant hardships.

Race and War

World War II had very different effects on Oregon's Japanese Americans and African Americans. It constituted an unprecedented disaster for the former and unparalleled growth and prosperity for the latter. It also drew large numbers of Latinos to the state for the first time, though they were excluded from well-paid jobs.

By 1940 people of Japanese descent had supplanted those of Chinese ancestry as the largest nonwhite ethnic group in Oregon. They had begun arriving in the late nineteenth century, when the restriction of Chinese emigration coupled with a need for labor on railroads, farms, and factories drew growing numbers of young Japanese men across the Pacific. Like the Chinese before them, most intended to stay for just a few years before returning with their savings to their homeland. Few women came at first. In 1910 they constituted less than 5 percent of Oregon's Japanese Americans.

By the 1910s the immigrants, or Issei, had become more at home in Oregon. Able to extract high yields of fruits and vegetables from even small plots of land, they leased and then purchased prime acreage east of Portland and near Hood River. Others moved to Portland, where they established hotels and businesses that serviced their largely self-sufficient community. Many brides arrived during this decade, and by the end of World War I a second generation, the Nisei, were growing up in Oregon, a state that they would regard as their home.

But most Oregonians, like their counterparts in Washington, California, and British Columbia, did not want the Issei or the Nisei to feel at home here. "We have no room for the yellow man and we don't want them," asserted the Madras newspaper in 1920.[19] Indeed, a Toledo mob drove a group of recently arrived Japanese Americans out of town in 1925. Citizens of La Grande and Woodburn had done so earlier. In 1923 Oregon passed a law making it illegal for people from Japan to own land, and in 1924 the U.S. Immigration Act essentially ended Japanese immigration.

But by this time Oregon's Japanese Americans were both numerous and able to reproduce themselves. Seventeen hundred lived in Portland alone by 1920, including ninety hotel operators and many other small-business people, such as grocers, who worked closely with the area's truck farmers. Most of Hood River's Issei and Nisei stuck to farming, and many did very well at it.

Though many of Oregon's Japanese Americans became Christians and the Nisei attended public schools, they constituted a very tight community. Intermarriage was unheard of. The Issei taught their sons and daughters to honor and serve their parents and to work hard in school and at home. This was the way to overcome the innumerable insults and other indignities that whites inflicted upon them. State

Japanese-American evacuees, with their luggage in hand, walk from the Pacific International Livestock Exposition Building that has been their temporary home to the train that will take them to an internment camp. Photo courtesy of Oregon Historical Society, OrHi 28157

and federal laws and whites' refusal to consider Japanese Americans for professional jobs made socioeconomic mobility difficult and their accomplishments all the more remarkable.

Yet the Nisei remained optimistic. "Undoubtedly our path in Oregon is going to be a great deal easier," remarked Minoru Yasui in 1940. "Much of the old race prejudice has disappeared."[20]

The internment that followed the nation's entry into World War II destroyed many of these accomplishments. The Roosevelt administration determined that Japanese Americans constituted a risk to national security if they remained on the West Coast, where they might commit acts of sabotage and espionage. The vast majority of Oregonians concurred. The exodus was humiliating and costly. Japanese Americans had but a few days to liquidate their property, to sell the many possessions that they could not take with them and to arrange for white neighbors to care for their land and businesses. They netted but a small fraction of their property's worth.

Many other humiliations followed. The internees were first taken to the Exposition Center in north Portland, where they were crowded together in unsanitary stalls for several months. From there most proceeded to isolated camps in the interior of the western United States. Conditions were not much better there, and relations in the highly ordered Japanese-American community and family frayed as children claimed independence from parents who no longer enjoyed economic authority. Many volunteered for the armed services or worked for farmers, and at the war's end some had already returned home to try to pick up the pieces of the life in Oregon they had been forced to leave behind.

People of African descent had come to Oregon long before their Japanese counterparts, but until World War II their numbers had remained modest.

In 1900 the census counted just 1,105 African Americans in Oregon, by 1940 just 2,565. By that date only a few hundred Blacks lived outside Portland. Many Oregon communities simply would not allow people of color to live in them. A sociologist studying Shevlin Hixon, a timber town near Bend, found that residents' "dislike for an oriental or a negro is so strong that when one comes into the community, conditions are made so unpleasant that he soon leaves."[21]

Which is not to say that Portland did not present its own problems. African Americans were excluded from most of its neighborhoods. Some theaters and restaurants refused to serve Blacks, and many employers refused to hire them. Kathryn Hall Bogle graduated from high school in the late 1930s to hear the same story again and again when she applied for openings at Portland stores, offices, and public utilities: "there was nothing about me in my disfavor—except the color of my skin."[22] Portland's African-American women were much more likely to work outside the home than were their white counterparts, most commonly as poorly paid maids. Most of the city's Black men also labored at or near the bottom of the service industry, as janitors, for example. The railway offered relatively good, stable jobs as porters and waiters. Other African Americans had their own small businesses: usually beauty parlors, barbershops, or shoeshine stands. The community included a smattering of professionals: several ministers and attorneys, and a few doctors or dentists. These business owners and professionals formed the backbone of the Black community's institutions: several churches, fraternal organizations, and a chapter of the National Association for the Advancement of Colored People that dated from 1914.

Edwin Berry arrived in Portland in the early 1940s to head the city's National Urban League and described the city's African Americans as "law-abiding, self-sustaining, and unobtrusive."[23] Portland's African-American leadership was seldom militant. But they were much more likely to protest injustices than their Japanese-American counterparts. Ordinary African Americans certainly stood up for themselves. A black first grader in Vernonia, for example, explained why she had shoved a white boy: "My Mama told me not to let any old white trash push me around, and he pushed me!"[24]

Race relations became more strained during the war. The number of Blacks in the Portland area increased fivefold by 1944, to over eleven thousand. By June 1945 over eight thousand worked for one of the Kaiser yards. Portland leaders did not exactly put out the welcome mat for these men and women. "Portland can absorb only a minimum of Negroes without upsetting the city's regular life," warned Mayor Earl Riley. "We Cater to White Trade Only" signs grew in number.[25] Vanport, where an increasing number of African Americans lived during the war, was segregated. Whites in northeast Portland stoutly resisted African-American residential expansion. One asserted that if Black families moved beyond Albina "it will soon be necessary to station a policeman on every block."[26] This intransigence caused the Albina community to become still more overcrowded. Its population density doubled during the war. Some longtime African-American residents of Portland at first blamed the newcomers, who tended to be less educated and more assertive, for these deteriorating conditions.

Yet, on the whole, the war was a great boon to Portland's African-American community. True, the area's shipyards discriminated against Blacks by excluding them from the best jobs and paying them less than whites for performing the same work. But they still paid much higher wages than African Americans had been accustomed to. True, the city's growing African-American population confronted rising racial tensions and prejudices. But there was also strength in numbers, and World War II made Oregon's Blacks a more potent social and political force.

The war brought similar difficulties and possibilities to Oregon's Mexican Americans. People of Latin American descent had a long if seldom documented history in Oregon as packers and laborers. By the 1920s more were working on Oregon farms, though their numbers remained slight compared to those in the southwestern part of the U.S. The census, which routinely undercounted minorities, recorded more than fifteen hundred people of Mexican descent in Oregon in 1930. Only about one out of five were female, so Oregon's Mexican Americans included few families. The hardships of the Great Depression drove roughly half of the nation's Latinos out, often with the active assistance of Anglos who argued that "aliens" should not be allowed to work at any sort of job when native-born Americans were going hungry.

World War II quickly reversed this dynamic. Now Oregon farmers were desperate for workers, and the *bracero* program brought some fifteen thousand Mexicans to them, ten times as many as had lived in Oregon at the Depression's outset. The arrangement worked well for Oregon's farmers. It offered them a fairly reliable and vulnerable stream of laborers at a time when unskilled workers outside the *bracero* program could demand high wages. The workers from Mexico were at first tractable, and by the time they became knowledgeable and bold enough to demand better wages and working conditions their contract would likely have expired and a fresh complement of *braceros* would appear. The "Mexican boys," a Columbia County farmer recalled, were "God-sent."[27]

Those who worked in the *bracero* program found it less edifying. Conditions were harsh, the meals poor. Some three hundred were hospitalized for food poisoning in a single outbreak at a hop farm near Grants Pass. Many suffered injuries from farm machinery. They had little recourse if their employees cheated them, though several camps staged work stoppages to protest their wages. The young men also missed their families and communities back home; about one of ten returned to Mexico before their contract expired. White

Oregonians treated them with contempt and occasionally with violence. In Medford, for example, the camp manager reported that five men beat a *bracero* "without provocation."[28] The assault staggered the man, who was promptly arrested for drunkenness.

Yet World War II also offered unprecedented opportunities to Mexican Americans. The *bracero* program, with all its faults, offered better wages than they were likely to find in Mexico. It brought some fifteen thousand Mexicans to Oregon. Many Mexicans, moreover, decided to work outside the system. They came north to Oregon on their own and found employers desperate for their labor. Many of them returned home after the war. But others did not. Mexican Americans who had worked inside and outside of the *bracero* program were beginning to make Oregon their home in the mid-1940s.

World War II temporarily pushed Oregon's Japanese Americans outside the boundaries of the state, and many of them would never return. But employment opportunities drew thousands of people of African and Mexican descent here, reversing Oregon's trend toward homogenization.

Women and War

World War II brought strains but also unprecedented possibilities to Oregon women. The strains were obvious enough. Many wives had to make do without their husbands, who were overseas, and that absence often created financial as well as emotional hardship. Wartime rationing meant that housewives had fewer resources with which to work. These women also bore the brunt of the wartime housing shortage. Many had to cook, clean, and care for their children under conditions that fell considerably short of ideal.

But the war brought opportunities along with privations. A young Portland woman, for example, "decided to get some of the attention the other girls did" and "started to go around with the Naval Air Cadets," who "took me to all the best places—no movie-cake dates!"[29] Any number of attractive, single women in Corvallis, Medford, Astoria, Portland, and other places where servicemen lived or tarried had the same chances.

As in earlier wars, wives left behind by these servicemen became more self-reliant in their husbands' absence. Indeed, divorce-seeking women routinely told judges that they neither wanted nor needed any financial support from their ex-husbands. "I work, and I feel capable of making my own living," asserted a Portland woman.[30] Acute labor shortages did in fact push many women, including wives and mothers, into the workforce. This was especially the case in Portland, whose shipyards desperately needed employees and where a woman might earn several times as much money as she had before the war. Broadly speaking, the shipyards drew two sorts of women: those who had already been working outside the home, but for poor pay and usually in another part of the country; and women who were drawn into the workforce as a way to support the war effort while making more money than they could have previously imagined possible.

Like their African-American counterparts, women shipyard workers faced pervasive discrimination. White men had first crack at the best jobs and earned more than women for doing the same work. Sexual harassment was commonplace. But no amount of male chauvinism could obscure these women's sense of accomplishment in doing work that men had asserted they could not do. "My husband was from Kentucky," recalled one woman, and "didn't think women knew anything. So I showed him."[31] She bought a house with her earnings.

World War II presented many thousands of women who had been scratching out a living as maids, factory workers, or farmers with their first good job. Beatrice Hadley had started supporting herself at age ten. Six years later she married a man who promised to rescue her from long hours as a chambermaid in a small Iowa town, but after three years of beatings she left him and her children, too, for she could not support them on her own. She and her second husband moved to Oregon in 1926, where she worked in a pickle factory. They spent much of the Depression eking out a living by raising chickens and calves on a small piece of land in Washington. The war dramatically changed her financial fortunes.

Many of the women who had gone to work outside the home to help win the war or to earn a bit of spending money were willing enough to give up their high-paying jobs at war's end. But for women like Hadley, long compelled by circumstance and necessity to make money to support themselves and their children, peace meant a dramatic and unwelcome drop in income and status.

About half of women war workers wanted to keep their jobs. A 1943 survey at the Kaiser yards found that 53 percent of women production workers intended to stay in an industrial occupation. They were disappointed. The war ended, the shipyards closed, and returning male veterans soaked up the well-paid industrial jobs that remained. In September 1945 women filed 60 percent of the state's unemployment claims. Others took low-paying jobs in food processing, did clerical work, or, if they could, went back to being housewives or students.

But the war had forever changed gender dynamics, in Oregon and in the nation. More and more women would work outside the home in the decades following the war, and many of them now knew that they could in fact do a "man's job" as well as or better than a man.

❧ ❧

The decade and a half encompassing the Depression and World War II brought dramatic changes to Oregon. Jobs were more scarce, then more abundant, than ever before. Cities, especially Portland, stagnated, then boomed. Many people made their way to the state: hard-pressed migrants from the Great Plains and Midwest in the 1930s, then people from across North America during the war, including thousands of African and Mexican descent.

Many of the changes proved ephemeral. The high unemployment rates of the Depression never returned. Nor did the rationing of World War II. Military bases closed. Even prejudice toward Japanese Americans would abate. But these exceptional years perpetuated and accelerated some durable and consequential trends. Government's size and power, and its willingness to work closely with big business, would outlive the war's end. So would Oregon's diverse social landscape.

In the twentieth century's last half, then, a state that had long been—by circumstance and design—insulated, thinly populated, and homogeneous would grow larger and more diverse, would find itself increasingly bound up in national and global economic, political, social, and cultural movements.

In this respect, then, the transformative power of external factors such as depression and war constituted not an aberration, but a harbinger.

Biographies

Charles McNary

The man who emerged as the leading light of Oregon politics during the 1920s was a moderate and often progressive Republican.

Charles McNary was born in 1874 in Keizer, on the farm north of Salem that his grandfather had homesteaded. His parents both died when he was young, and his older siblings raised him.

McNary's star rose quickly. Inspired by the example of his friend Herbert Hoover, another promising orphan, he attended Stanford University but soon returned home to clerk in his brother's law office. He quickly gained admission to the state bar and became a full partner in the firm. He also farmed and taught and in 1908 became dean of Willamette University's law school. He was a Republican supporter of the Oregon System. As the state's special counsel for the railroad commission he worked for lower freight and passenger rates.

His big political break came in 1917, when Governor Withycombe appointed him to take the deceased Harry Lane's seat in the U.S. Senate. Elected in his own right a year later, he would stay there until his death in 1944.

McNary quickly established himself as an able and well-liked western progressive. His relations with the decade's Republican presidents were often strained. He was at sword points with President Coolidge, especially over the McNary-Haugen bill that proposed using the federal government's resources to stabilize farms. What the President "doesn't know about 'sech' things," remarked McNary privately, "would fill a great big library."[32] He also found his old friend President Hoover doctrinaire and stubborn.

McNary championed diverse causes during his quarter century in the Senate. He broke with the Republican leadership early in his tenure by backing the League of Nations. He also promoted reforestation, expanding the U.S. Forest Service, most of President Roosevelt's New Deal, and federal dam building on the Columbia River. Indeed, Roosevelt and McNary cooperated in this venture and others, though the senator from Oregon was among the most vocal critics of the president's attempt to pack the Supreme Court. In 1939 the president considered putting McNary on a bipartisan ticket. McNary instead ran for the Republican nomination, but the isolationism he had espoused earlier in the decade as the Senate

minority leader harmed him, and he instead became Wendell
Willkie's running mate.

McNary was the first Oregonian to gain such prominence since
Joe Lane's run for the vice presidency as a southern Democrat in
1860. He is better remembered as one of Oregon's most effective,
courteous, and long-standing Senators.

Julius L. Meier

German Jews constituted one of the largest ethnic groups in early
Portland, and many of them became successful and influential
businessmen. Immigrant Aaron Meier founded Oregon's largest
department store, Meier and Frank. His son Julius, born in 1874,
would continue and build on that legacy.

Julius was graduated from the University of Oregon Law School
in 1895 and was for a few years an attorney before joining the family
business, where he soon became general manager and then, in
1930, president. He also invested in resort hotels and a bank and
took an active part in civic affairs. In World War I he headed Liberty
Loan drives and the regional Council of National Defense. He
boosted the Columbia River Scenic Highway and the stillborn
world's fair for Portland. The *Oregon Journal* praised him in 1929 as
"a progressive spirit," with "supreme confidence in the future of this
territory and the institutions which reflect its growth."[33]

Meier entered politics in 1930, when he ran for governor as an
independent. The only proponent of public power among the three
leading candidates, he was elected easily, with more than twice as
many votes as his Democratic and Republican opponents
combined. Historian George Turnbull describes him as "sometimes
arbitrary and personally imperious in dealing with his associates in
the government," but concludes that "he gave Oregon a generally
efficient and money-saving administration."[34] It was not a
propitious time for bold legislation, but Meier began the state
police and worked for parks and scenic areas.

He declined to run for reelection, citing poor health, and died
less than three years after leaving office.

A wealthy Jewish businessman running for Oregon's highest
office provoked not a little anti-Semitism in a state where the Ku
Klux Klan had recently enjoyed so much popularity. Critics
repeatedly referred to him as "the Merchant Prince" and praised a
Republican opponent as "a regular guy."[35] That Meier nevertheless
won election so easily suggests that most Oregonians were able to
overcome such bigotry.

Dr. DeNormal Unthank

The onset of the Great Depression was not a promising time for a
young physician to begin practicing. Being a Black doctor in an
overwhelmingly white city like Portland compounded matters. Yet
Dr. DeNormal Unthank would become, by his death in 1977, one of
Portland's most honored residents.

Born in Pennsylvania and raised by a physician uncle, Unthank
studied at the University of Michigan, the University of Kansas, and
Howard University. He moved to Portland in 1929, at age twenty-
nine, from Kansas City.

Portland had fewer than two thousand African Americans at that
time. "I never tried to say I came here to treat Negroes," Unthank
later recalled. "My approach always has been to say, 'I'm a doctor—
and incidentally, I'm a Negro.'"[36] But many white Portlanders saw
only his color. Residents of several communities chased the
Unthanks out. Neighbors at Ladd's Addition signed a petition, broke
windows, and threw a dead cat on their lawn. Tenants of the
Panama Building objected when he set up his office there, and
Unthank moved his office to Burnside.

His persistence paid off. White loggers joined his African-
American clients, as did many gypsies, whom Unthank helped with
medical and personal difficulties. Unthank "had a special kind of
dignity and gentle persuasiveness that was right for his generation
and his environment,"[37] noted Reverend John Jackson of the
National Association for the Advancement of Colored People in
1977.

Unthank's practice grew along with Portland's African-American
community and improved interracial relations. Unthank played a
key role in those changes. He co-founded Portland's Urban League,
was the first Black member of the City Club, and helped start what
would become the Metropolitan Human Relations Commission. He
was active in many other organizations, including St Philip's
Episcopal Church. When he retired, in 1970, about half of his
patients were white, including some retired loggers who had chosen
him as their doctor some forty years before.

A park in North Portland bears Dr. Unthank's name.

Pat Koehler

Thousands of women who had been laboring as domestics, factory hands, and sales clerks came to Portland's shipyards in World War II. So did many locals for whom working outside the home was a choice, not a necessity.

Pat Koehler was just eighteen, with one year of college under her belt, when she and a friend decided to do their part to win the war by becoming electrician helpers at Kaiser's Vancouver shipyard. They entered "a world of strangers who did not step aside for teenage girls." She and her friend learned how to tell a Brooklyn accent from a New Jersey one and to harden their ears to the obscenities lacing their workplace.

The work was hard. They studied at night and advanced quickly, becoming journeyman electricians earning $1.20. Koehler worked every day, up to twelve hours a day. She broke a toe, got it taped up, and went back to the job. She broke her elbow, took a day to get it set, then "learned to work left-handed." She became so anemic that the Red Cross would no longer accept her blood. Each night she and her friend returned to their homes in northeast Portland and "fell into bed exhausted, our hands chapped and our hair smelling of paint," with "no time to spend our money."

Koehler later recalled hoping that the five-inch gun she was wiring "would be well tested before battle. What was a nineteen-year-old girl doing up there in such a job, anyway?"

But she was proud of her work. The escort carriers she helped to build "helped to win the war in 1945." The war bonds that she and her friend purchased paid for two years of college. "Best of all," she concludes, "we had acquired new confidence and maturity."[38]

Koehler married, raised four children, and in 1974 received a B.A. in political science.

Chapter Eight

Prosperity and Its Problems

1945-1975

---

*"We ... thought we were making a paradise on
earth, a perfection of fields."*
William Kittredge on growing up in the Warner Valley

Oregonians, like their counterparts across the U.S., were overjoyed when World War II ended. By 1945 they had endured more than fifteen years of economic hardship or warfare. Now, they hoped, they could at last enjoy both prosperity and peace.

Those hopes were to a large extent fulfilled over the next three decades. Oregon's economy and population expanded steadily from the mid-1940s to the mid-1970s. Here, as elsewhere, technology finally trumped nature. Chainsaws and logging trucks fuelled logging's expansion. Modern chemicals, farm machinery, and irrigation multiplied agricultural yields. Improved automobiles and highways spread the easy movement of people and goods. Electricity reached even the most remote parts of the state, including the scattered farms of southeastern Oregon's Fort Rock Valley.

But problems persisted and festered beneath this veneer of growth and prosperity. African Americans and other people of color were still largely excluded from the center of Oregon's economic and social life. Some of Oregon's leading writers worried about the impact of success itself and wondered if people were not squandering their rugged pioneer heritage for comfort and complacency. Others noticed, certainly by the early 1970s, that Oregonians were consuming their natural resources, their trees and their fish, at an alarming rate.

Many Oregonians remember the postwar decades as a golden age. But those decades were characterized by both the persistence of old problems and the appearance of new ones.

Prosperity and Dislocation

Oregon manufacturing declined with the close of World War II and the Portland-area shipyards, but the state's economy soon recovered and became stronger than ever.

The state's population grew steadily. It was more than 1.5 million in 1950, up from just under 1.1 million ten years before. The next two decades saw more gradual growth, to about 2.1 million in 1970. The gains were highest in the Willamette Valley, around Portland, Eugene, and Salem—especially in Washington and Clackamas counties.

Eastern Oregon grew more slowly, in part because most of it continued to rely on agriculture. In 1970 farmers constituted 7.5 percent or more of the population in eleven counties east of the Cascades, none west of the mountains. Farmers by then made up only about 5 percent of the entire state's population, down from over 20 percent in 1940. Oregon had been settled largely by people who wanted to make a living farming. That occupation employed a shrinking, small fraction of Oregonians after World War II.

This is not to say that Oregon's agricultural production lagged. The value of farms and farm produce increased nearly fourfold from 1950 to 1974. Wheat, beef, milk, and hay constituted the major crops. Expanded irrigation helped fuel this increase. So did improved seeds, fertilizers, herbicides, and pesticides.

Farming became more concentrated as it became more intensive. The number of farms fell by more than 50 percent in the quarter century following 1950, and the farms that remained roughly doubled in size. In other words, half the farmers were farming the same amount of land and producing crops worth four times as much. The trend toward consolidation would have been still more pronounced if so many Oregonians had not farmed a few acres to supplement their incomes. In 1969, 40 percent of the state's farms created less than $2,500 worth of products. On the other extreme, just 10 percent of Oregon farms sold at least $40,000 worth of products, nearly two thirds of the state's total.

William Kittredge's account of growing up in southeastern Oregon's Warner Valley after the war reveals how the new agricultural order worked. His father drained and plowed hundreds of acres of marshlands and constructed canals to control the flow of the water that remained. Chemicals killed pests from clover mites to coyotes. Tractors and other machines displaced humans and other animals. Haying that had occupied one hundred sweating men and twice as many horses was now accomplished by a handful of workers guiding powerful tractors and harvesters. The raising of animals also became more intense and calculated. A huge feed mill mixed hay, grains, and "additives from molasses to growth-inducing chemicals like stilbestrol." Cows were becoming meat-making machines. Every year the operation shipped some five thousand head to slaughterhouses. "We were doing God's work," Kittredge remembers, "and thought we were making a paradise on earth, a perfection of fields."[1] Most of the farmers who could not keep up found another way to make a living.

The same process happened in the Willamette Valley, long one of the state's most intensively farmed areas. There many farmers had turned to grass seed in the 1920s and 1930s. The industry boomed soon after World War II ended as tractors, combines, swathers, commercial fertilizers, more robust seeds, and field burning boosted output while reducing labor. Yet each increased efficiency required increased investment. Horses had been slow but drew their energy from hay, which could be cheaply grown on the farm, and they reproduced themselves. The new tractors ate gasoline and oil, which cost money, and when they wore out farmers had to buy new ones. Many farmers literally could not afford to keep up. The farms of those who could got larger.

Manufacturing followed much the same pattern as farming. The number of factories decreased as their output increased.

The production of machinery had overtaken food processing as the second largest industrial employer by the mid-1970s, followed by metal and electricity. When combined with wood processing, these

Penguins at Washington Park Zoo, in Portland, 1961. As Oregonians became more removed from the natural world, their attention increasingly turned to more exotic animals. Photo courtesy of the Historic Photograph Collections, Salem (Oregon) Public Library

five sectors employed 87 percent of the one in four Oregonians working in manufacturing. The great majority of these workers lived in western Oregon, and only a few major industries besides wood manufacturing were outside the Willamette Valley.

Craft skills declined with mechanization. Oregon's building trades, always tied closely to the state of its general economy, did very well in the decades following the war, as homes and larger construction projects proliferated. But the work of building was becoming easier as sheetrock supplanted lathe and plaster and machine-made products replaced a host of features that had once been shaped by experienced carpenters. The new order, notes historian Craig Wollner, was "cost-efficient and productive."[2] It turned out serviceable and inexpensive homes for Oregon's growing population. But skilled carpenters suffered.

Mechanization both created and destroyed jobs. By 1970 Oregonians were much less apt to be engaged in creating food or other products, much more likely to be employed distributing or tracking goods, in sales and service. Clerical work grew dramatically, as did white-collar and government jobs.

But retail work was reshaped by the forces of rationalization even as it expanded. The state had been dotted by thousands of small stores early in the century, including many neighborhood grocery stores. By 1929, though, regional or national chain stores had captured nearly a quarter of Oregonians' business. These new stores were larger and more uniform and offered cheaper goods. But they offered fewer people the opportunity to run their own business, and they threatened to undercut local economies. Critics decried the spread of Safeway, Piggly Wiggly, and Wonder Bread and urged Oregonians to realize "that natural man differs in many ways from the corporate man," and "that the individual merchant differs from the chain store man."[3] In 1931 Portland's city council even passed an ordinance that taxed chain stores, and Portland voters supported it. But the ordinance was repealed during the war, and by the 1950s stores, like farms and factories, had become both larger and less numerous.

These stores served a spreading population. Portland's suburbs had less than two hundred thousand people in 1940. By 1970 they had more than six hundred thousand, 62 percent of the metropolitan area's population. The city had been expanding eastward for years, and the trend continued after the end of the war as houses sprang up between Portland and Gresham. By the 1960s most of the growth had moved west, as Interstate 5 and the Sunset Highway tunnel provided quick access to downtown. These homes in Beaverton, Lake Oswego, Tigard, and elsewhere were, as historian Carl Abbott puts it, "bigger, newer, better equipped, and probably more stylish than" were their counterparts to the east.[4]

Suburban residents jealously guarded their autonomy. A proposal to incorporate a portion of Clackamas County into Portland was turned down by a margin of nearly three to one in 1962 and elicited the charge that Portland was trying to pick residents' pockets through "Deceit, Deception, and Doubletalk!"[5] Planners of the 1950s took note and gave Oregonians what they wanted: low taxes and minimal regulations. The amount of land consumed by the metropolitan area's homes therefore grew much more quickly than its population, and its population was growing very quickly indeed.

A subsequent generation of planners and residents would find much to criticize in this quarter century of aggressive and largely unregulated expansion. But most people enjoying new homes and roads seemed very well pleased with the fruits of progress.

The interstates spread goods as well as people. The Portland-Salem highway opened in 1952, and it soon joined a broader federal network of interstates running between Portland and Ashland (north-south) and Portland and Ontario (east-west) and around Portland itself. These multi-lane roads made it possible for trucks to at last meet or

Paved roads in 1920 and 1950. Images reproduced from the Atlas of Oregon, Second Edition *courtesy of the University of Oregon Press. © 2001 University of Oregon Press*

Tractor-trailer built in Portland, 1955. Photo courtesy of Oregon Historical Society, OrHi 79646

exceed the speed of trains. Industries could now relocate away from railways, on cheaper land. Between 1955 and 1969 some seventy manufacturers employing nearly ten thousand workers left Portland for its suburbs.

Many stores also relocated. This trend had begun well before World War II, as goods and services proliferated along streets such as Sandy Boulevard in Portland. Fred Meyer had opened his first store squarely in downtown Portland, in 1922. Between 1945 and 1960 he opened seven new stores between five and fifteen miles from the city center, and in the next two decades his shopping centers followed suburban sprawl to Gresham, Beaverton, and beyond. Lloyd Center was one of the nation's largest malls when it opened in 1960 in inner northeast Portland. But developers more often chose locales where land and shoppers were easy to come by. Lloyd Center tucked most of its parking spaces out of view. Suburban malls such as Eastport Plaza and Gateway Center on Portland's eastern boundary did not and "were essentially retailing strips set behind great, gray parking lots," observes Abbott.[6]

Many of Portland's white-collar workers stayed downtown, for the city's office buildings multiplied as its stores moved away. Thousands of commuters from Beaverton, Gresham, and elsewhere came and went daily, for modern automobiles and highways made a twenty-mile commute commonplace. But suburbanites who worked in Portland did not necessarily shop there. From 1946 to 1960 the number of daily personal trips to Portland's business core declined by more than 10 percent.

The downtowns of smaller places suffered more dramatically. A survey of eighteen Willamette Valley towns found that both the number and range of businesses had decreased by the late 1940s even as their populations had grown. Hotels, movie theatres, medical services, and a host of specialty stores had disappeared from main streets as improved transportation systems carried residents and visitors to larger centers.

The new highway system caused some towns to boom. Wilsonville, located just south of the confluence of Interstates 5 and 205, was transformed from an agricultural community with a few stores to a growing city incorporating a large planned community (Charbonneau) and a score of factories and warehouses drawn by easy access to highways and airports. Burns Brothers truck stop opened at the interchange in 1969 and constituted a village in its own right, with two restaurants, a motel, office complex, and barbershop.

Interstates affected other towns and cities, too. Service stations, motels, and restaurants commonly migrated to or opened at freeway interchanges, where locals and visitors alike congregated. Businesses that catered to residents only—grocery stores and barber shops, for example—often stayed put on decaying main streets. A few smaller cities like Eugene and Coos Bay opened downtown pedestrian malls. But the automobile drew a substantial chunk of residents, shoppers, and workers out of downtowns across the state in the decades following the war.

Other areas were affected by the spread of vacationers. Barely two million tourists visited Oregon in 1950. More than nine million did two decades later, when they spent well over $300 million here. About one half of these tourists came from neighboring California, which enjoyed easy access to western Oregon via I-5. Oregonians also took

Getting away from it all meant bringing a lot of it with you in the 1950s. Beverly Beach State Park in Lincoln County, 1958. Photo courtesy of the Historic Photograph Collections, Salem (Oregon) Public Library

to the roads in pursuit of relaxation and pleasure. The well-to-do enjoyed weekends and second homes at central Oregon's Sunriver or at Salishan, on the coast. Their working-class counterparts were more apt to rent a motel room in Seaside or camp in one of the state's hundreds of parks.

The postwar decades, then, brought substantial and sustained economic growth to Oregon. Most people enjoyed a much higher material standard of living than they had before, and many parts of the state boomed. College attendance grew in the 1950s, and late in the decade the state inaugurated a network of community colleges that would soon offer courses in a burgeoning range of vocations.

But these gains too often obscure less obvious losses. Opportunities to run one's own business declined as the economy expanded. Communities were fragmented or transformed as automobility transformed the geographies of small towns and big cities alike.

Few people of the time counted these costs. Their children would.

Timber

World War II and the boom that followed it did not dislodge timber as Oregon's leading industry. But the industry would both grow and change dramatically.

The site of timber production shifted. By the 1950s much of northwestern Oregon's old growth had been consumed. Logging and milling moved east and especially south, to the richly forested hills of Lane, Douglas, and Coos counties.

The amount of timber, including much from national forests, harvested in Oregon shot up dramatically during the 1940s and then remained relatively steady, at about 9 million board feet per year, from the mid-1950s to the mid-1960s. A variety of developments made the timber industry much more economically efficient than before, at least in the short term. The proliferation of chain saws widened the remaining bottleneck in timber production by greatly reducing the amount of time that it took to fell and buck (cut into manageable lengths) a tree. Tractors or cats offered unprecedented flexibility for yarding or dragging logs to loading sites. Cats also carved out logging roads that could penetrate areas that had been too rugged for railroads.

Technology also made mills more productive. The kraft process made it possible to produce wood pulp for paper from scraps that had once been discarded. Plywood created a stronger, thinner board, and particleboard utilized sawdust, which had been a troublesome waste product. In sum, modern mills wasted much less wood than their prewar predecessors had.

Foresters also became more efficient. The Tillamook burns, as we saw in Chapter Seven, quickened concerns over forest conservation, as did various New Deal programs. After the war companies and governments alike devoted more money to researching how to grow trees more quickly. Tree farms, tree planting, and fire suppression spread. Timber managers were treating trees like a crop by replanting what they harvested, speeding their growth cycles, and guarding against fire and disease.

Times were flush, and not just for big concerns. The transition to logging roads and trucks meant that small operators, usually referred to as gyppos, could claim a piece of the market. Buying a few log trucks, a cat or two, a diesel-powered donkey, and some chain saws was much cheaper than outfitting an operation that required rails, trains, and steam-powered donkey engines, and small-town bankers loaned them the money to do so. "Just one guy goes out, he cuts the trees down, he cuts it up in logs, loads it on his truck, and takes it to town all by himself," summed up one logger. Nor did the new outfits have to house their workers in camps. Loggers now drove to work, like everybody else. Gyppo outfits of several workers specialized in logging small, easily accessible tracts of second- or third-growth timber. Small mills did well, too, at least if they were oriented toward niche markets and marginal raw materials. A former Coos County logging inspector recalled that some five hundred spread across the south coast in the 1950s. Most of them produced railway ties and sent semi-finished lumber to the area's big mills. Some were family businesses. A Coos County resident remembered one in which "the mother did the firing for the steam engine, the father was head sawyer, and the son ran the dogs on the carriage. Two other sons did all the other off-bearings from the saw."[7] Making a decent living from such operations required more than just hard work. Small operators had to scramble to find reliable supplies of timber and markets, and it required considerable ingenuity to keep their worn-out equipment running.

By the late 1950s, however, a set of new problems worried gyppo loggers and small mill owners. Technology kept improving. Those who couldn't afford it suffered in relation to the larger mills that could. They also had trouble meeting the growing number of government regulations, such as creating wigwam burners to dispose of waste. Markets were tightening up and becoming more centralized, another development that worked against small operators. Supply presented a similar set of problems. By 1960s the gyppos had already logged just about all the small stands on local farms and ranches. They didn't own forests of their own, and they were not large enough to bid on large government contracts. The gyppo's golden age had hardly lasted a generation.

Weyerhaeuser and Georgia-Pacific expanded their already considerable influence in Coos County as the gyppos declined. Weyerhaeuser had established a vertically integrated operation in 1951, with land, roads, loggers, and a huge mill. It started with more than five hundred employees and soon grew. Georgia-Pacific arrived from the southern United States a few years later, buying up more than a hundred thousand acres of prime timberland. These concerns had a steady supply of trees, the wherewithal to abide by government regulations, and the national and international connections to market their products effectively.

But what was good for Georgia-Pacific was not necessarily good for Coos Bay. Georgia-Pacific had spent money so rapidly that it needed to cut and sell its Coos County timber to meet its obligations elsewhere. The sea of logs created hundreds of jobs, but not for long. Technological changes meant that fewer and fewer people were needed to cut and process timber. Jobs increased, then, only because the rate of harvesting had risen even more steeply than the rate at which machines replaced workers. But that harvesting rate could not be sustained. Old-growth timber would run out long before replanted stands would be ready to cut. Many people saw trouble ahead. Georgia-Pacific asserted in 1959 that "we will grow a volume of timber at least equal to the volume harvested." Yet the Coos Bay newspaper, certainly no enemy of the timber industry, had warned in 1951 that the area's mills could not "operate at capacity without depleting the supply of green timber."[8] Even before Weyerhaeuser and Georgia-Pacific had arrived, then, locals realized that timber was in danger of being harvested too quickly. That Weyerhaeuser was sending raw logs to Japan to be processed exacerbated the local impact of overharvesting.

Jobs in Coos County's forest industry began to shrink in 1960. As late as 1975, 44.5 percent of Oregonians employed in manufacturing worked with wood. Timber was still the only game in town for communities such as Gardiner, Wauna, Hines, Veneta, Dillard, and Toledo. But Oregon's timber industry was by then declining fast.

Minorities and Progress

Most Oregonians of color were still trying to enter the state's economic and social mainstream as white timber workers began to leave it. They were aided by an unprecedented wave of civil rights activism that began among African Americans in the South in the 1950s and spread across the nation and to many peoples in the 1960s.

Oregon's non-white population declined in the years following World War II as war jobs in industry and agriculture dried up. But the state would never again be as homogeneous as it had been in 1940, when more than ninety-eight in one hundred Oregonians were white.

World War II inflicted deep and lasting trauma on Oregon's Japanese Americans. Those who returned near the war's end met with bitter disappointment. Their homes had been looted, their orchards and fields disregarded, their forebears' gravestones broken. White neighbors were openly hostile. Many residents of Hood River, Gresham, Sherwood, and Forest Grove argued that all people of Japanese descent ought to be deported. "We should never be satisfied until every last Jap has been run out of United States and our Constitution changed so they can never get back," asserted former Governor Walter Pierce. Issei and Nisei endured boycotts of their fruits and vegetables, snubs and verbal abuse, and occasional physical assaults. Mrs. Bettsworth of Hood River had traded cookies and milk for songs and stories with young Mitzi Asai before the war. But when the Asais returned from internment, she lay in wait every school day so that no opportunity would be missed to sic her dog on the terrified Nisei. Hood River saw the most determined and notorious campaign against people of Japanese descent. Its American Legion Post went so far as to deny recognition of the sixteen local Nisei who had fought for their country during the war, including two who had died. Magazines and newspapers across the country condemned this proposal, as did many white soldiers. "We're ashamed to say we're from Oregon now, much less Hood River," wrote Sergeant David White.[9]

Word quickly spread of these abuses, and many Japanese Americans elected not to return to Oregon. Yet many did. When a Hood River man yelled, "Why don't you go back where you're from?" at Min Asai, he replied: "I'm from here," that "I was born here."[10] Some whites such as Sherman Burgoyne, the minister of a Hood River Methodist church, braved local opinion by sticking up for and helping their

Japanese-American friends. The Issei and Nisei, long accustomed to racial hostility, kept a low profile and waited for the hatred fanned by four years of war to subside.

Their patience was rewarded. Anti-Japanese sentiment declined at war's end, albeit in part because Oregon's Japanese now wielded only a fraction of the economic power that they had enjoyed at the war's outset. After a year and a half of being shunned, Mitzi Asai was once again included in the social activities of her school and church. Late in the 1940s the federal government reimbursed Japanese Americans for a small portion of the economic losses caused by internment. Congress in 1952 made citizenship available to Japanese-born Americans, a possibility that hundreds of Oregon Issei pursued, and in 1965 it overturned racist immigration quotas set in the 1920s. Employment discrimination also eased. The Sansei, or third-generation Japanese Americans, pursued educational and professional opportunities that had been denied their hard-working parents. Their successes won them the appellation "model minority."

But fitting in inflicted a cost. Many Nisei, in the judgement of historian Lauren Kessler, were so eager to "spare their children the ostracism they had suffered" that they surrendered "any vestige of their ethnic identity."[11] The Sansei were likely to live in communities that were overwhelmingly white, to marry outside their ethnic group, and to possess little knowledge of their language, culture, or history, including the hardships visited upon their parents and grandparents before and during the war. Only later would Japanese Americans explore publicly what had been lost since 1941.

White leaders in Oregon and the nation hoped in the postwar years that Native Americans, who had long constituted its most impoverished and marginal residents, would also assimilate into broader society. Many of Oregon's indigenous peoples had left their reservations during the war to serve in the military or for defense work. In the 1950s and 1960s Bureau of Indian Affairs (BIA) employees encouraged those on Oregon reservations to move to Portland or even Denver or Chicago to find employment. Portland's BIA office steered many Native peoples to the Adult Vocational Training Program. This program was no panacea. Administrators closely monitored their behavior and discouraged visiting home or other expressions of ethnicity. But the training, like urban life more generally, helped participants to "create a better life," as many applicants put it.[12] Some graduates confounded the BIA's expectations by returning to their reservations upon graduating. But most stayed, as did their counterparts who moved to urban areas without enrolling in the Adult Vocational Training Program. In 1950 just 15 percent of the state's Indians lived in urban areas. Two decades later 48 percent did.

Federal officials of the postwar years also hoped to more fully acculturate those who remained on reservations. Termination of treaty rights would, they believed, speed that process.

Termination directly affected nearly one half of Oregon's Native Americans: those living in western Oregon and the Klamath. Severing Native Americans' relations with the federal government had wide-ranging consequences. Those who had land were no longer exempt from taxes, and many could not pay those taxes and therefore lost their land. Indians from terminated tribes could no longer attend Chemawa School in Salem and had to pay for medical services. The government closed the Grand Ronde and Siletz reservations in 1956, along with dozens of small bands in western Oregon. Many of their members dispersed to larger reservations or to Oregon cities. Their tribal councils disbanded.

The Klamath seemed particularly well suited for termination. More prosperous and acculturated than most other tribes, they appeared to be eager to take charge of their own affairs, to get out from under the federal government's oversight. They also held in common, as tribal property, some of the state's most coveted timber. But the Klamath were much more vulnerable than they seemed. Local whites, including employers, looked down on and discriminated against them. The Klamath's relative prosperity, moreover, came largely from per capita timber payments. These payments enabled the Klamath to enjoy a relatively high standard of living, but unemployment and racism fostered high levels of violence, alcoholism, and truancy. Less than one Klamath student per year was graduating from high school, and only six out of ten were promoted to the next grade in 1954. The annual timber payments would disappear upon termination.

Divisions within the Klamath, confusion over exactly what termination entailed, determined federal officials, and a desire to acquire Klamath lands added up to termination. In 1958, 78 percent of the Klamath voted to withdraw from their tribe in return for a lump payment.

Termination brought many problems to the Klamath. Unaccustomed to handling large sums of money and bilked by local business people and lawyers, many quickly exhausted the $43,000 they had received in compensation for their share of tribal lands. They were left with few if any assets. Having surrendered their Indian status, they now had to pay for their health care. The state of Oregon ruled that they could no longer hunt and fish uninhibited on tribal lands. Two thirds of those who enrolled in an educational program linked to termination dropped out. The minority who had elected to remain tribal members were also weakened. Tribal government disappeared. Many left the community to find work. "After termination we were just left wide open and people scattered out," tribal elder Reid David later recalled."[13] Those who remained were divided and often hopeless.

The Paiute, Wasco, and Sahaptin peoples of the Warm Springs Reservation in Central Oregon fared much better after the war. In 1957 The Dalles Dam covered Celilo Falls, the rich fishing grounds that had sustained the economic well-being and cultural identity of the mid-Columbia River's peoples for millennia. But the Warms Springs tribes received $4 million in compensation and spent most of it on economic development, in timber and tourism. They rehabilitated a spa early in the 1960s and soon built Kah-Nee-Ta, a well-appointed resort. Many members worked in the tribe's sawmill. Yet per capita income at Warm Springs was only high compared to other Native peoples. It continued to lag far behind the rest of the state's.

Celilo Falls on the Columbia River at The Dalles. This photo was taken in September 1954, less than three years before The Dalles Dam, which would flood these Native fishing grounds, was completed. Photo courtesy of the Historic Photograph Collections, Salem (Oregon) Public Library

A growing sense of pride and initiative combined with expanded federal government programs in the 1960s to reinvigorate Oregon's Native Americans. Many availed themselves of educational, health-care, and job-training programs. Political activism and lobbying blossomed. The Burns Paiute won recognition from the Department of the Interior as a tribe in 1968, and four years later they had a small reservation. The Siletz and Grand Ronde tribal councils reconstituted themselves in 1973 and 1975, respectively. The Klamath and the Coos-Lower Umpqua-Siuslaw also stepped up their political activities. In 1975 the Oregon State Commission on Indian Services began lobbying on behalf of Oregon's Native Americans.

To be sure, poverty and lack of opportunities still dogged Oregon's indigenous peoples. The unemployment rate for Indians in Lincoln County was 44 percent in 1975, and more than four out of ten Indians between seventeen and twenty-five in the town of Siletz had not graduated from high school. But now Indians and some whites were both talking and doing something about such problems.

Being indigenous was no longer a source of shame. More Oregonians identified themselves as "Indian" in the census. The figure increased more than fivefold from 1950 to 1980, rising from just over five thousand to more than twenty-six thousand in just thirty years. Urban Indians, encouraged by government officials to assimilate in the 1950s and 1960s, reclaimed their heritage. The Portland American Indian Center sponsored the city's first powwow in 1965, which featured traditional dress and dances. Other Indian-led organizations offered programs for sobriety and education. By the early 1970s, many Portland Indians had joined organizations devoted to radical political change, including a chapter of the American Indian Movement (AIM). Indeed, AIM leader Dennis Banks briefly moved the radical movement's national office to Portland in 1976.

Oregon's Latinos resembled its Native peoples in many respects. The vast majority through the 1970s originated in the Southwest, especially Texas, or Mexico, and most had at least some Native ancestry. Like Native Americans they were a largely rural people who eked out a living on the edges of Oregon's economy. But in the decades after the war they constituted a rapidly growing and often successful component of the state's population.

The war's end reduced but did not end the migration of Mexican laborers to Oregon, and some of them made Oregon their year-round home by the late 1940s. A few families who had for years worked seasonally around Woodburn, Independence, Nyssa, The Dalles, Klamath Falls, Wasco, or elsewhere decided to leave Texas, California, or Mexico for good. Their numbers quickly grew: new individuals and families arrived, children were born. Adults moved out of the lowest rungs of agricultural work and became year-round employees on farms or in factories. Their children began filling up local schools and gaining admittance to colleges and universities. In 1970 about eighty entered the University of Oregon, and in 1975 the Chicano Cultural Center (which became the Centro Cultural Cesar Chavez) opened at Oregon State University.

Latinos created and utilized a wide range of organizations to help them gain a place in Oregon's economy. Catholic parishes formed. The Valley Migrant League and Treasure Valley Community College— located in the Willamette Valley and eastern Oregon, respectively— appeared in the mid-1960s and offered a wide range of services to Latinos. Governor Tom McCall instituted an Advisory Committee on Chicano Affairs. By 1970 six Oregon counties each counted more than two thousand Latino residents.

Oregon's Latinos, permanent and seasonal, maintained an ambivalent relationship with larger society. On the one hand, Oregon generally offered better pay and working conditions than Mexico— or Texas, for that matter. Yet better was not the same thing as good. At Eolo Village, near Dayton, forty-five hundred migrants lived in a camp built for one third that number. Employers routinely ignored laws stipulating decent housing and sanitation. State senator Don Wilner

Mexican workers harvesting onions in Marion County, September 1962. Photo courtesy of the Historic Photograph Collections, Salem (Oregon) Public Library

remarked in the 1950s that "discriminations have contributed in making migrant workers the poorest members of our society."[14] Nyssa-area taverns displayed signs reading "No Mexicans Allowed" in the early 1960s.[15] Latinos in Woodburn schools were disciplined for speaking Spanish, and few were graduated.

Latinos began to organize in the mid 1960s. In 1970 they took over the Valley Migrant League, which had been dominated by well-meaning but paternalistic whites, and worked inside and outside the system to improve farm workers' living and working conditions. In 1972 they collaborated with the Portland Catholic Archdiocese to establish Centro Chicano Cultural in Gervais, which served farm workers' social, educational, and cultural needs. El Movimiento, or the Chicano Movement, spread to Oregon and emphasized a broad range of reforms to create educational and occupational opportunities. The former Mount Angel College became Colegio Cesar Chavez, a college devoted to educating Latinos and other people of color. In 1977 it graduated twenty-two.

Colegio Cesar Chavez and some other expressions of the Chicano movement of the 1970s would not survive the 1980s. But many did, including MECHa (Movimiento Estudiantil Chicano de Aztlan) in Oregon's high schools and colleges. The political and cultural activities of the 1970s would lay the groundwork for renewed activism by Oregon Latinos near the century's end.

The same could be said of the state's African-American community. Black Oregonians had a long legacy of combatting racist practices and attitudes. Those efforts grew along with their numbers in the three decades following World War II.

The close of the war brought temporary setbacks for Portland's Black community. Well-paying jobs disappeared, driving many from the community. The Vanport flood of 1948, which literally washed away a city of over seventeen thousand, left many without affordable housing. Oregon's African-American population declined to just over twelve thousand for the state as a whole in 1950, but grew steadily to over twenty-six thousand in 1970. Most lived in Portland, where, as historian Stuart McElderry puts it, the city's "continued resistance to public housing ... combined with real-estate industry discrimination" created "an unprecedented level of black concentration in the Albina district."[16]

Those who sought new homes faced discrimination. "Until now I didn't know there were so many places Negroes can't live," remarked one woman.[17] Portland's growing Black community moved north and east, into communities that had been dominated by white working-class families who had left for the suburbs. By 1960 nearly one in five students at Jefferson High School, in north Albina, was Black. Just ten years later nearly one half were.

Movement out of central Albina was not always voluntary. Thousands of Portland residents, most of them Black, lost their homes to a series of urban renewal projects beginning in the late 1950s. Memorial Coliseum, Interstate 5, and Emmanuel Hospital destroyed many homes and businesses.

Discrimination in housing and employment prompted much political activism among Portland's African Americans after the war. The Urban League convinced the managers of Portland department stores to hire Black elevator operators. The National Association for the Advancement of Colored People and other organizations inside and outside Portland's African-American community advocated for more public housing and decried realty practices that excluded Blacks from many Portland neighborhoods.

Their efforts bore fruit. The state passed a fair employment law in 1949 and a public accommodation law in 1953. Fair housing laws followed in 1957 and 1959. Portland African Americans gained well-paying positions with the fire department, the Columbia Athletic Club,

African Americans march in Portland in June 1963, mourning the murder of Medgar Evers in Mississippi. Photo courtesy of Oregon Historical Society, OrHi 59874

the *Oregonian* and *Oregon Journal,* and several manufacturing concerns in the 1950s.

Yet progress was fitful. Some Portland employers agreed to hire people of African descent—but not dark-skinned ones. When residents of Northeast 140th Avenue learned that a Black couple, Rowan and Parthina Wiley, had purchased a lot in their neighborhood they first tried legal means to exclude them. When that failed, explosives destroyed the Wiley's half-completed home. The Wileys rebuilt. In Eugene, employed African Americans made less than one half, on average, as much as their white counterparts in the early 1960s. Oregon's Black community continued to lag far behind the state's average in education, occupational status, and income—and discrimination in every aspect of life endured.

Political activity quickened in the 1960s. The NAACP led a boycott of Fred Meyer stores in 1962 for not hiring African Americans, and soon of Sears and Allstate, too. Proliferating federal programs funded a variety of community programs, including education, job training, legal services, and culture. Young, more militant African Americans abjured traditional, integration-oriented churches and organizations in favor of the Black Muslims and Black Panthers, organizations that emphasized Black power and autonomy. A riot broke out in northeast Portland in the summer of 1967 involving about two hundred African Americans. It resulted in considerable damage to property but few injuries. All forty-five of Oregon State University's African-American students left the school to protest coach Dee Andros's decree that a Black football player had to shave his beard in the off-season.

African-American radicals paid a price for their outspokenness. Black residents remember their health, breakfast, and tutoring programs. White residents and law-enforcement officials saw them as a threat that needed to be eradicated. Kent Ford, a leader of Portland's Black Panthers, felt as if he was "being hunted" and recalled long nights sitting "at the front door with a shotgun, waiting for a raid."[18]

By the mid-1970s African Americans enjoyed more opportunities than ever before. But the rising expectations that accompanied these improvements were not fully realized.

For most of Oregon's growing minority population, then, the three decades following World War II brought more changes in perception than in condition. African Americans, Native Americans, and Latinos became more politically aware and active. But racism and poverty remained deeply entrenched problems for Oregon's people of color in 1975.

Prosperity's Discontented

Dissatisfied Oregonians included some people from the socio-economic mainstream. Most people of comfortable means spent their leisure time watching television and otherwise enjoying the fruits of prosperity. Indeed, much youthful rebellion in the 1950s entailed buying something: rock and roll records or tickets to a James Dean movie, for example. Yet a growing number of prosperous, well-educated people expressed concern over the direction of their state and nation in the postwar decades.

Novelist Don Berry, born in 1932 in Minnesota, came to Portland during the war. He left home a few years later, at age fifteen, and returned to attend Reed College, one of the nation's premier liberal arts colleges, from 1949 to '51. At Reed Berry joined a gifted and iconoclastic group of young writers who would soon become leaders of the countercultural "beat" movement. Several years later he became fascinated in the settlement of Tillamook County while conducting research for Reed professor Dorothy Johansen. The result was *Trask*, a well-received novel published by Viking in 1960. Berry quickly followed this up with two more novels set in mid-nineteenth-century Oregon: *Moontrap* and *To Build a Ship*.

Readers engrossed by these novels' well-researched historical details may overlook the author's implicit and insistent critique of life in modern Oregon. The protagonist in *Trask*, like Berry and his friends at Reed, is attracted to Indian religion. After a harrowing vision quest in which he mistakenly kills his Native friend, he understands that the world is "made not for mastery but for living."[19] But such realizations put Berry's protagonists at war with Oregon's new order. In *Moontrap*, a retired mountain man learns that getting along in the young society of Willamette Valley farmers and missionaries required that one "float along with the surface, say the expected things."[20] Both books, as literary scholar Glen Love observes, represent "a rejection of, or a turning from, the social compact in favor of meaningful insight and action by the individual alone in nature."[21] Berry's trilogy—and its popularity—sounded a discordant note in the early 1960s in a state and nation that appeared well satisfied and optimistic.

Ken Kesey made the same arguments as Berry, and on a larger stage. Born in Colorado, Kesey moved to Oregon with his parents in 1946. He was graduated from Springfield High School and the University of Oregon. In 1959 he entered the graduate program in writing at Stanford University, where he worked with Wallace Stegner. Kesey became a national figure in the mid-1960s, cavorting across North America with the Merry Pranksters, high on marijuana and LSD, partying with the Hells Angels, and serving as the main character of Tom Wolfe's *Electric Kool-Aid Acid Test*. But before becoming a famous hippie he published two novels set in Oregon that were well received by readers and critics: *One Flew Over the Cuckoo's Nest* and *Sometimes a Great Notion*.

Both books argue that modern Oregon men are in danger of being emasculated and debilitated by modern society. *Cuckoo's Nest* is set in a sanitarium, and it soon becomes clear that the sanitarium is a metaphor for American society, a place in which men are compelled to lead anesthetized lives of sedate conformity. Likewise, in *Sometimes a Great Notion*, logger Hank Stamper comes home from the Korean War "to find the Dodgers in a slump, frozen apple pie just like Mom useta make in all the supermarkets, and a sour stench in the sweet land of liberty he'd risked his life defending." His friends were "tired, scared, asleep."[22] Only Hank's capacity for flouting community pressure and remaining his own man gives his neighbors hope that there is more to life than mind-numbing predictability and prosperity.

Julia Ruuttila, then 59, being arrested by Portland police at a 1966 peace march. Ruuttila (1907-91) was a social and labor activist. Photo courtesy of Oregon Historical Society, OrHi 23930

By the mid-1960s, more and more Oregonians were questioning the certitudes and platitudes that Berry and Kesey had taken issue with. Kittredge recalls that John F. Kennedy's assassination implied a destabilizing question: "What was the use of caution or circumspection or good manners or prudence or good looks if somebody would shoot you anyway?"[23] For many Oregonians, the dissolution of traditional restraints and hopes paired with new drugs and birth control added up to a sort of moral weightlessness in which the pursuit of pleasure became the only good and certain thing.

Many other Oregonians became more idealistic, especially on college campuses. The first uprising of the 1960s at the University of Oregon seemed innocuous enough. Some one hundred fifty male students rampaged through a women's dormitory upon hearing that said women had resolved not to go on any dates during homecoming. But the university's students were soon protesting tuition increases and demanding more autonomy in their personal lives and authority in college affairs. By 1965 they were expressing concern over the Vietnam War. In the fall of 1969 approximately four thousand people marched at the University of Oregon to protest the conflict. The protests became more extreme as their numbers swelled. "All we are saying is give peace a chance" gave way to more profane utterances.[24] Eugene's ROTC building was the target of many rocks and a bombing. That year also saw a determined protest at Portland State University that shut the institution down for several days.

Well-educated Oregon women began to organize around their own oppression in the late 1960s. In 1969 a women's liberation group appeared at the University of Oregon. More diffuse than most other protest groups, feminists at first spent much of their time raising each others' consciousness about male dominance and struggling to create more equitable marriages with their husbands. "I feel just like it's awakened me," said a Eugene member. "For years I tried hard to be like a man, because I knew it wasn't cool to be a woman if you had any brains. But now I think it's marvellous to be a woman."[25] Women who never formally joined a feminist group were very much affected by them. By the mid-1970s, young women, in particular, had stopped wearing dresses and were pursuing jobs in fields previously closed to them. Legislative changes in the state included the nation's first law recognizing marital rape.

Feminism flourished in Portland. Bonnie Tinker was one of many young women who arrived in the city fresh from well-regarded liberal arts colleges like Grinnell and Oberlin determined to create politically active communities. Like many radicals, most feminists settled in southeast Portland, along Hawthorne Boulevard, where they began conscious-raising groups, a women's bookstore, a women's health center, and many other woman-centered activities. Prescott House began as a home for women who had been living on the streets or in prison and mixed people like Tinker with women from poorer backgrounds, including many who had been sexually and physically abused in their homes, marriages, or as prostitutes. "We already had a perspective of class politics, … the peace movement and nonviolence," recalls Tinker. Now the middle-class activists learned from these survivors "that oppression was not just a theoretical construct, but that there were real material consequences" to living without money or education and suffering from violence.[26] This cross-cultural and cross-class collaboration helped create Bradley-Angle House, one of the nation's first shelters for battered women, and many families, as feminists from diverse backgrounds became partners and raised children together.

By the 1970s many young radical Oregonians were becoming more inwardly focused. Communalists had began filtering into the Takilma area of southern Oregon in the late 1960s. A reporter described the members of the Fanatic Family commune as "into a … love trip with various religious overtones and backgrounds."[27] Communalists, by definition, emphasized cooperation and self-sufficiency. Living together on the land served to limit reliance on the market, keep expenses low, bring one closer to nature, and facilitate the creation of nontraditional family structures. Indeed, many gay and lesbian communes sprouted in western Oregon in the 1970s.

Other communes stressed interaction with the broader community. Quakers founded the Alpha community of Deadwood in the Coast Range foothills west of Eugene. They operated a store, delivered mail, and sold farm products. A group of urban Quakers formed Terrasquirma, in southeast Portland. An observer described them as striving "to make their way of life completely consistent with what they want to achieve on a larger scale in society."[28] They lived very simply, pooled all their earnings, made decisions by consensus, and men did the same household chores as women. This frugality and communalism served to free up time for political work, such as founding the path-breaking Rape Relief Hotline and Sunflower Recycling Collective, though Terrasquirma never exceeded more than a dozen or so members.

Shiloh occupied the opposite end of the theological spectrum. Located in Dexter and Eugene, it had attracted several hundred people by the late 1970s and was part of the decade's Jesus Movement. Many of its members were recovering drug addicts who found in Shiloh a sense of purpose and structure. Shiloh operated several economic ventures, but its *raison d'etre* was to bring people to Jesus.

Like most of its smaller counterparts, Shiloh had fragmented by the decade's close. But to this day one can find communities sprinkled across western Oregon in which people of varying religious, sexual, and political orientations are striving to live lives of simplicity, creativity, and relatedness.

Politics

Oregon politics changed dramatically from 1945 to 1975, and in several ways.

The size of state and local government grew dramatically in the postwar years. Government regulated an increasing array of services and procedures, everything from the size of trailers hauled behind trucks to the intricacies of used-car sales. State spending for education, social services, roads, and other amenities grew. In 1941, for example, about 80 percent of Oregon homes flushed their sewage into public waterways. Thirteen years later, in 1954, just 20 percent of the state's homes remained unlinked to sewage treatment plants. Progress had its price. Oregon led the nation in tax increases from 1940 to 1950.

Oregon's Democratic Party also grew during these years. This was partly a matter of demographics. Oregon was becoming more urban and attracting residents from other states, a pair of trends that benefited the Democrats more than their Republican counterparts. By 1954 there were more registered Democrats than Republicans in Oregon.

The Democrats also profited from new leadership. Liberals captured the state party in 1952, after six years of factionalism. They set up party organizations in all but a few Oregon counties. They made the party more issue oriented and emphasized causes that many Oregonians cared about: better education, public housing, national health insurance, and public power. The rejuvenated party attracted and nurtured dynamic and popular leaders, people such as Al Ullman, Robert Holmes, Edith Green, and Richard Neuberger.

The year 1954 brought two impressive victories. Green was elected the U.S. House of Representatives, Neuberger to the U.S. Senate. They were soon joined by the irascible Senator Wayne Morse, who had left the Republican Party in 1952. Oregon's Democrats had gone four decades without a U.S. Senator. Now they held both seats.

The 1956 elections brought a breakthrough at the state level. Oregon Democrats shared power in the Senate, with each party holding fifteen seats, but had an absolute majority in the House. In the next session they controlled both houses for the first time in eighty long years. Republicans, buoyed by Mark Hatfield's classy nonpartisanship and young Bob Packwood's innovative campaign strategies, took the House back in 1965. But they would never approach the dominance they had enjoyed for the first half of the twentieth century.

By the 1960s the legislature was turning its attention to environmental issues. In 1961, inspired by the smell emanating from bottles of effluents collected from Georgia-Pacific's Newport mill, legislators granted the State Sanitary Authority the wherewithal to insist that polluters clean up the waters they had fouled. Such environmental legislation quickened several years later, when Tom McCall became governor.

Other laws also reflected the growing power of Oregon liberals. In 1965 the legislature established a minimum wage for men as well as women workers and revamped the state's workers' compensation system. In 1971 it followed California in passing a no-fault divorce law. Another piece of legislation set aside 1 percent of state highway funds for bicycle trails and paths. Watergate scandals helped Democrats to a comfortable majority in both houses in 1973, when the legislature passed Senate Bill 100, a highly controversial and innovative measure that initiated comprehensive land-use planning. Two years later, in 1975, Oregon became evidently the first state in the nation to ban chlorofluorocarbon gases that were destroying the atmosphere's ozone layer.

Oregon's Democrats returned from the dead in the decades following World War II, and the state was regaining its reputation as a progressive, path-breaking state.

Tom McCall

Probably no Oregonian—if we may discount the accomplishments and antics of figure skater Tonya Harding—has attracted as much attention to the state as Tom McCall. His ambition, charisma, and programs were crucial in forming Oregon's modern identity, inside and outside the state.

McCall's fraternity brothers at the University of Oregon laughed out loud when he told them that he would one day become president of the United States. By the early 1930s McCall seemed to be squandering a promising legacy. His grandfathers had been a prosperous, self-made Boston financier and a Massachusetts congressman. His father, smitten by Oregon while visiting wealthy Portland friends, moved his young bride to West World, a ranch near Prineville. Tom came along three years later, in 1913, and spent the first decade of his childhood moving between the opulence of his maternal grandfather's Boston mansion and a more modest Crook County home that nevertheless featured four indoor toilets. Tom was persuasive and bright, but an indifferent student. He graduated near the bottom of his class at the University of Oregon and was best known for club activities and such stunts as building a still in his fraternity's basement.

McCall's ambition and talents eventually drew him to politics. A hard drinker and gambler, he was fired from his reporting position with a Moscow, Idaho, newspaper. He then served in World War II and turned to the emerging field of broadcast journalism in Portland, where he became active in the Young Republicans. In 1949 the newly elected governor, Doug McKay, asked McCall to become his chief assistant, a job that showcased McCall's charm and speaking abilities. McCall was blindsided by the rise of Oregon's Democratic Party and lost to Green after capturing the Republican nomination for Congress in 1954. But his job with KGW, a Portland TV station, kept him in the public eye and involved with Oregon politics.

McCall emerged as the frontrunner for governor when he narrated KGW's "Pollution in Paradise," a 1962 exposé of environmental degradation that focused on the Willamette River. He pulled few punches in the broadcast, singling out large corporations such as Crown Zellerbach and Georgia-Pacific as offenders and accusing federal agencies of failing to enforce the law. His performance signaled voters that he was no hostage to the conservative wing of Oregon's Republican Party and vaulted him to the forefront of a rising tide of concern over environmental problems. In 1964, in the same election that saw Republican nominee Barry Goldwater buried in President Johnson's landslide, McCall convincingly beat his Democratic rival to become secretary of state, and two years later he beat Democrat Bob Straub handily to become the state's governor.

Once in office, McCall solidified his reputation as a reformer willing to take on wealthy Republicans. In 1967, when Oregon's beaches seemed to be in danger of becoming partially privatized, McCall leaked a letter to the press warning of "the encroachment of crass commercialism."[29] When conservative legislators countered with an offer that didn't suit him, McCall flew to Seaside and Cannon Beach with a team of scientists, surveyors, and of course reporters and camera crews to illustrate the difference between his proposal and theirs. The opposition quickly backed down, and Oregon's beaches remained public.

McCall could soon boast of several other environmental accomplishments. In 1971 he overcame intense out-of-state lobbying by powerful corporations to spearhead passage of the nation's first effective bottle bill, which served to reduce dramatically the number of cans and bottles littering Oregon. In 1972 he approved shutting down Boise Cascade's Salem pulp mill for failure to cut its emissions into the Willamette River. When angry workers confronted McCall on the capitol steps, he retorted that the plant's managers were "using you as pawns," and led them back to the plant, where company officials soon recanted their accusations. Troubled by unfettered sprawl and the paving over of fertile Willamette Valley fields by "the grasping wastrels of the land," McCall played a critical role in founding the Land Conservation and Development Commission, an agency that both created and enforced much tougher planning regulations. During the energy crisis of the early 1970s, McCall tried to convince Oregonians to consume less electricity and gas. "We've gotten careless," he warned. "We've installed all the modern conveniences, used them without regard to energy supply, and now the piper must be paid." State employees were soon working in office buildings without air conditioning and washing their hands in bathrooms without hot water. An emboldened McCall moved his campaign to the private sector by issuing an executive order banning nonessential lighting in advertising and business. McCall had no such authority, but business owners hesitated to disobey their popular governor. *Time* magazine described Portland's office towers as "abandoned hulks, their silhouettes illuminated only by a handful of office lights and the winking red beacons that warn aircraft the buildings still stand."[30] McCall boasted to a *New York Times* reporter that even his dog had caught a cold from their home's low thermostat setting.

"The Oregon Story," as Tom McCall liked to call his measures, put the state on the nation's map for the first time since the Oregon System had blossomed some seventy years before. In 1974, under the title "Where the Future Works," *Newsweek* observed that "Oregonians don't seem to have come across anything they can't handle."[31] McCall was interviewed at length by NBC and PBS and profiled in most of the nation's leading newspapers.

All of this served to conceal the many flaws of the man and the politician who left office to such widespread national acclaim early in 1975. McCall was not always a bold environmentalist. An implied promise to Glenn Jackson, a peerless force in Oregon business and politics, caused him to equivocate on whether or not to allow a highway to be built alongside a scenic beach south of Pacific City. Like many Oregon politicians before and since, he failed to revise the state's tax system. He also took criticism personally. He aspired to the U.S. Senate but could never quite muster the courage to take on Senators Morse, Hatfield, or Packwood. His memoir, *Tom McCall: Maverick*, was so disparaging of these politicians and others that one target remarked that "a class-action suit" would have ensued if everyone slandered in McCall's book had decided to sue.[32] Even obscure Oregonians who wrote letters to the editor critical of McCall might receive an irate call from the governor.

Yet to say that McCall was thin-skinned and ambitious is to imply that he was also charismatic and passionate. He became a bold politician who helped to heal or at least obscure the political, social, and cultural divisions that were driving most of the rest of the nation into separate corners. When, for example, in 1970 radical Portland activists planned a rock concert at McIver Park near Estacada, McCall's administration both sponsored it and agreed to tolerate drug use and nudity. McCall's motive for this tolerance was political: the rock concert would draw thousands of potential protestors out of downtown Portland, where twenty-five thousand members of the American Legion were meeting. Vortex, the rock concert, probably played only a minor role in helping Portland avoid violence and riot that weekend. Yet the episode burnished McCall's reputation as a different kind of politician, one who did not simply react punitively to youthful protest.

But it was McCall's invitation to "visit us again and again ... . But for heaven's sake, don't come here to live" that identified him as peculiar. The quip generated considerable heat outside and inside of Oregon, and McCall hastened to clarify that he was not opposed to new residents and new industry. "But we are not willing to take any industry at any price," he explained. "The industry must come here on our terms, play the game by our environmental rules, and be members of the Oregon family."[33] McCall's bold assertion of selectiveness sounded a chord that, once again, crossed generational and political lines, appealing both to tradition-minded Oregonians who loathed growth-happy California and Seattle and to a growing counterculture who both opposed growth for growth's sake and enjoyed having a governor who did not mind challenging the status quo.

❧ ❧

Tom McCall governed Oregon from 1967 to 1975 and bought the state eight years of relative comity at a time when most parts of the nation were riven by political and cultural disputes. He quarreled openly with the Nixon administration, the symbol of everything that disaffected youth despised about America, and took tangible, meaningful steps to preserve Oregon's environmental and social distinctiveness.

But Oregon could not stave off these forces indefinitely. Time bombs and anxieties lay beneath the surface of consensus in the 1950s. Timber companies could not keep cutting at the same rate, especially while technology continued to eliminate jobs. Protests against the established order grew more intense as the 1960s progressed, as anti-war protestors, Black radicals, feminists, communitarians, and others insisted that the American dream had gone rotten and needed a radical overhaul.

Modern Oregon's divisions were becoming too deep for even Tom McCall to bridge. In 1978, predictably restless out of office and eager to build on his legacy, he ran again for governor. He did not make it out of the Republican primary, losing to Victor Atiyeh, who ran a well-organized, pro-business campaign.

There are many reasons for McCall's defeat in 1978. His appeal to Democrats did not help him in the Republican primary, Atiyeh had much more money to work with, and McCall, buoyed by his popularity, did not work hard enough.

But McCall also lost in 1978 because the times had passed him by. Long villified by some of the state's corporate interests, he was now attacked on his left flank for not being radical enough. Environmentalists were no longer content with cleaning up litter. Developments such as nuclear power, which McCall found perfectly reasonable, drew their harsh opposition.

Disaffection with McCall's legacy grew after the election, as the state settled into a deep recession. Governor Atiyeh, amidst much fanfare, replaced the sign at the I-5 Oregon-California border that read "We Hope You Enjoy Your Visit" with "Welcome to Oregon." Oregon was now open, and desperate, for business.

Prosperity would soon return to Oregon. But prosperity would restore neither unity nor peace.

Biography

Barbara Mackenzie

Women's issues and changing roles have attracted much attention in Oregon from the 1970s to the present. But women's economic and social roles had in fact been shifting a great deal in preceding decades, though few observers seemed to notice. Barbara Mackenzie was one of many women who participated in this quiet revolution.

Barbara Mackenzie was born in 1905 to restless parents. Her father, Ezra Tudor, was an engineer whose work took the family to several parts of Oregon. Ida Jane, her mother, suffered several mental breakdowns, and she and Ezra eventually separated. Barbara ended up boarding at Portland's St. Mary's Academy, where she enjoyed "the first security I had experienced." She eventually earned a teaching degree from Monmouth's Oregon Normal School in 1926.

Her life quickly took a conventional turn. After a few months of teaching and waitressing in Deschutes County she married Thomas Mackenzie and moved to Roseburg, where Barbara and Thomas taught school. Barbara was asked to resign her teaching job when she became pregnant. The young family moved to Salem and then Santa Barbara during the Depression before returning to Oregon in 1941 so that Thomas could teach at Oregon State College.

Mackenzie was one of many Oregon wives and mothers drawn out of the home by World War II. She volunteered with the Red Cross and quickly won additional responsibilities. She became the Executive Director for Lincoln County's chapter after the war. Mackenzie was now a social worker who looked after military families whose husbands had gone overseas, helped veterans return to civilian life, and responded to local disasters.

Like other professional women of her day, Barbara moved when her husband found a better job elsewhere, this time near The Dalles. Barbara was soon working for Wasco County as a Veteran's Service and Juvenile Court Officer. It was 1952, with the construction of The Dalles Dam in full swing, and people and social problems were proliferating. The indigenous peoples of Celilo Village were especially vulnerable, as the new dam would destroy their homes and perhaps their livelihood. Mackenzie became an advocate for Native people even as she helped to relocate them. She confronted local educators who asserted that "Indians can't learn after the fourth grade" and construction workers who made no effort to preserve indigenous burial grounds or artifacts.

Barbara Mackenzie soon moved, this time to the San Francisco Bay Area, where she continued her social work until the 1980s. But, long after retirement, she recalled her work with at Celilo as "the most interesting and certainly the most varied I have ever participated in."

Barbara Mackenzie's life work attracted little public notice and acclaim. But, as her biographers point out, that work "personifies the sweeping changes that expanded nineteenth-century women's lives from the limited private sphere of home and family to a broader sphere where women claimed important public roles."[34]

Glenn Jackson

Most of the thousands of commuters who pour across the I-205 bridge between Oregon and Washington every Monday to Friday cannot tell you much about the man the bridge is named for. Yet Glenn Jackson, "Mr. Oregon," was probably the most powerful person in the state for a quarter century.

The grandchild of pioneers, Jackson was born in Albany in 1902. He was graduated from Oregon State College, married, and went to work for a utility company. He started out selling electrical appliances, rose quickly, then served as a colonel in the Air Force during World War II.

Jackson soon became wealthy. Back home in Medford he bought property north of the city and turned it into a profitable business park, White City. He engineered a merger between the California Oregon Power Company and Pacific Power & Light in 1961 and became vice chairman and eventually chairman of its board. He served on the boards of Standard Insurance, U.S. National Bank of Oregon, Fred Meyer, Western Minerals, and the U.S. Chamber of Commerce and owned several newspapers and other businesses and a great deal of land.

But it was Jackson's political work that brought him the most acclaim. Though never elected to public office, Jackson worked closely with Senator Wayne Morse, who had alienated other powerful Republican business people by leaving the party in 1952. Jackson, who routinely crossed party lines, boosted Mark Hatfield, who, upon becoming governor, made Jackson head of the state's

Highway Commission. Upon being asked if having a powerful businessman decide on the location of the state's highways might constitute a conflict of interest, Hatfield replied that Jackson "has so many conflicts they cancel each other out." No one could dispute that Jackson accomplished a lot in this position. He built seven hundred miles of interstate freeways promptly and efficiently. Congresswoman Edith Green called for an investigation to see whether Jackson had used his position to profit himself. But most powerful Oregonians respected or feared Jackson too much to tangle with him. "You had a regard for him and knew you should respond to whatever he might be asking to be done," recalled a Hatfield aid.[35]

Jackson was in many respects a moderate. Like McCall, he urged Oregonians to "get away from the old Chamber of Commerce notion that added payroll is worth any cost," and he helped create 1,000 Friends of Oregon, a group that has long frustrated developers.[36] But he also noted that "I don't think I've ever got involved in anything in my life that hasn't had a growth factor in it."[37] Like most Oregonians, Jackson wanted Oregon to both retain its natural beauty and become more prosperous.

Described by his wife as a man who "can't play," Jackson gave his time and money to scores of causes, including colleges, hospitals, and the arts.[38] Upon his death the *Oregonian* called him "Oregon's uncrowned governor" who "unabashedly used" his "power." Jackson would not have disagreed. "One thing I couldn't stand was for someone to say something couldn't be done," he remarked. "So then I'd go out and do it, just to prove the bastards were wrong."[39]

Celia D. Mariscal

Celia Dominguez arrived in Hood River in 1964, with her parents and a dozen younger siblings. They had a Chevy station wagon and a few hundred dollars to their name and planned to return soon to California.

The family got a job harvesting green beans. Then her father found a rare year-round job as a foreman on a fruit farm that enabled them to stay. They were the only Mexican family in Hood River.

Dominguez went to school during the daytime and cared for her sisters and brothers at night. At age sixteen she left high school, got her GED, and began working as a secretary with the Forest Service.

By this time large numbers of Latinos were arriving in Hood River; Dominguez became an interpreter, married Santos Mariscal, had a child, and bought a home.

In 1969, with family members, she began a long-anticipated business producing tortillas. Every night they made some thirty boxes of them. By 1972 they had quit their jobs and devoted themselves to the business. By the late 1970s they were making some $4 million a year. They eventually employed seventy people as their product spread across the western U.S.

Mariscal insisted that her ethnicity made the business distinctive not just in what it made, but in how it was run. She and the other family members in the business paid homage to their ancestors and to "Our Lady of Guadalupe." Her brothers respected her business acumen "because I am the oldest."[40]

She and her family had achieved the American dream—without ceasing to be Mexican.

Bill Naito

Just two months after Bill Naito's death in 1996 Portland renamed one if its major arteries, Front Street, after him. That's how highly the city thought of the "idiosyncratic merchant prince who," in the words of *Willamette Week* editor Mark Zusman, "did well by doing good."[41] But those successes came at a much higher private price than his many admirers realized.

Born in Portland in 1925, Naito was the second son of Japanese immigrants, or Issei, who owned a small store that sold imported goods from Japan. Pearl Harbor drove the Naitos and other Japanese-American families from the West Coast, and years later he still recalled the shame he felt emptying his locker at Portland's Washington High School.

But adversity never slowed Bill Naito for long. He joined the Army, was graduated from Reed College and then the University of Chicago, where he met his wife, Micki. In the early 1950s they moved to Portland, where Bill rejoined the family business. Bill's older brother, Sam, handled retail as Bill moved into property development in the 1960s.

Bill's timing seemed poor. Portland's core was deteriorating, with businesses and home owners alike moving to the suburbs. But Bill saw opportunity where more cautious investors predicted defeat. He began buying up run-down properties and refurbishing them.

He purchased an old building on Southwest 10th for $565,000, made $3 million of renovations, and produced the Galleria, a glittering collection of upscale shops. Neglected warehouses along the waterfront became the McCormick Pier apartments, which drew hundreds of middle-income people back to downtown. His most ambitious gambit was to borrow $25 million to purchase the Montgomery Ward warehouses in Northwest Portland, a structure that other investors viewed as a ponderous white elephant. Today the building houses stylish offices and banquet rooms. There are many other examples.

These projects, and many more, put Bill Naito at the heart of downtown Portland's revitalization. He also improved its social and cultural life. Naito chaired the county library board, spearheaded urban forestry, helped create Saturday Market, founded Artquake, and offered his time and money to many other causes. Diminutive and often shabbily dressed, Naito seemed to personify the city's understated, offbeat style.

But Bill Naito was not easy to live with or work for. Former employees recalled a boss who insisted on loyalty but was distrustful and penurious. His widow recalled Bill's business as "my white whale, my rival. It always seemed to to be more important … than me or the family."[42] While vacationing he preferred finding other people's lost golf balls to playing golf, hammering out bent dimes to relaxing on the beach.

Though he became the driving force behind Portland's Japanese American Historical Plaza, Naito was ambivalent or even hostile to his heritage for much of his life. He resented going to Japanese language school, Americanized the pronunciation of his last name, and was even known to refer to other Japanese Americans as "Japs."[43] Bill also failed to offer his older brother the respect and deference prescribed by Japanese tradition, and upon his death resentments long in the making split the family and its business.

Bill Naito's unflagging energy and determination brought to the city that had once expelled him rare gifts, but trouble and strife to the people he loved.

Chapter Nine

A Polarized State

1975-2003

" Somebody crossed over a line out there."
Tom Hirons

Tom McCall's version of the good life, the Oregon Story, offered Oregonians a compelling vision of a state in which quality of life was defined broadly, where citizens chose preservation and sustainability over evanescent riches and quick fixes. The dream has persisted, but generally only during selected periods of time and among Oregon's more privileged residents. A sharp downturn in the state's economy during the mid-1970s made the state's vaunted "livability" seem like a luxury that many Oregonians could not afford. The 1990s restored prosperity to the state and drew a blend of people who enriched its ethnic and cultural diversity. Portland gained a national reputation for doing things right, for growing and prospering without selling its soul.

But many Oregonians felt excluded from or hostile to the new Oregon. People of color still suffered from low incomes and racism. White Oregonians from Beaverton to Burns worried that Latinos were injuring their communities. A series of ballot measures designed to exclude gays and lesbians from full civil and political rights engendered angry debates and even violence, suggesting that both sexual minorities and the people who opposed them felt marginalized and threatened in modern Oregon. Controversies over whether to log the state's remaining old-growth forests also precipitated bitter disagreements.

These acrimonious debates both suggested and disguised Oregon's widening economic and social divisions. Well-educated, urban Oregonians were doing better than ever. Buoyed by an expansive and lucrative high-tech industry, the Portland metropolitan area blossomed. Those who worked on the lower rungs of the burgeoning service industry or in manufacturing were not so fortunate, especially if they lived outside the Willamette Valley. Many rural and small-town Oregonians weren't making it during Oregon's economic boom.

Political polarization ensued, as many of these residents identified taxes, government, environmentalists, homosexuals, liberals, or simply "Portland" as the cause of their decline.

Prosperity for Some

The history of the Oregon economy in the last quarter of the twentieth century was, in many respects, a tale of two states—or two components of the state. But the overall or aggregate numbers were impressive. Oregon's population surged to over 2.5 million in the 1970s, slowed during the 1980s, then spurted to nearly 3.5 million by 2000. Oregon was again growing more quickly than the nation as a whole, and people were coming to Oregon to work. The state's unemployment rate generally declined during the 1980s and 1990s and was near 4 percent by 2000.

As elsewhere, the service industry led the charge. About three Oregon workers out of ten labored in that sector by 2000. Retail passed manufacturing in the 1970s and employed nearly 18 percent of working Oregonians by 2000. Manufacturing and government jobs constituted a declining proportion of the workforce after 1970. The number of farmers grew only slightly, though the number of farm workers increased dramatically. The timber and especially fishing industries fell precipitously. The days when agriculture, timber, and other extractive industries dominated Oregon's economy were long past.

But one sort of manufacturing concern was doing very well indeed. Oregon's high-tech industry had its roots in the early postwar period, when several Portlanders developed an oscilloscope, a machine to measure electrical signals. Their company would eventually become Tektronix, and by 1954 it boasted nearly seven hundred employees and had left Portland for the expansive environs of Beaverton.

Tektronix and related companies grew dramatically in the 1970s. By the decade's end Tektronix was the state's biggest private-sector employer, and several major out-of-state concerns had moved here. Intel arrived in 1976 and soon had more than two thousand employees in Aloha. Hewlett-Packard also came that year.

This growth built on itself, attracting other companies and creating opportunities for subcontractors. The Oregon Graduate Center opened its doors in 1969, next door to Tektronix. Along with the state's public and private colleges, it trained the thousands of skilled workers that the new industry required.

Corporate offices and product engineering laboratory for Lattice Semiconductor Company, Hillsboro, about 1980. Photo courtesy of Oregon Historical Society, CN 023401

The high-tech boom brought many benefits to Oregon. By the late 1990s its more than eighteen hundred establishments employed nearly sixty thousand people. Intel alone employed around twelve thousand in 2000, Tektronix more than nine thousand. They provided tax revenues for governments, and a large fraction of their jobs paid well. These companies prompted growth in related industries, such as housing and retail. They made Oregon less subject to the boom and bust cycle of extractive industries. High-tech industries also fit Oregon's new clean image, for they did not belch smoke or mow down forests.

But high tech was no panacea. The roads of Washington County were soon choked by commuters, as the number of passenger cars rose fivefold from 1960 to 1986. The generous tax breaks offered to some companies made it difficult for local governments to provide the necessary infrastructure—roads, sewers, and schools—that Beaverton, Hillsboro, and other rapidly growing cities required. Though microchip and software manufacturers appeared to be environmentally innocuous, they often used toxic chemicals that leaked into groundwater. Nor was this industry bulletproof. In the recession of the early 1980s, for example, companies cut several thousand workers and jobs declined again later, in the 1990s, particularly those that could be done more cheaply overseas.

Most tellingly, Oregon's modern economy has exacerbated social and regional differences. Poverty and inequality alike grew in the 1980s and 1990s, even as the state's economy boomed. In 2000 the richest one percent had 17 percent of the state's income, more than twice its share in 1979. The poorest 20 percent's portion of Oregon's income fell during those twenty-one years from 1.7 to 0.6 percent. In 2002 Oregon had the highest proportion of hungry people in the nation. The fruits of prosperity have been unequally distributed. The overwhelming majority of high-tech employees, for example, worked and lived in the urban Willamette Valley, in Corvallis, Eugene, and especially in the Portland metropolitan area.

Portland as Model City

The prosperity generated by the high-tech industry was but one of many developments that blessed Portland in the late twentieth century and won for it the sobriquet "the city that works."

The renaissance began in the mid-1970s, after Neil Goldschmidt became mayor. Goldschmidt, elected at age thirty-two, was both a practical coalition builder and a visionary. He emphasized public transit, downtown planning, and stronger neighborhoods. The mix worked.

In 1974 the Portland City Council established an Office of Neighborhood Associations that fostered such grass-roots organizations. Neighborhood groups have been invited to make annual needs reports that city bureaus are required to consider when creating their budgets, and the city must notify the neighborhood associations of any anticipated zoning or other changes in land use. The plan has given city residents substantial control over their communities. A 1981 study found that poorer people and people of color were just as apt as their more privileged counterparts to participate in neighborhood associations.

During the last quarter of the twentieth century Portland leaders and residents made several choices that set the city aside from others of the U.S. West. They turned down a major highway and instead added light rail to an expansive bus system. They created perhaps the nation's most ambitious network of urban bicycle lanes. Portland commuters are therefore more apt than their counterparts in Seattle, let alone Los Angeles, to leave their cars at home. Some manage to get along without owning an automobile at all, as a "bumper" sticker declaring that "my other bicycle is a bicycle" suggests.

Goldschmidt also helped turn the tide in Portland's downtown. Portlanders began refurbishing rather than destroying its remaining historic buildings, a trend that marked the city's determination to fight for business on its own terms. Goldschmidt talked some retailers into staying, or even moving in: J. C. Penney, Nordstrom's, and Meier and Frank. Bill and Sam Naito created the Galleria, an indoor shopping mall on the west edge of downtown. Office buildings sprouted. So did public spaces: the Forecourt (now Ira Keller) Fountain, Pioneer Courthouse Square, and the sprawling Tom McCall Waterfront Park along the Willamette River's west bank. Downtown Portland became a place to work, shop, attend cultural events, and to relax.

Portland's residential areas have also flourished, and for much the same reason as its downtown. They offer amenities that cannot be created from scratch. Much of the city has a traditional feel. Although nondescript buildings materialized in the 1960s and 1970s, Portland's growth has been more gradual than most twentieth-century western cities, and it therefore possesses scores of quaint apartment buildings and thousands of older homes graced with inviting front porches and surrounded by stately trees. Homeowners can get more house for their money in the suburbs, but are willing to pay extra for the feel of what real estate agents like to call "old Portland": original glass doorknobs, box-beam ceilings, and a strong sense of community that manifests itself at neighborhood association meetings, block parties, and

Tri-Met's light-rail train, MAX, in downtown Portland. Photo courtesy of Oregon Historical Society, CN 019560

progressive dinners. Planners favor high-density housing, with small lots. Single-family, infill dwellings therefore tend to be two or three stories, and of modest width. Diverse businesses line the major streets of many neighborhoods, enabling residents to eat, drop off their dry cleaning, and shop for groceries, clothes, a bewildering and expensive variety of coffees and juices, and a host of more specialized items ranging from cockatoos to vibrators—all within a few blocks of their front door. Portland's crime rate is lower than most cities', and many neighborhoods have a lot of sidewalk traffic, a sense of shared public space. Portlanders tend to be active in local political, social, and cultural affairs. A very high proportion of its children attend public schools. Market analysts report that Portlanders rank near the top in buying products related to gardening, natural foods, and the outdoors. Powell's immense "city of books," the nation's largest bookstore and "Portland's living room," is the most obvious manifestation of Portlanders' interest in the printed word.

There has, however, been an underside to Portland's vaunted livability. It is pricey. Downtown revitalization has been great for well-heeled shoppers, but a disaster for low-income residents, who have lost thousands of housing units since the 1970s. Renters and homeowners on fixed incomes have found it more and more difficult to pay their rent or property taxes as a seemingly inevitable succession of artists, Starbucks coffee shops, and young, often childless professionals have moved into and gentrified trendy neighborhoods such as Hawthorne and Irvington. By the late 1990s many neighborhoods along Martin Luther King Boulevard or Alberta Street in northeast Portland were becoming more desirable for the city's white majority, but less affordable for low-income, largely African-American residents who had made their homes there.

Many parts of Portland and the Portland metropolitan area, furthermore, remained or became decidedly untrendy and unattractive. The gentrification of inner Portland moved prostitution and drug dealing eastward, along Sandy Boulevard, into such places as Parkrose. Much of the city's eastern fringe consisted of gritty apartment complexes interspersed with tedious strip malls. Here a mixture of low-income transplants from rural Oregon, Latin America, and Russia have struggled to carve out a piece of the American dream—and to oppose many of the expensive projects championed by Portland's liberal establishment.

Nor has Portland's renaissance healed the breaches between city and suburbs. Residents of Beaverton and West Linn have had fewer and fewer reasons to go downtown. Historian Carl Abbott refers to

Washington Square's great concentration of goods and services in Tigard as the outer city's "rainproof main street."[1] But Metro (the regional decision-making body first known as the Metropolitan Service District) has continued to frustrate suburban people and companies by favoring public transit over new highways and high-density housing over continued sprawl.

The shortage of affordable homes on large lots in or near Portland led to the creation of new bedroom communities. Sherwood and St. Helens grew dramatically in the 1990s as commuters went farther and farther afield in search of low mortgage payments and the amenities of what they hoped would be small-town living, though not a few long-time residents worried that the newcomers were destroying the very qualities that they sought. Jeff VanNatta of Columbia County put it this way in 1998: "They work in Portland, they shop in Portland, and they drive home and they complain about the roads."[2] The Portland area's economic boom even began to transform the north coast in the 1990s, as increasing numbers of well-heeled urbanites spawned a wave of high-end shops and restaurants in Cannon Beach and elsewhere. This shift, coupled with continued job losses in the timber and fishing industries, helped tilt Clatsop, Tillamook, and Lincoln counties leftward politically—and generated resentment among many locals, in spite or because of the infusion of Portland dollars.

For many low-income people outside and inside the city, the new, prosperous Portland represents the abuses of power and privilege.

The Browning of Oregon

Racial divisions have accompanied and exacerbated class divisions in Oregon's recent history.

Oregon is well on its way to becoming a diverse state. Few would have predicted so in 1960, when African Americans, Native Americans, and Asian Americans combined to constitute just 2 percent of the state's population. But by 1990 people of color (including Latinos) made up more than 9 percent of the state's residents. A decade later their numbers had doubled, growing much more quickly than their white counterparts were. People of color constituted over 15 percent of Oregon's population in 2000.

Numbers of Latinos grew most quickly. By 1980 they had become the state's most populous minority, with more than sixty-five thousand people—not counting those missed by census takers. Two decades later their numbers had increased to over 275,000. They were concentrated in the lower Willamette Valley, in Washington, Multnomah, and Marion counties. But their growth was most striking and noticeable in less populated areas. More than two thousand Latinos lived in Lincoln County at the turn of the century. They constituted about 10 percent of Newport's population. One in four of the residents of eastern Oregon's Morrow County was Latino by 2000.

Oregon's Latinos were becoming more diverse. People of Mexican descent were joined by emigrants from South and especially Central America. Many newcomers worked in agriculture, but others moved into construction or the service industry. These recent immigrants joined second- and third-generation Chicanos whose parents or grandparents had come to Oregon in the mid-twentieth century. Many Latinos live in poverty. But increasing numbers are well-educated and prosperous.

Oregonians with Asian or Pacific Island ancestors were also growing more numerous and diverse. Their numbers swelled by 75 percent during the 1990s. They made up 3.5 percent of Oregon's population at the turn of the century, up from under 1 percent in 1960. Some three out of four lived in the Portland metropolitan area. Indeed, they made up 7 and 8 percent of Multnomah and Washington counties' population, respectively.

Oregon's Asian Americans had become extremely diverse. Japanese Americans remained the majority only in a few pockets of eastern Oregon by 2000. Many people of Chinese, Vietnamese, Korean, and Filipino descent were making themselves at home in Oregon, together with Cambodians and Laotians. Many of Oregon's Asian Americans identify themselves as multiracial.

African Americans and Native Americans expanded more slowly than their Latino and Asian-American counterparts, though still much more rapidly than the population as a whole. Blacks numbered over sixty-three thousand by 2000, up from just over eighteen thousand four decades before. Nearly two thirds lived in Portland, though the termination of explicit housing discrimination enabled many to disperse across the metropolitan area. Native Americans also continued to grow more numerous, in part because many people of mixed heritage chose to identify themselves as Indian. Most of Oregon's indigenous peoples lived in or near Portland, Salem, or Eugene, though several thousand remained on reservations.

The rapid expansion of people of color in Oregon suggested that the state's tradition of racial exclusion and segregation was crumbling. So did the growing number of Oregonians identifying themselves as multiracial: more than one hundred thousand by 2000, or some 3

*Dancers from La Amistad Youth Center in Independence
open the program at Terry Schrunk Plaza, Portland, for
National Hispanic Week, 1981. Photo courtesy of Oregon
Historical Society, OrHi 85258*

percent of the state's population. This category included a very broad
range of people, from light-skinned men and women who had a
grandparent of Mexican descent to people deemed African Americans
who also acknowledged their Native American or European ancestry.

More and more Oregon minorities have become educated and
prosperous. Approximately two thousand Latino businesses operated
in Oregon by 1990. More Blacks than ever before were graduating from
high school and college, running successful businesses, entering
lucrative professions, and joining the middle class. The same can be
said for Native Americans, and unemployment rates have dropped
even on Oregon's reservations. The incomes and graduation rates of
some Asian-American groups has approached or exceeded the state's
average.

Yet a disproportionate number of Oregon's people of color are
poorly educated and in poverty. A state study published in 1990 found
that the state's many seasonal Latino workers had high accident rates
and commonly lived in crowded conditions and were exposed to
noxious pesticides. A 2000 study found that Oregon's African
Americans, Latinos, and Native Americans were about twice as likely
to live in poverty as their white counterparts. More than one in four
lived below the poverty line. Some 44 percent of African-American

children dropped out of high school. About one half of Portland's Blacks remained concentrated in six census tracts, where poverty and crime rates exceeded the city's average. Unemployment for Native Americans remained high: about 20 percent at the Umatilla Reservation. It was 56 percent for the Klamath in 1989.

Escaping racism proved to be more difficult than escaping poverty.

Many of Oregon's people of color report feeling out of place here. Oregon is still homogeneous, at least compared to most other parts of the U.S. Portland, the state's melting pot, was the nation's whitest metropolis late in the century. African Americans who arrive from more diverse cities are often shocked by the sea of white faces that confront them in most of the city. They also find that Portland's white liberals tend to avoid talking about race and racism—beyond denying that it is a problem here.

Mexican Americans and other Latinos, who possess a distinctive and much-prized culture of their own, also feel pressured to acculturate in Oregon. In 1980 several Mexican-American mothers shared their fears that Lane County schools were teaching their children to be overly individualist and competitive. "When people do not know how to get along with others, to share and be part of a group, who are they going to turn to?" asked one.[3] Disagreements have also broken out over language. Latinos have been ejected from Oregon taverns for using their native tongue. Oregon's courts denied business owners such rights, and in 1989 the State Legislature passed a resolution asserting: "That the use of diverse languages in business, government, and private affairs, and the presence of diverse cultures is welcomed, encouraged and protected in Oregon."[4] Yet English-only advocates argue that bilingualism ought to be discouraged.

Oregon's minorities continue to suffer from direct expressions of racism. People of color relate a broad and saddening range of indignities, from being ignored at restaurants to enduring racial epithets to being stopped by police for "driving while Black" to physical threats and assaults. An African-American pastor at Cottage Grove's Methodist church left in 1992 because her life and property had been threatened.

White Oregonians have long discouraged Blacks and other people of color from living here, and many remain uncomfortable with the state's growing diversity. "I saw my first black person in town twelve years ago," remarked a Cottage Grove resident in the 1990s. "You gotta stare when that happens," she added.[5] In 2000 white visitors to Hillsboro's Washington County Fair were disturbed to find themselves, at least temporarily, in the minority. Hillsboro—like Newport, Burns,

Salem, and innumerable other Oregon towns—had been virtually all white not that long before. Most white Oregonians who lived outside selected pockets of north and northeast Portland saw people of color only occasionally, if at all. But now, in a growing number of moments and places, from county fairs to convenience stores, white Oregonians were the ones outnumbered.

Many Oregonians, to be sure, applauded racial diversity. Indeed, many people were drawn to inner Portland's eclectic—by Oregon standards—blend of cultures, ethnicities, and sexual orientations. But Oregonians who elected to stay put or to move in search of an old Oregon of traditional values and a homogeneous society have been more alarmed than delighted by the state's transformation, especially when Latinos or interracial couples have shown up not in faraway Portland, but next door.

White supremacy groups have drawn only a small fraction of Oregonians. Southeast Portland was home to a group of explicitly racist skinheads in the 1980s who attacked and, in one instance, killed people of color. Racism typically expressed itself more subtly. Oregon's growing ethnic diversity has contributed to white traditionalists' sense of unease, their fear that the state is becoming an alien environment where their privileges and assumptions will be challenged.

Battle Lines: The Environment

High-profile protests over racism and other injustices declined in Oregon after the early 1970s. The Black Panthers disappeared. The Vietnam War wound down, as did the immense marches in opposition to it. Hippies seemed less numerous, youth more conservative.

Yet a growing array of radical and reform groups continued to work at transforming Oregon politics and society, though their goals became more modest and less millennial. College campuses housed scores of eclectic organizations: recyclers, Black and Latino student unions, women's centers, and many, many more. Green Party and Socialist candidates did not come close to winning any major elections, but they did much better in Oregon than in most of the rest of the nation in the 1990s. Communes persisted or appeared. Homeless people organized. So did many gays and lesbians. Feminist organizations shifted from consciousness raising to creating and maintaining an impressive network of services for survivors of domestic violence and rape. African Americans, Latino farm workers, and other people of color continued advocating for full civil rights and economic opportunities, though now they were more likely to work within or in cooperation with the system than had their more militant counterparts of the 1960s. A small but determined group of white anarchists in Eugene and Portland, on the other hand, cultivated conflict with authorities by the late 1990s.

Most Oregonians were only vaguely aware of these movements. Environmentalists constituted the exception.

Oregonians had been concerned with the preservation of the state's scenic areas and salmon runs since the late nineteenth century. By the late 1960s, however, environmentalists had become both more focussed and more numerous. Some fifteen hundred or more gathered in Eugene in 1969 to protest the logging of the French Pete Wilderness.

The movement to save Oregon's remaining old-growth forests had been part of the mosaic of causes in the late sixties. In the 1970s it became *the* cause for many Oregonians.

The movement began a string of impressive victories in 1978. The Endangered American Wilderness Act created seventeen wilderness areas, and some one third of the acreage was in Oregon, including the hotly contested French Pete watershed. The Oregon Wilderness Coalition, which soon changed its name to the Oregon Natural Resources Council (ONRC), played a key role in passing that legislation.

The environmental movement became more powerful and radical in the 1980s. Earth First! appeared, with its slogan: "No Compromise in the Defense of Mother Earth." In 1983 some activists blocked logging near the boundary of southern Oregon's Kalmiopsis Wilderness. Meanwhile, the ONRC had become dismayed with the more cautious, conciliatory approach of the Sierra Club. It joined with Earth First! in a pioneering 1983 lawsuit to halt logging in roadless areas administered by the Forest Service. Local radicals helped by removing survey stakes from an old-growth forest of Port Orford cedar, which stalled the building of a logging road until Congress intervened by creating wilderness areas of 853,000 acres.

Most of this activism sprang from a strong if intangible sense of connection to forested wilderness, from a conviction that the small fraction of remaining old growth ought to be preserved, regardless of the economic consequences. But science, long the handmaiden of the forestry industry, was beginning to add its voice to these less tangible concerns. Biologists began to study forests as ecosystems rather than as plantations for pumping out a stream of Douglas firs and ponderosa pines. "Nature designed Pacific Northwest forests to live 500-1200 years," wrote Chris Maser, a former employee of the

Bureau of Land Management, in 1988. "We are designing a forest that may seldom live 100 years."[6] Maser and other biologists argued that the Pacific Northwest's old-growth forests (made up of trees of varying species and ages, living and dead) nurtured a rich, complex, and unique ecosystem of animals, insects, and other plants, that scientists were only beginning to understand. To clear-cut the region's remaining ancient forests, to turn them into homogeneous and sterile tree plantations, was to commit ecological genocide and to invite unforeseeable, perhaps catastrophic, biological consequences.

The northern spotted owl emerged as the poster child in the battle for Oregon's ancient forests. Researchers found that this endangered bird could flourish only in large tracts of old growth. Federal law stipulated that economic activity that threatened endangered species could be halted and that federal foresters were required to maintain "viable populations" of vertebrates in national forests.[7] Environmentalists had science and law on their side. Their lawsuits could save forests from the chainsaws. In 1989 a federal judge ruled that logging in forests inhabited by the owl must stop until the Forest Service created a plan to preserve the bird's habitat. Pacific Northwest lawmakers and the Bush administration tried to override such

Clearcuts like this one in the Oregon Coast Range outraged and mobilized many Oregonians. Photo courtesy of Oregon Historical Society, CN 006067

decisions. But environmentalists, aided by money from the Sierra Club Legal Defense Fund, now had more than emotion and aesthetics on their side.

President Clinton's 1993 Northwest Forest Conference in Portland brought national attention to the region's old-growth forests. The administration eventually sought a compromise that protected about two thirds of the region's remaining ancient forests, though it would allow thinning and salvage logging even there. But environmentalists often succeeded in blocking, with lawsuits and bodies, many of these cuts. Liberals donated money, radicals sat in trees. Alarm over logging grew with concerns about the viability of Columbia River salmon, whose habitats had been ravaged by poor logging practices and dams. Economic concerns over the decline of logging receded during the decade's prosperity—and as newcomers with no ties to the timber industry poured into Oregon.

These developments added up to many defeats for the state's timber industry. Logging on the state's extensive federal lands shrank dramatically during the 1990s.

Oregon's environmental movement coincided with hard times for the timber industry. Employment had been declining for years by the mid-1970s. Then it plummeted. Mill closures in and around Coos Bay threw more than a thousand out of work at the decade's close. The industry recovered somewhat but then sank late in the 1980s and throughout the 1990s, as timber from federal lands virtually dried up. More than 152 mills closed from 1980 to 1991. In 1988 about sixty-nine thousand people worked in the forest industry. Eleven years later, in 1999, there were just forty-nine thousand. Oregon's economy had by this time diversified, so the decline impacted the state's overall economy less dramatically than previous contractions had. But to residents of timber-dependent communities in Lane, Coos, Douglas, Lincoln, and other counties, the last twenty-five years of the twentieth century were a series of economic disasters.

Timber workers and especially loggers have seldom viewed their jobs as just another way to make a living. A sociologist who worked as a choker setter for a small operation on the Oregon-California border in the early 1980s repeatedly heard co-workers proclaim that logging "gets in your blood."[8] Timber workers also tended to strongly identify with their communities. Many had been born and raised in the towns they worked in. To leave town was to leave home. Shannon Chamness left Coos Bay to work in another Georgia-Pacific mill so that she could keep her income up. But: "I hated Springfield. I hated the people. I hated the town. I hated the mill."[9] She quit her job so that she could come home, where she worked for $3.35 an hour washing dishes. Most of the people who lost their jobs found other ones. But few of them paid as well. "This means not buying a new Ford every two years, not taking your family on vacation in the camper" explained a Cottage Grove resident.[10] Many older workers simply could not find other jobs. Coos Bay's Harold "Cardy" Walton, who had been working in the industry for more than forty years, summed up how mill closures affected his generation: "Losing their cars, losing their homes. People with their homes almost paid for. No way to finish it. ... Forcing the older people into early retirement, taking a reduced pension. Trying to survive."[11] For thousands of rural and small-town Oregonians, the good life ended when the mills shut down.

The loss of thousands of high-paying jobs devastated Oregon's many timber-dependent communities. All sorts of businesses, save taverns and pawn shops, lost money and closed. School budgets fell along with timber revenues. More and more wives went to work outside the home, usually in low-paying jobs as service or clerical workers. Masculine unemployment often brought violence and divorce. Many families moved away, separating children from their grandparents and sundering lifelong friendships. Drug use and other signs of malaise grew.

The Pacific Northwest's timber industry declined for many reasons. The most obvious was a shortage of timber. In the 1950s and 1960s, as described in Chapter Eight, Oregon's timber companies cut their lands at an unsustainable rate. The piper had to be paid. Much of the postwar boom had been fuelled by publicly owned timber, but these forests were also growing more scarce and, by the 1980s, restricted. The Pacific Northwest's timber industry also found that it was no longer the "Persian Gulf of Timber." Products from British Columbia and a rejuvenated Southeast penetrated its markets. Oregon's timber industry also continued to be buffeted by factors endemic to any extractive industry: fluctuations in demand. Companies turned to mechanization and, at times, the export of raw logs to maximize profits and stay in business. But these measures cost jobs in Oregon.

The thousands of loggers and mill workers thrown out of work in the late 1980s usually focused their ire on just one of these many interlocking factors: the northern spotted owl. For more nuanced environmentalists, saving spotted owls was not primarily an end in itself. The bird was an indicator species, a canary in a coal mine whose extinction would signal the disappearance of a forest containing thousands of interdependent organisms whose relationships and even identities remained obscure. But such subtleties were lost in most public debates of the issue, which boiled down to "jobs versus owls."

By the spring of 1989 yellow ribbons bloomed on automobile antennae across rural and small-town Oregon as timber workers, their neighbors, and sympathizers argued that people were more important than birds. "My husband took a $12,000 drop in wages," reported a tearful woman at a Lebanon meeting. "How am I going to feed my unborn child? I deserve food on my plate, not an owl." In May 1989 more than two hundred log and chip trucks paraded through Hood River, one bearing a sign reading: "Eat an owl, save the economy!"[12] Loggers began wearing baseball caps proclaiming: "I LIKE SPOTTED OWLS FRIED."[13]

The movement brought friction to many of Oregon's small communities. Rural environmentalists were harassed. Store owners who did not show sufficient enthusiasm for the yellow-ribbon campaign were boycotted.

The spotted owl controversy illustrated for many rural and small-town Oregonians that urbanites neither understood nor cared about them. Trucker Stanley Norman blamed Bay-Area Californians for blocking logging: "They're not getting hurt. They're getting a point across. They're creating problems." Ralph Pendleson, another Grants Pass resident, concurred, asserting that environmental activists "are getting paid for it. It's just something to get in someone's way, I guess. Cause a ruckus and try to get their way."[14] Timber workers and their sympathizers perceived themselves as "realists in a naive world" overpopulated by environmentalists, government employees, and urbanites who did not realize where their houses, books, and toilet paper came from.[15] Such people, summarizes Beverly Brown, viewed prosperous newcomers and environmentalists in much the same way as they looked at the heads of timber companies: "people with more education, money, and powerful connections who would impose their will on the local working-class community, even when their lives might be torn apart by the consequences."[16]

The jobs-versus-owls controversy will be with us for a long time. Feelings, to be sure, died down in the 1990s. The yellow ribbons faded after another round of mill closures ran its course. Many former timber workers moved away, retired, or found jobs as truckers or builders, or in some corner of the growing service industry. But, early in the new millennium, Oregonians are far from agreed on how Oregon's forests ought to be managed. Rural and small-town Oregonians still feel betrayed by their urban, more educated counterparts.

Battle Lines: Homosexuality

Gay rights displaced owls and old-growth forests as the lightning rod for Oregon's rural/urban tensions in the 1990s. This time, however, Oregon's culture wars would be framed in religious rather than environmental terms.

The state has long been one of the nation's most secular, with a low proportion of church members. But in Oregon and across the nation many people turned to fundamentalist churches during the economically and culturally tumultuous decades of the late twentieth century. Membership in Pentecostal, Assembly of God, Foursquare, and nondenominational churches grew as mainline Protestant congregations—Episcopalians, Methodists, Presbyterians, and the United Church of Christ—aged and shrank.

Oregon's fundamentalist Christians began flexing their political muscle in the 1980s. The state's leading Republicans, as we have seen, had been moderates: Charles McNary and Mark Hatfield were often left of center. Tom McCall was perhaps more popular with Democrats than with Republicans. Bob Packwood was the most visible of many Republican politicians who favored abortion rights. Fundamentalists, including ex-hippie Lon Mabon, formed the Oregon Citizens Alliance and tried to capture the Republican Party in the late 1980s. They opposed state-aided preschools, parental leave, and state divestment from companies that did business in South Africa. None of these issues resonated with conservative evangelicals like homosexuality did. The OCA soon, in the words of sociologist Arlene Stein, "swarmed shopping malls and churches calling Christian believers to arms."[17] Thousands of Oregonians responded by joining the organization and writing checks to it.

The OCA argued that Oregon, like the nation as a whole, had made a wrong turn away from God and its political traditions. "Teen rebellion, drug abuse, promiscuity, pregnancy, and suicide all continue to rise," asserted Mabon in 1989, as did abortion, divorce, taxes, government, pornography, and homosexuality. Free enterprise, private property, family values, the right to life, and the nation's Judeo-Christian heritage were besieged. Why? Because of the pernicious spread of "atheistic, humanistic liberalism," an "anti-God, anti-American, anti-Family philosophy."[18]

The OCA was not especially hopeful of getting sinful Oregonians to repent. It intended to elect people and pass laws. In 1990 it ran a candidate for governor who probably drew enough votes from

Republican moderate and pro-choice Dave Frohnmayer to put Democrat Barbara Roberts into office. Indeed, Republicans like Frohnmayer were becoming scarce. The OCA's deputy director was soon chair of the state's Republican Central Committee. Oregon's old-guard, centrist Republicans no longer controlled the party.

But if the OCA had turned the state's Republicans toward pro-life, the state as a whole remained unconvinced. Voters decisively defeated the alliance's 1990 ballot measure to ban abortion.

Oregonians were more receptive to anti-gay initiatives. In 1988 voters approved an OCA-sponsored ballot measure rescinding Governor Neil Goldschmidt's edict forbidding discrimination on the basis of sexual orientation in Oregon's executive branch. Oregon's Supreme Court overturned the legislation, but the OCA had found a winning issue. The group returned in 1992 with an ambitious ballot measure that would amend the state's constitution to declare that homosexuality was "abnormal, wrong, unnatural, and perverse" and that those who practiced it should therefore not be entitled to minority status or protections. The precise import of the proposed law was vague and contested, yet far reaching. Gays and lesbians who were discriminated against by employees or landlords would have no recourse. Oregon's public educators would be enjoined to condemn homosexuality if they discussed it.

Ballot Measure 9 generated a great deal of opposition. The state's leading newspapers and elected officials—including Senator Hatfield, an evangelical Christian—opposed it. Thousands of Oregonians, gay and straight, organized against the measure, and they outspent the OCA by a margin of six to one.

Yet Ballot Measure 9 won 44 percent of the vote. It also illustrated Oregon's deepening political divide. Homes, businesses, and not a few people along and around Hawthorne Boulevard, in Southeast Portland, became veritable thickets of "No on 9" signage. Multnomah County voters turned back the proposal by a more than three-to-one margin. But their counterparts in many eastern Oregon counties favored the measure two to one.

The OCA, cheered by the measure's strong showing, quickly returned to the fray in 1993. Its mailing list swelled to 265,000. It proposed equivalents to Measure 9 in counties and cities that had backed the initiative, and won in elections in Josephine, Douglas, Linn, and Klamath counties, and in Junction City and Canby. Oregon's legislature and courts voided the new legislation. The OCA persisted. In 2000 it asked the state's voters to prevent educators from discussing homosexuality or bisexuality "in a manner which encourages, promotes, or sanctions such behavior." Voters narrowly defeated the measure, which was much more moderate in its scope and language than the 1992 initiative.

The OCA seemed spent after this defeat. More than a decade of intense organizing and politicking had not made a dent in Oregon's statutes. Indeed, the campaign emboldened many of Oregon's gay and lesbian residents to "come out" to family members and coworkers. A Portland resident raised in a "very, very Catholic family" wrote some one hundred family members: "The reason for this letter is that many people say they don't know any homosexuals. Well, if you didn't know any before, now you do!"[19] This is not to minimize the hardships, emotional and tangible, that the OCA's campaigns have inflicted on such Oregonians. But these people and their communities proved to be resilient and enduring.

One of the ironies of Oregon's contentious debate over homosexuality is that the OCA did best where gays and lesbians had the lowest profile. The campaign resonated with rural and small-town Oregonians for whom homosexuality represented a cluster of often inchoate fears and resentments over the direction in which their state was headed. The one dozen Cottage Grove residents who attended a 1993 OCA meeting complained about much more than gays and lesbians: divorce, decrepit schools, bureaucratic requirements for building, and, as one woman put it, the fact that "men didn't know how to be men anymore."[20]

Cottage Grove's conservatives blamed these troubles on outsiders. "There are lots of people moving here," asserted a local pastor. "Gay people are coming in, and they're gonna try to propagate themselves. People from Asia, who are nonbelievers, people with a New Age mentality, who believe they've lived two or three lives." "'Special rights,'" explains sociologist Stein, "symbolized what happened when arriviste groups—hippies, environmentalists, Californians, racial minorities, lesbians and gays, and elites—were permitted to freely stake out political and cultural claims and make demands upon the state, driving up taxes and regulations, and taking rights and privileges from their rightful owner: the good, upstanding citizens of" Cottage Grove.[21]

Yet the OCA's campaign seemed only to widen and create social breaches. Cottage Grove merchants who opposed the OCA lost business. A group of high school boys wore necklaces sporting figures dangling from nooses with the words "kill fags" written on them.[22] The son of a lesbian who wore a pro-gay campaign button was routinely attacked—verbally and physically.

Cottage Grove's volatile social relations eased over time. Many conservatives once attracted to the OCA became distressed by how divided and hostile their city had become and backed away. Alarm over gay rights waned later in the decade, in Cottage Grove and in Oregon.

But, like the battle between environmentalists and loggers, the conditions that had spawned the furor remained. An OCA activist in Cottage Grove had asserted that "protecting gay rights is analogous to protecting the spotted owl."[23] This was to say that gay people and owls were doing more than fine on their own, without any help from government, that hard-working, tradition-minded Oregonians, not owls or transsexuals, were the endangered species struggling to stave off extinction.

The Hidden Divider: Class

The notion that Cottage Grove or Grants Pass was in danger of being overrun by gays and lesbians was, on the face of it, absurd. But OCA sympathizers were not really thinking about marginal old queens whom they could easily laugh off. A 1992 publication warned Oregonians that "homosexuals" constituted a *rich class* demanding 'special rights.'"[24] Gays, then, represented an economic and political as well as a moral threat, and anti-gay rhetoric expressed, if obliquely, rural and small-town Oregonians' resentment over their declining fortunes.

☐ <7.5%	▨ 12.5–14.9%	■ 20.0–22.4%
☐ 7.5–9.9%	■ 15.0–17.4%	■ 22.5–24.9%
☐ 10.0–12.4%	■ 17.5–19.9%	■ ≥ 25.0 %

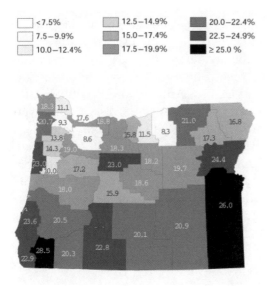

This 1997 map shows the percentage of people under eighteen in poverty in Oregon counties. Image reproduced from Atlas of Oregon, Second Edition *courtesy of the University of Oregon Press. © 2001 University of Oregon Press*

In 1969 the Oregon counties with the highest average median incomes were Washington, Multnomah, and Clackamas, the Portland metropolitan area. The seven lowest were located outside the Willamette Valley. Five were in eastern Oregon.

These regional gaps grew. By 1999 residents of the three metropolitan counties again led the state, with per capita incomes of between $31,500 and $32,200. All seven of Oregon's poorest counties were east of the Cascades. Gilliam County residents made an average of $11,500 in 1999, Sherman County's $12,000. That was a very wide gap. The percentage of people living below the poverty line was just 6.4 and 6.7 in Clackamas and Washington counties, respectively, but 19.6 in eastern Oregon's Malheur and 18.7 in southern Oregon's Josephine. More than a quarter of the latter two counties' children lived in poverty in 1997. Unemployment figures told much the same story. Rates tended to be low in the Willamette Valley, high outside it. Average unemployment exceeded 10 percent in Grant, Wheeler, and Wallowa counties during the 1990s, about twice the state's overall rate.

Political cleavages, as we have seen, mirrored these economic divides. Eastern Oregonians were much more likely to express alarm over homosexuality than were Portlanders. The yellow-ribbon campaign of the late 1980s and early 1990s swept small, timber-dependent communities and caused hardly a ripple in metropolitan Oregon. A 1994 measure to restrict the hunting of bears and cougars won 65 percent of Multnomah County votes, 30 percent or less of the votes in nine eastern Oregon counties. The 2000 ballot measure to require the state to compensate property owners for zoning and land-use planning regulations that lowered the value of the property also fared best in eastern Oregon and failed only in Benton, Multnomah, and Lane counties, home to Oregon's three largest universities.

The political and economic divide was local as well as regional, particularly in southern Oregon. Distinctive newcomers began arriving in and around such places as Ashland and Roseburg in the 1970s. Some, as we have seen, were communalists. Many were determined to live semi-subsistence lifestyles in a region where land was cheap and the winters mild. The old guard did not exactly welcome these "hippies," but the clashes were more cultural than economic. Then a larger and more powerful contingent arrived, so-called "equity migrants" who brought small fortunes gained from selling their homes in California. They bought or built spacious homes, often in the country. Southern Oregon's urban and rural landscapes became gentrified.

Displacement accompanied gentrification. The newcomers tended to be well educated, highly skilled, and confident. They took active roles in local politics, challenging and shouldering aside established leaders. They assumed well-paying jobs once filled by residents of long standing. Their arrival of course drove up the price of housing. This trend was exacerbated by the impact of state land-use regulations that made it increasingly difficult to live and build on small pieces of rural land but offered tax breaks to people with enough money to buy ten- or twenty-acre parcels. The rural commons shrank as property owners became more suspicious. "The land-based informal economy of firewood and plant gathering, gardening, hunting, poaching, fishing, low-income home construction, and free leisure use of the woods was transformed," Beverly Brown notes.[25]

John Darling, who came to Ashland in the early 1970s, in 2001 catalogued the differences between the first set of migrants and the second. "In the '70s," he recalls, "you had to pay a price to be here. … You found ways to survive. You gardened a little here, taught a college class there, gave a seminar, fixed bikes, did a gig on your guitar." Then, in the 1980s, growth-minded leaders got "the word out" to the "overrun, sprawled-out, megapriced megacities to the south." Ashland moved up the best-town lists and ceased to be a special place. "Ghastly trophy homes with … too many bedrooms began attaching themselves to the upper periphery of Ashland like a bathtub ring."[26] Backyards and orchards disappeared. Neighbors stopped talking to each other. People who had moved to Ashland because it was unique found that it had stopped being so—and that they could no longer afford to live there, anyway.

Like most jeremiads, Darling's was overdrawn. But there was no denying that life in Ashland had become very different—and more expensive.

Bend underwent a similar transformation. Its first boom had been decidedly blue-collar. In the 1910s two great timber companies began logging and milling central Oregon's expansive stands of ponderosa pines. Tourism—camping and fishing, then skiing—attracted vacationists early in Bend's history, but remained a secondary employer. Then tourism took off in the late twentieth century, fed by Mt. Bachelor, Oregon's most popular ski area, and some of the state's leading resorts: Sunriver, Black Butte Ranch, and Eagle Crest. Bend drew wealthy retirees or younger millionaires looking for a second home in a beautiful, outdoor setting. "I earn my living in Southeast Asia, the Mideast, wherever," commented a well-paid consultant. "I want Bend to be my playground."[27]

As in Ashland, the gentrification of Bend has left many people behind. Most jobs in the ascendant tourist industry pay much less than the shrinking ones in the timber industry. The service industry employs many more convenience-store attendants earning minimum wage than aroma therapists charging $50.00 an hour. Traffic has become heavy, housing expensive. Local cynics refer to life in Bend as "poverty with a view."

The contrast between residents with modest incomes and well-to-do newcomers and tourists has been strongest in and around Ashland, Bend, and affluent communities on the Oregon coast such as Cannon Beach. But more pedestrian communities have also been affected. The *New York Times* reported in 1998 that class war had come even to the tiny southeastern Oregon town of French Glen. Missy Litchy, who in three years had "transformed the local general store into an upscale tourist shop and a bed and breakfast," did not see eye to eye with Josh Warburton, who operated an R.V. park that catered to hunters. Warburton and other longtime residents worried that Litchy was attracting anti-ranching environmentalists to the area, and they were put off when she staged a champagne brunch that competed with Warburton's annual pancake feed. They also wondered why she stopped selling things that people needed, like canned goods, in favor of "curios and jewelry and all that kind of stuff."[28] In Cottage Grove and other small cities pricey latte shops rub shoulders with hardware and gun stores, and department stores have become scarce.

The new and the old, the upper middle class and the working class, often viewed each other with suspicion. Cottage Grove Presbyterians referred to the town's evangelical congregations as "parking lot churches" in which, as one architect sniffed, "you don't even need a degree to get up and preach." The conservatives gave as good as they got. One charged the liberal congregation with "trying to do a lot of social work with pedophiles, child molesters, alcoholics, and people we don't need in our community."[29]

These sorts of pronouncements tended to confirm liberals in their own prejudices about the ignorance and bigotry of Oregon's rural conservatives. That Grant County voters in 2002 passed a ballot measure banning the United Nations from its environs out of fear that it was conspiring to confiscate residents' lands and guns and impose an alien system of education did not exactly challenge well-educated, urban Oregonians' unflattering stereotypes of folks living east of the mountains.

But Oregon's regional divide is economic as well as cultural. Environmentalists, gays, lesbians, and the United Nations all represent outsiders, people thought not to understand or care about rural people's problems. The targets are indiscriminate. One would be hard put to blame any of Oregon's many problems on homosexuals or the United Nations. But tough, unforgiving economic realities lay behind rural Oregonians' anger. Prosperous, urban Oregonians can in fact afford to buy homes made from lumber cut and milled outside the state and to pay higher electricity rates to preserve fish runs. Many rural Oregonians cannot. Unemployment and its attendant problems have soared in communities largely excluded from federally owned timber, where cheap electricity is for many a necessity. A Redmond resident asserted in 1997 that he "would rather have a light in my cold refrigerator than a warm salmon on the shelf."[30] Such Oregonians are angered when distant people enjoying a much higher standard of living expect them to risk hunger for the sake of forests and fish. Urban Oregonians, whose economy is much less reliant than before on the countryside's timber and wheat, in fact tend to view rural Oregon as a place to vacation, not work.

❧❧ ❧❧

Modern Oregon is a divided state. Always hostile to people of color, it is now home to many people of Latin-American, African, Asian, Native, and eastern-European descent. These peoples face less economic and social discrimination than their earlier, less numerous counterparts in Oregon did. But the state has not exactly put out the welcome mat for them, and they still constitute a disproportionate number of Oregon's poor.

Class has become an increasingly important socioeconomic divider in modern Oregon. The boom times of the late twentieth century focused on the urban Willamette Valley. Residents in most of the rest of the state did not keep up. Many, especially those dependent upon timber, saw their standard of living fall precipitously. Rural Oregon men can no longer expect to go straight from high school to a high-paying job in the mill.

I have oversimplified Oregon's divisions. The OCA did well in many prosperous suburbs. Rural Democrats and urban Republicans, though beleaguered, are hardly extinct. Parts of Portland are considered conservative, the north coast, Hood River, and Bend areas increasingly liberal.

But class and region have become more closely correlated, and the state's divergent economic history has created stark contrasts: trendy Portland streets full of well-educated people trying to find interesting ways to spend their ample incomes and depressed small towns full of families struggling to eat.

At this writing, early in the new millennium, the two sides seem not much interested in talking to each other, and, when they do, it is often through the filter of polarized political positions on issues like environmentalism or gay rights or taxes, disagreements that both inflame and obscure the source of our differences—and will continue to until we care to listen to each other.

Oregon will remain a polarized state until the fruits of its prosperity are more evenly spread across racial, occupational, and geographic divides and until its residents are more interested in understanding than reviling each other.

Biographies

Tom Hirons

Born around 1940, Tom Hirons grew up in Salem and started working hard at a young age. At seven or eight he was picking strawberries to pay for school clothes. Later he rose at 4:00 a.m. to complete his seven-mile paper route. Adulthood brought the Navy, college, and a succession of unsatisfying jobs. Then, in 1977, he founded his own small company: Mad Creek Logging in Mill City, east of Salem.

The timing was not propitious. One of Hirons's biggest mistakes, by his own admission, was laying out a quarter of a million dollars for a massive yarder. The capacity to drag old-growth logs out of the forest promised to help Mad Creek bid for big, profitable jobs. But by the late 1980s environmentalists were filing suits and the Forest Service was restricting logging. Hirons was left with a huge debt that he could not pay off. "It's like having a damn combine with no wheatfields," he complained.

These reverses struck Hirons as unfair. He took pains to log safely and effectively. The Oregon Associated Loggers named him Logger of the Year for 1989. He worked hard, rising at 4:00 a.m. or earlier and laboring in rain and heat. Even a small mistake could shut down his operation for hours, costing him thousands of dollars that would take days to recoup. Meanwhile, "smart-asses and manipulators" like Donald Trump were getting rich and being lionized. The days when honest hard work sufficed to secure a man a good living seemed to be long gone.

Hirons reserved much of his anger for the environmentalist movement and became one of its leading Oregon critics. He lamented that growing numbers of city dwellers "think milk comes from cartons, beef from the beef case." "If you're gonna build a hot tub or a house," he concluded, " a tree is going to fall."[31]

In 1989, at the peak of the spotted owl controversy, he became the founding president of the Oregon Lands Coalition, a strong advocate for logging federal forests. "My sense of morality got offended in this whole thing," he recalled three years later. "Somebody crossed over a line out there and I felt I had to defend a set of values my old man tried to teach me."[32]

Ramon Ramirez

In Oregon, as across the United States, the power of unions has declined steadily over the past several decades. That an Oregon union has increased its membership from less than a hundred in 1985 to more than four thousand five hundred in 2000 is therefore noteworthy. That these members are among the state's most impoverished and vulnerable residents makes the accomplishment remarkable.

Ramon Ramirez, the president of Pineros y Campesinos Unidos del Noroeste (PCUN), is influenced by Cesar Chavez, the legendary leader of the United Farm Workers, who visited his east Los Angeles high school in 1971. The son of a commercial painter and former farm worker, Ramirez became active in the farm worker and Chicano movements.

Ramirez went to college in Olympia and Mount Angel, at Colegio Cesar Chavez, where he started the work of organizing Oregon farm laborers. He became PCUN's president in 1995.

He works hard. Organizing requires long hours, and Ramirez is seldom at home with his wife and children. Yet he made just $24,000 in 2001 and lives in a Hubbard mobile home.

Ramirez is a bold leader. In 1995, faced with proposed legislation much like Proposition 187 in California that would have cut services to Latinos, Ramirez turned to what at first seemed like an unlikely community: Oregon's gays and lesbians. Criticized by some Latino conservatives, Ramirez reasoned that his new allies had themselves turned away discriminatory ballot measures and could offer invaluable advice and resources. The coalition worked; the measures failed. Latino organizers returned the favor in 2000 by working to defeat another anti-gay initiative.

Ramirez spearheaded many other successes, including fighting a new *bracero* (guest worker) program and proposals mandating the use of English only. A 2000 march in Salem opposing *bracero* programs and calling for immigrant legalization drew three thousand participants. And, all the while, he has attracted more and more of Oregon's farm workers to PCUN. In 2002 the PCUN-sponsored boycott of NORPAC Foods at last drove the food processor to bargain with the once-tiny union.

Not everyone is a fan of Ramirez and his work. Oregon farmers have struggled to compete against inexpensive imports and understandably try to keep labor costs low. The vice president of one agricultural company charges PCUN with being more "interested in the union" than "in farm workers." Ramirez counters that his organizers do not force workers to join the union—and that the union is for workers. "We're the only force in this country that doesn't have benefits, for example, paid vacations, health," he explained in 2002. "If we work overtime, they don't pay us."

"My question to you is: Is this just, [is it] right?"[33]

At this writing, Oregonians have not yet settled on an answer.

Bill Sizemore

Glenn Jackson arguably wielded more power than Oregon's elected officials in the 1960s and 1970s. Much the same could be said of Bill Sizemore in the 1990s, though Sizemore has attracted much more attention and criticism than his earlier and quieter counterpart did.

Sizemore moved to Portland in 1972 from Washington. He was graduated from Portland Bible College, married, had children, and ran several small businesses. He entered politics in 1980 by running, unsuccessfully, for Portland's City Council. The *Willamette Week*, no friend of conservatives, then predicted that "Christian right-wing" candidates like the "young, attractive, energetic … Sizemore, can work the increasingly fertile ground of the public's ignorance, apathy and anti government sentiment."[34]

Whether one believes that Sizemore's message has converted the ignorant or the prescient of course depends on one's political point of view. But no one can gainsay that he has rallied plenty of Oregonians to his cause.

Sizemore reemerged in the early 1990s, after the success of anti-tax activist Don McIntire's Ballot Measure 5. Sizemore formed Oregon Taxpayers United and in 1994 offered two measures. One required a public vote for all new or raised taxes. It failed. The other, Measure 8, stipulated that public employees pay part of their pensions. It narrowly passed, but was later nullified by courts.

Two years later, though, Sizemore hit the jackpot. Voters approved by comfortable margins his measures to cut property taxes and kill a light-rail project in Portland. In 1998 he won the Republican nomination for governor and ran on a platform of traditional schools, less government regulation, new roads, longer sentences for criminals, and, of course, no new taxes. He lost, badly. But Sizemore had learned that Oregon's initiative and referendum, crafted a century before by people near the other end of the political spectrum, allowed him to go over the heads of elected officials. His intricate political organization turned money and indignation into laws. An educational foundation drew tax-deductible donations that paid staff salaries ($70,000 for Sizemore in 2002), office, and legal expenses. His political-action committee drew more than $2 million from 1993 to 2002, money that went to pay for signature drives and polling. Sizemore spread his message through daily talk shows on the radio station that he co-owned.

Oregonians have disagreed sharply over what all this added up to. Supporters have argued that Sizemore is a populist who found a way for ordinary working people to frustrate Oregon's liberal elite by at last slowing the growth of big government and high taxes. Detractors counter that Sizemore has simply used money from wealthy individuals and businesses to make a mockery of direct democracy, buy petition gatherers and perhaps even signatures, and enrich himself while taking money out of schools and social services and giving it to his well-heeled backers.

Sizemore was battling for his political life near the end of 2002. A jury decided that Oregon Taxpayers United had used forged signatures and distorted campaign finance and tax reports. Oregon's attorney general was investigating whether it had violated Oregon laws governing tax-exempt organizations.

It remains to be seen, at this writing, if Sizemore can survive this setback. It seems highly unlikely, however, that Sizemore's demise would much deflate the resentment and anger toward government that he has so deftly utilized.

Sima Teherani

Teherani's life changed dramatically during a vacation to Florida in the mid-1990s, when she fell in love with a woman. She was then married with two children and teaching at Hidden Valley High School, near Grants Pass.

Teherani and her daughters then moved to Portland, where she had grown up, and began looking for support. She found Love Makes a Family, one of the nation's first organizations for gay, lesbian, bi-sexual, and transgendered parents and their children. The group gave her daughters the chance to "see other families like mine." Love Makes a Family also drew Teherani's considerable energies; she began volunteering and was soon president of its board.

In 2000 she became the staff member in charge of a new program bringing Love Makes a Family to Portland middle schools. Lesbian and gay parents were reporting that homophobic language and behavior was commonplace in these schools and that their children were often terrified that classmates would discover that they had lesbian or gay parents. Such children often discouraged their parents from going to school events or never brought friends over to their homes. Some simply became depressed and withdrawn.

Teherani works with administrators, teachers, and students to create a more inclusive school climate. She persuades administrators that there are children in their schools who "feel alienated and alone," who "don't feel safe." Some of the solutions are subtle. Children can be given the option of making more than one Mothers' Day card, for example. Other steps are more elaborate, such as bringing panels of older students to middle-school classrooms to talk of how they have been harmed by hateful, homophobic language. Teherani looks forward to the day when when gay and lesbian teachers and administrators feel safe to "come out," to put their partner's picture on their desks "so our children could see" that people like their parents are all around them.

That so many gay and lesbian professionals feel compelled to disguise their sexual identities reveals that Portland is less progressive than it seems. Teherani is saddened that so many of her friends cannot even "go to a store and act like a family … and feel safe," that Love Makes a Family gatherings remain, for many gay and lesbian parents, the only secure public place for them and their children.[35]

But she also celebrates the changes that she and others have helped to create. She served a year as the PTA president at Irvington Elementary School, whose principal describes her as a "very supportive parent, eager and willing to help and get anything accomplished in the school."[36]

Indeed, when school gets out at Irvington, with a daughter at her side and dozens of people—young and old, gay and straight, Black and white—sharing with her a word or a smile, it is easy to see that Sima Teherani is simply a mother and friend and community member, as well as a lesbian activist.

Conclusion

Lewis and Clark or Ralph and Marie

When I think of Oregon history I think of Ralph and Marie Wright—maybe because they were an important part of my childhood on the banks of the Lewis and Clark River, or maybe because they eventually told me quite a bit about their long lives.

Ralph was a retired logger, Marie a housewife who relentlessly kept their tiny house free of dust specks or any other disorder—this despite the tremendous log trucks that regularly roared past just a few feet from it. The Wrights had married around World War I. They remembered the awful depression that had followed that conflict, recounting how they lived off the land along a stream far out in the country until times got good enough for Ralph to find work. Now, in the 1960s, they had a television and let me come over every Thursday night to watch Batman. From expeditions to central Oregon they brought coarse-looking "thunder eggs," rocks that they cut open and polished to reveal interiors that shimmered in a confusion of color and light. They had lived through the great cataclysms of the first two thirds of the twentieth century and were now enjoying the good life.

I gained a more intimate understanding of the Wrights many years later, after I had grown and they had been pushed out of their home to accommodate a wider logging road—a road that would itself be abandoned some years later. They now enjoyed a larger house in Springfield, though they missed their home along the Lewis and Clark River. Both had grown feeble. Ralph's health was the most precarious, though he retained his puckish sense of humor. Years before he had regaled me with stories of trips to the moon and money buried under stumps. Marie had no time for such foolishness, and she was now consumed with concern for her husband. She would get after him about some habit she didn't approve of, he would laugh off her cares and pronounce that he felt fine. And then they would begin again.

Then Marie died. No one had expected her to go first. I saw Ralph the next day. "She worried too much," he asserted, as if pleased to have the uncontested last word. Then his grief overran his triumph and he convulsed into tears. They had lived together for more than half a century and had never spent a night away from each other. Now she was irretrievably gone. Ralph died a few weeks later. "They kept each other going," observed my father, and he was surely right.

It seems to me that the lives of Ralph and Marie lay much closer to the heart of the Oregon experience than Lewis and Clark's. They were, for starters, much more enamored with the Lewis and Clark Valley than were the explorers whom said valley is named after. A discerning eye can still detect the plants they cultivated in their little yard. They were not trying to get somewhere else. They tended their flowers, polished their rocks, looked after their two sets of neighbors, and loved each other.

Lewis and Clark were not, to be sure, the last Oregonians to be consumed with getting somewhere, and the state's ambitious and driven citizens have no doubt enriched us all by their determination to get us from here to there.

But if Oregon has a unique history to offer up, it consists of a peculiar blending of western opportunity with more traditional norms of community and stability. Ralph and Marie, like my maternal grandparents, escaped poverty in Oregon. But they aspired to become comfortable, not wealthy or famous. In this they participated in an Oregon legacy that includes millennia of indigenous peoples, the overlanders who settled most of the Willamette Valley, and many other peoples who came before and after them, from across the nation and the globe. Oregonians, as Gordon Dodds points out in his fine history of the state, have often been "satisfied with the competent, not the distinguished."[1] Why not, then, go with our strengths? Why not look to the past to discern how ordinary Oregonians have worked to create meaningful and sustainable communities rather than totting up the number of nights that Lewis and Clark and other exotic celebrities slept here?

It seems to me that this Oregon tradition of moderate accomplishment is threatened by four broad and powerful factors. First, as the history of such places as Coos County illustrates, we must find a way to utilize our environment in a sustainable fashion. We can do this out of a sense of deep respect for the nonhuman environment. Or we can do so from a sense of enlightened self-interest, for it ought to be clear by now that Oregon's soils, waters, animals, plants, and fish will not support us for long if we do not use them more judiciously than we have.

We must also find a way for rural and small-town Oregonians to stay and prosper in their communities. Surely our state is enriched by people who so love the places in which they live that only poverty can drive them away. Large income gaps between urban and rural areas tear people from their homes and breed social malaise and political resentment. Solving these problems will be very difficult. But we can't begin unless urban people acknowledge the need.

The growing economic and political gap between rural and urban Oregon is related to a more general fraying of Oregon's social fabric. The distance between rich and poor Oregonians is widening. We have moved near or to the top of some shameful lists: shortest school years, highest proportion of hungry people, and most expensive college tuition. Solutions do not seem to be around the corner. The legislature has for several years been hamstrung by partisan factionalism, and the general public's distrust of government has spawned voting for term limits, a refusal to approve taxes, and criticism of government employees. A rejuvenated economy would of course salve some of these wounds. But many of our differences reside in obdurate philosophical and political disagreements that must be discussed and resolved.

Finally, Oregon must address and reverse the racist legacy that stands at the center of its history. We must confront the fact that white settlers shunted aside and killed the peoples who had flourished here, an attempted ethnic cleansing that still haunts the state's indigenous peoples—and ought to trouble us all. We must come to terms with the repeated efforts of leading and ordinary Oregonians alike to keep away and drive out dark-skinned peoples of African, Asian, and Mexican descent. We must understand that, at least until recently, when white Oregonians spoke of pursuing the good life in Oregon, they assumed and asserted that this required excluding people of color.

Marie Wright once illustrated to me their youthful poverty by describing how she and Ralph spent their wedding night in a boarding house where the beds were separated only by a cloth screen. "You didn't even know what color the person on the other side was!" she exclaimed, her voice contorted by remembered fear and revulsion.

Most Oregonians would today say that color doesn't matter. But its historical weight is far too considerable to be vanquished by glib reassurances.

In addressing my first two concerns, environmental sustainability and economic equity, Oregonians can draw from our history, our peculiarities. Industrialization and globalization are extraordinarily powerful, to be sure, and they have already reworked Oregon. But we have a long tradition of prizing community and other intangibles.

Racism will be more difficult to vanquish. Here Ralph and Marie and most of our white ancestors offer us few models and precious little encouragement. Here white Oregonians will have to set aside our pride in being different from everywhere else, in being better than the South or New York City or California, if we are going to be even able to just *listen*, to try to fathom something of what it has been and continues to be like to live in this white place with dark skin.

To come to terms with racism and factionalism we must surrender our pretensions of innocence and exceptionalism. Oregon has been no Eden, welcoming and granting opportunities to all people with a ready mind and willing hands. Its promise remains unfulfilled.

But we can change that.

Notes

Introduction

1. Helen E. Nelson, *Annie Ripley: Right Side Up With Care* ([n.p.:n.p., ca. 1985]).
2. John M. Findlay, "A Fishy Proposition: Regional Identity in the Pacific Northwest," in *Many Wests: Place, Culture, & Regional Identity*, ed. David M. Wrobel and Michael C. Steiner (Lawrence: University Press of Kansas, 1997), 37-70.

Chapter 1

1. Jarold Ramsey, comp. and ed., *Coyote Was Going There: Indian Literature of the Oregon Country* (Seattle: University of Washington Press, 1977), 185-86.
2. Ramsey, *Coyote Was Going There*, 73-74.
3. Ramsey, *Coyote Was Going There*, 213.
4. Ramsey, *Coyote Was Going There*, 222.
5. Ramsey, *Coyote Was Going There*, 64-65.
6. Ramsey, *Reading the Fire: The Traditional Indian Literatures of America*, 2nd ed. (Seattle: University of Washington Press, 1999), 86.
7. Ramsey, *Coyote Was Going There*, 186.
8. Ramsey, *Coyote Was Going There*, 257.
9. Joseph E. Taylor, III, *Making Salmon: An Environmental History of the Northwest Fisheries Crisis* (Seattle: University of Washington Press, 1999), 31.
10. Ramsey, *Coyote Was Going There*, 58-60.
11. Alfred W. Crosby, Jr., *The Columbian Exchange: Biological and Cultural Consequences of 1492* (Westport, Connecticut: Greenwood Press, 1972), 56.
12. Christopher L. Miller, *Prophetic Worlds: Indians and Whites on the Columbia Plateau* (New Brunswick, New Jersey: Rutgers University Press, 1985), 55.
13. Taylor, *Making Salmon*, 34.

14. Keith A. Murray, *The Modocs and Their War* (Norman: University of Oklahoma Press, 1959), 13.
15. Alvin M. Josephy, Jr., *The Nez Perce Indians and the Opening of the Northwest*. (Boston: Houghton Mifflin, 1997, orig. 1965), 37-38.
16. Josephy, *Nez Perce Indians*, 38.
17. Robert H. Ruby and John A. Brown, *The Chinook Indians: Traders of the Lower Columbia River* (Norman: University of Oklahoma Press, 1976), 148-49.

Chapter 2

1. [Rick Steber], *Union Centennial Album* (Union, Oregon: Union Centennial Productions, 1978), Chapter 3 [the book is not paginated].
2. Dorothy O. Johansen and Charles M. Gates, *Empire of the Columbia: A History of the Pacific Northwest*, 2nd ed. (New York: Harper & Row, 1967), 25.
3. Roy E. Appleman, *Lewis and Clark: Historic Places Associated with Their Transcontinental Exploration (1804-06)*, (Washington, D.C.: National Park Service, 1975), 34-35.
4. John A. Hussey, *The History of Fort Vancouver and its Physical Structure*, ([Tacoma]" Washington State Historical Society, [1957]), 7.
5. Douglas Cole and David Darling, "History of the Early Period," in *Northwest Coast*, ed., Wayne Suttles (Washington, D.C.: Smithsonian Institution, 1990), 133.
6. David Peterson del Mar, "Intermarriage and Agency: A Chinookan Case Study," *Ethnohistory* 42 (Winter 1995): 13-14.
7. Stephen Dow Beckham, *Requiem for a People: The Rogue Indians and the Frontiersmen* (Norman: University of Oklahoma Press, 1971, repr. Corvallis: Oregon State University Press, 1996), 48.
8. Julie Roy Jeffrey, *Converting the West: A Biography of Narcissa Whitman* (Norman: University of Oklahoma Press, 1991), 39.

9. Jeffrey, *Converting the West*, 126.
10. Jeffrey, *Converting the West*, 220.
11. Alvin M. Josephy, Jr., *The Nez Perce Indians and the Opening of the Northwest.* (Boston: Houghton Mifflin, 1997, orig. 1965), 328.
12. Josephy, *Nez Perce Indians*, 503.
13. Kyle Ewing, term paper, History 468, University of Oregon, 2000.
14. Cole Harris, *The Resettlement of British Columbia: Essays on Colonialism and Geographical Change* (Vancouver: University of British Columbia Press, 1997), xii.
15. Hussey, *History of Fort Vancouve,* 31
16. Hamar Foster, "Killing Mr. John: Law and Jurisdiction at Fort Stikine, 1842-1846," in *Law for the Elephant, Law for the Beaver: Essays in the Legal History of the North American West*, ed. John McLaren, Foster, and Chet Orloff (Regina, Saskatchewan: Canadian Plains Research Center and Pasadena, California: Ninth Judicial Circuit Historical Society, 1992), 176-77.
17. Edward Curtis, *The North American Indian* (New York: Johnson Reprint Corporation, 1970, orig. 1924), vol. 13: 93-95.

Chapter 3

1. Dorothy O. Johansen and Charles M. Gates, *Empire of the Columbia: A History of the Pacific Northwest*, 2nd ed. (New York: Harper & Row, 1967), 144.
2. John Mack Faragher, *Women and Men on the Overland Trail* (New Haven: Yale University Press, 1979), 175.
3. Faragher, *Women and Men on the Overland Trail*, 27.
4. Margaret Jewett Bailey, *The Grains, or Passages in the Life of Ruth Rover, with Occasional Pictures of Oregon, Natural and Moral*, ed. Evelyn Leasher and Robert J. Frank (Oregon, 1854, repr. Corvallis: Oregon State University Press, 1986), 236.
5. Paul Bourke and Donald DeBats, *Washington County: Politics and Community in Antebellum America* (Baltimore: The Johns Hopkins University Press, 1995), 90.
6. David Alan Johnson, *Founding the Far West: California, Oregon, and Nevada, 1840-1890* (Berkeley: University of California Press, 1992), 41.
7. William A. Bowen, *The Willamette Valley: Migration and Settlement on the Oregon Frontier* (Seattle: University of Washington Press, 1978), 25.
8. Lynne Ertle, "Antique Ladies: Women and Newspapers on the Oregon Frontier, 1846-1859" (M.A. thesis, University of Oregon, 1995), 141.
9. James Jeffery Roberson, "An Historical Geography of Banking in Oregon from 1859 to 1968, with Emphasis on Unit Banking from 1900 to 1933" (M.A. thesis, University of Oregon, 1971), 6.
10. Ruth Barnes Moynihan, *Rebel for Rights: Abigail Scott Duniway* (New Haven: Yale University Press, 1983), 56.
11. David Peterson del Mar, *What Trouble I Have Seen: A History of Violence against Wives* (Cambridge: Harvard University Press, 1996), 15.
12. Bailey, *The Grains,* , 12.
13. G. Thomas Edwards, "Dr. Ada M. Weed: Northwest Reformer," in *Experiences in a Promised Land: Essays in Pacific Northwest History*, ed. Edwards and Carlos A. Schwantes (Seattle: University of Washington Press, 1986), 164.
14. Peterson del Mar, *What Trouble I Have Seen*, 21.
15. Peterson del Mar, *What Trouble I Have Seen*, 28.
16. Elizabeth McLagan, *A Peculiar Paradise: A History of Blacks in Oregon, 1788-1940* (Portland: The Oregon Black History Project and the Georgian Press, 1980), 24, 29.
17. Johansen and Gates, *Empire of the Columbia*, 184.
18. Johansen and Gates, *Empire of the Columbia*, 220.
19. Johnson, *Founding the Far West*, 61.
20. James E. Hendrickson, *Joe Lane of Oregon: Machine Politics and the Sectional Crisis, 1849-1861* (New Haven: Yale University Press, 1967), 48.

21. Robert M. Utley, *A Life Wild and Perilous: Mountain Men and the Paths to the Pacific* (New York: Henry Holt, 1997), 221.

22. Harvey Elmer Tobie, *No Man Like Joe: The Life and Times of Joseph L. Meek* (Portland: Binfords & Mort for the Oregon Historical Society, 1949), 165.

23. Tobie, *No Man Like Joe*, 279.

24. Abner S. Baker, III, "Experience, Personality and Memory: Jesse Applegate and John Minto Recall Pioneer Days" (*Oregon Historical Quarterly* 81 (Fall 1980): 249.

25. Malcolm Clark, Jr., *Eden Seekers: The Settlement of Oregon, 1818-1862* (Boston: Houghton Mifflin, 1981), 189.

26. Johansen and Gates, *Empire on the Columbia*, 219.

27. Jeff LaLande, "'Dixie' of the Pacific Northwest: Southern Oregon's Civil War," *Oregon Historical Quarterly* 100 (Spring 1999): 42.

28. Edwards, "Dr. Ada M. Weed," 169, 166.

Chapter 4

1. Randall V. Mills, *Railroads Down the Valleys: Some Short Lines of the Oregon Country* (Palo Alto, California: Pacific Books, 1950), 32.

2. Dean L. May, *Three Frontiers: Family, Land, and Society in the American West, 1850-1900* (Cambridge: Cambridge University Press, 1994), 253.

3. David Peterson del Mar, *Beaten Down: A History of Interpersonal Violence in the West* (Seattle: University of Washington Press, 2002), 51-52, 76.

4. Margaret L. Sullivan, "Conflict on the Frontier: The Case of Harney County, Oregon, 1870-1900," *Pacific Northwest Quarterly* 66 (October 1975): 181.

5. William G. Robbins, *Landscapes of Promise: The Oregon Story, 1800-1940* (Seattle: University of Washington Press, 1997), 99.

6. *New York Times*, 20 August 1995, sect. 1, p. 30.

7. Randall E. Rohe, "After the Gold Rush: Chinese Mining in the Far West, 1850-1890," *Montana: The Magazine of Western History* 32 (Autumn 1982): 9.

8. Jeff Zucker, Kay Hummel, and Bob Høgfoss, *Oregon Indians: Culture, History & Current Affairs, An Atlas & Introduction* (Portland: Oregon Historical Society, 1983), 114.

9. David Peterson del Mar, *What Trouble I Have Seen: A History of Violence against Wives* (Cambridge: Harvard University Press, 1996), 49.

10. Sister Miriam Teresa, *Legislation for Women in Oregon* (New York: C. P. Young, 1924), 8-14.

11. Peterson del Mar, *What Trouble I Have Seen*, 50.

12. Gordon B. Dodds, *The Salmon King of Oregon: R. D. Hume and the Pacific Fisheries* (Chapel Hill: University of North Carolina Press, 1959), 95.

13. Jeffrey Max LaLande, "'It Can't Happen Here' in Oregon: The Jackson County Rebellion, 1932-1933, and its 1890s-1920s Background" (Ph.D. diss., University of Oregon, 1993), 52.

14. Dorothy O. Johansen and Charles M. Gates, *Empire of the Columbia: A History of the Pacific Northwest*, 2nd ed. (New York: Harper & Row, 1967), 368.

15. Ruth Barnes Moynihan, *Rebel for Rights: Abigail Scott Duniway* (New Haven: Yale University Press, 1983), 120, 101.

16. Johansen and Gates, *Empire of the Columbia*, 311.

17. Anne Shannon Monroe, ed., *Feelin' Fine! Bill Hanley's Book* (Garden City: Doubleday, Doran, 1930), 63, 155.

18. Priscilla Knuth, "Images of the Deschutes Country," in *High & Mighty: Select Sketches about the Deschutes Country*, ed. Thomas Vaughan (Portland: Oregon Historical Society, 1981), 179.

19. Jeff LaLande, "A Wilderness Journey with Judge John B. Waldo, Oregon's First 'Preservationist,'" *Oregon Historical Quarterly* 90 (Summer 1989): 118, 132, 155, 158.

Chapter 5

1. Robert D. Johnston, *The Radical Middle Class: Populist Democracy and the Question of Capitalism in Progressive Era Portland, Oregon*, (Princeton: Princeton University Press, 2003), 121.

2. Esther G. Weinstein, "William Simon U'Ren: A Study of Persistence in Political Reform" (Ph.D. diss., Syracuse University, 1967), 12.

3. Weinstein, "William Simon U'Ren," 24.

4. Johnston, *Radical Middle Class*, 124.

5. Tony Howard Evans, "Oregon Progressive Reform, 1902-1924" (Ph.D. diss., University of California, Berkeley, 1966), 211.

6. Evans, "Oregon Progressive Reform," 271.

7. David Elvin Lindstrom, "W.S. U'Ren and the Fight for Government Reform and the Single Tax, 1908-1912" (M.S. thesis, Portland State University, 1972), 138-39.

8. Evans, "Oregon Progressive Reform," 154.

9. Paul Thomas Culbertson, "A History of the Initiative and Referendum in Oregon" (Ph.D. diss., University of Oregon, 1941), 196.

10. David Peterson del Mar, *What Trouble I Have Seen: A History of Violence against Wives* (Cambridge: Harvard University Press, 1996), 73.

11. David Peterson del Mar, *Beaten Down: A History of Interpersonal Violence in the West* (Seattle: University of Washington Press, 2002), 104.

12. Gloria E. Myers, *A Municipal Mother: Portland's Lola Greene Baldwin, America's First Policewoman* (Corvallis: Oregon State University Press, 1996), 46.

13. Hayes Perkins, "Here and There: An Itinerant Worker In the Pacific Northwest, 1989," *Oregon Historical Quarterly* 102 (Fall 2001): 371.

14. Carl Abbott, *Portland: Gateway to the Northwest* (Tarzana, California: American Historical Press, 1985), 67.

15. E. Kimbark MacColl, with Harry Stein, *Merchants, Money, and Power: The Portland Establishment, 1843-1913* (Portland: Georgian Press, 1988), 435.

16. Dennis E. Hoffman and Vincent J. Webb, "Police Response to Labor Radicalism in Portland and Seattle, 1913-19," *Oregon Historical Quarterly* 87 (Winter 1986): 355.

17. Jack Smolensky, "A History of Public Health in Oregon" (Ph.D. diss., University of Oregon 1957), 111-12.

18. Mansel G. Blackford, *The Lost Dream: Businessmen and City Planning on the Pacific Coast, 1890-1920* (Columbus: Ohio State University Press, 1993), 129-30.

19. Blackford, *The Lost Dream*, 141.

20. Peterson del Mar, *What Trouble I Have Seen*, 80.

21. Ward M. McAfee, "The Formation of Prison-Management Philosophy In Oregon, 1843-1915," *Oregon Historical Quarterly* 91 (Fall 1990): 274.

22. Hoffman and Webb, "Police Response to Labor Radicalism," 344.

23. Wayne A. Wiegand, "Oregon's Public Libraries during the First World War" *Oregon Historical Quarterly* 90 (Spring 1989): 54.

24. John E. Caswell, "The Prohibition Movement in Oregon," *Oregon Historical Quarterly* 39 (September 1938): 254.

25. F[rances] F[uller] Victor, *The Women's War with Whisky; or, Crusading in Portland* (Portland: Geo. H. Himes, 1874), 59.

26. Martha Killian Barefoot, "Between 'True Woman' and 'New Woman': Oregon Women's Clubs, 1890-1916" (M.A. thesis, University of Oregon, 1994), 25.

27. Peterson del Mar, *What Trouble I Have Seen*, 74.

28. G. Thomas Edwards, *Sowing Good Seeds: The Northwest Suffrage Campaigns of Susan B. Anthony* (Portland: Oregon Historical Society Press, 1990), 132.

29. Gordon B. Dodds, *Oregon: A Bicentennial History* (New York: Norton, 1977), 176.

30. Evans, "Oregon Progressive Reform," 133.

31. Robert Hamburger, *Two Rooms: The Life of Charles Erskine Scott Wood* (Lincoln: University of Nebraska Press, 1998), 122, 253.

32. Quintard Taylor, Jr., "Susie Revels Cayton, Beatrice Morrow Cannady, and the Campaign for Social Justice in the Pacific Northwest," in *The Great Northwest: The Search for Regional Identity*, ed. William G. Robbins (Corvallis: Oregon State University Press, 2001), 43.

33. David Peterson del Mar, "'A Great Mystre of Sorrow': The Secret History of Foster Children," manuscript in author's possession.

34. Robert D. Johnston, "The Myth of the Harmonious City: Will Daly, Lora Little, and the Hidden Face of Progressive-Era Portland," *Oregon Historical Quarterly* 99 (Fall 1998): 257, 260, 264.

Chapter 6

1. Barbara Allen, *Homesteading the High Desert* (Salt Lake City: University of Utah Press, 1987), 46.

2. William G. Robbins, *Landscapes of Promise: The Oregon Story, 1800-1940* (Seattle: University of Washington Press, 1997), 248.

3. Robbins, *Landscapes of Promise*, 253.

4. Douglas Heider and David Dietz, *Legislative Perspectives: A 150-Year History of the Oregon Legislatures from 1843 to 1993* (Portland: Oregon Historical Society Press, 1995), 123.

5. Carol Ann Krenelka, "Entertainments at Jantzen Beach Amusement Park, 1928-1970" (M.A. thesis, University of Oregon, 1981), 26.

6. Erik Lawrence Weiselberg, "Ascendency of the Mazamas: Environment, Identity and Mountain Climbing in Oregon, 1870 to 1930" (Ph.D. diss., University of Oregon, 1999), 365.

7. Nard Jones, *Oregon Detour* (Corvallis: Oregon State University Press, 1990, orig. 1930), 11, 131, 143.

8. Ray Nelson, *Memoirs of an Oregon Moonshiner* (Caldwell, Idaho: Caxton, 1980), 19-20.

9. Nelson, *Memoirs of an Oregon Moonshiner*, 20.

10. David Peterson del Mar, *What Trouble I Have Seen: A History of Violence against Wives* (Cambridge: Harvard University Press, 1996), 100, 112.

11. David Peterson, "Ready for War: Oregon Mennonites from Versailles to Pearl Harbor," *Mennonite Quarterly Review* 64 (July 1990): 214.

12. Peterson del Mar, *What Trouble I Have Seen*, 102.

13. Peterson del Mar, *What Trouble I Have Seen*, 103.

14. David Peterson del Mar, *Beaten Down: A History of Interpersonal Violence in the West* (Seattle: University of Washington Press, 2002), 125.

15. Peterson del Mar, *Beaten Down*, 123.

16. Peterson del Mar, *What Trouble I Have Seen*, 107, 102, 104.

17. Abner Sylvester Baker, III, "The Oregon Pioneer Tradition in the Nineteenth Century: A Study of Recollection and Self-Definition" (Ph.D. diss., University of Oregon, 1968), 144.

18. Glen A. Love, "Stemming the Avalanche of Tripe," in *H. L. Davis: Collected Essays and Short Stories* (Moscow: University of Idaho Press, 1986), 328.

19. Charles A. Povlovich, ed., "Lest We Forget: World War I Diary of Kirby Ross," *Oregon Historical Quarterly* 84 (Spring 1983): 25-28.

20. *H. L. Davis: Collected Essays and Short Stories*, 359, 361-62, 365-66.

21. Warren L. Clare, "Big Jim Stevens: A Study in Pacific Northwest Literature" (Ph.D. diss., Washington State University, 1967), 5.

22. H. L. Davis, *Honey in the Horn* (New York: Avon, 1962, orig. 1935), 236, 21.

23. George M. Armstrong, "An Unworn and Edged Tool: H. L. Davis's Last Word on the West, 'The Kettle of Fire,'" in *Northwest Perspectives:*

Essays on the Culture of the Pacific Northwest, ed. Edwin R. Bingham and Glen A. Love (Seattle: University of Washington, 1979), 176.

24. Clare, "Big Jim Stevens," 7.

25. James Stevens, *Brawny Man* (New York: Alfred A. Knopf, 1926), 53.

26. David Tyack, "The Perils of Pluralism: The Background of the Pierce Case," *American Historical Review* 74 (October 1968): 79.

27. Steve Neal, *McNary of Oregon: A Political Biography* (Portland: Oregon Historical Society Press, 1985), 72.

28. Neal, *McNary of Oregon*, 75.

29. Eckard V. Toy, "The Ku Klux Klan in Oregon," in *Experiences in a Promised Land: Essays I in Pacific Northwest History*, ed. G. Thomas Edwards and Carlos Schwantes (Seattle: University of Washington Press, 1986), 276.

30. Tyack, "Perils of Pluralism," 82.

31. William Toll, *Women, Men and Ethnicity: Essays on the Structure of Thought of American Jewry* (Lanham, Maryland: University Press of America, 1991), 131.

32. Robert E. Burton, *Democrats of Oregon: The Pattern of Minority Politics, 1900-1956* (Eugene: University of Oregon, 1970), 12.

33. Alice Day Pratt, *A Homesteader's Portfolio* (Corvallis: Oregon State University Press, 1993; orig. 1922), 178, 87, 115, 176.

34. Worth Mathewson, *William L. Finley: Pioneer Wildlife Photographer* (Corvallis: Oregon State University Press, 1986), 8.

35. Jeffrey Barlow and Christine Richardson, *China Doctor of John Day* (Portland: Binford & Mort, 1979), 67, 81-82.

36. Meredith L. Clausen, *Pietro Belluschi: Modern American Architect* (Cambridge, MIT Press, 1994), 90-91, 347.

Chapter 7

1. William H. Mullins, "'I'll Wreck the Town If It Will give Employment': Portland in the Hoover Years of the Depression," *Pacific Northwest Quarterly* 79 (July 1988): 111.

2. Gary Murrell, *Iron Pants: Oregon's Anti-New Deal Governor, Charles Henry Martin* (Pullman: Washington State University Press, 2000), 157-58.

3. Jeffrey Max Lalande, "'It Can't Happen Here' in Oregon: The Jackson County Rebellion, 1932-1933, and its 1890s-1920s Background" (Ph.D. diss., University of Oregon, 1993), 170.

4. William Bigelow and Norman Diamond, "Agitate, Educate, Organize: Portland, 1934," *Oregon Historical Quarterly* 89 (Spring 1988): 6.

5. Thomas R. Cox, *The Park Builders: A History of State Parks in the Pacific Northwest* (Seattle: University of Washington Press, 1988), 36.

6. Cox, *The Park Builders*, 95.

7. William G. Robbins, "The Good Fight: Forest Fire Protection and the Pacific Northwest," *Oregon Historical Quarterly* 102 (Fall 2001): 279.

8. Nancy Langston, *Forest Dreams, Forest Nightmares: The Paradox of Old Growth in the Inland West* (Seattle: University of Washington Press, 1995), 228.

9. Langston, *Forest Dreams*, 226.

10. William Kittredge, *Hole in the Sky: A Memoir* (New York: Vintage, 1993), 77.

11. Richard White, *"It's Your Misfortune and None of My Own": A History of the American West* (Norman: University of Oklahoma Press, 1991), 500.

12. Manly Maben, *Vanport* (Portland: Oregon Historical Society Press, 1987), 33.

13. Mark S. Foster, *Henry J. Kaiser: Builder in the Modern American West* (Austin: University of Texas Press, 1989), 77.

14. David Peterson, "The Quiet Pacifists: Oregon's Old Mennonites, 1914-1945," *Oregon Historical Quarterly* 93 (Summer 1992): 136.

15. Carl Abbott, *Portland: Gateway to the Northwest* (Tarzana, California: American Historical Press, 1997), 120.

16. Maben, *Vanport*, 5.

17. Maben, *Vanport*, 98.

18. Abbott, *Portland,* 121.

19. Marjorie R. Stearns, "The History of the Japanese People in Oregon" (M.A. thesis, University of Oregon, 1937), 66.

20. Barbara Yasui, "The Nikkei in Oregon, 1834-1940," *Oregon Historical Quarterly* 76 (September 1975): 254.

21. Virgil Davis Jackson, "Social Conflicts in Rural Communities of Oregon" (M.S. thesis, Oregon State Agricultural College, 1932), 112-13.

22. "Kathryn Hall Bogle's 'An American Negro Speaks of Color,'" *Oregon Historical Quarterly* 89 (Spring 1988): 79.

23. Edwin C. Berry, "Profiles: Portland," *Journal of Educational Sociology* 19 (October 1945): 158-59.

24. David Peterson del Mar, *Beaten Down: A History of Interpersonal Violence in the West* (Seattle: University of Washington Press, 2002), 143.

25. Rudy N. Pearson, "African Americans in Portland, Oregon, 1940-1950: Work and Living Conditions—A Social History" (Ph.D. diss., Washington State University, 1996), 29-30.

26. Rudy Pearson, "'A Menace to the Neighborhood': Housing and African Americans in Portland, 1941-1945," *Oregon Historical Quarterly* 102 (Summer 2001): 171.

27. Erasmo Gamboa, "The Bracero Program," in *Nosotros: The Hispanic People of Oregon,* ed Gamboa and Carolyn M. Buan (Portland: Oregon Council for the Humanities, 1995), 44.

28. Erasmo Gamboa, *Mexican Labor & World War II: Braceros in the Pacific Northwest, 1942-1947* (Seattle: University of Washington Press, 2000, orig. 1990), 113.

29. David Peterson del Mar, *What Trouble I Have Seen: A History of Violence against Wives* (Cambridge: Harvard University Press, 1996), 103.

30. Peterson del Mar, *What Trouble I Have Seen,* 129.

31. Amy Kesselman, *Fleeting Opportunities: Women Shipyard Workers in Portland and Vancouver During World War II and Reconversion* (Albany: State University of New York Press, 1990), 29.

32. Neal, *McNary of Oregon,* 105.

33. E. Kimbark MacColl, *The Growth of a City: Power and Politics in Portland, Oregon, 1915 to 1950* (Portland: Georgian Press, 1979), 390.

34. George S. Turnbull, *Governors of Oregon* (Portland: Binfords & Mort, 1959), 79-80.

35. Floyd J. McKay, *An Editor for Oregon: Charles A. Sprague and the Politics of Change* (Corvallis: Oregon State University Press, 1998), 66.

36. Portland *Oregonian,* 22 September 1977, p. 1.

37. (Portland*) Daily Journal,* 22 September 1977, p. 1.

38. Pat Koehler, "Reminiscence," *Oregon Historical Quarterly* 91 (Fall 1990): 285-91.

Chapter 8

1. William Kittredge, *Hole in the Sky: A Memoir* (New York: Vintage, 1993), 154, 171.

2. Craig Wollner, *The City Builders: One Hundred Years of Union Carpentry in Portland, Oregon, 1883-1983* (Portland: Oregon Historical Society Press, 1990), 114.

3. David A. Horowitz, "The Crusade against Chain Stores: Portland's Independent Merchants, 1928-1935," *Oregon Historical Quarterly* 89 (Winter 1988): 345.

4. Carl Abbott, *Portland: Planning, Politics, and Growth in a Twentieth-Century City* (Lincoln: University of Nebraska Press, 1983), 241.

5. Abbott, *Portland,* 244.

6. Abbott, *Portland,* 238.

7. William G. Robbins, *Hard Times in Paradise: Coos Bay, Oregon, 1850-1986* (Seattle: University of Washington Press, 1988), 131, 113.

8. Robbins, *Hard Times in Paradise,* 119, 131.

9. Lauren Kessler, *Stubborn Twig: Three Generations in the Life of a Japanese American Family* (New York: Random House, 1993), 238, 244.

10. Kessler, *Stubborn Twig*, 240.

11. Kessler, *Stubborn Twig*, 284.

12. Nicolas G. Rosenthal, "'Walk Across the Bridge … An' You'll Find Your People': Native Americans in Portland, Oregon, 1945-1980 (M.A. thesis, University of Oregon, 2000), 33.

13. Patrick Haynal, "Termination and Tribal Survival: The Klamath Tribes of Oregon," *Oregon Historical Quarterly* 101 (Fall 2000): 289.

14. Erasmo Gamboa, "El Movimiento: Oregon's Mexican-American Civil Rights Movement," in *Nosotros: The Hispanic People of Oregon, Essays and Recollections*, ed. Gamboa and Carolyn M. Buan (Portland: Oregon Council for the Humanities, 1995), 48.

15. Richard Wayne Slatta," Chicanos in Oregon: An Historical Overview" (M.A. thesis, Portland State University, 1974), 70.

16. Stuart McElderry, "Building a West Coast Ghetto: African-American Housing in Portland, 1910-1960," *Pacific Northwest Quarterly* 92 (Summer 2001): 143.

17. McElderry, "Building a West Coast Ghetto," 144.

18. *Portland Tribune*, 20 September 2002, p. A3.

19. Don Berry, *Trask* (Sausalito, California: Comstock, 1969, orig. 1960), 372.

20. Berry, *Moontrap* (Sausalito, California: Comstock, 1971, orig. 1962), 181.

21. Glen A. Love, *Don Berry* (Boise: Boise State University, 1978), 24.

22. Ken Kesey, *Sometimes a Great Notion* (New York: Bantam, 1965), 144, 150.

23. Kittredge, *Hole in the Sky*, 186-87.

24. Neil Dennis Murray, "A Comparative Historical Study of Student Protest at the University of Oregon and Oregon State University during the Sixties" (Ph.D. diss., University of Oregon, 1971), 147.

25. Myrna Ewart Tonkinson, "Changing Consciousness: The Impact of the Women's Liberation Movement on Non-Activist Women in a University Community" (Ph.D. diss., University of Oregon, 1976), 122-23.

26. Bonnie Tinker, interview by author, 28 October 2002.

27. Joseph Bear Wilner, "All My Sisters and Brothers: Redefinitions of Family in Oregon Intentional Communities During the Late Twentieth Century" (M.A. thesis, University of Oregon, 2000), 31.

28. Alexander Patterson, "Terrasquirma and the Engines of Social Change in 1970s Portland," *Oregon Historical Quarterly* 101 (Summer 2000): 168.

29. Brent Walth, *Fire at Eden's Gate: Tom McCall & the Oregon Story* (Portland: Oregon Historical Society, 1994), 188.

30. Walth, *Fire at Eden's Gate*, 330, 356, 378, 379-80.

31. Walth, *Fire at Eden's Gate*, 385.

32. Walth, *Fire at Eden's Gate*, 420.

33. Walth, *Fire at Eden's Gate*, 314, 315.

34. Katrine Barber and Janice Dilg, "'I Didn't Do Anything Anyone Else Wouldn't Have Done': A View of Oregon History through the Ordinary Life of Barbara Mackenzie," *Oregon Historical Quarterly* 103 (Winter 2002):487, 501, 505, 482.

35. Walth, *Fire at Eden's Gate*, 165-66.

36. (Portland*) Oregon Labor Press*, 5 December 1969, p . 3.

37. *Eugene Register-Guard*, 22 June 1980, p. 19.

38. Portland *Oregonian*, 20 March 1977, p. mag. 11.

39. Walth, *Fire at Eden's Gate*, 165.

40. *Nosotros*, 142.

41. (Portland*) Willamette Week*, 15 May 1996, p. 4.

42. (Portland*) Willamette Week*, 29 July 1998, p. 29.

43. Portland *Oregonian*, 15 February 1999, p. A1.

Chapter 9

1. Carl Abbott, *Portland: Planning, Politics, and Growth in a Twentieth-Century City* (Lincoln: University of Nebraska Press, 1983), 247.

2. Carl Abbott, *Portland: Urban Life and Landscape in the Pacific Northwest* (Philadelphia:

University of Pennsylvania Press, 2001), 121.

3. Carmen Cecilia Ramirez, "A Study of the Value Orientation of Lane County, Oregon, Mexican American Mothers with a Special Focus on Family/School Relationships" (Ph.D. diss., University of Oregon, 1981), 94.

4. Steven W. Bender, "Spanish Language Rights and Law in Oregon," in *Nosotros: The Hispanic People of Oregon, Essays and Recollections*, ed. Erasmo Gamboa and Carolyn M. Buan (Portland: Oregon Council for the Humanities, 1995), 81.

5. Arlene Stein, *The Stranger Next Door: The Story of a Small Community's Battle Over Sex, Faith, and Civil Rights* (Boston: Beacon Press, 2001), 62.

6. Kathie Durbin, *Tree Huggers: Victory, Defeat & Renewal in the Northwest Ancient Forest Campaign* (Seattle: Mountaineers, 1996), 82.

7. Durbin, *Tree Huggers*, 90.

8. Matthew S. Carroll, *Community and the Northwestern Logger: Continuities and Changes in the Era of the Spotted Owl* (Boulder: Westview Press, 1995), 92.

9. William G. Robbins, *Hard Times in Paradise: Coos Bay, Oregon, 1850-1986* (Seattle: University of Washington Press, 1988), 158.

10. Stein, *The Stranger Next Door*, 51.

11. Robbins, *Hard Times in Paradise*, 162.

12. Durbin, *Tree Huggers*, 96, 97.

13. David Seideman, *Showdown at Opal Creek: The Battle for America's Last Wilderness* (New York: Carroll & Graf, 1993), 31.

14. Beverly A. Brown, *In Timber Country: Working People's Stories of Environmental Conflict and Urban Flight* (Philadelphia: Temple University Press, 1995), 192, 227.

15. Carroll, *Community and the Northwestern Logger*, 102.

16. Brown, *In Timber Country*, 248.

17. Stein, *The Stranger Next Door*, 25.

18. S. L. Gardner, *Rolling Back Civil Rights: The Oregon Citizens' Alliance at Religious War* (Portland: Coalition for Human Dignity, 1992), 28.

19. Patricia Jean Young, "Measure 9: Oregon's 1992 Anti-Gay Initiative" (MA thesis, Portland State University, 1997), 143.

20. Stein, *The Stranger Next Door*, 28.

21. Stein, *The Stranger Next Door*, 34-35, 113.

22. Stein, *The Stranger Next Door*, 199.

23. Stein, *The Stranger Next Door*, 121.

24. Susan Johnston, "Paradoxes of Identity: Liberalism, Bio-Power and 'Homosexual' Politics in Oregon (Ph.D. diss., University of Oregon, 1996), 111, emphasis in original.

25. Brown, *In Timber Country* 21.

26. *(Portland) Oregonian*, 29 April 2001, p. B2

27. *(Portland) Oregonian*, 26 August 2001, p. F3

28. *New York Times*, 20 November 1998, p. A20.

29. Stein, *The Stranger Next Door*, 90-91.

30. Joseph E. Taylor, III, *Making Salmon: An Environmental History of the Northwest Fisheries Crisis* (Seattle: University of Washington Press, 1999), 248.

31. Seideman, *Showdown at Opal Creek*, 84, 88, 79.

32. Durbin, *Tree Huggers*, 101.

33. Portland *Oregonian*, 4 March 2002, p. A8.

34. *(Portland) Willamette Week*, 27 October 1980, p. 14.

35. Sima Teherani, interview by author, 18 October 2002.

36. Jack Turteltaub, "Mother Knows Best," *Just Out*, 4 January 2002, 13.

Conclusion

37. Gordon B. Dodds, *Oregon: A Bicentennial History* (New York: W. W. Norton, 1977), 228.

Selected Secondary Sources

Published

Those wishing to read more deeply about the events and processes described in a given chapter are referred to the books and articles cited in that chapter's notes.

Abbott, Carl. *The Great Extravaganza: Portland and the Lewis and Clark Exposition,* rev. ed. Portland: Oregon Historical Society Press, 1996.

———. *Portland: Gateway to the Northwest.* Northridge, California: Windsore Publications, 1985.

———. *Portland: Planning, Politics, and Growth in a Twentieth-Century City.* Lincoln: University of Nebraska Press, 1983.

———. *Portland: Urban Life and Landscape in the Pacific Northwest.* Philadelphia: University of Pennsylvania Press, 2001.

Ackerman, Lillian A. "The Effect of Missionary Ideals on Family Structure and Women's Roles in Plateau Indian Culture." *Idaho Yesterdays* 31 (Spring/Summer, 1987): 64-73.

Aikens, C. Melvin. *Archaeology of Oregon.* Portland: Bureau of Land Management, 1993.

Allen, Barbara. *Homesteading the High Desert.* Salt Lake City: University of Utah Press, 1987.

Applegate, Shannon. *Skookum: An Oregon Pioneer Family's History and Lore.* New York: Beech Tree Books, 1988.

Appleman, Roy E. *Lewis and Clark: Historic Places Associated with Their Transcontinental Exploration (1804-06).* Washington: National Park Service, 1975.

Azuma, Eiichiro. "A History of Oregon's Issei, 1880-1952." *Oregon Historical Quarterly* 94 (Winter 1993-1994): 315-67.

Bailey, Barbara Ruth. *Main Street, Northeastern Oregon: The Founding and Development of Small Towns.* Portland: Oregon Historical Society Press, 1982.

Abner S. Baker III, "Experience, Personality and Memory: Jesse Applegate and John Minto Recall Pioneer Days." *Oregon Historical Quarterly* 81 (Fall 1980): 229-59.

Barber, Katrine, and Janice Dilg. "From Homework to Home Service: Building a Social Service Career in Oregon." *Oregon Historical Quarterly* 103 (Winter 2002): 480-509.

Barlow, Jeffrey, and Christine Richardson. *China Doctor of John Day.* Portland: Binford & Mort, 1979.

Barnett, H. G. *Indian Shakers: A Messianic Cult of the Pacific Northwest.* Carbondale: Southern Illinois University Press, 1957.

Beckham, Stephen Dow. *The Indians of Western Oregon: This Land Was Theirs.* Coos Bay: Arago Books, 1977.

———. *Requiem for a People: The Rogue Indians and the Frontiersmen.* Norman: University of Oklahoma Press, 1971. Reprinted Corvallis: Oregon State University Press, 1996.

Bedwell, Stephen F. *Fort Rock Basin: Prehistory and Environment.* Eugene: University of Oregon Books, 1973.

Bingham, Edwin R., and Glen A. Love, eds. *Northwest Perspectives: Essays on the Culture of the Pacific Northwest.* Seattle: University of Washington Press, 1979.

Blackford, Mansel G. "The Lost Dream: Businessmen and City Planning in Portland, Oregon, 1903-1914." *Western Historical Quarterly* 15 (January 1984): 39-56.

———. *The Lost Dream: Businessmen and City Planning on the Pacific Coast, 1890-1920.* Columbus: Ohio State University Press, 1993.

Blair, Karen J., ed. *Women in Pacific Northwest History,* revised ed. Seattle: University of Washington Press, 2001.

Boag, Peter G. "Ashwood on Trout Creek: A Study in Continuity and

Change in Central Oregon." *Oregon Historical Quarterly* 91 (Summer 1990): 117-53.

———. *Environment and Experience: Settlement Culture in Nineteenth-Century Oregon.* Berkeley: University of California Press, 1992.

———. "Sex and Politics in Progressive-Era Portland & Eugene: The 1912 Same-Sex Vice Scandal." *Oregon Historical Quarterly* 100 (Summer 1999): 158-81.

Bosker, Gideon, and Lena Lencek. *Frozen Music: A History of Portland Architecture.* Portland: Oregon Historical Society Press, 1985.

Bourke, Paul, and Donald DeBats. *Washington County: Politics and Community in Antebellum America.* Baltimore: The Johns Hopkins University Press, 1995.

Bowen, William A. *The Willamette Valley: Migration and Settlement on the Oregon Frontier.* Seattle: University of Washington Press, 1978.

Boyd, Robert T. "Another Look at the 'Fever and Ague' of Western Oregon." *Ethnohistory* 22 (Spring 1975): 135-54.

———, ed. *Indians, Fire, and the Land in the Pacific Northwest.* Corvallis: Oregon State University Press, 1999.

———. *People of the Dalles, the Indians of Wascopam Mission: A Historical Ethnography Based on the Papers of the Methodist Missionaries.* Lincoln: University of Nebraska Press, 1996.

Brandt, Patricia. "Organized Free Thought in Oregon: The Oregon State Secular Union." *Oregon Historical Quarterly* 87 (Summer 1986): 167-204.

Brown, Beverly A. *In Timber Country: Working People's Stories of Environmental Conflict and Urban Flight.* Philadelphia: Temple University Press, 1995.

Buan, Carolyn M., and Richard Lewis, eds. *First Oregonians: An Illustrated Collection of Essays on Traditional Lifeways, Federal-Indian Relations, and the State's*

Native People Today. Portland: Oregon Council for the Humanities, 1991.

Bunting, Robert. "The Environment and Settler Society in Western Oregon." *Pacific Historical Review* 64 (August 1995): 413-32.

———. *The Pacific Raincoast: Environment and Culture in an American Eden, 1778-1900.* Lawrence: University Press of Kansas, 1997.

Burton, Robert E. *Democrats of Oregon: The Pattern of Minority Politics, 1900-1956.* Eugene: University of Oregon, 1970.

Canfield, Gae Whitney. *Sarah Winnemucca of the Northern Paiutes.* Norman: University of Oklahoma Press, 1983.

Carey, Charles H. *General History of Oregon: Through Early Statehood.* Portland: Binfords and Mort, 1971.

Clark, Malcolm, Jr. *Eden Seekers: The Settlement of Oregon, 1818-1862.* Boston: Houghton Mifflin, 1981.

Carroll, Matthew S. *Community and the Northwestern Logger: Continuities and Changes in the Era of the Spotted Owl.* Boulder: Westview Press, 1995.

Caswell, John E. "The Prohibition Movement in Oregon." *Oregon Historical Quarterly* 39 (September 1938): 235-61.

Clausen, Meredith L. *Pietro Belluschi: Modern American Architect.* Cambridge: MIT Press, 1994.

Collins, Cary C. "Through the Lens of Assimilation: Edwin L. Chalcraft and Chemawa Indian School." *Oregon Historical Quarterly* 98 (Winter 1997-1998): 398-425.

Cornerstones of Community: Buildings of Portland's African American History, rev. ed. Portland: Bosco-Milligan Foundation, 1997.

Connolly, Thomas J. *Newberry Crater: A Ten-Thousand-Year Record of Human Occupation and Environmental Change in the Basin-Plateau Borderlands.* Salt Lake City: University of Utah Press, 1999.

Cook, Warren L. *Flood Tide of Empire: Spain and the Pacific Northwest, 1543-1819.* New Haven: Yale University Press, 1973.

Cox, Thomas R. *Mills and Markets: A History of the Pacific Coast Lumber Industry to 1900*. Seattle: University of Washington Press, 1974.

——. *The Park Builders: A History of State Parks in the Pacific Northwest*. Seattle: University of Washington Press, 1988.

Cressman, L. S. *Prehistory of the Far West: Homes of Vanished Peoples*. Salt Lake City University of Utah Press, 1977.

——. *The Sandal and the Cave: The Indians of Oregon: Archaeological Studies in the Northern Great Basin*. Portland: Beaver Books, 1962. Reprinted Corvallis, Oregon State University Press, 1981.

——, Howel Williams, and Alex D. Krieger. *Early Man in Oregon: Archaeological Studies in the Northern Great Basin*. Eugene: University of Oregon, 1940.

Crosby, Alfred W., Jr. *The Columbian Exchange: Biological and Cultural Consequences of 1492*. Westport, Connecticut: Greenwood Press, 1972.

Davis, Everett H. "Rural Oregon Lights Up." *Oregon Historical Quarterly* 80 (Fall 1979): 323-28.

Dean, Jonathan R. "The Hudson's Bay Company and Its Use of Foce, 1828-1829." *Oregon Historical Quarterly* 98 (Fall 1997): 262-95.

Dicken, Samuel N., and Emily F. Dicken. *The Making of Oregon: A Study in Historical Geography*. Portland: Oregon Historical Society Press, 1979.

Dodds, Gordon. *The College that Would Not Die: The First Fifty Years of Portland State University, 1946-1996*. Portland: Oregon Historical Society Press and Portland State University, 2000.

——. *Oregon: A Bicentennial History*. New York: Norton, 1977.

——. *The Salmon King of Oregon: R. D. Hume and the Pacific Fisheries*. Chapel Hill: Universitiy of North Carolina Press, 1959.

——, and Craig E. Wollner, with the assistance of Marshall M. Lee. *The Silicon Forest: High Tech in the Portland Area, 1945-1986*. Portland: Oregon Historical Society Press, 1990.

Douthit, Nathan. "The Hudson's Bay Company and the Indians of Southern Oregon." *Oregon Historical Quarterly* 93 (Spring 1992): 25-64.

——. "Joseph Lane and the Rogue River Indians: Personal Relations Across a Cultural Divide." *Oregon Historical Quarterly* 95 (Winter 1994-1995): 472-515.

Drukman, Mason. *Wayne Morse: A Political Biography*. Portland: Oregon Historical Society Press, 1997.

Drury, Clifford M. *Chief Lawyer of the Nez Perce Indians, 1796-1876*. Glendale California: Arthur H. Clark, 1979.

Due, John F., and Giles French. *Rails to the Mid-Columbia Wheatlands: The Columbia Southern and Great Southern Railroads and the Development of Sherman and Wasco Counties, Oregon*. Washington: University Press of America, 1979.

——, and Frances Juris. *Rails to the Ochoco Country: The City of Prineville Railway*. San Marino, California: Golden West Books, 1968.

Durbin, Kathie. *Tree Huggers: Victory, Defeat & Renewal in the Northwest Ancient Forest Campaign*. Seattle: Mountaineers, 1996.

Edson, Christopher Howard. *The Chinese in Eastern Oregon: 1860-1890*. San Francisco: R and E Research Associates, 1974.

Edwards, G. Thomas. *Sowing Good Seeds: The Northwest Suffrage Campaigns of Susan B. Anthony*. Portland: Oregon Historical Society Press, 1990.

——, and Carlos A. Schwantes, eds. *Experiences in a Promised Land: Essays in Pacific Northwest History*. Seattle: University of Washington Press, 1986.

Faragher, John Mack. *Women and Men on the Overland Trail*. New Haven: Yale University Press, 1979.

Findlay, John M. "A Fishy Proposition: Regional Identity in the Pacific Northwest." In *Many Wests: Place, Culture, & Regional Identity*, edited by David M. Wrobel and Michael C. Steiner, 37-70. Lawrence: University Press of Kansas, 1997.

Etulain, Richard W. *Ernest Haycox.* Boise: Boise State University Press, 1988.

Foster, Doug. "Refuges and Reclamation: Conflicts in the Klamath Basin." *Oregon Historical Quarterly* 103 (Summer 2002): 150-87.

French, David. "Wasco-Wishram." In *Perspectives in American Indian Culture Change*, edited by Edward H. Spicer, 337-430. Chicago: University of Chicago Press, 1961.

Friday, Chris. *Organizing Asian American Labor: The Pacific Coast Canned Salmon Industry, 1870-1942.* Philadelphia: Temple University Press, 1994.

Gamboa, Erasmo. *Mexican Labor & World War II: Braceros in the Pacific Northwest, 1942-1947.* Seattle: University of Washington Press, 2000, orig. 1990.

———. "The Mexican Mule Pack System of Transportation in the Pacific Northwest and British Columbia." *Journal of the West* 29 (January 1990): 16-27.

Gardner, S. L. *Rolling Back Civil Rights: The Oregon Citizens' Alliance at Religious War.* Portland: Coalition for Human Dignity, 1992.

Gastil, Raymond D. "The Pacific Northwest as a Cultural Region." *Pacific Northwest Quarterly* 64 (October 1973): 147-56.

Gaston, Joseph. *Portland, Oregon: Its History and Builders*, 3 vols. Chicago: S. J. Clarke, 1911.

Gunns, Albert F. *Civil Liberties in Crisis: The Pacific Northwest, 1917-1940.* New York: Garland: 1983.

Haarsager, Sandra. *Organized Womanhood: Cultural Politics in the Pacific Northwest, 1840-1920.* Norman: University of Oklahoma Press, 1997.

Hall, H. J. "A Paleoscatalogical Study of Diet and Disease at Dirty Shame Rockshelter, Southeast Oregon." *Tebiwa* 8 (October 1977): 1-15.

Hamburger, Robert. *Two Rooms: The Life of Charles Erskine Scott Wood.* Lincoln: University of Nebraska Press, 1998.

Hanson, David E. "Home-Front Casualties of War Mobilization: Portland Public Schools, 1941-1945." *Oregon Historical Quarterly* 96 (Summer/Fall 1995): 192-225.

Harmon, Rick. *Crater Lake National Park: A History.* Corvallis: Oregon State University Press, 2002.

Haynal, Patrick. "Termination and Tribal Survival: The Klamath Tribes of Oregon." *Oregon Historical Quarterly* 101 (Fall 2000): 271-301.

Hedges, James Blaine. *Henry Villard and the Railways of the Northwest.* New York: Russell & Russell, 1930.

Heider, Douglas, and David Dietz. *Legislative Perspectives: A 150-Year History of the Oregon Legislatures from 1843 to 1993.* Portland: Oregon Historical Society Press, 1995.

Hendrickson, James E. *Joe Lane of Oregon: Machine Politics and the Sectional Crisis, 1849-1861.* New Haven: Yale University Press, 1967.

Higgens-Evenson, R. Rudy. "The Political Asylum: State Making and the Medical Profession in Oregon, 1862-1900." *Pacific Northwest Quarterly* 89 (Summer 1998): 136-47.

History of Portland's African American Community (1805 to the Present). Portland: Portland Bureau of Planning, 1993.

Hitchman, James H. *Liberal Arts Colleges in Oregon & Washington, 1842-1980.* Bellingham: Center for Pacific Northwest Studies, Western Washington University, 1981.

Hoffman, Dennis E., and Vincent J. Webb, "Police Response to Labor Radicalism in Portland and Seattle, 1913-19." *Oregon Historical Quarterly* 87 (Winter 1986): 340-66.

Hogg, Thomas C. "Black Man in a White Town." *Pacific Northwest Quarterly* 63 (January 1972): 14-21.

Holden, Margaret K. "Gender and Protest Ideology: Sue Ross Keenan and the Oregon Anti-Chinese Movement." *Western Legal History* 7 (Summer/Fall 1994): 223-43.

Holsinger, M. Paul. "The Oregon School Bill Controversy, 1922-1925." *Pacific Historical Review* 37 (August 1968): 327-41.

Horowitz, David. "The 'Cross of Culture': La Grande, Oregon, in the 1920." *Oregon Historical Quarterly* 93 (Summer 1992): 147-67.

———. "The Klansman as Outsider: Ethnocultural Solidarity and Antielitism in the Oregon Ku Klux Klan of the 1920s." *Pacific Northwest Quarterly* 80 (January 1989): 12-20.

Hummasti, P. G. "Ethnicity and Radicalism: The Finns of Astoria and the *Toveri*, 1860-1930." *Oregon Historical Quarterly* 96 (Winter 1995-1996): 362-93.

———. *Finnish Radicals in Astoria, Oregon, 1904-1940: A Study in Immigrant Socialism.* New York: Arno Press, 1979.

Hussey, John A. *Champoeg: Place of Transition, A Disputed History.* Portland: Oregon Historical Society Press, 1967.

———. *The History of Fort Vancouver and its Physical Structure.* [Tacoma]: Washington State Historical Society, [1957].

———. "The Women of Fort Vancouver." *Oregon Historical Quarterly* 92 (Fall 1991): 265-308.

Jackson, Philip L., and A. Jon Kimerling, eds. *Atlas of the Pacific Northwest*, 8th ed. Corvallis: Oregon State University Press, 1993.

Jacobs, Melville. *The People are Coming Soon: Analyses of Clackamas Chinook Myths and Tales.* Seattle: University of Washington Press, 1960.

Jansson, Kyle R. "The Changing Climate of Oregon's Driest Town: Monmouth's Prohibition Ordinances, 1859-2001." *Oregon Historical Quarterly* 102 (Fall 2001): 337-51.

Jeffrey, Julie Roy. *Converting the West: A Biography of Narcissa Whitman.* Norman: University of Oklahoma Press, 1991.

Jobanek, George A. "Searching for the Tree Vole: An Episode in the 1914 Biological Survey of Oregon." *Oregon Historical Quarterly* 89 (Winter 1988): 369-400.

Johannsen, Robert W. *Frontier Politics and the Sectional Conflict: The Pacific Northwest on the Eve of the Civil War.* Seattle: University of Washington Press, 1955.

Johansen, Dorothy O. "Oregon's Role in American History: An Old Theme Recast." *Pacific Northwest Quarterly* 40 (April 1949): 85-92.

———, and Charles M. Gates. *Empire of the Columbia: A History of the Pacific Northwest*, 2nd ed. New York: Harper & Row, 1967.

Johnson, Daniel P. "Anti-Japanese Legislation in Oregon, 1917-1923." *Oregon Historical Quarterly* 97 (Summer 1996): 176-210.

Johnson, David Alan. *Founding the Far West: California, Oregon, and Nevada, 1840-1890.* Berkeley: University of California Press, 1992.

Johnston, Robert D. *The Radical Middle Class: Populist Democracy and the Question of Capitalism in Progressive Era Portland, Oregon.* Princeton Princeton University Press, 2003.

Josephy, Alvin M., Jr. *The Nez Perce Indians and the Opening of the Northwest.* Boston: Houghton Mifflin: 1997, orig. 1965.

Kent, William Eugene. *The Siletz Indian Reservation, 1855-1900.* Newport, Oregon: Lincoln County Historical Society, 1977.

Kesselman, Amy. *Fleeting Opportunities: Women Shipyard Workers in Portland and Vancouver During World War II and Reconversion.* Albany: State University of New York Press, 1990.

Kessler, Lauren. "The Ideas of Woman Suffrage and the Mainstream Press." *Oregon Historical Quarterly* 84 (Fall 1983): 257-75.

———. "A Siege of the Citadels: Search for a Public Forum for the Ideas of Oregon Woman Suffrage." *Oregon Historical Quarterly* 84 (Summer 1983): 117-49.

———. *Stubborn Twig: Three Generations in the Life of a Japanese American Family.* New York: Random House, 1993.

Kirchmeier, Mark. *Packwood: The Public and Private Life from Acclaim to Outrage.* New York: Harper Collins, 1995.

Komar, Paul D. *The Pacific Northwest Coast: Living with the Shores of*

Oregon and Washington. Durham: Duke University Press, 1997.

LaLande, Jeff. "Beneath the Hooded Robe: Newspapermen, Local Politics, and the Ku Klux Klan in Jackson County, Oregon, 1921-1923." *Pacific Northwest Quarterly* 83 (April 1992): 42-52.

———. *The Indians of Southwestern Oregon: An Ethnohistorical Review.* Corvallis: Oregon State University Department of Anthropology, 1991.

———. "The 'Jackson County Rebellion': Social Turmoil and Political Insurgence in Southern Oregon during the Great Depression." *Oregon Historical Quarterly* 95 (Winter 1994-1995): 406-71.

Lang, William L., and Robert C. Carriker, editors. *Great River of the West: Essays on the Columbia River.* Seattle: University of Washington Press, 1999.

Langston, Nancy. *Forest Dreams, Forest Nightmares: The Paradox of Old Growth in the Inland West.* Seattle: University of Washington Press, 1995.

Largent, Mark A. "'The Greatest Cause of the Race': Eugenic Sterilization in Oregon, 1909-1983." *Oregon Historical Quarterly* 103 (Summer 2002): 188-209.

Lay, Shawn, editor. *The Invisible Empire in the West: Toward a New Historical Appraisal of the Ku Klux Klan of the 1920s.* Urbana: University of Illinois Press, 1992.

Lewty, Peter J. *Across the Columbia Plain: Railroad Expansion in the Interior Northwest, 1885-1893.* Pullman: Washington State University Press, 1995.

Little, William A., and James E. Weiss, editors. *Blacks in Oregon: A Statistical and Historical Report.* Portland: Portland State University, 1978.

Loewenberg, Robert J. *Equality on the Oregon Frontier: Jason Lee and the Methodist Mission, 1834-43.* Seattle: University of Washington Press, 1976.

Love, Glen A. *Don Berry.* Boise: Boise State University, 1978.

Lowenstein, Steven. *The Jews of Oregon, 1850-1950.* Portland: Jewish Historical Society of Oregon, 1987.

Loy, William G., et al., editor. *Atlas of Oregon,* 2nd ed. Eugene: University of Oregon Press, 2001.

Maben, Manly. *Vanport.* Portland: Oregon Historical Society Press, 1987.

MacColl, E. Kimbark. *The Growth of a City: Power and Politics in Portland, Oregon, 1915 to 1950.* Portland: Georgian Press, 1979.

———, with Harry H. Stein. *Merchants, Money, & Power: The Portland Establishment, 1843-1913.* Portland: Georgian Press, 1988.

Marsh, Kevin R. "'This Is Just the First Round': Designating Wilderness in the Central Oregon Cascades, 1950-1964." *Oregon Historical Quarterly* 103 (Summer 2002): 210-33.

Mathewson, Worth. *William L. Finley: Pioneer Wildlife Photographer.* Corvallis: Oregon State University Press, 1986.

May, Dean L. *Three Frontiers: Family, Land, and Society in the American West, 1850-1900.* Cambridge: Cambridge University Press, 1994.

McAfee, Ward M. "The Formation of Prison-Management Philosophy in Oregon, 1843-1915." *Oregon Historical Quarterly* 91 (Fall 1990: 259-84.

McClintock, Thomas C. "Seth Lewelling, William S. U'Ren, and the Birth of the Oregon Progressive Movement." *Oregon Historical Quarterly* 68 (September 1967): 196-220.

McElderry, Stuart. "Building a West Coast Ghetto: African-American Housing in Portland, 1910-1960." *Pacific Northwest Quarterly* 92 (Summer 2001): 137-48.

———. "Vanport Conspiracy Rumors and Social Relations in Portland, 1940-1950." *Oregon Historical Quarterly* 99 (Summer 1998): 134-63.

McKay, Floyd J. "After Cool Deliberation: Reed College, Oregon Editors, and the Red Scare of

1954." *Pacific Northwest Quarterly* 89 (Winter 1997/1998): 12-20.

———. *An Editor for Oregon: Charles A. Sprague and the Politics of Change.* Corvallis: Oregon State University Press, 1998.

McLagan, Elizabeth. *A Peculiar Paradise: A History of Blacks in Oregon, 1788-1940.* Portland: Georgian Press, 1980.

McVoy, Arthur D. "A History of City Planning in Portland, Oregon." *Oregon Historical Quarterly* 46 (March 1945): 3-21.

Meinig, D. W. *The Great Columbia Plain: A Historical Geography, 1805-1910.* Seattle: University of Washington Press, 1968.

Merk, Frederick. *The Oregon Question: Essays in Anglo-American Diplomacy and Politics.* Cambridge: Harvard University Press, 1967.

Messing, John. "Public Lands, Politics, and Progresives: The Oregon Land Fraud Trials, 1903-1910." *Pacific Historical Review* 35 (February 1966): 35-66.

Metzler, Ken. *Confrontation: The Destruction of a College President.* Los Angeles: Nash Publishing, 1973.

Miller, Christopher L. *Prophetic Worlds: Indians and Whites on the Columbia Plateau.* New Brunswick: Rutgers University Press, 1985.

Mills, Randall V. "Development of the Mass Transit Pattern of Portland, Oregon." In *Selections from the Oregon Business Review, 1941-1964,* edited by Catherine Lauris, 8-16.

———. *Railroads Down the Valleys: Some Short Lines of the Oregon Country.* Palo Alto, California: Pacific Books, 1950.

Minor, Rick, Stephen Dow Beckham, Phyllis E. Lancefield-Steeves, and Kathryn Anne Toepel. "Cultural Resource Overview of BLM Lands in Northwestern Oregon: Archaeology, Ethnography, History." *University of Oregon Anthropological Papers* 20 (1980): 1-198.

Mitchell, Donald. "A Demographic Profile of Northwest Coast Slavery."

In *Status, Structure and Stratification: Current Archaeological Reconstructions,* edited by Marc Thompson, Maria Teresa Garcia, and Francois J. Kense, 227-36. Calgary: University of Calgary Archaeological Association, 1985.

Morrison, Dorothy Nafus. *Outpost: John McLoughlin & the Far Northwest.* Portland: Oregon Historical Society Press, 1999.

Moynihan, Ruth Barnes. *Rebel for Rights: Abigail Scott Duniway.* New Haven: Yale University Press, 1983.

Mullins, William H. "'I'll Wreck the Town If It Will Give Employment': Portland in the Hoover Years of the Depression." *Pacific Northwest Quarterly* 79 (July 1988): 109-18.

Munk, Michael. "Portland's 'Silk Stocking Mob': The Citizens Emergency League in the 1934 Maritime Strike." *Pacific Northwest Quarterly* 91 (Summer 2000): 150-60.

Murray, Keith A. *The Modocs and Their War.* Norman: University of Oklahoma Press, 1959.

Murrell, Gary. *Iron Pants: Oregon's Anti-New Deal Governor, Charles Henry Martin.* Pullman: Washington State University Press, 2000.

Myers, Gloria E. *A Municipal Mother: Portland's Lola Greene Baldwin, America's First Policewoman.* Corvallis: Oregon State University Press, 1995.

Nash, Lee. "Scott of the *Oregonian:* Literary Frontiersman." *Pacific Historical Review* 45 (August 1976): 357-78.

Neal, Steve. *McNary of Oregon: A Political Biography.* Portland: Oregon Historical Society Press, 1985.

Norwood, Frederick A. "Two Contrasting Views of the Indians: Methodist Involvement in the Indian Troubles in Oregon and Washington." *Church History* 49 (June 1980): 178-87.

O'Connor, Richard, and Dale L. Walker. *The Lost Revolutionary: A Biography of John Reed.* New York: Harcourt, Brace & World, 1967.

O'Donnell, Terence. *An Arrow in the Earth: General Joel Palmer and the Indians of Oregon.* Portland: Oregon Historical Society Press, 1991.

———. *That Balance So Rare: The Story of Oregon.* Portland: Oregon Historical Society Press, 1997.

Oliphant, J. Orin. *On the Cattle Ranges of the Oregon Country.* Seattle: University of Washington Press, 1968.

Ostler, Jeffrey. "The Origins of the Central Oregon Range War of 1904." *Pacific Northwest Quarterly* 79 (January 1988): 2-9.

Patterson, Alexander. "Terrasquirma and the Engines of Social Change in 1970s Portland." *Oregon Historical Quarterly* 101 (Summer 2000): 163-91.

Paul, Rodman W. "After the Gold Rush: San Francisco and Portland." *Pacific Historical Review* 51 (February 1982): 1-21.

Peterson del Mar, David. *Beaten Down: A History of Intimate Violence in the West.* Seattle: University of Washington Press, 2002.

———. "Intermarriage and Agency: A Chinookan Case Study." *Ethnohistory* 42 (Winter 1995): 1-30.

———. "The Quiet Pacifists: Oregon's Old Mennonites, 1914-1945." *Oregon Historical Quarterly* 93 (Summer 1992): 116-40.

———. "Ready for War: Oregon Mennonites from Versailles to Pearl Harbor." *Mennonite Quarterly Review* 64 (July 1990): 209-29.

———. *What Trouble I Have Seen: A History of Violence against Wives.* Cambridge: Harvard University Press, 1996.

Pilcher, William W. *The Portland Longshoremen: A Dispersed Urban Community.* New York: Holt, Rinehart and Winston, 1972.

Pitzer, Paul C. "The Atmosphere Tasted Like Turnips: The Pacific Northwest Dust Storm of 1931." *Pacific Northwest Quarterly* 79 (April 1988): 50-55.

Pomeroy, Earl. *The Pacific Slope: A History of California, Oregon, Washington, Idaho, Utah, and Nevada.* New York: Alfred A. Knopf, 1965.

Porter, Kenneth Wiggins. "'The Boy's War': A Study in Frontier Racial Conflict, Journalism, and Folk History." *Pacific Northwest Quarterly* 68 (October 1977): 175-90.

Potts, James T. "H. L. Davis' View: Reclaiming and Recovering the Land." *Oregon Historical Quarterly* 82 (Summer 1981): 117-51.

Rakestraw, Lawrence. "Before McNary: The Northwestern Conservationist, 1889-1913." *Pacific Northwest Quarterly* 51 (April 1960): 49-56.

———. *A History of Forest Conservation in the Pacific Northwest, 1891-1913.* New York: Arno Press, 1979.

Ramsey, Jarold, comp. and ed. *Coyote Was Going There: Indian Literature of the Oregon Country.* Seattle: University of Washington Press, 1977.

———. *Reading the Fire: The Traditional Indian Literatures of America,* rev. ed. Seattle: University of Washington Press, 1999.

Reichwein, Jeffrey C. *Emergence of Native American Nationalism in the Columbia Plateau.* New York: Garland, 1990.

Reid, John Phillip. "Restraints of Vengeance: Retaliations-in-Kind and the Use of Indian Law in the Old Oregon Country." *Oregon Historical Quarterly* 95 (Spring 1994): 48-92.

Richard, K. Keith. "Unwelcome Settlers: Black and Mulatto Oregon Pioneers, Part II." *Oregon Historical Quarterly* 84 (Summer 1983): 173-205.

Richardson, Elmo. *David T. Mason: Forestry Advocate.* Santa Cruz, California: Forest History Society, 1983.

Robbins, William G. "Community Conflict in Roseburg, Oregon, 1870-1885." *Journal of the West* 12 (October 1973): 618-32.

——. *Hard Times in Paradise: Coos Bay, Oregon, 1850-1986*. Seattle: University of Washington Press, 1988.

——. *Landscapes of Promise: The Oregon Story, 1800-1940*. Seattle: University of Washington Press, 1997.

——. "Opportunity and Persistence in the Pacific Northwest: A Quantitative Study of Early Roseburg, Oregon." *Pacific Historical Review* 39 (August 1970): 279-96.

——. "Social and Economic Change in Roseburg, Oregon, 1850-1885: A Quantitative View." *Pacific Northwest Quarterly* 64 (April 1973): 80-87.

——. "Some Perspectives on Law and Order in Frontier Newspapers." *Journal of the West* 17 (January 1978): 53-61.

——, editor. *The Great Northwest: The Search for Regional Identity*. Corvallis: Oregon State University Press, 2001.

——, Robert J. Frank, and Richard E. Ross, editors. *Regionalism and the Pacific Northwest*. Corvallis: Oregon State University Press, 1983.

Rohe, Randall E. "After the Gold Rush: Chinese Mining in the Far West, 1850-1890." *Montana: The Magazine of Western History* 32 (Autumn 1982): 2-19.

Ronda, James P. *Astoria & Empire*. Lincoln: University of Nebraska Press, 1990.

——. *Lewis and Clark among the Indians*. Lincoln: University of Nebraska Press, 1984.

Ruby, Robert H., and John A. Brown. *The Cayuse Indians: Imperial Tribesmen of Old Oregon*. Norman: Oklahoma University Press, 1972.

Schlup, Leonard. "Republican Insurgent: Jonathan Bourne and the Politics of Progressivism, 1908-1912." *Oregon Historical Quarterly* 87 (Fall 1986): 229-44.

Schwantes, Carlos Arnaldo. *The Pacific Northwest: An Interpretive History*, rev. ed. Lincoln: University of Nebraska Press, 1996.

——, editor. *The Pacific Northwest in World War II*. Manhattan, Kansas: Sunflower University Press, 1986.

——, editor, assisted by Evelyne Stitt Pickett. *Encounters in a Distant Land: Exploration and the Great Northwest*. Moscow: University of Idaho Press, 1994.

Schwartz, E. A. *The Rogue River Indian War and Its Aftermath, 1850-1980*. Norman: University of Oklahoma Press, 1997.

Schwartz, Gerald. "Walter M. Pierce and the Birth Control Movement." *Oregon Historical Quarterly* 88 (Winter 1987): 370-83.

Seideman, David. *Showdown at Opal Creek: The Battle for America's Last Wilderness*. New York: Carroll & Graf, 1993.

Shinn, Paul L. "Eugene in the Depression, 1929-1935." *Oregon Historical Quarterly* 86 (Winter 1985): 341-69.

Simpson, Peter K. *The Community of Cattlemen: A Social History of the Cattle Industry in Southeastern Oregon, 1869-1912*. Moscow: University of Idaho Press, 1987.

Slatta, Richard W. "Chicanos in the Pacific Northwest: A Demographic and Socioeconomic Portrait." *Pacific Northwest Quarterly* 70 (October 1979): 155-62.

——, and Maxine P. Atkinson. "The 'Spanish Origin' Population of Oregon and Washington: A Demographic Profile, 1980." *Pacific Northwest Quarterly* 75 (July 1984): 108-16.

Spores, Ronald. "Too Small a Place: The Removal of the Willamette Valley Indians, 1850-1856." *American Indian Quarterly* 17 (Spring 1993): 171-91.

Stein, Arlene. *The Stranger Next Door: The Story of a Small Community's Battle Over Sex, Faith, and Civil Rights*. Boston: Beacon Press, 2001.

Stern, Theodore. *Chiefs and Chief Traders: Indian Relations at Fort Nez Perces, 1818-1855*, vol 1. Corvallis: Oregon State University Press, 1993.

——. *Chiefs and Change in the Oregon Country: Indian Relations* at Fort Nez Perces, 1818-1855, vol 2. Corvallis: Oregon State University Press, 1996.

———. "Ideal and Expected Behavior as Seen in Klamath Mythology." Journal of American Folklore 76 (January-March 1963): 21-30.

———. The Klamath Tribe: A People and their Reservation. Seattle: University of Washington Press, 1965.

Steward, Julian H., and Erminie Wheeler-Voegelin, The Northern Paiute Indians. New York: Garland Publishing, 1974.

Stone, Harry W. "Beginning of Labor Movement in the Pacific Northwest." Oregon Historical Quarterly 47 (June 1946): 155-64.

Stratton, David H., and George A. Frykman, editors. The Changing Pacific Northwest: Interpreting its Past. Pullman: Washington State University Press, 1988.

Sullivan, Margaret L. "Conflict on the Frontier: The Case of Harney County, Oregon, 1870-1900." Pacific Northwest Quarterly 66 (October 1975): 174-81.

Suttles, Wayne, ed. Northwest Coast. Washington: Smithsonian Institution, 1990.

Tamura, Linda. The Hood River Issei: An Oral History of Japanese Settlers in Oregon's Hood River Valley. Urbana: University of Illinois Press, 1993.

Tanaka, Stefan. "The Toledo Incident: The Deportation of the Nikkei from an Oregon Mill Town." Pacific Northwest Quarterly 69 (July 1978): 116-26.

Tanner, Stephen L. Ernest Haycox. New York: Twayne, 1996.

Taylor, Joseph E., III. Making Salmon: An Environmental History of the Northwest Fisheries Crisis. Seattle: University of Washington Press, 1999.

Taylor, Quintard. "The Emergence of Black Communities in the Pacific Northwest." Journal of Negro History 64 (Fall 1979): 342-55.

———. "The Great Migration: The Afro-American Communities of Seattle and Portland During the 1940s." Arizona and the West 23 (Summer 1981): 109-26.

———. "Slaves and Free Men: Blacks in the Oregon County, 1840-1860." Oregon Historical Quarterly 83 (Summer 1982): 153-70.

Teresa, Miriam. Legislation for Women in Oregon. New York: C. P. Young, 1924.

———. "Oregon Legislation for Women in Industry." Bulletin of the Women's Bureau 90 (1931): 1-37.

Thompson, Jeff, and Michael Leachman. Boom, Bust, and Beyond: The State of Working Oregon 2002. Silverton: Oregon Center for Public Policy, 2002.

Toll, William. The Making of an Ethnic Middle Class: Portland Jewry Over Four Generations. Albany: State University of New York Press, 1982.

———. "Permanent Settlement: Japanese Families in Portland in 1920." Western Historical Quarterly 28 (Spring 1997): 18-43.

———. Women, Men and Ethnicity: Essays on the Structure and Thought of American Jewry. Lanham, Maryland: University Press of America, 1991.

Turnbull, George S. Governors of Oregon. Portland: Binfords & Mort, 1959.

Twining, Charles E. George S. Long: Timber Statesman. Seattle: University of Washington Press, 1994.

Tyack, David B. "The Perils of Pluralism: The Background of the Pierce Case." American Historical Review 74 (October 1968): 74-98.

Tyler, Robert L. Rebels of the Woods: The I.W.W. in the Pacific Northwest. Eugene: University of Oregon, 1967.

Unruh, John D., Jr. The Plains Across: The Overland Emigrants and the Transmississippi West, 1840-60. Urbana: University of Illinois Press, 1982.

Utley, Robert M. A Life Wild and Perilous: Mountain Men and the Paths to the Pacific. New York: Henry Holt, 1997.

Vaughan, Thomas, editor. High & Mighty: Select Sketches about the Deschutes Country. Portland: Oregon Historical Society Press, 1981.

———, editor. *The Western Shore: Oregon Country Essays Honoring the American Revolution*. Portland: Oregon Historical Society Press, n.d.

———, and Virginia Guest Ferriday, editors. *Space, Style, and Structure: Building in Northwest America*, 2 vols. Portland: Oregon Historical Society Press, 1974.

Vibert, Elizabeth. "'The Natives Were Strong to Live': Reinterpreting Early-Nineteenth-Century Prophetic Movements in the Columbia Plateau." *Ethnohistory* 42 (Spring 1995): 197-229.

———. *Traders' Tales: Narratives of Cultural Encounters in the Columbia Plateau, 1807-1846*. Norman: University of Oklahoma Press, 1997.

Voeltz, Herman C. "Coxey's Army in Oregon, 1894." *Oregon Historical Quarterly* 65 (September 1964): 263-95.

Walker, Deward E., editor. *Plateau*. Washington: Smithsonian Institution, 1998.

Walth, Brent. *Fire At Eden's Gate: Tom McCall & the Oregon Story*. Portland: Oregon Historical Society, 1994.

Wardin, Albert W., Jr. *Baptists in Oregon*. Portland: Judson Baptist College, 1969.

Wells, Gail. *The Tillamook: A Created Forest Comes of Age*. Corvallis: Oregon State University Press, 1999.

White, Richard. *"It's Your Misfortune and None of My Own": A History of the American West*. Norman: University of Oklahoma Press, 1991.

———. *The Organic Machine: The Remaking of the Columbia River*. New York: Hill and Wang, 1995.

Whitelaw, Ed. "Rich Oregonian, Poor Oregonian." *Oregon Quarterly*, Summer 1995, 28-30.

Wiegand, Wayne A. "Oregon's Public Libraries during the First World War." *Oregon Historical Quarterly* 90 (Spring 1989): 39-63.

Wiley, Leonard. *The Granite Boulder: A Biography of Frederick Homer Balch, Author of The Bridge of the Gods*. Portland: Dunham, 1970.

Wollner, Craig. *The City Builders: One Hundred Years of Union Carpentry in Portland, Oregon, 1883-1983*. Portland: Oregon Historical Society Press, 1990.

Wright, Mary C. "Economic Development and Native American Women in the Early Nineteenth Century." *American Quarterly* 33 (Winter 1981): 525-536.

Wynne, Robert Edward. *Reaction to the Chinese in the Pacific Northwest and British Columbia, 1850 to 1910*. New York: Arno Press, 1978.

Youst, Lionel. *She's Tricky Like Coyote: Annie Miner Peterson, an Oregon Coast Indian Woman*. Norman: University of Oklahoma Press, 1997.

Zucker, Jeff, Kay Hummel, and Bob Høgfoss, *Oregon Indians, Culture, History & Current Affairs: An Atlas & Introduction*. Portland: Oregon Historical Society Press, 1983.

Unpublished

Baisinger, Janet Lynn. "Nordic Immigrants in Portland, 1870-1920: The First Fifty Years." Master's Thesis, Portland State University, 1981.

Baker, Abner Sylvester, III. "The Oregon Pioneer Tradition in the Nineteenth Century: A Study of Recollection and Self-Definition." Ph.D. diss., University of Oregon, 1968.

Barefoot, Martha Killian. "Between 'True Woman' and 'New Woman': Oregon Women's Clubs, 1890-1916." Master's Thesis, University of Oregon, 1994.

Beers, Christian Robert Nicholas. "Basque Settlement in Jordan Valley, Oregon." Master's thesis, University of Oregon, 1982.

Blankenship, Warren Marion. "Progressives and the Progressive Party in Oregon, 1906-1916." Ph.D. diss., University of Oregon, 1966.

Buck, Amy K. "Alien Land Laws: The Curtailing of Japanese Agricultural Pursuits in Oregon." Master's thesis, Portland State University, 1999.

Buckley, Geoffrey L. "Desertification of the Camp Creek Drainage in Central Oregon, 1826-1905." Master's thesis, University of Oregon, 1992.

Carlson, Christopher Dean. "The Rural Family in the Nineteenth Century: A Case Study in Oregon's Willamette Valley." Ph.D. diss., University of Oregon, 1980.

Carson, James Leonard. "A Social History of the Willamette Valley: 1890-1900." Master's thesis, University of Oregon, 1953.

Chapman, Maude Davis. "Sylvester Pennoyer, Governor of Oregon." Master's thesis, University of Oregon, 1943.

Chen, Chia-Lin. "A Gold Dream in the Blue Mountains: A Study of the Chinese Immigrants in the John Day Area, Oregon, 1870-1910." Master's thesis, Portland State University, 1972.

Clare, Warren L. "Big Jim Stevens: A Study in Pacific Northwest Literature." Ph.D. diss., Washington State University, 1967.

Cliff, Thelma Drake. "A History of the Warm Springs Reservation, 1855-1900." Master's thesis, University of Oregon, 1942.

Cocks, James Fraser, III. "The Selfish Savage: Protestant Missionaries and Nez Perce and Cayuse Indians, 1835-1847." Ph.D. diss., University of Michigan, 1975.

Culbertson, Paul Thomas. "A History of the Initiative and Referendum in Oregon." Ph.D. diss., University of Oregon, 1941.

Cummings, Hilary Anne. "John H. Mitchell, a Man of His Time: Foundations of His Political Career, 1860-1879." Master's thesis, University of Oregon, 1985.

Dawson, Deborah Lynn. "'Laboring in My Savior's Vineyard': The Mission of Eliza Hart Spalding." Ph.D. diss., Bowling Green State University, 1988.

Dougherty, Clifford. "A History of Education in Tillamook County, Oregon." Master's thesis, University of Oregon, 1942.

Edson, Christopher Howard. "The Chinese in Eastern Oregon, 1860-1890." Master's thesis, University of Oregon, 1970.

Ertle, Lynne. "Antique Ladies: Women and Newspapers on the Oregon Frontier, 1846-1859." Master's thesis, University of Oregon, 1995.

Evans, Tony Howard. "Oregon Progressive Reform, 1902-1914." Ph.D. diss., University of California, Berkeley, 1966.

Ferrell, John S. "Indians and Criminal Justice in Early Oregon, 1842-1859." Master's thesis, Portland State University, 1973.

Fahl, Ronald Jenks. "Joseph Watt: Pioneer of Commerce and Industry." Master's thesis, University of Oregon, 1966.

Gregor, Kyung Sook Cho. "Korean Immigrants in Gresham, Oregon: Community Life and Social Adjustment." Master's thesis, University of Oregon, 1963.

Guzowski, Kenneth James. "Portland's Olmsted Vision (1897-1915): A Study of the Public Landscapes Designed by Emanuel T. Mische in Portland, Oregon." Master's thesis, University of Oregon, 1990.

Haines, Margaret Nan. "Women in Jackson County, Oregon, 1875-1885: A Group Portrait." Master's thesis, University of Oregon, 1980.

Hajda, Yvonne P. "Regional Social Organization in the Greater Lower Columbia, 1792-1830." Ph.D. diss., University of Washington, 1984.

Hanson, David E. "A Pyrrhic Victory on the Home Front: Portland, Oregon, Schools in World War II." Ph.D. diss., University of Oregon, 1985.

Harger, Jane Marie. "The History of the Siletz Reservation, 1856-1877." Master's thesis, University of Oregon, 1972.

Harvison, Robert Guy. "The Indian Reorganization Act of 1934 and the Indians of Oregon and their Land." Master's thesis, University of Oregon, 1970.

Hatton, Raymond Robert. "Impact of Tourism on Central Oregon." Master's thesis, University of Oregon, 1969.

Herzog, June. "A Study of the Negro Defense Worker in the Portland-

Vancouver Area." B.A. thesis, Reed College, 1944.

Hilden, Clark Gilbert. "An Historical Geography of Small Town Main Streets in the Willamette Valley, Oregon." Ph.D. diss., University of Oregon, 1980.

Hill, Daniel G., Jr. "The Negro in Oregon: A Survey." Master's thesis, University of Oregon, 1932.

Hinken, Susan Elizabeth. "The Woman's Christian Temperance Union of Oregon, 1880-1916." Master's thesis, Portland State University, 1987.

Holden, Margaret Kolb. "The Rise and Fall of Oregon Populism: Legal Theory, Political Culture and Public Policy, 1868-1895." Ph.D. diss., University of Virginia, 1993.

Hylton, Dory J. "The Portland State University Student Strike of May 1970: Student Protest as Social Drama." Ph.D. diss., University of Oregon, 1993.

Jackson, Virgil Davis. "Social Conflicts in Rural Communities of Oregon." Master's thesis, Oregon State Agricultural College, 1932.

Jepsen, Victor L. "A General History of Klamath Falls from its Beginning Until the Coming of the Railroad in 1909." Master's thesis, University of Oregon, 1939.

Johnson, Elaine Gale Zahad. "Protective Legislation and Women's Work: Oregon's Ten-Hour Law and the Muller v. Oregon Case, 1900-1913." Ph.D. diss., University of Oregon, 1982.

Johnston, Susan. "Paradoxes of Identity: Liberalism, Bio-Power and 'Homosexual' Politics in Oregon." Ph.D. diss., University of Oregon, 1996.

Kardas, Susan. "'The People Bought this and the Clatsop Became Rich': A View of Nineteenth Century Fur Trade Relationships on the Lower Columbia between Chinookan Speakers, Whites, and Kanakas." Ph.D. diss., Bryn Mawr College, 1971.

Kazin, Michael. "Irish Families in Portland, Oregon: 1850-1880, an Immigrant Culture in the Far West." Master's thesis, Portland State University, 1975.

Keeler, Elizabeth. "The Landscape of Horticultural Crops in the Northern Willamette Valley from 1850-1920." Ph.D. diss., University of Oregon, 1994.

Kessler, Lillian. "The Social Structure of a War Housing Community: East Vanport City." B.A. thesis, Reed College, 1945.

Koehler, Paul P. "Integration of the Mexican People in Woodburn, Oregon." Independent study thesis, University of Oregon, 1982.

Krenelka, Carol Ann. "Entertainments at Jantzen Beach Amusement Park, 1928-1970." Master's thesis, University of Oregon, 1981.

LaLande, Jeffrey Max. "'It Can't Happen Here' in Oregon: The Jackson County Rebellion, 1932-1933, and its 1890s-1920s Background." Ph.D. diss., University of Oregon, 1993.

La Plante, Bernard Raymond. "The Negro at Jefferson High School: A Historical Study of Racial Change." Ph.D. diss., University of Oregon, 1970.

Laythe, Joseph Willard. "Bandits and Badges: Crime and Punishment in Oregon, 1875-1915." Ph.D. diss., University of Oregon, 1996.

Lindstrom, David Elvin. "W.S. U'Ren and the Fight for Government Reform and the Single Tax, 1908-1912." M.S.T. thesis, Portland State University, 1972.

Livingston, Marilyn Gerber. "Klamath Indians in Two Non-Indian Communities: Klamath Falls and Eugene-Springfield." Master's thesis, University of Oregon, 1959.

Loprinzi, Colleen Marie. "Hispanic Migrant Labor in Oregon, 1940-1990." Master's thesis, Portland State University, 1991.

Lyon, Cherstin M. "Chinese Immigrants, Cultural Hegemony, and the Politics of Everyday Crime in Portland, Oregon, 1859-1908." Master's thesis, University of Oregon, 1998.

Malarkey, Deirdre Pruyn Dexter. "Processes of Land Conversion: An Example of Wilsonville, Oregon." Ph.D. diss., University of Oregon, 1978.

Manchester, Scott. "The History of Mutual Support Organizations Among the Chinese in Portland, Oregon." Master's thesis, Portland State University, 1978.

McConnell, Gregory Clark. "An Historical Geography of the Chinese in Oregon." Master's thesis, University of Oregon , 1979.

McElderry, Stuart John. "The Problem of the Color Line: Civil Rights and Racial Ideology in Portland, Oregon, 1944-1965." Ph.D. diss., University of Oregon, 1998.

McFarland, Carol Kirkby. "Bethenia Owens-Adair: Oregon Pioneer Physician, Feminist, and Reformer, 1840-1926." Master's thesis, University of Oregon, 1984.

Merriam, Paul Gilman. "Portland, Oregon, 1840-1890: A Social and Economic History." Ph.D. diss., University of Oregon, 1971.

Miller, Gary Kenneth. "A History of Transportation in Nineteenth Century Umatilla County, Oregon." Master's thesis, Portland State University, 1996.

Miller, Heather Lee. "From Moral Suasion to Moral Coercion: Persistence and Transformation in Prostitution Reform, Portland, Oregon, 1888-1916." Master's thesis, University of Oregon, 1996.

Minor, Rick. "Aboriginal Settlement and Subsistence at the Mouth of the Columbia River." Ph.D. diss., University of Oregon, 1983.

Moon, Katherine Lee. "Nan Wood Honeyman and the Politicization of Women in Oregon, 1870-1942." Master's thesis, Portland State University, 2001.

Moser, Douglas Steven. "An Ethnographic Study of the Southern Willamette Valley Grass Seed Industry." Ph.D. diss., University of Oregon, 1975.

Murray, Neil Dennis. "A Comparative Historical Study of Student Protest at the University of Oregon and Oregon State University during the Sixties." Ph.D. diss., University of Oregon, 1971.

Nash, Lee M. "Refining a Frontier: The Cultural Interests and Activities of Harvey W. Scott." Ph.D. diss., University of Oregon, 1961.

Niles, Aliscia. "The Power of Culture, Place and Agency: Understanding Struggles Over Agrarian Land Use and Practices in Oregon's Willamette Valley." Master's thesis, University of Oregon, 1999.

Ostler, Jeffrey Don. "The Meaning of Place in an Eastern Oregon Locality: The Antelope-Shaniko Country, 1863-1915." Master's thesis, University of Oregon, 1984.

Pearson, Rudy N. "African Americans in Portland, Oregon, 1940-1950: Work and Living Conditions—A Social History." Ph.D. diss., Washington State University, 1996.

Peters, Robert Norton. "From Sect to Church: A Study in the Permutation of Methodism on the Oregon Frontier." Ph.D. diss., University of Washington, 1973.

Pintarich, Richard Mark. "The Swamp Land Act in Oregon, 1870-1895." Master's thesis, Portland State University, 1980.

Poulton, Helen Jean. "The Progressive Movement in Oregon." Ph.D. diss., University of Oregon, 1949.

Pricco, Jeff David. "Homeless Strangers Among Us: The Chinese Community in Portland, Oregon, 1860-1900." Master's thesis, University of Oregon, 1978.

Ptacek, Thomas James. "The Federal Writers' Project in Oregon, 1935-1942: A Case Study." Master's thesis, Portland State University, 1979.

Ramirez, Carmen Cecilia. "A Study of the Value Orientation of Lane County, Oregon, Mexican American Mothers with a Special Focus on Family/School Relationships." Ph.D. diss., University of Oregon, 1981.

Rhodes, Ethel Camille. "Negroes in Pacific Coast History Prior to 1865." Master's thesis, Howard University, 1940.

Robbins, Marcus Christoph. "Striving to Loosen the Bonds of Dependence: Eugene, Oregon, 1890 to 1929." Master's thesis, University of Oregon, 1990.

Robert, Frank Livezey. "The Public Speaking of George Earle Chamberlain: A Study of the Utilization of Speech by a

Prominent Politician." Ph.D. diss., Stanford University, 1954.

Roberson, James Jeffery. "An Historical Geography of Banking in Oregon from 1859 to 1968, with Emphasis on Unit Banking from 1900 to 1933." Master's thesis, University of Oregon, 1971.

Rosenthal, Nicolas G. "'Walk Across the Bridge. . . an' You'll Find Your People': Native Americans in Portland, Oregon, 1945-1980." Master's thesis, University of Oregon, 2000.

Roulston, Thomas B. "A Social History of Fort Vancouver, 1829-1849." Master's thesis, Utah State University, 1975.

Schmalenberger, Roberta Lee. "The German-Oregonians, 1850-1918." Master's thesis, Portland State University, 1983.

Scott, Edna. "The Grange Movement in Oregon, 1873-1900." Master's thesis, University of Oregon, 1923.

Shroyer, Peter Anthony. "Railroad Regulation in Oregon to 1898." Master's thesis, University of Oregon, 1965.

Slatta, Richard Wayne. "Chicanos is Oregon: An Historical Overview." Master's thesis, Portland State University, 1974.

Smith, Steven L. "The Oregon Farmers Union, 1930-1940: A Study in Farm Values and Adjustment." Master's thesis, University of Oregon, 1973.

Smolensky, Jack. "A History of Public Health in Oregon." Ph.D. diss., University of Oregon, 1957.

Stearns, Marjorie R. "The History of the Japanese People in Oregon." Master's thesis, University of Oregon, 1937.

Stone, Harry W., Jr. "Oregon Criminal Syndicalism Laws and the Suppression of Radicalism by State and Local Officials." Master's thesis, University of Oregon, 1933.

Sturdivant, Fred D. "The W. A. Woodard Lumber Company: A Case Study in 'Rugged Individualism.'" Master's thesis, University of Oregon, 1961.

Sutherland, Johnnie David. "Umatilla Agricultural Landscapes, 1700-1973: An Historical Geography of a Region of the Oregon Country."

Master's thesis, University of Oregon, 1973.

Swenson, Steven Robert. "Political Culture, Voting Behavior, and Political Realignment: The Case of Eugene, Oregon, 1864-1920." Master's thesis, University of Oregon, 1983.

Tattam, William Marquis. "Sawmill Workers and Radicalism: Portland, Oregon, 1929-1941." Master's thesis, University of Oregon, 1970.

Tetzlaff, Thomas Edwin. "Settlement and Landscape Transitions: The Coquille Valley, Oregon." Masters thesis, University of Oregon, 1973.

Tims, Melinda. "Discovering the Forty-Three Percent Minority: Pioneer Women in Pleasant Hill, Oregon, 1848-1900." Master's thesis, L'Universite de Poitiers, 1982.

Tonkinson, Myrna Ewart. "Changing Consciousness: The Impact of the Women's Liberation Movement on Non-Activist Women in a University Community." Ph.D. diss., University of Oregon, 1976.

Tracy, Charles Abbott. "The Evolution of the Police Function in Portland, Oregon, 1811-1974." Ph.D. diss., University of California, Berkeley, 1976.

Triplett, Jack E., Jr. "History of the Oregon Labor Movement Prior to the New Deal." Master's thesis, University of California, 1961.

Valadez, Senon Monreal. "An Exploratory Study of Chicano Parent Perceptions of School and the Education of their Children in Two Oregon Community Settings." Ph.D. diss., University of Oregon, 1974.

Weinstein, Esther G. "William Simon U'Ren: A Study of Persistence in Political Reform." Ph.D. diss., Syracuse University, 1967.

Weiselberg, Erick Lawrence. "Ascendency of the Mazamas: Environment, Identity and Mountain Climbing in Oregon, 1870-1930." Ph.D. diss., University of Oregon, 1999.

Wilner, Joseph Bear. "All My Sisters and Brothers: Redefinitions of Family in Oregon Intentional Communities During the Late

Twentieth Century." Master's thesis, University of Oregon, 2000.

Wilson, John Donald. "The Knights of Labor in Oregon, 1880-1897." Master's thesis, University of Oregon, 1997

Woodell, Marshall E. "Grange Influence on Direct Legislation in Oregon, 1903-1934." Master's thesis, University of Oregon, 1936.

Wong, Rose Marie. "Sweet Cakes, Long Journey: A Social and Urban History of Portland, Oregon's First Chinatown." Ph.D. diss., University of Washington, 1994.

Wright, Mary C. "The Circle, Broken: Gender, Family, and Difference in the Pacific Northwest, 1811-1850." Ph.D. diss., Rutgers University, 1996.

———. "The World of Women: Portland, Oregon, 1860-1880." Master's thesis, Portland State University, 1973.

Young, Patricia Jean. "Measure 9: Oregon's 1992 Anti-Gay Initiative." Master's thesis, Portland State University, 1997.

Zakoji, Hiroto. "Klamath Culture Change." Master's thesis, University of Oregon, 1953.

Zink, Laurie A. "Women in the Oregon Political Elite, 1960-1990: Changing Profiles of State Participation." Ph.D. diss., University of Oregon, 1993.

Index

What thought leaders and management professionals have to say about *Restore Yourself*:

"Like *Good to Great* and *Built to Last*, Edy Greenblatt's *Restore Yourself* unlocks the secrets of creating sustainable organizations. She explains how busy executives and professionals have it within their grasps to rejuvenate themselves and lead more fulfilling and satisfying professional lives ... even when the odds seem stacked against them. A must read for anyone who makes it through the day on espressos and lattes."

— **DAVID AGER, PH.D.**
Co-Director of Undergraduate Studies and Lecturer on Sociology, Harvard University

"Relax, take a moment – or if you're still on 24/7 time – **make** a moment to enjoy this book and learn from it the great secrets to a life free from professional exhaustion!"

— **MARSHALL GOLDSMITH**
Executive Coaching Guru and *New York Times* best-selling author of *What Got You Here Won't Get You There*

"In this important book, Edy Greenblatt shows us the way to achieve a higher quality of life and how to eliminate so many of the stressors that plague and tire us – especially the self-imposed ones. In these challenging times, it's hard to find a more necessary or more welcome set of strategies for rejuvenation."

— **BRONWYN FRYER**
Senior Editor, Harvard Business Review

More praise for Edy Greenblatt's *Restore Yourself*

"In our spastic 24/7 world, this book is astonishingly timely, useful and important. Please read it before you die. It might add a few years to your life."

—WARREN BENNIS

Distinguished Professor of Business, University of Southern California; leadership guru; multiple bestselling author and most recently, co-author of *Transparency and Judgment*

"A much-needed primer on living in the age of perpetual depletion. In today's environment, organizations, groups and teams feed off the individual like ant colonies live off the bodily resources of individual ants and the illusion that work happens only in the cognitive realm of the mind has become the unquestioned major premise. The worker's whole being – mind and body – need to be brought, together, to the light of consciousness. This is what Dr. Greenblatt accomplishes, with characteristic authenticity, wit, and *savoir-faire*. Read it to *do* differently – and read it to *see* differently."

—MIHNEA MOLDOVEANU

Professor & Director, Desautels Centre for Integrative Thinking, Rotman School of Management, University of Toronto; Founder & CTO, Redline Communications Group

"This inspiring book translates years of thoughtful social scientific research into actionable strategies for bringing positive energy back into our work and lives. *Restore Yourself* not only advances the argument that restoration is critical to both productivity and happiness, it shows us *how* to find that energy and then capitalize on it every day."

—MONICA C. HIGGINS, PH.D.

Associate Professor, Harvard Graduate School of Education, Author, *Career Imprints: Creating Leaders Across an Industry*

Restore Yourself

Restore Yourself

The Antidote for Professional Exhaustion

Edy Greenblatt, Ph.D.
with Michael Allan Kirk and Erin V. Lehman, Ph.D.

Execu-Care Press
Los Angeles

Cover design by Renee Frisbie,
Guru of Brands, Los Angeles, CA
Cover photograph by
Frank Richardson, FDR Photo, San Jose, CA
Cover model is Pierre-Herve Giauque
Back cover author's photograph by
Alex Huber and Sara Jacobson, New York, NY
Book block design by Oscar Cragwell

ISBN: 9780981929910

For inquires about author appearances or permission to
reprint, please visit www.RestoreYourselfBook.com

FIRST EDITION

10 9 8 7 6 5 4 3 2 1

To The Farmer

"If I am not for myself, who will be for me?

If I am only for myself, what am I?

And, if not now, when?"

Rabbi Hillel
Pirkei Avot 1:14

Contents

Foreword

Twenty-five years ago, I had the opportunity to work as a consultant at several of America's largest organizations. By 5 p.m. each day the hallways were empty. As a matter of fact, I could have shot a torpedo down the hall and no one would have known until the next day!

In those days, professionals and leaders alike worked a 40-hour week. They took vacations — sometimes four to five weeks of the year! Job security, benefits, healthcare, and pensions—these were all available for the taking. Those days are gone.

Today, we work hard, perhaps too hard, often past the point of exhaustion. Yet, it doesn't matter how much we learn, how skilled we become, or what we know if we cannot generate and manage the necessary energy to do what needs doing.

In *Restore Yourself*, Edy Greenblatt provides views, approaches, and strategies for rejuvenation that will help you accomplish what you want to accomplish. This comprehensive volume is the synthesis of Dr. Edy's many years of experience and research. *Restore Yourself* will not just help you achieve more. It will also teach you to draw positive energy back into your life consistently and successfully, time and time again.

Relax, take a moment – or if you're still on 24/7 time – **make** a moment to enjoy this book and learn from it the great secrets to a life free from professional exhaustion!

Marshall Goldsmith

New York Times best-selling author of
What Got You Here Won't Get You There
International best-seller and winner of the
Harold Longman Award – Best Business Book of 2007

Introduction

I suspect that you've opened this book because you or some important people in your life are exhausted. Perhaps, in spite of all of your multi-tasking, optimizing, and time juggling, life still feels unmanageable. If so, you have opened the right book.

Are you distraught because the 'to-die-for' job is killing you? I understand how you feel. I spent the first half of my adult life helping repair personal and social damage done by work. Then, one day, I awoke professionally exhausted myself and decided to get on the other side of that equation.

At the Harvard Business School, I focused my doctoral research on how to make work less damaging to people like you and me. After receiving my Ph.D. in Organizational Behavior, I spent the next seven years working as an executive coach, consultant, and researcher. I have helped thousands of professional people learn to be more resilient. This book is the culmination of that research- and experience-based journey.

This chapter details the book's origins. If you are eager to get started on your personal journey to restoration, then skip mine and go directly to Chapter One to start to restore yourself!

MY TALE OF PROFESSIONAL EXHAUSTION

In my first career, I helped people recover. I was neither a physician, nurse, social worker, nor a therapist. I was a dance ethnologist. As a trained and practicing artist and

social scientist, I examined what we learn about human values, minds, and societies by examining the physical and social artifacts that humans create. Speaking more plainly, I looked at culture and dancing.

Unlike other cultural anthropologists, the dance ethnologist's primary window into culture and human behavior is the dance event. (To try out that role, think about what a visitor from rural Ghana could ascertain about American high school culture by spending one hour at your high school prom. Or, think about why you loved the movie *My Big Fat Greek Wedding*.) I worked as a dance professional, scholar, assistant professor, choreographer and master teacher travelling throughout the world to teach ethnic dance. For additional income, I taught social dancing to adults in recreational settings in Los Angeles.

Living the artist's dream had included completing a B.S. in world arts & cultures (including the pre–med curriculum) and an M.A. in dance ethnology, both from the University of California at Los Angeles (UCLA). My career included running an arts and education business that linked travel and corporate trainings with the dance people and skills that inspired me. I achieved my childhood goal of dancing for a living. It made me happy but often physically tired, sleep deprived and poorer than I preferred. It was a good life nonetheless.

My adult students came to my classes on weeknights at seven or eight in the evening, often directly from work. They spent their scarce free time learning Israeli, Balkan, or North American social dances from me. Often I was paid per head and so my continued ability to eat sushi depended on my students' sustained and growing weekly satisfaction. In business terms, to succeed I had to know my customer value proposition and exactly what differentiated my product from all the competing uses of people's free time.

At one point, I realized that my customers weren't just paying for dance lessons. *They were buying restorative experiences.* As I became more and more mindful of the experiences that my customers really craved, I also started noticing some paradoxes in my own professional experience.

I was living three different professional lives. When I spoke with people about my work, I described an enviably happy existence. I was proud that, among other things, I enabled people to heal from the damage done by work. The dance events I ran created conditions that replenished people's personal resources, that is, their life energies. For between $3 and $15 per session, clients of all ages had fun, expressed themselves through physical exercise, learned some new skills, met an achievable cognitive challenge, and often received a hug or two.

When asked about my seemingly boundless energy and passion, I shared that my work/life was free from draining process losses, impossible deadlines, and other liabilities typically attributed to employment in corporate America. I rarely needed to get approvals, sit in meetings, wait in lines, face crowds or get stuck in rush-hour traffic. I also mentioned that my work included lots of artistic expression, music, exercise, joy, and passion. To my audience, that made sense. What I did wasn't *really* work because it was fun! For a while, I believed that as well.

The second manifestation of my professional life was my "on stage" experience. Whether performing or teaching, engaging with and for an audience gave me a buzz. I often got into the state of optimal experience called flow.[1] On stage, I was an elated, high-performing, effective, efficient and beloved artist-educator-friend-scholar at the top of my tiny little field. Jewish mothers lined up to proffer their single sons' phone numbers and photographs. When I finished performing at an event, though parts of me were exhausted, I

was content and still resilient. These first two work/life experiences were complimentary enough.

Over time, however, professional exhaustion became my third career experience. Increasingly, I felt physically, socially, cognitively, and emotionally drained. Some days I hated myself, my students, and the entire world. I was short-tempered with my family, my dry cleaner, my boyfriend and stray cats. I was getting sick more often. Although objectively I knew that my classes were comprised of wonderful, lovely, committed, supportive, generous people, there were days during which all I could see was a room full of energy vampires poised to extract their pint.

Pouring my vitality into my students' leaky buckets without a reliable source of replenishment for myself was leaving *me* drained. I began avoiding calls and didn't go dancing in my free time. I rarely recall my dreams, but at the time in a particularly vivid one, I was joyously living alone with a large dog on a vast property dotted with large 'No Trespassing' signs. I had a shotgun for those who refused to obey the signs.

My dream career eventually became a nightmare. My three loves: dancing, teaching and helping people had morphed from sweet treats into bitter toxins and I was burnt out. I had come down with a severe case of professional exhaustion.

Even in my pooped-out state, I noticed that my students arrived tired and grumpy but continued to leave my classes inspired and energized. That was good. Yet I became hyper-aware that they would come back each week just as beleaguered. Often, I imagined hearing the taunts of Bad Luck telling the spirit of Good Luck in a famous children's book, "What it takes you one year to create; I can destroy in one second.[2]" I became increasingly frustrated that I could not cure my own chronic depletion, let alone others'.

I thought, "If my dream job was burning me out, what hope was there for ANYONE to survive much less thrive in the workplace? What was it about working that depleted people so much? And why did this affect almost every adult I met?"

Contemporary Western society didn't have the answer. The Dilbertesque, thank-G-d-it's-Friday view that attributes chronic exhaustion to the corporate cubical was obviously insufficient. Granted, when you don't enjoy what you do, each hour worked can feel like torture. But, many of my students had wonderful, creative, fulfilling jobs or ran their own businesses. And those who spent their days managing their households, family, health and financial matters were equally *kaput*.

My goal became to discover a way to significantly reduce the damage typically attributed to work. Achieving that goal would make my career as the fleet-footed depletion repairwoman obsolete. In a world with a readily available antidote for professional exhaustion, dance students would take dance classes only because they wanted to be better dancers, not because they were craving the balm of Gilead.

Moreover, in a post-antidote world, people would have enough energy to discipline themselves to deposit their trash in a bin, be more patient with their two-year-olds, and get enough sleep to safely operate their motor vehicles. All of us would have the cognitive fuel to make better decisions, lead more responsibly, and collaborate more effectively. If less mentally and physically exhausted, the stewards of commerce and policy could better focus sufficient attention on **our** interests, homes, lives and portfolios. In a world of more resilient coworkers and neighbors, tough times would be shorter and markedly less tough because each person would be able to contribute more, faster and better. A more

energized world could not help but be better than an exhausted one.

There HAD to be an answer. So, off I went to the joint Ph.D. Program in Organizational Behavior at Harvard University and Harvard Business School with my lay theory that professional exhaustion did not have to be an inevitable part of contemporary urban life. Though at the time I could not articulate it as such, I had a hunch that the problem's root cause was a complex interaction between job design, leadership, organizational culture, common assumptions, folklore, habits, and unexamined expectations and that interacting together, they made our work/lives unmanageable. I was confident that somewhere, at the intersection of psychology, physiology, sociology, management science, neuropsycho-pharmacology, anthropology, organizational behavior, nutrition, occupational therapy, dance, grandma's wisdom, experience and some common sense there awaited a palatable antidote.

I conducted the initial research for this book while in the doctoral program at Harvard. That work was generously funded by the Division of Research at the Harvard Business School, the Department of Psychology at Harvard University, Club Med North American Zone, Club Med Asian Zone, Bank of Ken, the Pavlovitch Family Fund for Academic Advancement, and Your Travel Agent. Subsequent work was either directly or indirectly supported by Execu-Care Coaching and Consulting and its clients, the Center for Effective Organizations at the Marshall School of Business at the University of Southern California, and recently, by a large, well-respected and very generous management consulting company that shall remain nameless.

The specifics of the original research and analyses, including Club Med village stories, are in my dissertation entitled, *A Paradox in Paradise: Depletion and Restoration of*

Personal Resources, Emotional Labor and Burnout in an Idyllic Total Institution (Edith Greenblatt, 2001, Harvard University). A shorter version of its key messages appear in a rather dry but managerially-relevant article called, "Work/life Balance: Wisdom or Whining," published in *Organizational Dynamics* (Edy Greenblatt, 2003). Research details are in those two publications. This book, by contrast, is intentionally light on research citations for faster, easier reading by busy people like you.

Restore Yourself is the synthesis of five years of doctoral research, including two year's studying and working alongside Club Med frontline resort hosts called *gentile organisateurs* (GO's). (Although GO's live and work in paradise, they burn out faster than securities traders!) I then spent another five years running seminars for and coaching thousands of men and women who worked in a broad range of professional occupations and organizations. What I have discovered about avoiding professional exhaustion has helped me to help them. Now, I hope I can help you.

The views, tools, and strategies that I present in this book have already made a difference in the lives of others who either learned them through my workshops, the *Dr. Edy Shows*, articles, executive coaching, or during casual airplane conversations. I am confident that you can benefit from being exposed to them here.

Now, it is time for the disclaimer. The materials in this book are NOT an alternative to or replacement for proper medical treatment, wellness care, social support, difficult conversations, formal management education, tough decisions, leadership coaching, curbing your inner four-year-old, self-discipline, or your having to change a particularly bad condition or relationship that you have suffered too long.

This book CAN help you regain your resilience so that you have more stamina, patience, focus and confidence to take

care of your own needs and commitments, whatever they are. If you diligently apply what you'll learn here, you should also have extra energy left over to help yourself and those around you become at least a bit more successful and content.

The time, money, love, support, and personal resources of many, many people made *Restore Yourself* possible. The list of those contributors is at the end of the book. The placement is intentional. By the time you finish reading this, I think you will have gleaned at least a few valuable insights. At that time, I hope you will skim the list of contributors and direct a moment of praise or gratitude to those who have helped me help you.

A special note of thanks is presently due to my coaches and colleagues Michael Allan Kirk and Dr. Erin V. Lehman without whose professional input and encouragement, this book would be far less clear, concise, and useful. Though many have been involved, all errors and omissions in this work are entirely mine. My wish is that this book starts some useful conversations in your head, your organization, and your family.

I hope this book helps you not just survive but thrive at work and in your personal life. If you have additional questions, find errors or would be willing to share some of your experiences with others, please visit our website at www.RestoreYourselfBook.com. I will be working to nurture an on-line community there and welcome your input.

Be well and good luck!

Edy Greenblatt

Restore Yourself

CHAPTER ONE

Vitameatavegamin

"Are you tired, rundown, listless? Do you poop out at parties? Are you unpopular?³" In the 1950s, *I Love Lucy* featured Lucille Ball inviting us to join the "thousands of happy peppy people" who had successfully rejuvenated themselves by drinking Vitameatavegamin.⁴ On her husband's mythical television special, Lucy hawked this equally mythical elixir – the 23% alcohol solution to cumulative urban fatigue.

To me, the Vitameatavegamin episode provided telling social commentary. Even 50 years ago, the man in the grey flannel suit was already often chronically exhausted, burned out, pooped, fuzzy, dull, or depressed.

Life surely hasn't gotten any easier and the real-life Vitameatavegamin has yet to appear. Though not clinically in physical, psychological, emotional or spiritual crisis, many of us are among the scores of walking wounded or nearly so.

I wrote this book to help you heal from and prevent future burnout. Through it, I will teach you to view, choreograph and manage your life in ways that will help you energize yourself and those around you. The research, tools and best practices shared in this book will allow you to take steps, right now, to improve the quality of your existence without quitting your job, moving to Costa Rica, or getting a divorce. If you or those you manage are professionally exhausted or on the verge, you'll want to implement at least some of these restorative strategies. My intention is to give

1

you the basic tools you'll need to prevent or recover from professional exhaustion.

Unlike many work/life balance strategies, my approach does not pit work against home nor does it force you to choose between yourself, your family or your career. *Au contraire*, with Personal Resource Management™ (PRM), my approach to lasting resilience, your net gains in energy, attitude and capability will benefit you, your family, AND your organization. A more resilient YOU will have more to bring to all aspects of your life. In this chapter, I present the book's main ideas and then briefly summarize each chapter so you can quickly locate what you need.

THE MAIN POINT

The useful and proven assumption underpinning *Restore Yourself* is:

If you know how to successfully increase your personal resources and then do so, you will have more available energy to mobilize in the service of those things most important to you.

Your personal resources are your founts of **physical, social, cognitive and psychological energies.** Notice that I am not talking about reallocating financial resources, downshifting, multi-tasking or managing time better. *Restore Yourself* is about learning to create and then mobilize more personal fuel in the service of the things that matter to you without costing you additional time, money or favors. Moreover, the skills required to restore yourself can be learned and practiced **while** you work, not in lieu of it.

On this journey, you will learn to see life in terms of restorative or depleting events instead of as a war between

work and life.   I'll provide research and case studies reminding you that in many instances, both your grandmother and your instincts were correct all along.   A satisfying, successful balance of work and life is possible if you have the right tools, skills and mindsets.   Personal Resource Management™ (PRM), the antidote for professional exhaustion, will provide them.

In many ways, you already know and understand the basics of PRM. To prove it, try this little quiz. How would your grandmother have answered this question, "What do children need when they get home from school?" Jot your answer down here.

_____

_____

_____

_____

_____

Great. Did your list include things like run around, play, tell someone about their day, take a nap, go outside, get a hug, sit quietly, or have milk and cookies? Would the answers have varied for different kids or under different circumstances? Of course they would have.

These answers support a core understanding that people's personal resources are part of a dynamic and individual cycle that ebbs and flows with who we are and what we do. Grammy could predict when and why energies would be up or down, and knew how to enable her loved ones to self-manage. She was using her instinctive version of PRM.

You face daunting demands as a manager, worker, leader, team player and family member. You are a corporate athlete who needs adequate breaks, proper nutrition and

coaching. Basic maintenance is **necessary but not sufficient** for life's performance. To be your best, you also need the skills to repair the damage done by work, and more importantly, the ability to diagnose the conditions and behaviors that depleted you in the first place. With these tools, you can recover from and prevent future burnout.

Grammy did not need a book describing a systematic approach to increasing her organization's productivity. She was pretty good at predicting what people needed because she personally (a) knew all the players well, (b) was a skilled and mindful observer of human behavior, (c) knew the working conditions, and (d) recognized and understood the daily energy demands on members of her staff. She also had social values on her side. The values of Grammy's world did not thwart her efforts; they actually guided her.

Grandma's job was in many ways easier than yours is. She did not have to contend with television and the web wide cacophony of contradictory experts. Nor did she confront external stakeholders' value conflicts driven by organizational mission statements. Experience and instinct, aided by ethics and religious values, informed her. And, Grammy's risks of making a mistake were lower. If Grammy miscalculated and her team started running on fumes, the Sabbath acted as a safety net that insured the extra rest, socializing, engagement or detachment that was needed.

In Grammy's era, human needs were basically the same, but, values were clearer and external influences were more limited. Life was neither global nor 24/7. Knowing how we were 'feeling' was part of her job description and a valued use of her time. Society understood that people were, well... human, and needed attention, care and maintenance. That was Grammy's job and she got little guff for doing it.

Times have changed. More than half of what we know we've learned in the last fifteen years. The need to remain

resilient in our complex world is great and growing ever greater. And the costs of failing to do so are dear and growing dearer. Professional exhaustion is expensive by every standard of measure because it disrupts our lives, companies, families and communities.

Restore Yourself teaches you Personal Resource Management™ (PRM), a research- and practice-based system to diagnose and treat the causes of your professional exhaustion. And Grammy would have approved of it. PRM has already helped thousands of professionals world-wide. As a manager, this approach will help you increase your own productivity, satisfaction and energy. It will also help you understand how to create conditions that will do the same for those around you without noticeably increasing your costs in time or money. In learning and mastering Personal Resource Management™, my proven method for increasing your energy and satisfaction with your entire work/life), you will become expert at diagnosing what most impacts your personal energies. This will help you make small but powerful changes that increase your personal and professional resilience.

Whether out of necessity, obligation or enjoyment, using PRM will make it natural for you to effectively restore yourself. This works whether you are currently running a company, raising a family, or managing a personal setback.

WHAT'S IN THE BOOK

In order to reliably and successfully restore yourself, you will need to (a) get clear on the problem, (b) understand what a solution would look like, (c) determine exactly what you will want to change, (d) learn techniques and tools to implement the solutions you come up with and then (e) implement. This book provides you with the tools, techniques and knowledge to get you started down the path to restoration.

First, you will need a clear vision of what the problem really is and what kind of results you want. Since one barrier to achieving a more resilient life is the myth of the work/life balance, we will approach professional exhaustion in ways that make solutions both tractable and attainable.

Chapter Two reveals the commonly held assumptions about work/life balance that have led most of us astray. Here, I explode the debilitating and pervasive myth that work is essentially depleting and non-work is restorative. Adopting a more accurate perspective of the situation will get you off the work/life balance merry-go-round and onto a mount headed down the road to resilience.

If the demands of your work and life have you feeling caught between a rock and a hard place, Chapter Three will help you understand how you got there and how to relocate. There I reveal how Personal Resource Management™ is the antidote for professional exhaustion. PRM was developed to help those employed in various 24/7 service industries and has made a difference for thousands of people living hectic professional lives. It will help you.

In Chapter Three you'll also learn about the *two agreements of PRM*: Learn to identify your depleters and restorers and commit to managing them on a regular basis.

In Chapter Four you will be introduced to three counterintuitive secrets that will help you master what depletes and restores your personal resources. These *three musketeers of resilience* will help you in your battle against professional exhaustion.

In Chapter Five, you will learn about the four kinds of energy – physical, social, psychological and cognitive that constitute your vital personal resources. You'll learn how they interact with each other and how to manage your Average Personal Resource Levels (APRLs).

With a basic understanding of Personal Resource Management, you'll be ready for some surprising findings in Chapters Six and Seven: Reliable Restorers and Sneaky Depleters. In these chapters you'll discover why fidgeting in your desk chair can increase your productivity and how even extroverts can become exhausted being around people. You will also learn how *overdose effects* can turn your favorite hobby into a draining experience.

In Chapter Eight you will diagnose your own energizing needs. You will complete an enlightening exercise; my proven Personal Resource Management Assessment™ (PRMA). Regardless of how traditional or untraditional your occupation or lifestyle, completing this exercise will immediately reveal to you specific, simple actions you can take today that will improve the quality of your life tomorrow. You will find this exercise helpful right now. It will also show you how to effectively prioritize your future actions as you progress towards a richer, more resilient future. You'll finish Chapter Eight with a first draft of a *Personal Energy Profile* (PEP) and action plan that will start you down your path to resilience.

Chapter Nine is about time and timing. Here I teach you about what I call *strategic sequencing.* This approach helps make even the most debilitating and inflexible schedule less daunting and exhausting. Strategic sequencing will help you hone your PEP to use timing to your advantage in ending professional exhaustion. Ever wonder if it's better to take lots of short breaks or push through and then take a longer break? You'll get the answer here. Even master time jugglers and calendar queens have honed their skills using my strategic sequencing protocols. You'll hone your action plan here.

Finally, Chapter Ten is your review and the launch of your more resilient life. That's the best part!

ARE YOU READY TO RESTORE YOURSELF?

Many people feel like unwilling participants trapped in a lose-lose game of overwork and fatigue. Some feel they've traded financial security and social comfort for chronic exhaustion. Others feel that they have unknowingly signed up to be a responsible, albeit slightly miserable drone. There are also those who do what I used to do; pretend that it is okay to exhaust yourself in the name of caring for others while ignoring the reality that if you collapse, everyone loses.

If you're okay with clinging to weekends like a rescue buoy and enduring each weekday by minimizing the time and energy you spend on work, then don't read the rest of this book. BUT, if your current existence simply is no longer good enough for you, or, if you want to coach your kids, employees, parents, teammates, mentees, clients and spouses towards a better way, then read on. I will equip you with the necessary tools to bust the myth of work/life balance and start to working on the things that you CAN change to bring positive energy into your work/life. That will put you and your team, company and/or family back on a path to living the lives that you know you are capable of and, dare I say, deserve. Are you ready? If so, go on to the next page and start to RESTORE YOURSELF!

CHAPTER TWO

The Work/Life Balance Myth

"I'm headed back to New York from Rome. I haven't been feeling well and will set up a time for us to meet when I'm back in Italy." The handsome, graying-at-the-temples dark-eyed man in the aisle seat next to me ended his call and started dialing again.

"... and please ask Roberto to follow up with Mr. Williams for me. I'll pick things up on Monday," he concluded.

"May I just slip out for a minute?" I asked. He nodded, obviously a bit irritated, and then started speaking to his headset again.

"I'm about to take off. The doctor said that I should" CLICK. As he had gotten up to let me out into the aisle, he had somehow disconnected his call.

"I'm sorry," I said as I passed close to his now even more irritated face. He snorted a little.

I smiled. "Arrogant jerk," I thought. "What makes him think he's so special that his call is more important than my work and my life?" I got my notes from the overhead and slid quickly past him back into my seat.

"Please turn off and stow away all portable electronic devices," declared the omnipresent voice of the flight steward.

"...doctor in Italy put some needles in my ears and said I really should take at least a few weeks off and stop flying so much," he said into his headset. Silence. "...much more useful than those New York doctors who ran me through 30

9

tests and still couldn't tell me why I'm suffering." Silence. "We'll talk when I get back. *Ciao*," he finished.

Many contemporary professional development books use a fabricated story that helps make it more *Who Moved My Cheese*-like. In my case, this encounter really did occur. I had been trying to finish this book for five years and was struggling to complete it when, yes, I really did meet a handsome, dark-eyed co-CEO guy on a plane. And yes, he really was the archetypal depleted professional this book aims to help. He actually did sit next to me and let me teach him how to use Personal Resource Management ™ to restore himself. (It was a long flight and all the other seats were full.)

Clearly, he was a gift from the heavens to help me get this book done. In return, I introduced him to ways by which he could help himself become more effective, satisfied and resilient. With your indulgence, I will tell this tale with the help of my Mediterranean travelling companion periodically appearing and disappearing from these pages. We're going to call him David – like Michelangelo's definitive statue. Yes, that's good – David.

I tried to ignore him. Honestly, I tried. "He's not your client. He's not your friend. It's none of your business," I told myself.

Just before take off, an uncommonly attentive flight attendant chatted charmingly with us. She clearly thought we were a married couple. Handsome guy seemed to lighten up.

"Wow, she's really enjoying this. How unusual," I commented after she had moved up the aisle.

"Yes, quite unusual," he answered to my surprise. "Service is almost dead on American carriers," he added. "But, you can't expect much more. Their job has gotten so much harder recently and, by the time people get on planes

these days, everyone is so exhausted and irritable that it certainly must make their work that much harder."

Clearly, I was sitting next to a passenger who understood and excelled in exhausted and irritable. At least he was aware that something was wrong with his own situation and was frustrated that he couldn't define or remedy it. (Those are often necessary first steps to recovering one's vitality.)

Several moments passed as each of us busied ourselves putting away our Blackberries and unpacking headphones while listening to the usual pre-flight drill. As the plane took off, we spoke of airlines and service workers.

Then, I just couldn't contain myself. After all, he really wasn't a jerk. He was a nice guy who was just professionally exhausted. And, I was sure that I could help him.

"It seems like you've been working really hard," I began. "I'm sorry; I couldn't help but overhear your calls. You said you haven't been feeling well. Usually, by the time a guy like you is telling others that he's exhausted, things are actually pretty bad." He nodded in agreement.

To my considerable surprise, my co-traveler's face softened and he shared the dilemma he was confronting. He was so burned out that he was considering leaving his dream job as co-CEO of a global professional services firm.

David is not alone. Work/life balance is the topic of thousands of books, articles and conversations throughout the Western world for a reason. Now more than ever, we have an escalating need for solutions to chronic depletion. Many of us find ourselves thrust into life and work situations that seem to constantly be at odds with each other. No longer do we have

the luxury of working a set eight hours whether it be nine to five or the graveyard shift. Given today's global economic difficulties, we not only have to work our set hours, but we also have to use our rare discretionary time working 'second shift' – holding down second jobs, running our households, and trying to develop entrepreneurial ventures to help free us from the risks of layoffs. We habitually do this by sacrificing time originally slated for sleep, self-care, family, friends and recreation.

All told, most of us are failing to lead well-rounded, healthy lifestyles. This is not unique to professionals who have families but applies to single people as well. Un-partnered individuals face the same struggles with work/life balance that their married counterparts do. They too are endlessly struggling to find time for their extended family, companionship, passions and other obligations while meeting the demands of staying professionally afloat.

Scores of books and articles have taught us about optimizing our time by becoming hyper-efficient through multi-tasking, priority setting and becoming more goal oriented. We also know from positive psychology that having a clear, compelling purpose and meaning for our lives inspires and invigorates. Those strategies all help. Even so, many of the most organized, optimized and noble of purpose among us still experience rampant depletion, exhaustion and frustration. David had clearly arrived at that place.

"First I thought I was exhausted because I'd been bad at making time for sleep and exercise" he admitted. "I'm really shocked. I actually just took a few weeks off and, frankly, I'm not much better off now than I was before I went on vacation. In the past, I could always catch up over the weekend or during vacation but that's not working any more."

"I've been watching my ability to think and to plan deteriorate, too. I'm trying to make more time for myself and my family but I just cannot seem to pull that off either. I've overheard my children's casual discussions about how Papa's burning the candle at both ends and it seems he's running out of wax," admitted David.

"Sounds like you're fighting a losing battle," I said. "Perhaps you're starting from a flawed set of assumptions. If so, those assumptions could be preventing you from addressing the underlying problem," I suggested.

At that moment, I wouldn't have been surprised if he had hauled off and clocked me one. Instead, the corners of David's mouth curled up and, with an inquisitive smile, he asked, "Do you have an approach that would help me do so?"

THE LIES THAT BIND US

"I might," I replied. "But first, I have a question for you. Are your colleagues and professional peers faring any better than you are?" I asked.

"No," he replied. "It seems we're an entire generation paddling ever harder but still failing to get upstream."

I continued. "Most professionals I meet are having the same experience. I think that's in part because they are running their businesses and lives based on a disabling world view. Here's a visual depiction of what I call the work/life balance myth." I handed him a PowerPoint slide I'd printed out for a recent workshop. It's Figure 1.

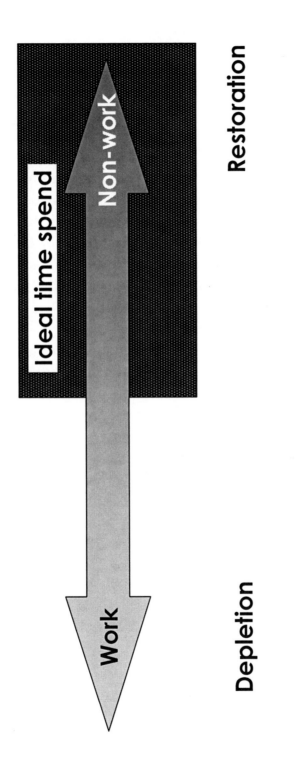

Reproduced with permission: Greenblatt, 2001

Figure 1: Work/Life Balance Myth

"A slide, eh? Your pedigree is showing," he joked.

"Forgive me," I replied. "This chart shows the common perception that work, on the left, is depleting and non-work – time devoted to family, friends, hobbies, and community – is restorative. If this is the case, how would you achieve an ideal, energized, restored, contented work/life?"

David replied quickly. "According to this picture, all you can do is quit working or at minimum, strive to work as little as possible."

He was right and as such, summarized the current problem. The fundamental assumption underlying the dominant view of work/life balance is that work and non-work are on the same continuum as depletion and restoration. Its message is clear: work is depleting and non-work is restorative.

"If work is always depleting and non-work is always restorative, then we should all retire in order to regain our resilience and verve," he continued. "But that's not only absurd, it's impossible."

"Is this model consistent with your professional experiences in the United States?" I asked.

"Yes. Actually, now I see what so shocked me about how Americans think. I remember when I opened the New York office, how surprised I was when my secretary explained the common phrases 'Thank G-d it's Friday' and "over-the-hump day."

"So, you've seen this model in action?" I asked.

"Yes, I have," he admitted.

"Though it may hurt to admit it, can you see how you have now successfully adopted this perspective?" I asked. He grimaced in agreement and took a sip of red wine.

"As a successful businessman," I continued, "you clearly have outstanding problem-solving skills. Tell me, David, what is wrong with this model?" I inquired.

"Okay, first of all, if this is true, we have only two choices in life – either to be chronically depleted from working or to be unemployed and energetic. That's a pretty dismal set of choices given that most of us need to and even like to work. It makes life appear to be indentured servitude for everyone but the super rich and that just feels wrong," he said.

David paused a moment. "Well, either that or you need to be a professional athlete, artist or owner of a little café on Avenue des Champs-Élysées," he mused.

In addition to being an impossible situation (for anyone but trust-fund babies), this dominant Western paradigm permanently and completely pits organizations against their workforces and vice versa. In our current world of both perceived and chronic scarcity, most employees end up forever trying to work less for more money. Simultaneously, their organizations are endlessly trying to motivate them out of this tendency. This duel interferes with creating the collaborative, empowered organizational cultures we know are most successful. And, this is likely a reason that job satisfaction and work/life balance issues don't get the attention they should in organizations. When defined in this way, they are losing battles that no HR director in her right mind would enthusiastically step into.

Entrepreneurs and artisans are not immune to chronic depletion, either. In many cases, they are even more susceptible to professional exhaustion than white collar workers because they actually think that they're operating on the right side of the model, pursuing their passions and therefore not subject to depletion at all. Many assume that they do not need to actively manage depletion because by definition, they don't really work. That's simply not true and I am living proof of that fallacy.

And, what else is wrong with this approach?" I continued. David took a moment to think and then smiled.

"Well, maybe you will think me a work-a-holic," he said, "but, I disagree with the part about work being depleting. There are aspects of my job that I find very restorative. For example, when I'm in a tough negotiation and I can tell we are gaining the upper hand, I feel like a million bucks, even if we're only going to net a half million." He smiled. "In fact, in my role as co-CEO, I'd say most of what I do, I really love," he concluded.

"Cool. So you're saying that all aspects of work aren't necessarily depleting. I agree," I said.

> Think about it for yourself. Remember a time when you became so completely absorbed in and energized by an interesting task that work just didn't feel like work? What you were doing? How did it feel?
>
> I recall how invigorating it was working 18-20 hour days as a lighting designer for an amazing modern dance company called Moving Arts. The dancers, the stage manager, the choreography, the ease of communication, the theater and the great equipment all made the project an incredibly restorative experience.

"Can you see any other flaws in the model?" I asked.

"Yes. Again, maybe something's wrong with me but, to be quite frank, spending time with my family at my mother-in-law's house in Tuscany is not the enviable holiday that my colleagues imagine. When I get back, I feel more like I've unsuccessfully negotiated a peace treaty than finished a vacation in the Italian countryside," sighed David.

David's experience is illustrative. The current urban myth touts the restorative benefits of all time spent away from work, whether spent with family or on recreation. To test the

validity of that assumption, one need only sit on a bench at Disneyland on any given day at 4 pm. The myth is debunked each time a quibbling, crabby, sugar-buzzed, sleep-deprived family stumbles past. I tested the validity of my hypothesis with David, "Were you surprised how you felt during your first family trip to Disneyland?"

"Oh my, I think I had blocked it from my memory," David exclaimed. "The first half of the day was great. Then, by mid afternoon, the twins were taking turns crying and my wife was sun burned, irritable and had a migraine. My ever-bored teenage daughter was whining about already spending her $150 and not having gotten anything good. What's really frightening was that by dinner time, my family seemed rather content compared to others around us."

"So, it sounds like we agree that there must be a more precise way to depict the challenges of maintaining one's resilience?"

"Yes. And, let me guess...you have a slide for that, too don't you Edy?" David teased.

"Well, I do happen to have this one that specifically addresses your objections to the first model. I used it yesterday. It's based on my research." I pulled out the resilience goal slide showing a more accurate depiction of the relationships between work, non-work, depletion and restoration. (See Figure 2.)

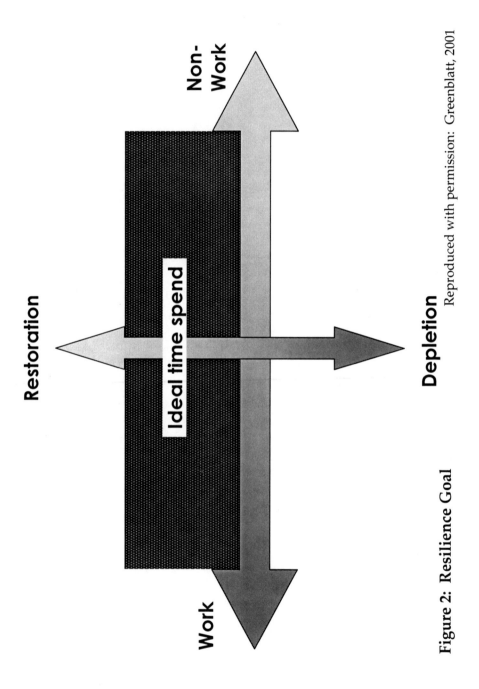

Figure 2: Resilience Goal

"In contrast with the first model, this chart depicts work and non-work on a separate continuum from depletion and restoration," I said. "Consistent with what you've explained David, it portrays how time working can be either restorative or depleting just as time away from work can be one or the other."

"So," said David, "it sounds like my goal should NOT be to work less, but rather to maximize my exposure to restorative things and minimize my exposure to depleting things, right?"

"Exactly!" I replied.

JUGGLING FOR BALANCE

Research and casual observation show that we cannot find work/life balance in part because we're starting from a disempowering and fundamentally flawed set of assumptions. Most of us are trying to balance or trade off resources that we neither understand nor control. This practice has made addressing the problem of work/life balance that much more vexing. Before we go onto the next chapter, let's take a few minutes to talk about time, money and the other things historically juggled in the name of work/life balance.

Work/life balance is the absence of unacceptable levels of conflict between work and non-work demands.[5]

Research on work/life balance usually focuses on how to manage competing demands for resources. Simply put, achieving work/life balance depends on obtaining and managing sufficient resources to do, have or be those things that are most important to us. For most, this means meeting our real and perceived obligations.

SHARED VERSUS PERSONAL RESOURCES

The three types of resources most frequently discussed in the work/life balance literature are: (a) temporal resources, (b) financial resources, and (c) control or power. *Temporal resources* provide the time to do everything one needs or wants to do. Telework (working from remote locations), multitasking (i.e., eating while driving), and using information technology systems are among the common approaches to optimizing time use.

Financial resources provide the currency to buy goods and services that either improve life satisfaction or create opportunities to free up time to do so. Budget-reducing lifestyle choices and downshifting are among the strategies used to address financial resource constraints. *Control and power* provide the ability to select when and how to create important outcomes. Empowerment, self-directed work teams, and flexible scheduling have all been used to increase an employee's locus of control. These policies can increase job satisfaction and performance.

What these three shared resources have in common is that they are the products of social contracts that, by definition, are rarely determined by a single person. In the normal course of work; time is allocated, money is earned, and power and control are established through social interactions. Obtaining and maintaining these shared resources are normally the result of a negotiation between an individual and another social entity.

If you really want to have impact on your personal energies, you will also need to start consciously managing those things that **you** alone control. Those are your *personal resources* or personal sources of energy. Because they reside within each individual, personal resources are often managed at low social and financial cost. This leads to improved satisfaction and resilience for you while improving your

performance and satisfaction at work. That's because you simply have more to give.

Having imbibed too much Vitameatavegamin, Lucy Ricardo ended up drunk and out of work. False panaceas such as Vitameatavegamin have been providing us with a modicum of temporary relief without providing a real and lasting solution to professional exhaustion. It's time to stop treating the symptoms and, instead, address the problem of professional exhaustion and solve it. That's what I offer you in the rest of this book.

CHAPTER THREE

The Antidote for Professional Exhaustion

David, you and I probably now agree that the accepted view of work/life balance is a self-limiting one at best. As such, you may have formulated some new questions. For instance, "How can I use this new knowledge to help me feel better?" or "How can I use it to better my organization?" You might even be asking, "Which strategies beyond staff dinners and paid time off should I be supporting to keep us going during these tough times?" Alternatively, the skeptic in you might be saying "Great idea, but this looks too difficult to implement." David's reaction was less subtle.

"How do you expect me to focus my time and attention on yet another issue without sinking the company, alienating stakeholders or slowing the earth's rotation enough to create a 27- hour day?" he asked.

The short answer is, **in order to succeed, you will need to become an expert at optimizing your personal resources. That will increase your capacity to get things done both at work and away.** I told David as much.

LEADERS NEED TO BE ENERGIZED

"Okay, I get how having more energy could help me feel better, but, how would that make me a better leader?" David asked.

"Great question," I commended him. "Here's how.

That which we are able to accomplish on any given day has significant impact on the web of stakeholders relying on us to lead, follow or get out of the way. At work, exhaustion directly or indirectly slows down, damages or prevents millions of actions that client teams, customers, bosses, peers, support staff, and entire organizations need every single day. These depletion-based losses are so common that corporate culture has developed a litany of acceptable excuses for them. Some of my favorites (and they usually start with 'sorry') are:

- My computer crashed,
- I left my Blackberry in the car,
- I'll get back to you on that,
- 80/20 will be plenty here,
- We've had an unavoidable setback, and
- The guy responsible for that had an emergency."

"Have you every heard any of those?" I asked in jest.

"Of course I have," enjoined David. "My favorite is 'circumstances beyond our control.'"

"So, you get it. The cascade of common disclaimers that we use to explain away accountability failures almost always has a substantial professional exhaustion back-story," I shared.

EXHAUSTION REDUCES ACCOUNTABILITY

"Interesting that you raise the issue of accountability," David said, a bit surprised. "It is a huge problem in my business. I thought people failing to keep their promises simply reflected their poor character and upbringing."

"That can be a part of it. But, the answer in organizational settings is a far more complex one. The extent to which we hold ourselves accountable is actually the result of multiple social and personal conditions," I said.

"There is a lot of great thinking and research out on organizational accountability, especially work being done by Mobius Executive Leadership and by Professor Michnea Molodoveanu at the Center for Integrative Thinking at the University of Toronto.[6] Yet, even in the best thinking on this topic, one often overlooked contributor to accountability failures is that people are often just simply too tired to do what they know is right," I pointed out.

"Indications of this are everywhere," I continued as suddenly found myself in lecture mode. He looked interested so I continued. "A significant contributing cause of most major environmental catastrophes, from oil spills to Chernobyl, is operator error due to sleep deprivation; a severe form of personal resource exhaustion. Some estimates show that sleep deprivation alone causes more than 100,000 car accidents each year.[7] Surely at least most of those drivers intended to do the right thing. When it came time to act responsibly, many simply did not have the energy to discipline themselves sufficiently to make better choices."

I continued. "We, as a society, tolerate these practices calling them necessary evils. Exhaustion compromises our performance as much as being drunk does, yet surgeons still do surgeries and attorneys still argue death sentence cases long after their windows of peak performance have closed." I had concluded my lecture.

David's eyes flashed. "You're right. It's a bait and switch," he realized. "I pay a premium for the best orthopedic surgeon to do my knee surgery. Then, the great physician arrives in the operating room so tired that he really cannot be the first-rate artist that I hired. Tired and distracted, he cannot perform much better than the resident assisting him."

"That's exactly the case," I agreed. "And, it's at the core of hiring and other selection challenges. Think about it. When we recruit someone into a professional position or even search

for a spouse, we are trying to match the role's requirements with our estimate of what that person can do, day in and day out. Basically, we're estimating not only a person's capabilities but also the average level of personal resources available to support and sustain their mobilization.

On the other hand, when on an interview or a date auditioning for a particular romantic role, we are careful to be upbeat, well-groomed and rested. We do so in order to convey the highest possible average capacity to our future partners. Then, both in business and in love, once 'hired', we can deliver only the level of enthusiasm and commitment that remain after our depleting habits and routines have worn us down."

"Even though we continue to create and tolerate lifestyles that sabotage our ability to be our best, we are still surprised when our relationships fall short of expectations," I pontificated.

David looked thoughtful and remained seated. I took that as permission to continue.

"Because we tolerate and excuse so much personal and professional exhaustion, I believe that most of the U.S. workforce is unintentionally working well below its capacity. Given this endemic professional exhaustion, is it any wonder that we're struggling to remain competitive in so many commercial arenas?" I asked.

"Makes sense to me," David shared. "Clearly, you have the problem diagnosed. Dr Edy, do you also have the cure?"

"I think I have at least part of it. I call it Personal Resource Management™ or PRM for short," I replied. "I have already seen many successful men and women identify and conquer chronic professional exhaustion by using PRM. And I am confident it can help most people significantly, including you."

I estimate that with organizational support for employee's adoption of basic Personal Resource Management™ strategies, work productivity and job satisfaction in United States businesses could increase by 10-20% within two years.[8]

PERSONAL RESOURCE MANAGEMENT™ (PRM)

Somewhere over the Atlantic, the jet engines had faded into the background. My conversation with David had given way to a necessary hour-long pause. The flight attendant was serving dinner and, with the cart blocking the aisle, my audience was captive. But before I could speak, David asked me to share the antidote for professional exhaustion that I had promised him previously.

"While my research exposed the liabilities of living under the influence of the work/life balance myth, it also provided the empirical data that led to my developing Personal Resource Management™. This approach has helped revitalize thousands of pooped professionals."

"Okay, I'll bite. Please tell me more about your energizing approach with the stuffy title," David asked mockingly.

"Yes sir, I will. But it will take me a few more minutes of management speak to get there. Can you handle it?" I asked.

"Yes, I can. They'll be serving the hot fudge sundaes soon so I'll have fortification," he replied.

Here's what I explained.

PRM DEFINED

Your personal resources are the founts of energy that you use to fuel everything that you do. In PRM, I refer specifically to four kinds of personal resources or energies: *physical, cognitive, social and psychological-emotional.* (I'll get

very specific about that in Chapter 4.) For now, when I say personal resources, think of *life fuel* or energy.

Personal Resource Management™ (PRM) is the active diagnosis and intentional regulation of the life features that impact our personal resources.

THE TWO AGREEMENTS OF PRM

To actively diagnose and intentionally regulate the aspects of your life that affect your energies, you will need to do two things. I call these the *Two Agreements of PRM*.

1. **Learn the distinguishing features of what restores and depletes you, and**

2. **Mindfully manage the conditions and behaviors in your life that most impact your personal resource levels.**

"The extent to which you keep these two agreements will determine how quickly and effectively you'll be able to reenergize yourself," I told David.

"Sounds right," said David, "though some of the terms are still a little confusing. I'll need you to elaborate on the agreements. But before you do, I'd appreciate a concrete example of how your PRM approach can help me."

"Okay," I agreed. "David, earlier you mentioned that winning a professional negotiation really restores you. Which parts of that scenario give you the rush you described?" I asked.

"Well, I like the intellectual challenge, engaging with smart people all focused on a single task and, well, the influencing and winning part," David answered.

"Great," I replied. "According to PRM, that would suggest that not only should you try to maximize your professional opportunities to negotiate, but you might also try to replicate those same social and cognitive conditions outside work, as well. For example, if you had a choice between volunteering to coach your son's debate team and making fundraising calls for it, I'd suggest you choose the former. The coaching is most likely to expose you to the conditions and behaviors that restore you. Do you get the idea?"

"Yes, that makes sense," David said sounding a bit surprised. "It's amazing how you figured that out so quickly. I've had mixed experiences helping my kids with school activities. Your explanation helps me start to understand why helping out at school is sometimes so wonderful and at other times so frustrating."

GET TO KNOW YOURSELF

Effective PRM requires that you make only two agreements in order to become more resilient. Let's take a closer look at the PRM's *first agreement*:

Know the distinguishing features of what restores and depletes you.

This agreement requires that you learn to recognize which behaviors and under which conditions you become restored—and, similarly, the behaviors and conditions that deplete you.

"I know what depletes me," David insisted. "Working too much, having too little family time, and being away from home exhaust me. Why do I have to make a specific commitment to doing what I'm already doing? Besides, doing so hasn't kept me from burning out so far."

"Great point," I replied.   "Your instincts that certain buckets of activities restore or deplete you (work, family time, travel) are good place to start."

Frankly, I was being a bit overly polite. The notion that big categories of activities such as work, home or vacation are fundamentally depleting or restorative is just plain wrong. I've found this rough-cut approach too imprecise to help most people get and remain resilient. (More on that later.)

Channeling Dr. Phil, I continued, "So, how's that working for ya?"

"Well, clearly its not," he admitted. "What am I missing?"

"First of all David, you're not alone," I offered in consolation. "Like so many others, your approach to burnout prevention is too imprecise to be reliably effective. Using this approach is rather like using a vacuum cleaner to clean your fine Swiss watch. You not only fail to get the outcome you want, but you're also likely to do some damage in the process. That's because using a blunt instrument prevents you from making critical distinctions between what you need to preserve, what needs replacing, and what actually needs gentle removal, " I shared.

"I get the metaphor. Now, please explain how this works for me in my life," he admonished.

"My research has shown that to be able to really prevent professional exhaustion, we need a precise instrument that helps accurately assess what affects our personal energy levels. With that, we can learn our own specific restoration and depletion triggers," I explained.

"So, how about an example Dr. Edy?" David asked.

"Okay, let's diagnose why volunteering at school has had an unpredictable effect on your energy," I suggested. "When assisting your son's debate team, do you run practice

sessions with them as well as coach them during actual debates with the other teams?" I asked.

He nodded.

"Ok, so in that scenario, you collaborate with kids who you know, providing feedback on how well they used data to help them win their negotiations, right?" I asked.

"Right," David concurred.

"In contrast, when you make fundraising calls for the team, you spend your time trying to convince community members, currently struggling to pay their mortgages, to donate money to a cause they may not yet support."

"Yes," he agreed.

"Then, although it is all volunteering and all involves negotiating, the latter exposes you to behaviors and conditions that are your known personal depleters – losing negotiations," I concluded.

"Wow, you're right. I hadn't really diagnosed the root cause of it's affect on me." David paused and then with a sly grin said, "I guess my goal should be to only work on the stuff I like and avoid the stuff that's frustrating."

"Well, not exactly," I replied.

"I know. But seriously," he continued, "this is a great strategy for volunteering but, what about for work? If you had figured out how I can run a business without ever doing anything I don't like to do, you'd be on a private jet instead of sitting next to me on commercial air. Even in my role as a co-CEO of a successful firm, I cannot offload ALL the unpleasant tasks to others. I might get away with it for a little while, but soon I'd get such a bad reputation that it would become impossible to get anyone to work with me in the future."

"Right again," I agreed. "And, I promise to get back to that shortly. But first, let me clarify the *second commitment of PRM* a bit.

PRM's SECOND AGREEMENT

Recall that the first agreement of PRM is to know what restores and depletes you. The second agreement of PRM is

Mindfully manage the features of your life that most impact your personal resource levels.

"Explain the terms, please," David requested.

"Let's start with mindfully manage," I suggested. "All successful professional people manage their lives or, frankly, they wouldn't be successful. A bit of mindless wandering and dithering is okay but not a reliable strategy to ensure long-term health and prosperity. Most of us do not wander through life in a completely mindless fashion. However, many of us are more mindless than we think. To be mindful is to be intentionally aware and actively make distinctions in your mental and physical world.[9] Harvard social psychology professor and mindfulness researcher Ellen Langer has proven that to be mindful, to carefully recognize (and therefore adapt to) what *is* instead of what our previous beliefs, experiences and hopes lead us to expect, improves almost all aspects of human existence.[10]

Importantly, this key aspect of what leadership guru Warren Bennis calls being 'a first-class-noticer' is a critical characteristic of great leaders.[11] Langer's important research-based book *Mindfulness* is a guidebook for acquiring this important skill. Until you hone that skill, PRM's tools and approach will teach you to draw the careful distinctions you'll need to help you get and stay restored," I concluded.

"You're saying that I can be less exhausted if I start to pay more attention to the behaviors and conditions under which I do things since they affect my personal resource levels?" David asked.

"Yes, that's exactly what I'm saying. Now, you've become mindful that simply volunteering does not have a predictable affect on you. Rather, it is the nature of the negotiations involved in volunteering that determine the quality of your experience," I explained.

"Okay, I've got the two commitments. Number one, get really good at what restores and depletes me and then, number two, continuously manage the behaviors and conditions that do so," David shared.

"Correct," I agreed.

"Great. Now, help me with my manpower shortage," David requested. I just don't have enough indentured servants to offload all of my nasty depleters onto others. Is there a website I should know about?" he joked.

I smiled. "Well, once you have made the two commitments to succeed at PRM, you'll need to know three key tactics to help you keep your agreements," I said.

"And what do you call these tactics, the three musketeers?" he mused.

"Well, I had been calling them the three secrets of resilience but actually, I like your term better. Thank you," I said gratefully.

Three Musketeers of Resilience

Over the years, I have learned three counterintuitive secrets that will help you master what depletes and restores your personal resources. These *three musketeers of resilience* will help you in your battle against professional exhaustion. They are:

- *VIVE LA DIFFÉRENCE*
  People differ in what restores and depletes them

- *LOOK BEHIND THE MASK*
  Social tags (such as *work* and *vacation*) can prevent us from seeing and acting on our true restoration and depletion triggers

- *WE CHANGE*
  Our sources of restoration and depletion change over time.

"Let's take them one at a time," I suggested. You joked that your answer to ongoing rejuvenation was impossible because you'd need to get someone else to do all of the tasks that frustrate you. That's a misconception from which you'll need our first musketeer to rescue you," I said.

"So d'Artagnan, you say I can make people do all my dirty work for me?" he jabbed.

"No, that's Bart Simpson's philosophy," I parried. "Seriously, it turns out that people respond very differently to particular tasks and environments and that can provide a great advantage when you're trying to create a more restored life, team or organization. Got it?" I teased.

"Of course not," he replied. "But, my belly is full of ice cream and I've seen all of these movies on previous flights. You have my undivided attention. Continue."

VIVE LA DIFFÉRENCE

The message of our first musketeer of resilience is not a complex one:

People differ in what restores and depletes them.

How **can** you offload even some of your most onerous tasks onto others and not suffer ill social consequences? No one these days has either enough friends or enough money to find, retain and pay people to be miserable for long. Not to mention that miserable people make really bad employees.

David had exposed a fundamental challenge in trying to improve people's work/lives. If certain tasks are just plain insufferable for everyone, then how do you get anyone to do them? One answer is to pay a premium for discomfort. That's in part why New York City garbage men working only three hours per day can earn more than a Manhattan-based nurse working a 12-hour shift. However, if this was universally the case, all salaries would be compensation for damage done by work, all people would dread coming to work each day, and, the entire workforce would arrive on Monday mornings fully restored and rejuvenated (after having been away from their

sole source of depletion). We know that's not true. I shared these thoughts with David.

"That sounds like part of the myth we busted earlier. Work isn't always depleting so salaries aren't simply a version of hazardous duty pay," David responded. "Moreover, I've read that retirement for many individuals increases the incidence of depression, disability and early death in some groups. So, at minimum, something about working is better for those people than not working is," he shared.

"Exactly," I remarked. Now, we had come to the first musketeer's message.

"Specifically, people differ in what restores and depletes them. Like the legendary three musketeers in Alexandre Dumas' novel, even those in the same occupation who share common goals and values are very different. And those differences can be cause for celebration. Even though by Thursday afternoon most people are looking forward to the weekend, the assumption that work depletes people the same way is just a corollary to the work/life balance myth," I said.

"I get the general idea," said David. "Now, give me an example of how this works."

"The first step is recognizing that in terms of what energizes and drains us, we are all more dissimilar than we think. We are pretty sure that our friends and colleagues are more like us than not. Don't you agree?" I asked.

"I accept that the world is full of different kinds of people, but yes, I do assume that my friends share many of my preferences, views and interests," David answered.

"I used to think the same way. As a result," I continued, "I spent years mindlessly missing how my friends were dramatically different from me on a few important dimensions. For example, I hate washing dirty dishes," I admitted. "Before I got a dishwasher, the dishes would often stack up in the sink waiting only for a sympathetic friend or

houseguest to wash them. I thought that their help was a painful sacrifice made by generous friends willing to suffer in my place. But, I was wrong. It turns out that washing the dishes didn't bother my friends the way it did me. Some of them even found it restorative. I was flabbergasted!"

Research and client feedback have subsequently supported this realization. Studies in organizational behavior show that no jobs, not even 'dirty jobs' are globally depleting.[12] In occupational settings, as with garage sales, one man's trash really is another's treasure. People really do differ in the extent to which certain sets of behaviors and conditions deplete or restore them. *Vive la différence.*

OUR DIFFERENCES HELP US ALL RESTORE

Imagine a hypothetical couple from Pasadena, California. Outgoing Jim works crunching numbers in a windowless cubical and shy Kim teaches Mommy-and-Me swim classes at the local outdoor pool. If one asked each of them to plan his/her perfect vacation, what do you think those vacations would look like? Moreover, if you compared the two vacation plans, how similar do you think they would be? My guess would be that Jim might want to be outdoors, active, meeting lots of people and Kim might be happy with the option to stay in or out of the sun, relaxing alone with a book or able to swim laps in the adult only pool. Jim and Kim's ideal vacations differ because our personalities, physiologies and lifestyles make us each restore and deplete in different ways.

Let's talk about three reasons why our personal resource triggers differ. First, people differ in how they view their work and their roles in society. Second, people differ in their physical and cognitive propensities. Third, people's experiences cause them to develop different strengths and vulnerabilities.

First, a combination of natural tendencies and learned behaviors causes people to view particular occupational tasks and roles very differently. This dramatically affects their ability to thrive in various occupations. Research shows that those who do "dirty work," including jobs that are socially stigmatized, can more than just survive their occupations. Some of them are inspired and energized by their work. This occurs because they construct a positive professional identity that reduces the social and psychological resource losses normally associated with difficult working conditions.[13] For example, hospital cleaning staff members that manage their social relationships and mentally frame what they do as helping people get well, actually find their work consistently invigorating and rewarding.[14]

David looked surprised and chimed in, "Okay, I understand that there are some people who can look at cleaning a toilet as a developmental opportunity. But, in my experience, most of us aren't wired that way. Were we all subscribers to Dr. Pangloss' view in Voltaire's *Candide*, we'd agree that the bowl in need of tidying is so because in this best of all possible worlds, it presents a remarkable growth opportunity for the cleaner," David shared. "What if your nature is to see the glass half full?" he asked.

"Those who are not natural optimists can intentionally train themselves to see a rosier perspective," I replied. "I'm sure that's what many of those who comfortably blow and shovel snow in 30 degree-below-zero weather have taught themselves. And, researchers concur. Positive psychologists and best-selling authors like Martin Seligman and Tal Ben-Shahar have shown that we can all learn to be happier regardless of the nature of our work and our natural tendencies to accentuate the positive." David nodded in acceptance.

"The second reason people react differently to different conditions and behaviors is that we vary widely in our natural preferences and sensitivities. While we easily accept that the six foot four inch personal trainer can lift more than the four foot six inch elderly cooking champion, we often overlook natural sensory, cognitive, and psychological differences. These natural but non-obvious differences dramatically alter the impact of various task experiences," I explained.

In my *Restore Yourself* workshops, I often ask "For who is folding warm clean towels direct from the dryer a restorative act?" Within three seconds, a few hands go up. Within ten seconds, between 30% and 50% of the room's participants raise their hands. When I ask people to look around the room at the show of hands, most seem stunned. The 'pro-folding' individuals say they thought they were alone in finding 'doing laundry' personally pleasing. Many with their hands down are dumbfounded that so many people could actually ENJOY what they experience as an onerous task.

"The third reason, David, that you can avoid some personally depleting tasks is that people's diverse life experiences cause them to develop different skills and preferences. And, life is much easier when we take advantage of other people's strengths and experiences," I suggested.

"Imagine two colleagues have the very same enthusiastic attitude about planning a huge retirement party for the CFO. One is a former professional party planner. The other went to a lot of parties in college. Who should plan the party? Often, we let our equity-at-all-costs attitude spill into domains where it is neither necessary nor appropriate. If all other things are equal, the company will benefit most if the ex-party planner leads the charge. She will not only spend less

time preparing, but she'll also use less physical and cognitive resources to recreate a familiar outcome than the novice who may know she likes party outcomes but hasn't had the experience doing the upfront work. Mind you, it is rare that all other things are equal but you get the idea," I said.

"Yes, I get it," David assured me.

Experience can also work against us. For my client Max who recently lost his job over what appeared to be a poorly-delivered final presentation, preparing a toast for his friend's wedding will cause him far more anxiety than it will the maid-of-honor Sarah, who runs the local Toastmasters' meeting. So, all of this is to say that our first musketeer is very robust and we should remember to use people's diverse restoration and depletion profiles to our collective advantage.

"I get it, Edy," David remarked. "I remember when I was recently out of school, I gave up my seat on an airplane to a man I'd never met. I didn't know why at the time. Now I realize what I intuited: It was less difficult and less depleting for me to sit comfortably in a middle seat in coach than it was for the nervous, 350-pound college linebacker next to me to do so," David shared. "So, the lesson is to recognize that people are different and use those differences to restore myself and conserve the energy of those around me."

"Yes, you do get it," I complimented. "Good managers should try to match tasks with appropriate individuals to minimize the resource hit to the entire team whenever possible. And, this knowledge can help prevent them from accidentally prescribing, suggesting or judging others' restorative sets inappropriately. In short, it is often best to have scared football players sitting in comforting seats and have pro-folders folding the towels."

"Actually, d'Artagnan, just like your three musketeer friends figured out how to use their skills complementarily, I realize that I already do this in my home," David said. "My

wife loves to cook, I like doing dishes and my kids don't like to do anything but use their iPhones and be waited on. When it's necessary to teach the kids to learn to share in domestic chores, we basically force them to struggle through the cooking and cleaning. If I work late and my kids have a lot of homework to do, my wife both cooks and does the dishes. But, if there are no other pressing agendas, what really works best is for each of us to do things that really restore us."

"Congratulations. Now, can you see how you can apply the same principles at work?" I asked.

"Not entirely," David replied. "My wife, kids and I are noticeably different from each other. Most of the guys I work with seem more similar to me so I'm having trouble seeing harnessable differences. As I said earlier, I'm hesitant to offload dirty work to subordinates. It just doesn't feel right," David confessed.

Often times we might feel like David in that we don't think we can offload any of our least favorite tasks. This is a common trait of many leaders and managers and one that can, unfortunately, increase susceptibility to professional exhaustion. When you find yourself making excuses to not delegate tasks that YOU find depleting, try to remember that what depletes you may just be restorative for someone else on your team. Your job as a leader or colleague is to find out what affects your team's resources so, together, you can decrease the net drain of a project on the entire group.

"Let's look at you and your business partner, for example," I suggested. "If you thrive on negotiating, but your business partner restores by doing strategic and financial tasks in the office, then exploiting your natural complementarities makes sense. When all else is equal, allocating tasks to reduce the net energy expended will result in higher performance and

satisfaction for everyone. Work will take less time, create less stress and often produce a better outcome because the expertise in the system is utilized optimally."

I continued. "Contrast that with the unnecessary stresses of trying to make everyone good at doing everything. This might be a necessary evil on a desert island or in emergency situations where all hands are often needed for all tasks.   However, if a system is well-established, taking advantage of skill and temperament complementarities, well...that's a no brainer. So, even if everyone is cross-trained, insisting everyone do everything at least some of the time can be less beneficial than encouraging people to focus what restores them (to the extent there is a reasonable business case to do so, of course)."

David unclicked his seatbelt. "Okay, I got it. Now, I'm getting up to stretch my back because my body is different from yours! When I get back, I'm sure you'll introduce me to the second musketeer of resilience," he said as he stood up.

LOOK BEHIND THE MASK

While our first musketeer insists that we celebrate each other's differences, the second musketeer of resilience reminds us that

> **Social tags, like 'work' or 'vacation,' can prevent us from seeing and acting on our true restoration and depletion triggers.**

David returned to his seat. I introduced him to the second musketeer's message.

"That sounds awfully academic," he said. "I'm not a professor and I used to get sleepy in class. Could you please explain to me what you mean using plain English?"

"Yes, of course. This musketeer protects us from the kind of confusion you suffered around volunteering," I began. Specifically, social tags like *volunteering, work* and *vacation* can prevent us from identifying our actual restoration and depletion triggers. This is true because our behaviors and the conditions under which we engage in activities determine how they impact our personal resources

"Example?" David asked.

"Okay," I agreed. "A common social tag for the daily going to and coming from work is *commuting*. Newspaper headlines and 'Best Cities to Live In' lists tell us that short commute times and distances are ideal and long commutes are something to avoid."

"That makes sense to me," David said. "In fact, when I moved to New York, I told the realtor I was only willing to commute 20 minutes or less to work."

"Fabulous. What happened?" I asked.

"Actually, you'll laugh," David replied. "We were shown five apartments. When I asked about my commute to work, the realtor assured me that each unit met all of our requirements, including commuting times. She said that for four of them, the commute would be a five-minute walk to the station, a ten-minute wait for and ride on the F train and then another five-minute walk from the station to my office. The fifth apartment was close enough for me to simply walk 20 minutes to my office. I had to explain to her that only the fifth apartment actually fit our requirements because it allowed me *to walk* through Central Park to get to work," he said.

I smiled. "Then you understand exactly what I'm talking about. A 'commute' is a social tag for a broad array of conditions and behaviors that occur during the period when one is *enroute* between home and work. The realtor did not understand that your home and neighborhood requirements included a location that avoided crowds, darkness, noise and

being in tunnels while going to and from work. And frankly, one should not expect her to understand that right away since for others, sitting in a relatively dark train reading the paper each morning is the most restful part of their day." The social tag 'a 20-minute commute' was too blunt an instrument to get the precise outcome you wanted," I concluded.

"Wow. I guess this is also part of the first musketeer – we're all different," David remarked. "Okay, I think I've got the second one. To paraphrase, it is the things that I do and the environment in which I do them that matter. Walking in the park is restorative but walking in noisy tunnels is depleting. The same with volunteering – it is not the activity, it's how and what I do when I'm engaged in it," David proclaimed.

"Great." I complimented him.

"I like the counter-intuitive nature of your musketeers, Dr. Edy," he said. "Like Dumas's triad, they are each different and one must not be fooled by the mask he wears. Instead, I should focus on the complexity behind the mask. What does my last protector offer me in my quest for restoration?"

WE CHANGE

Dumas's literary heroes discovered that life changes us. That is the third musketeer's message. Although at core we remain the same in many ways, over time, some of our energizing needs change. When we actively try to increase our resilience by engaging in or avoiding particular activities, we often do not take into account the message of the third musketeer:

What restores and depletes us changes over time.

Often during my workshops I ask, "Who here can think of something that used to be restorative that has become

depleting?" I frequently hear that people used to look forward to checking e-mail, staying at nice hotels, attending client dinners, flying first class and drinking alcohol but now dread them. Similarly, people are often surprised when they suddenly discover that they enjoy lawn mowing, cooking and being alone. These changes in preference may be catalyzed by various lifestyle changes or by 'overdose effects'.[15] Regardless of the cause, the third musketeer of resilience encourages us to become more mindful of our changing personal resource needs.

I summarized the third musketeer for David and then continued. "My research on Club Med GO's demonstrated that ability to effectively scan for and adapt to otherwise surprising changes in restoration needs can be a professional advantage. Especially in 24/7 work environments and total institutions, where the lines between home and work are virtually non-existent, one should heed the GO's precautionary tale.

"Predominantly a population of extroverts, successful GO's learned to intentionally limit discretionary group socializing (e.g., going to parties, hanging out in the disco, etc.) because the nature of their work caused these social settings to shift from sources of restoration to depletion. Many other extroverted team members who continued to view group interactions with virtual strangers as unmitigated 'fun' often found themselves burnt out by it," I explained.

"To avoid making life even more depleting than it has to be, I need to get and stay aware of those things that affect my personal resources and then manage them," David synthesized.

"Yep," I acknowledged. "To recap specifically on our three musketeers, remember first, we differ in what restores and depletes us; second, we need to watch out for the imprecision of social tags that disguise our real resource sinks

and oases; and third, we should regularly scan to determine if old hobbies and habits need adjusting since our restoration needs change over time." I concluded.

"That was fascinating," David replied. "Thanks for sharing all the great information. Not to be impolite, but, well, after all that, I really need a nap. I know you'll be here when I wake up, so do you think we can finish all that stuff about types and levels of *personal resources* when I wake up?" David asked.

"No problem. I need a nap myself. Sweet dreams," I said as I curled up under my blanket and closed my eyes.

Four Tigers in Your Tank

"Put a tiger in your tank" was Esso's famous ad campaign to encourage its customers to buy premium gas. The gas was formulated to help release the latent capacity in car engines. Your life runs on *personal resources* and you can upgrade your performance by knowing how to best fill your tank and care for your personal engine. Now that you know the two agreements of PRM and have met the three musketeers of resilience, its time to improve your performance by deepening your knowledge of the four personal resource types. To start, let's talk about how PRM looks at energy. The more completely you understand this system, the better you can use it to your advantage.

David and I had both awoken from our naps. A few minutes and a cup of tea later, he turned to me and said, "Now that I've had a nice restoration break, how about telling me about the personal resources that I've just replenished?"

"Okay," I agreed. "I'll dive straight in. The relationships among personal resources, depletion, and restoration can be viewed as an energy system not unlike your car's fuel system," I began. "Imagine that your personal performance is like the performance you get from your BMW and your personal resources, the fuel it uses. For your car, filling up, using a fuel additive and getting a tune up are all restorative activities – they increase the capacity of your car to perform. Similarly running the car on low octane gas, under-

49

inflated tires or with the emergency brake on creates depleting conditions that reduce its performance. In general, to increase your 'vehicular resources' you can either enhance restorative behaviors and conditions, reduce depleting ones, or both. The same goes for your personal resources."

"I get it," he said. "To have access to more personal fuel to run my life, I should get and keep more of the good stuff and minimize waste and losses. Now, you promised me four tigers for my tank. So, I guess you mean that there are four different kinds of personal fuel. Is that right?" he asked.

"Yes, you are exactly right," I replied.

"Then I'm ready to hear about tigers for my tank and how they will keep me from burnout and professional exhaustion," David declared.

FOUR TYPES OF PERSONAL RESOURCES

The four tigers are your four types of personal resources or personal fuel. Each person is a holistic, integrated system. Trying to divide our use and acquisition of energy into discrete parts is, as such, somewhat unnatural. However, I find it helpful if we subdivide the multiple kinds of energies that ebb, flow and carry us through the day into four intuitive categories.

The four personal resource types are *physical, social, cognitive,* and *psychological.* You can think of these four energy groups as the old four food groups – breads and cereals; fruits and vegetables; dairy products; and meat, fish and poultry. They are both rough categorizations of raw materials from which you derive what you need to sustain yourself.

"Here's the overview of the four types of personal resources," I said as I handed him these definitions:

- *Physical resources* include physical and psychophysical real time capabilities — strength to lift your roll-aboard

suitcase, endurance to climb the stairs, and restfulness to stay alert during your 4 o'clock staff meeting. Catching a cold or experiencing physical fatigue may signal that these resources are low.

- *Social resources* include one's social capital — both your sense of connectedness to and ability to access other humans in your various networks of interpersonal ties. These social resources also include your faith and ability to experience and benefit from ties with natural and supernatural entities. For example, if you are on the floor in fetal position whimpering because you feel stupid, unworthy and fat, you probably lack the social resources to ask your ex-boyfriend to help change your flat tire. Similarly, if your professional network could provide access to a favor from an old college friend but you are convinced, incorrectly, that this outcome is either impossible or will harm your social capital, your accessible social resources are probably compromised.

- *Cognitive resources* include your natural and learned intellectual capacities, as well as your metacognitive abilities, that is, the ability to access them. These are the resources that you would need to plan a complex family vacation, do your taxes or write a new resume. The human resource executive who has just debriefed eight 360 degree assessments is no less smart than he was 10 hours prior. Only the personal resources necessary to utilize that cognitive capacity have become depleted.

- *Psychological resources* include all types of affective and psychological capabilities and their emotional manifestations. These include, of course, those

necessary for competent leadership and parenting such as patience, self-discipline, self-esteem, capacity to resist temptation, and empathy. The typically patient father who loses his temper with two cranky children doesn't love them any less today than yesterday nor is he a different person. He is simply psychologically depleted and needs to regroup and restore.

MOST RESTORATION IS ACTIVE

David finished reading the definitions and looked up.

"I understand," he said. "I have different kinds of energy. When I use some up, I need to replace it. So, if my brain is tired from doing performance reviews, I need to watch *Gilligan's Island* reruns and let my brain rest until it recovers."

"Not necessarily so. What you've suggested is that **not** burning a particular resource for a period of time allows us to restore ourselves. In your tired brain example, personal experience suggests that if you stop thinking for a while, your ability to think will return. Often, that may be true, but it is a coincidence more than a natural outcome of ceasing to think. As a matter of fact, waiting for recovery is often the least effective, least efficient way to restore a particular resource," I told him.

"Let me share an example," I continued. "Many people think that an effective way to recover from muscle soreness is to passively wait for the muscles to naturally recover. In most cases, its better to actively help them recover using gentle massage, ice, and stretching, in addition to rest. The active, not passive use of your four personal resource founts is a key to successful PRM. When we get to talking about strategic sequencing and such, you'll see how intentional, active restoration strategies are often the most effective," I finished.

PERSONAL RESOURCE OVERLAP

Our four personal resources often act together and are not mutually exclusive. Think of lasagna in relation to the four food groups. Lasagna is comprised of all four food groups. It is mostly pasta with meat, cheese and vegetables. Most restorative or depleting conditions are like lasagna, composed of more than one type of resource ingredient.

You know this from experience. Take a basic social interaction – a disagreement with your boss. Though the interaction is social, it can certainly trigger multiple kinds of resource losses. The disagreement could cause a headache, make you angry, engender fear and/or, reduce your ability to think clearly. So, it's clear that an assault on one tiger can affect them all.

"Though it is convenient to talk about physical, social, cognitive and psychological resources as separate entities, in reality, few behaviors, conditions or responses are pure in any way," I said to David. "For example, my swim in the morning not only enhances my physical sense of wellbeing, it also clears my head, calms me down and prepares me to cope with others' declared needs and senses of urgency. Swimming restores me by raising all of my personal resource levels synergistically and simultaneously."

"So Dr. Edy, do I need to get a Ph.D. to be able to diagnose what I need to restore myself?" David asked.

"No," I answered, "you don't have to understand every detail of physiology and psychology to make informed decisions on how to maximize your personal resources right away. These synergies will reveal themselves naturally if you'll fill out my Personal Resource Assessment™."

"And I bet you've got some in your bag, right?" he teased.

"Of course," I replied. "But, you're not ready for it just yet."

He smiled. I continued. "First, it will help you to understand that the causes of depletion do not automatically point to the appropriate sources of restoration. In many cases, there is no direct connection between the depletion trigger's resource type and the appropriate restoration tiger. For example, imagine an amateur runner finishing his first marathon. He is near collapse at mile 25. You'd say he's out of physical resources. Yet, the cheering crowd and his vision of crossing the finish line enable him to continue. His psychological and social resources get him across the finish line. Eating a candy bar absent the vision and support would not have," I pointed out.

"I understand," said David. "My neighbor Francisco would often end his work day at 5 pm feeling physically exhausted. When he went home and relaxed by playing video games, he usually awoke the next day feeling almost equally exhausted. When, instead, he played soccer for an hour after a grueling work day, he would arise the next day feeling alert and rested. I guess that's because his sense of physical tiredness was created by inactivity and lack of social stimulation. Exerting himself a bit more by playing sports was always the best remedy to his feeling tired," David said.

NOTHING IS FREE

"So, I guess I should not just manage particular energy sources. I need to also watch my overall resource levels," David realized.

"Correct. I call overall energy levels your Average Personal Resource Levels (APRLs) or your 'Aprils'," I replied. "Calculating an activity's effect on them should soon become a habit since most personal resource enhancements not only come in mixed packages, but also come with a resource price to pay. You already know that nothing is free. I can tell you more about APRLs, if you want."

"Yes, but not yet. First, go back to the nothing-is-free idea. I understand the concept in general, but, give me a specific example of what you're talking about," David asked.

"Okay. Take going out salsa dancing with friends on a Wednesday night," I began. "How should you decide whether to go or not?" I didn't pause. It was a rhetorical question. "On the one hand, dancing with friends and missing a couple of hours sleep will burn some of your physical resources. On the other hand, the movement, the music, the social contact and the fun will likely make you and the other Wednesday night party animals feel socially and spiritually uplifted," I suggested.

"In many cases, you might correctly decide to exchange the increased patience, sense of well being and other effects of having had fun, danced, and felt socially significant for a bit of Thursday morning dimness. It depends on where you think you most need the boost and what you can afford to pay for it," I said.

There are always some costs associated with resource gains and often some gains associated with overall APRL depleters. That's alright. With the diagnostic precision you gain from using the PRMA, you'll get really good at making the right restoration decisions.

KEEPING YOUR APRLS UP

Personal Resource Management™ focuses on the whole person and on that person's global energies and available abilities. While it would be fabulous to precisely measure and regulate our energy flows, precision is not necessary to become a master of resilience. Because we bring our entire selves to everything we do, what is most reliably managed at any given time is our overall energy level. That suggests we focus on managing the average of all four of our personal

resource levels or APRLs. (I often just call it your personal resource level for short.) Because more often than not, accomplishing a single task requires multiple personal resources, we need to try to keep our APRL's up as high and for as long as possible on a regular basis. If you can also help others around you to do so, that's even better.

SUPPORT APRL RAISING

Think about what it takes to have a good meeting. Once you've done all the usual things (like proper agenda setting and participant selection), you can still do more to make the time well spent. Activities that increase any of the participants' personal resource levels will contribute to a more effective meeting by creating more capable participants. Here's how.

Actively participating in a meeting requires the expenditure of all four resource types: physical, social, cognitive and psychological. One must stay alert, be patient with tedious agenda items, contribute useful ideas to the discussions, and enlist the cooperation of colleagues to create consensus on important decisions. If you are able to facilitate the increase of any personal resource in any member, the quality of meeting's outcome will likely improve because the team's APRL is elevated. That would suggest that bringing high quality snacks, encouraging sufficient breaks and keeping the physical conditions and the emotional tenor of the meeting comfortable for everyone can have real payoffs. Can you think of other ways to easily raise personal, team or office APRLs?

"As a manager, how else can I choreograph work in order to optimize workers' personal resources in general, and more particularly, those personal resources critical to high occupational performance?" David asked. (Well, he didn't phrase it exactly that way but, yes, he did ask about this how

he can use PRM to better manage his people.)

"Start by helping each with his or her own personal mastery of PRM," I suggested. "Once they become familiar with and have practiced these techniques, managers can use their own resulting capacity gains to make a difference in team-level and organizational-level APRLs. Mostly, what you need to do is avoid interfering with people's ability to optimize their own APRLs once they know how themselves.

TWO DIRECT WAYS TO RAISE APRLS

There are two direct ways to increase APRLs. The first direct way is to increase exposure to known resource-enhancing conditions and behaviors or simply put, increase your restoration. If you are tired, for example, you can get more sleep. Because insufficient sleep also reduces cognitive, social, and psychological resources, getting a good night's sleep or taking a quick nap will directly enhance the other three types of resources as well.

"As a leader, you can help support direct restoration. It is a good idea, for example, to structurally and culturally encourage employees to get the rest they need," I suggested. "You will see performance gains from higher individual APRLs. To do that, place a cot and an alarm clock in a quiet corner of the employee lounge to send this signal. The time spent napping will, in most cases, be more than offset by the increased productivity of refreshed workers."

"I understand," said David. He took out a piece of paper and jotted down 'support power naps.'

"The second direct way to directly increase APRLs," I said, "is to reduce losses from depleting conditions and behaviors; that is, reduce depletion. For example, visual clutter and loud sounds reduce the cognitive and psychological resources of many people. As such, organizing their working spaces to prevent clutter and using earplugs to

dampen sound can directly reduce environmental sources depletion. Making these actions socially acceptable goes a long way toward individual depletion reduction. These actions, just like getting more sleep, directly increase APRLs at work," I concluded.

I was done. So was David. It was time to watch a movie or listen to some music. This lovely conversation was starting to become depleting for both of us and we knew it. You're probably having a similar experience. So, here's a quick review before you take a break.

We have covered considerable ground in the past several chapters. First, recognizing the root cause of professional exhaustion is the first step towards recovering from and then preventing its recurrence. Early recognition allows us to implement the proper restorers before things get out of control and we become too depleted. Through practice and by developing some personalized tools, you will begin to master this.

You have four primary tigers in your personal resource tank: physical, social, cognitive and psychological resources. These resources work synergistically, interact, cross react and are not mutually exclusive. It is not necessary to identify exactly how each resource becomes restored or depleted. We can instead work to manage our overall or Average Personal Resource Levels (APRLs).

Two ways to directly increase your APRLs are to increase restorative behaviors and conditions (like getting more sleep) and reduce exposure to depleting behaviors and conditions (like clutter).

Keep in mind that our goal is to become able to bounce back before things reach a tipping point. As an expert restorer, you will become able to embed specific strategies into your normal work routine that energetically optimize regularly-encountered situations. With practice, you will

recognize opportunities to improvise restorative moments and approaches in unique situations based on your understanding of how and why they became depleting.

Now that it's clear why we should craft customized energizing strategies, let's look at a few *reliable restorers* and *sneaky depleters* common to all of us. Then, you'll be ready to dive into your very personal diagnostic (PRMA) and action planning.

CHAPTER SIX

Reliable Restorers

Dating is difficult. And, if you've been reading along carefully, you may discover that dating just got more difficult. Why? Because in describing your favorite activities on Match.com, you now may have to reconsider if, indeed, long walks on the beach and flying trapeze lessons are always your favorite activities. Regardless of your need for full disclosure in relationships, please do refrain from sharing the more accurate description, "the effects of certain activities vary dramatically in their resource impact on me depending on my starting APRL" during your first phone conversation with a potential blind date. (Don't ask me how I know this.)

At some point in the last chapter, you must have said, "Come on Edy, SOME things must be universally exhausting or rejuvenating! Surely we cannot escape the human condition. Decades of research on fitness, sleep, psychology, health, marketing, nutrition and sociology cannot all be wrong."

Yes, you are correct. I call these universals *reliable restorers*. They are, however, fewer and farther between than most of us realize. Like folding towels and washing dishes, most activities can affect people differentially.

Most of my clients find success focusing on five reliable restorers. In this chapter, I will share some notable characteristics and surprises about the reliably restorative

nature of:

- sleep,
- sunlight,
- flow,
- sensory integration, and
- movement

"What about exercise, massage, pets, hugs, and prayer?" you might ask. Well, it turns out that they are not always restorative for everyone all the time. At the end of the chapter, I'll talk about why that is, along with a quick discussion of sex, drugs and rock 'n roll!

SLEEP

"Are you going to sleep some more on this flight?" I asked David. I sure was. We were in those fully-reclining transatlantic first class seats, the greatest gift ever for road warriors.

"I've been having back trouble and frankly, I haven't had a good night's sleep in months," he replied. "I'm thinking that the back problem and my worrying about things all the time have kept me from sleeping enough."

"Do you think the sleep deprivation has been having a negative affect on you?"

"Of course, I'm a wreck," he replied.

"What time is your bedtime?" I queried.

He laughed. "Bedtime? What am I, six years old? I go to sleep when I can and wake up when I have to."

A major contributor to professional exhaustion is sleep deprivation. And, in most cases, it is a passive choice that each of us makes.

"How often do you change the oil in your car?" I asked.

"Every three months or six thousand kilometers," he said.

"How often do you brush your teeth?"

He squinted at me – unable to detach and strangely curious. "Twice a day; when I arise and when I go to bed."

"Why do you change the oil and brush your teeth?" I persisted.

"Okay, okay. I got your point," David conceded.

"Let's continue" I suggested. "You do so because they are basic maintenance activities – minimal requirements to keep your car and your teeth working properly. They are 'no brainers' because the investment required is relatively low compared to the exponentially higher costs of running your car and teeth to failure."

He nodded unconvincingly.

I rephrased. "You can choose to risk substantial damage by not performing the minimum maintenance, or you can easily prevent possible devastating problems with a small investment of time and discipline, right?" He nodded more convincingly and then spoke.

"So you're suggesting that by not getting enough sleep, I am pushing my engine too hard and am setting myself up for unnecessary damage and major repair."

"Exactly," I said.

David sighed. "Sometimes I feel like a complete failure when it comes to the basics of being human."

SLEEP DENIAL

Clearly, David is not a failure as a human being. He is functioning drowsily like most members of today's professional world. That's because David's choices about

sleep which, at one time were strategically advantageous, no longer serve. This is the case for most of us.

Beginning in high school, we start treating sleep as though it is 'free' time. We treat time for sleep like a big, nightly bank account that we can borrow from whenever we need some extra time to work, party, or unwind. Coffee, tea, so called energy drinks and exciting social settings help us make withdrawals. This ability to borrow a few hours from sleep when we miscalculate the actual time we'll need to finish a project or wish to overindulge helps support procrastination and encourages us to remain poor at prioritizing.

In high school and college, the pattern looks like this. We pull a few 'all-nighters' each semester and, with some regularity, keep our fair share of late nights. During the semester, we repay the sleep debt by sleeping until noon on weekends. We really top off our sleep tanks the week after finals by sleeping part way through semester break and/or when we come down with the flu (the two of which usually coincide).

Although this strategy was probably successful and even satisfying in high school and college, as a working adult, you chronically carry that debt only managing to make minimum payments since you almost never 'have' the time to fully catch up. (Well, that is until you burn out.)

Most of us in Western society not only endure life chronically exhausted, we also wear our sleep deprivation as a parental medal of honor or symbol of professional commitment. This passive choice has compromised our productivity and satisfaction with our collective work lives. Moreover, our personal relationships and physical resilience suffer.

For those like David, mental and physical health begin to noticeably deteriorate first. (Well-functioning immune systems require sufficient sleep. If you are experiencing a

series of unrelated little health issues or problems, perhaps your sleep-deprived immune system is crying out for attention.)

A SLEEP SOLUTION YOU CAN USE

By now, you're probably thinking, I KNOW I need more sleep, but I just don't have the time to sleep more! I have a super busy schedule. I have responsibilities. I have commitments. And, sometimes, I even want to have a life. So, yes Dr. Edy, I know you're right but I just cannot do this. If that's your reaction, read on. Here is a solution that just might work for you.

I have discussed the sleep challenge in many *Restore Yourself* workshops worldwide. Here's what I've found:

- More than 85% of the professionals I met felt that they did not get enough sleep.
- European and Latin American women were a bit less exhausted than North American women but, really, not by much.
- More than half of those who completed the following 10 minute exercise got more rest in the subsequent 3 months.

Before trying the following exercise, most of my students were convinced that they could not keep their current jobs, maintain family responsibilities AND get more sleep. After this 10-minute exercise, most recognized that they could easily find two to three more hours of sleep per week without making any major lifestyle changes, and, many did so.

Try this exercise with a few friends, colleagues, or family members. Only spend ten minutes on it. Discuss and then write down the answer to this question,

"How can I find myself and my team two to three more hours of sleep each week?"

I suggest looking for time in places where you waste time or make decisions that are habitual instead of mindful. Do not be afraid to question all assumptions about things that may not be true anymore. (For example, since I can record any TV program I want with TiVo, do I really need to stay awake until my favorite show comes on?) Can you think about managing your technology to help you instead of allowing it to lead you astray? Now, spend the ten minutes and jot down some of your ideas here. Go ahead, just do it, okay?

_____

_____

_____

_____

_____

Well done. Here are just a few ideas from the scores that my participants generated:[16]

- Skip the news at night and skim the headlines in the morning when you check your email
- Set a bedtime with your housemates or work colleagues and ask them to help you enforce it a few nights a week
- Turn off your Blackberry and cell phone when you are sleeping. Buy and use a travel alarm clock to wake you up from a nap or night's sleep (not your phone)
- Do not take the first flight out in the morning and arrange to take your first calls on the road
- Take naps
- Turn off the TV

- Cluster the emails you send so that you get one email back instead of four
- Take a holiday from Facebook, MySpace or Twitter
- Discuss team norms and expectations with the express intent of getting everyone more sleep
- Start and end meetings on time so people don't wait around
- Avoid working 1 hour before bedtime so you fall asleep more easily
- Set time limits on social events – e.g., go to a club on the condition that you leave at midnight
- Get a babysitter for the children one night a week and then go to bed early instead of going out

No doubt you'll find others. I hope you are noticing that much of our sleep deprivation is self-imposed and that we can and should make better choices. When you have a chance, please take a moment to share your ideas for getting more sleep by logging on to www.RestoreYourselfBook.com. Or, then again, you could take a little nap first.

SUNLIGHT

We have been taught to avoid too much sunlight because, over a lifetime, it blurs our vision and damages our skin. But most of us have not yet learned that we must also be mindful to seek out sufficient sunlight to restore ourselves. Unless you are lucky enough to live in Western Samoa or its latitudinal equivalent, you are probably not soaking up optimal amounts of full spectrum light all year round. Working long days in windowless environments almost guarantees cubical dwellers insufficient exposure to full spectrum light.

Most people experience some seasonal changes in feelings of well-being (usually in the fall and winter as the

days get shorter.)[17] Research shows that between 6 and 14% of Americans at work suffer from a seasonal reduction in physical, cognitive, social and psychological resources caused by insufficient exposure to sunlight.[18]

"The more severe form of winter blues, Seasonal Affective Disorder (SAD), causes changes in mood and behavior so powerful that they produce significant problems in people's lives," says Dr. Norman Rosenthal, medical director of Capital Clinical Research Associates and author of the seminal book *Winter Blues*. Some estimate that this seasonal depression affects up to 20% of those who live in less temperate climes such as Ireland, New England, New Zealand and Alaska. Importantly, Rosenthal and others' research shows that symptoms of SAD are more common and more often misdiagnosed in women than in men.

So, if as the days get shorter, your temper is growing shorter, your waistline is growing larger, your craving for carbohydrates is growing insatiable, you're growing impatient getting lost in neighborhoods you know and your emotional resilience is getting brittle, think twice. You have not suddenly become senile or become in need a divorce, lobotomy or new career. You probably just need to spend more time outside, get a full-spectrum light box and/or schedule a weekend in Florida. If you think you might have SAD or subclinical SAD, start by reading *Winter Blues* and speak with a knowledgeable physician about your symptoms.

FLOW

Have you ever skied the perfect run? Do you recall ever becoming so involved in a conversation with a friend that you completely lost track of the time. Have you ever become so engrossed in thinking through a problem that you missed your train stop? If yes you've experienced that wonderful state called flow.[19] The state of *optimal experience*, flow occurs

when, amongst other things, your skill level and the task you are performing are perfectly matched causing you enter into an enjoyable altered state.[20] Musicians and other artists call it being 'in the groove.'

Extensive research by social psychologist Mihaly Csikszentmihalyi has shown that when you are in this psychophysical state, fully engaged in activities that capture your attention and allow you to become one with the activity, many if not all of your personal resource levels rise. Most often, flow creates and sustains a psychologically and emotionally restored state of being.

While flow is pretty close to a universal restorer of emotional and psychological resources, learning which behaviors and conditions cause you to personally achieve flow and how to create them is the work of each individual. For me, one reliable flow-inducing scenario is dancing Zydeco (a form of swing dance) with Rob and other excellent partners at the Gator by the Bay Zydeco and Blues Festival in California. When I find myself feeling tired and unmotivated, I force myself to go to this type of dance event because I KNOW that my flow experience from this activity will entirely refill my personal resource tank.

In addition to knowing what helps achieve flow, one should also be mindful to avoid conditions that impede flow. My client Abby frequently achieves flow writing poetry but only when she is not interrupted and can manage her blood sugar properly. So now, when she is trying to get into flow, she sits alone with her pad and favorite pen, keeps food and water nearby and turns off her Blackberry. She then sets a travel alarm so that she can comfortably lose track of time without messing up the rest of her schedule and gets a lot of great work done.

Later in this book you will discover some of the behaviors and conditions that help you personally get into

flow. To begin that journey, try taking a few minutes to reflect on where flow experiences most often turn up in your life and how you might arrange to encounter them more often. For detailed information on this fabulous restorer, start by reading *Flow* the seminal book by Dr. Csikszentmihalyi.

WHAT ABOUT EXERCISE?

In my *Restore Yourself* workshops, I have had many participants ask me, "Well, isn't exercise restorative for everyone?" The answer is, not exactly. Exercise of various forms is amazingly restorative for most people under many conditions. But remember, to be a reliable restorer, an activity must be restorative under pretty much all conditions for pretty much all people, all the time. So, yes, there is certainly at least one particular type of exercise and/or set of exercise conditions that will restore each person at a given time but, they are different for different people.

To best understand the restorative impact of various types of exercise, we can dissect each into its two primary reliable restoration levers: sensory stimulation and movement. To be more specific, athletic activities are often restorative because they revive us by (a) meeting our sensory integration needs and by (b) providing us with the right kind and amount of physical movement (and related outcomes.) I will get very specific here because exercise is a social tag for a very broad and complex set of widely disparate activities and we all know how social tags can be distracting masks.

SENSORY INTEGRATION

A giant part of the human experience we get from our senses. Seeing, smelling, hearing, tasting and touching the world around us not only enriches our experiences, but also dramatically impacts our brains, bodies and, as such, our personal resources. Sensory integration theory, developed by

occupational therapist A.J. Ayers at University of California at Los Angeles (UCLA), holds that the correct balance of sensory stimuli received within the body and the lower brain's successful integration of those signals result in enhanced emotional, cognitive and physical resources.[21]

To move, learn and behave normally, the brain must receive and organize all categories of sensations. Those include the five conscious sensations that we all learned to name in kindergarten and, the semi-conscious senses that, among others, include the proprioceptive and vestibular. Simply put, proprioception tells you when your muscles and joints are moving and vestibular tells you about your current relationship to gravity. The sensations you get driving on a windy road, turning a somersault or swinging on a swing are proprioceptive. (Fluid moving in your inner ears triggers these sensations.)

Research led by scholars in the Occupational Sciences at the University of Southern California (USC) and most recently, research on play and adult sensory needs conducted at USC by Dr. Erna Blanche, director of Therapy West in Los Angeles, and, Dr. Diane Parham, now at University of New Mexico, have shown that whether you are an autistic child or an electrical engineer, your cognitive, emotional and physical resources are improved when the amount and intensity of sensory input you get is properly balanced. That means that fidgeting, playing video solitaire, pacing, thumb twiddling, whistling, and subconsciously rocking in that $500 desk chair are at least in part self-medicating actions that are most likely helping you to restore yourself in real time.

Different forms of exercise have different sensory profiles. For example, downhill skiing provides a great deal of vestibular and proprioceptive stimulation but little auditory and olfactory stimulation. On the other hand, golf has a very different sensory profile (much lower in vestibular and

proprioceptive stimulation) but is similar in how quiet and mild-smelling it is. When you do your Personal Resource Assessment in Chapter Eight, I'll direct you to watch for the sensory conditions that affect your APRLs.

MOVEMENT

The second salient restorative feature of exercise is movement. Various types of physical activity have different effects on brain chemistry, physiology and general metabolism. Libraries full of research show that physical activity is necessary and often fabulously beneficial to humans. Improved blood circulation, increased heart rate, deeper breathing, muscle movement, and significant changes in neurotransmitters including increased secretion of endorphins all contribute to creating a heightened sense of well-being. I don't have to make the argument for restorative capacity of human movement. Even the most sedentary of us knows it is a good thing.

The most important message here is that the social tag "exercise" does not guarantee a reliably restorative outcome. For example, if you are a runner, you know that all runs are not created equal. For each person, running at a specific pace, at a certain speed under particular physical, psychological, social and emotional conditions is reliably restorative.

Increased APRLs occur under a broad range of conditions. For Patsy, any run from one to four miles at between four and seven miles an hour in temperatures between 55 and 80 degrees, either alone or with a good conversationalist feels like a mini-vacation. In contrast, sprinting two miles down on a smoggy, crowded street in 105 degree heat because she's late for a meeting is unlikely to result in a happy, peppy Patsy. In sum, regardless of how broad the range, it is the specific set of behaviors and

conditions, not the social tag, that determine the rejuvenation potential of any exercise.

PRAYER, FOOD, SEX, DRUGS AND ROCK 'N ROLL

"You know, petting my dog and going to church always make me feel better. Why aren't they on your list?" David asked. "And, my 20-year-old son would say that nothing restores him more than sex, drugs and rock 'n roll. Aren't they universal?" David mused. His questions were fair.

"Instead of talking about particular social tags, let's see if we can't pick out their distinguishing features to see what makes them less than universal," I suggested. Caring for a pet can lower your blood pressure, blood lipid levels, and feelings of loneliness.[22] Pets can provide opportunities for exercise, socialization and unconditional love.[23] They also provide a great source of tactile and proprioceptive stimulation. That's all good. But, pets can also be a source of increased time pressure, financial burden and personal stress. Some catalyze physical depletion by causing allergic reactions as well as contributing to sleep loss by jumping on your bed at 5 am," I said.

"I get it. You're saying that most things are mixed blessings," remarked David.

"Yes. Now, let's talk sex," I suggested. He smiled. "Physical forms of affection like hugs and sex can change our moods, brain chemistry, relationships, emotions and bodies in very positive ways. Intimacy, for many, is hugely restorative. But, those same manifestations can also be sources of stress or trauma when the interactions are unexpected, deemed inappropriate, cause anxiety or, are poorly timed. For example, a big hug and romantic kiss delivered by a naked man running on stage halfway through her keynote speech

would qualify as a depleter for most Princeton University commencement speakers," I said.

"The positive effects of prayer and meditation on health and overall well being have been known for millennia.[24] Focus and relaxation associated with these altered states replenish many people's personal resources, especially the social and spiritual ones. However, sitting in church with your angry neighbor glaring at you or forcing yourself to engage in spiritual practices inconsistent with your current beliefs can sometimes do more harm than good. For some, trying to sit and meditate only makes the self-critical voice in their heads become unbearably loud," I shared.

By now, you're getting the hang of these kinds of distinctions. Therefore, let's finish the rest of the list handily. Food and drink can be refreshing, rejuvenating and beneficial. Eating food to which we are sensitive or allergic depletes but sometimes less so than skipping a meal. Consuming a pound of ribs and a quart of Häagen Dazs at midnight washed down by three martinis will likely diminish you on at least one resource dimension. The same goes for many drugs. While drugs can have intended positive effects, they also carry risks and side effects; in PRM terms, the potential capacity to deplete.

Different sounds affect individuals differently. Music and dance have enormous capacity to restore us. As for the universal value of rock 'n roll, ask your elementary school music teacher. Silence disturbs some of my clients more than cacophony. A few enjoy Bulgarian bagpipe music while others think it sounds like cats fighting in trash cans. The frequent stereo wars blasting six simultaneous radio stations through my college apartment measurably reduced many of the neighbors' cognitive and social resources. (I have to believe that at least six people were somehow restored by it.) Finally, in many cases, waltzing together at a wedding

reception can simultaneously be torture for him and heaven for her. Yes, it's back to the musketeers again.

To summarize, keep in mind that the five reliable restorers: sleep, flow, sunlight, sensory integration and movement can help recharge almost everyone, every time. You'll use these common energy boosters plus your personally identified restorers to help you create your Personal Energy Profile (PEP) and action plan at the end of the book. Now, why not get up, go outside and move around a bit before you read on? And while you're up, consider planning how you're going to go to bed a little earlier tonight. When you return, I will tell you about sneaky depleters.

CHAPTER SEVEN

Sneaky Depleters

Think about things that deplete you. It doesn't take long for a list of things to pop into your mind, does it? What came up? Spending the weekend with your in-laws; seemingly endless meetings that result in nothing but frustration; sitting alone writing a document that you know no one will read; traveling in a noisy, crowded subway for 45 minutes at dawn? How about trying to present something important to someone who is not paying attention or trying to follow a leader unsure about where he wants to go?

This chapter is about sharing some of the less-than-obvious sources of personal resource depletion. My work has revealed some common depleters that often sneak up on us unawares. These common contributors to professional exhaustion are insidious and some of them even masquerade as sources of entertainment and restoration. That's why I call them *sneaky depleters*.

Four of the most common sneaky depleters of personal resources are:

- emotional labor,
- overdose effects,
- interruptions, and
- cultures of relentless enthusiasm.

Let's explore them one at a time.

EMOTIONAL LABOR

Emotional labor is essentially the effort needed to keep your feelings from surfacing in ways that interfere with your job. More than twenty years ago, sociologist Arly Hochschild coined the term emotional labor to describe a salient feature of the work demands placed on flight attendants.[25] Job requirements of front-line flight crew members still include smiling and cheerily handling customers regardless of passengers' bad behaviors or the difficult working conditions.

Emotional labor is that kind of behavior and emotion management that includes both holding your tongue when a customer is being an idiot and forcing yourself to remain calm when your hostile supervisor announces the hostile takeover that now threatens your job. You engage in this kind of work pretty much any time you are not alone – when you are with clients, customers, children, neighbors, other drivers on the road and, yes, sometimes with your significant other.

In PRM terms, emotion management of any kind, whether in the service of the firm or the family, is a sneaky depleter. Managing what you express and feel for the sake of others' experience is a powerful, often underestimated energy drain.[26]

What's so sneaky about emotional labor is that you naturally do it when you're in the presence of others – even if you love being around other people. That means virtually all 'face time' burns resources. So, for example, if for three consecutive days you sell all day, have dinner with customers, and then go out for drinks with a blind date, you'll likely need to schedule some time to restore your social resources by the end of the week.

Some tactics that work for Club Med frontline vacation hosts, as well as less evenly-tanned management consultants, include intentionally scheduling alone-time whenever possible. (Indeed, for most people, it's the only time they can

be free to emote with reckless abandon.) Scheduling alone time requires the same discipline and commitment that you use to meet your flight check-in deadlines and doctor's appointments.

Ah, but you are an extreme extrovert, you say, so this probably does not apply to you. Well, in studying Club Med GO's, more than 75% of whom were extroverts, it was emotional labor that significantly contributed to workers' premature intent to quit.[27] That's because extroverts also burn through social, psychological, and emotional resources when engaging with others too much. Extroversion does not protect you from the depletion caused by managing too many social interactions. It just means that the process is often more enjoyable and, at least sometimes, more restorative compared to others. What often happens to extroverts with high presentation demands is that they actually suffer from our second sneaky depleter, *overdose effects.*

OVERDOSE EFFECTS

Imagine you live to SCUBA dive. Your one-room apartment, complete with roommate, allows you to spend the money saved on rent for exotic diving trips and gear. You don't go to movies, you don't drink Starbucks. You dive! You live on financial fumes; thus, allowing you to create discretionary money to dive. You work at the local dive shop on evenings and weekends for minimum wage just to get the employee discount on SCUBA stuff. You have taken every dive class your budget allows. Now, among other things, you have become a certified PADI Open Water Diving Instructor.

You have taught a few classes for money. That was the coolest accomplishment ever! For you, work and life happen between dive trips. Your land-based, full-time job keeps you clothed, fed, and sheltered. As long as it doesn't interfere with

diving, the job is fine. You dream of owning and operating a beach-front dive shop anywhere in the tropics.

One morning, the phone rings with the answer to your prayers. The voice on the other end belongs to a dive buddy living and working in the Caribbean. He announces that Club Med desperately needs a SCUBA instructor at its singles' village in Turks & Caicos.

Your buddy asks, "Can you come for a year to live in an all-inclusive, beach-side resort to teach diving to vacationing singles?"

"Yes!" you answer without hesitation.

This is the true tale of Michael, one of my research subjects. Just days after receiving the call, he left Chicago on a plane destined for the Caribbean. Within 24 hours of landing in Providenciales, he was having the time of his life. Every minute underwater was a gift. Taking money to guide good-looking single women (and some men) through calm, clear waters felt almost like stealing. Time on land wasn't bad either; gourmet meals, fawning women, a beachside room.

Like all SCUBA GO's of his era, Michael typically dove with guests five or six days a week (depending on the weather) and then did maintenance and paperwork one day a week. Michael negotiated to have his weekly afternoon off on a dive day so that he could go out exploring dive sites too deep or difficult for guests.

After one month in his new-found paradise, Michael had a severe sinus infection that knocked him flat for almost two weeks. After two months, he felt lonely even while sitting at the bar with two guys from the beach team. After five months, every minute underwater seemed like ten. While he waited for the clients to finish putting on their gear, he fantasized about sitting in his warm Chicago apartment sharing a Domino's pizza and watching *Friends* reruns with his former roommate.

Michael was suffering from *overdose effects*, the sneaky depleter most common among those passionate about their hobbies and/or vocations, and anyone overexposed to particular circumstances. Overdose effects sneak up when activities that are restorative in small doses become depleting in larger ones.

TOO MUCH OF A GOOD THING

Here's how too much of a good thing can lead to serious depletion. Activity overdose resembles vitamin overdose. Take Vitamin D, for example. Too low an intake may result in rickets and osteoporosis, whereas a sufficient amount of vitamin D sustains general health. An optimum amount of vitamin D strengthens the immune, cardiovascular, and skeletal systems while too much can cause gastrointestinal problems and kidney damage.[28]

We experience a similar progression of outcomes when we escalate exposure to our passions past a personally optimal level. Here is an example of how social overdosing happens and how you can help avoid it. Imagine Bernard and Leona are your friends. For Bernard, speaking with his new girlfriend just makes his heart sing. He loves Leona. He loves how her voice sounds and the images it evokes. Recently, however, each conversation between them has started to include her laments about her messy divorce and her ex-husband's past transgressions.

Bernard becomes increasingly frustrated that his advice seems unappreciated and that he cannot change the past for the women he loves. You, having read this chapter, are able to decompose the situation enough to see that the cause of his unhappiness is overdosing on the divorce topic, not that he is speaking too often with his beloved. You suggest that he simply learns to redirect the conversation when necessary in order to keep their discussions restorative and their

relationship in tact. He does. It all works out. You are a hero and they live happily ever after.

Before we wrap up overdoing, one brief caution about exercise overdosing. Exercise, for those of us who are a bit driven to 'overdo it', can quite easily become a source of socially supported depletion. For those who are susceptible, be sure to watch for exercise overdosing as carefully as the more sedentary should remain mindful to move around enough.

So, watch out for overdose effects and move rapidly to ameliorate their causes. Remember that just because some is good, more is not always better. If indeed, you find the things that used to restore your energy have lost their positive impact, first consider if you've overdosed before attributing the lost impact to the third musketeer of resilience, you've changed.

INTERRUPTIONS

The cell phone starts to vibrate. A moment later you hear, "This is why I'm hot. This is why I'm hot. This is why, this is why…" – your cell phone is ringing. You answer the phone. It's your boss Aaron. You start explaining how getting the estimate to him will take longer than anticipated.

"Yes, I'll definitely get it finished in the next hour and that…"

PING "You've got mail." Oops, you forgot to lower the volume on your personal in-box.

"Yes, I'm still with you, Aaron," you confirm. "Sorry, could you repeat what you were saying? Okay thanks, I'll get right on it."

You hang up and turn to the open spreadsheet. Projections for next year need to be calculated at 15% higher because of the 2008 fuel spike…

CLICK. An IM from your colleague in the neighboring cubical pops up. It says "please turn down the ringer on your phone and while you're at it, get a ring tone that's not so last decade."

"Thanks, Sean, will do" you type back. You now try to refocus on the numbers. It's hard. Darn, you need information from the field manager. "Argh, no time to talk, I'll send an email," you think to yourself. You open a new email, type it up, hit 'replicate'.

"Oh no, 40 new emails, I am SO behind," you say to yourself. Suddenly you feel deflated. Another IM from cubical guy says "I just downloaded the theme from Gilligan's Island – want a copy?"

Does this scenario seem familiar? If so, I'm not surprised. Unnecessary interruptions consume about 28 percent of the knowledge worker's day. That translates into an annual 28 billion hours wasted in U.S. companies alone.[29] This amount represents approximately a $600 billion annual loss![30] Many of these costs accrue because recovering from interruptions takes a lot of time and yes, energy. Various studies place that recovery time somewhere between 8 and 15 minute each time we are interrupted!

David and I were still on the plane now discussing sneaky depleters. "Why are interruptions among the MOST important sneaky depleters to manage?" he asked.

"Because every interruption requires you to burn psychological and cognitive resources; first to address the new issues that the interruption raised and then, more resources to regain your original focus," I replied.

"Wow, I had no idea. Maybe you can help settle a little domestic disagreement," David wondered out loud. "My wife keeps telling me to turn off my cell phone at night because it disrupts our personal life. I tell her I just like to know who is

calling when it rings. I only take the call if it looks urgent. Is she right? Is what I'm doing supporting interruptions?"

"First of all, she's your wife so you already know that she is always right," I joked. "With regards to the specific phone issue, she has science on her side. I've coached many clients in this situation. Let's walk through a hypothetical scenario similar to the ones I often see," I suggested.

"The phone rings and shows your mother-in-law's caller identification. You are in a meeting and do not take the call. Even though you didn't answer the phone, the part of your brain dedicated to worrying about your in-laws' leaky roof and the pending hurricane has 'lit up' and has you at least somewhat distracted. The moment you looked at the phone number, you were psychologically hijacked, even though you did not answer the call. Moreover, if you were in flow when that call came in, you disabled a highly restorative process to boot," I concluded.

"Makes sense to me," said David. "That suggests that I really have to manage my personal boundaries and stay open to my wife's ideas."

"It couldn't hurt," I agreed.

For more information on the mechanism by which interruptions contribute to professional exhaustion, I recommend you start with Leslie Perlow's book *Time Bind* in which she writes about Fortune 500 company's software development teams and how their ability to manage interruptions improved their overall productivity and satisfaction.

In the meantime, think about some possible strategies for you to avoid this sneaky depleter?" Jot those down here.

_____

_____

_____

Thank you. Now, here are a few tips that my clients have found helpful:

- close your door
- turn off your cell phone, ringers, dingers and buzzers as often as possible (especially when you are sleeping)
- set your voicemail and 'out-of-office' message to announce that you check messages at regular intervals throughout the day and do so
- try working from a home office or a coffee shop if your office provides too many social or sensory distractions
- designate 'interruption free' zones and times

In general, be mindful that you must actively manage your vulnerability to interruptions and, when possible, modify your behaviors to lead by example. Now is a great time to practice this. Is there a ringer or dinger near you that you might be able to turn down until you have completed this chapter?

CULTURES OF RELENTLESS ENTHUSIASM

In today's world, we are all susceptible to overwork and professional exhaustion. This susceptibility is increased by the relentlessness of client and work team demands in our 24/7 society. Boundaries between work and non-work easily become blurred, making it difficult to shut off the 'go-for-it' culture of our communities. This leads us to keep working when we should stop and, and, similarly, remain awake socializing when we should go to sleep. The buzz of the group's happiness or success compels us to continue to engage when what we really need is to disengage—if only for a little while.

The positive benefits that accrue from encouragement and doing what one really loves are powerful and restorative.

However, when we really identify with our work and our peers, we can easily become seduced into self-depletion by our colleagues' enthusiasm and our own sensitivity to emotional contagion.[31] Organizations that enact this kind of occupational value system have what I call *cultures of relentless enthusiasm*.[32] These cultures not only encourage and reward our going the extra mile but also make us really **want** to attend the extra team dinner, work extra late and 'take one for the team' whenever asked to do so.

Cultures of relentless enthusiasm attract and cultivate enthusiastic, happy, capable, productive and engaged workers who gladly give-it-all-they've-got. That's great until the day comes when employees suddenly wake up to find themselves completely spent. At that moment, the response is often, "I don't know how I got this way but I can't go on like this. I quit. [33]"

HOW'S YOUR CULTURE?

Are you part of a culture of relentless enthusiasm? Consider the following. You stay up all night to get the bi-weekly progress report done. What does your team do? They congratulate you of course! Way to go! You're a rock star! After working in an environment that generates this kind of support and encouragement for such "heroics", why on earth would you ever want to get things done on time or at a reasonable pace? No one would pay you any mind nor appreciate you much.

Is this always the case in your world? Is there no minute except the last minute? Do you manage from emergency to emergency without any normalcy in between? Is it possible that in more than some of these cases, the heroes who saved the day needed to do so because they didn't scope or manage the work properly in the first place?

In your company, do those who propose longer timelines, a more measured pace, or clearly bounded working hours get labeled plodders, slackers, or whiners? Is it okay for a mother to say she has to leave by 6 pm to put her child to bed, but unacceptable for a single man to leave at 6 pm to get to his spinning class? If so, you might be living in a most difficult situation — a poorly disciplined culture of relentless enthusiasm. If so, you're in great company.

Why are these cultures so prevalent? Clearly, they can drive very high organizational performance. People work really hard when encouraged to and so, these organizations often succeed until the pipeline of willing participants dries up and/or too much of the organization's tacit knowledge walks out the door.

Colleagues and cultures that drive you to 'go the extra mile' unintentionally support self-depletion in the name of high performance. And without the self-awareness to prevent it, you slowly compromise your capacity to deliver. Intermittent positive reinforcement, one of the most powerful strategies for influencing behavior, feeds this cycle.[34]

Why do these organizations continue to exist? Because, if an organization can keep the talent pipeline flowing, it can get the maximum performance from people right up until they prematurely exhaust themselves and quit. For most firms, this is a risky strategy since turnover can cost organizations dearly. But unless someone is looking long term at the damage to knowledge and culture, these organizational systems rarely change. As such, we need to learn how to thrive in them.

MANAGING CULTURES OF RELENTLESS ENTHUSIASM

If you manage a firm with a culture of relentless enthusiasm, you may not want people to stop going the extra mile for you. That's fine. How about a *both and* approach?[35] Consider the low cost benefits of ALSO supporting and

rewarding the people who got things done on time without creating drama and undue stress? Not only would the quality of the product improve but so would the experience and output of the team. With both options on the organizational table, your team might reduce turnover and burnout while increasing long-term productivity.

The key to this win-win approach is to establish appropriate norms up front. Know the tradeoffs and create a climate of support around you. Although you probably don't want to discourage the guy who likes to go the extra mile, you may also want to be careful that he is not driven to seek out less exhausting work while his co-workers appreciatively applaud his most recent heroic act. Encourage planning, communication and moderation. Share these strategies with those around you and reward those who practice them effectively.

In closing this chapter, let's take a moment to recap. You now have the core components of Personal Resource Management. You understand how personal resources work. In addition to optimizing your reliable restorers, you will now be mindful of and manage the four sneaky personal resource depleters: emotional labor, overdose effects, interruptions, and cultures of relentless enthusiasm. With this clarity and knowledge, you are ready to create your personal energizing plan. The most important next step in making that plan is taking the Personal Resource Management Assessment™ (PRMA). Let's go!

CHAPTER EIGHT

Assessing Your Unique Energizing Needs

It's time to talk about you, you, you! That is, it's time to assess YOUR unique energizing needs. When you are done with the next two chapters, you will know and understand your Personal Energy Profile and have an actionable strategy to begin restoring yourself immediately. The first step towards that goal is to complete the Personal Resource Management Assessment™ (PRMA). This is an effective tool to uncover precisely what restores and depletes your personal resources. You'll want to routinely revisit the exercise and, over time, build a repertoire of responses you can deploy to remain ever mindful of and responsive to your Personal Resource Management needs.

Speaking of which, it's time to get back to my conversation with David. We had shared yet another meal and another nap on that long transatlantic journey. I opened my file and handed David the assessment.

"I just happen to have an extra fifty copies of the PRMA in my bag. Now that you've had a nap, do you want to try it out?" I asked enthusiastically. He nodded in agreement as he skimmed the exercise.

"Hmm, only two spaces for what depletes me?" He chuckled.

"Feel free to write on the back," I said.

There is a great chasm between knowing what to do and actually doing it. I really encourage you to be a doer in this chapter. Would YOU please try to fill out the form now? I know some of you will just go get a pen and write all over this book knowing there's a website where you can get more forms when you need them. That's good. For those of you who don't write in books, you can go to www.RestoreYourselfBook and print out a copy of the form before you do anything else. Or, just sketch it onto a piece of paper and fill that out. That way you won't worry (which could distract you and deplete your cognitive resources).

For the others of you who are thinking to yourselves – "I'll just read through this first and then decide if I want to fill it out or not," I have a request. Please, let this once be an exception and agree to DOING this exercise. It's a nice idea to read first. However, the exercise is not as powerful a change agent unless you actually DO the thinking and the writing. So, please, consider just 'doing it.' Besides, by the time you've "just read through" the exercise you could have already been well on your way to finishing it!

We're now going to complete the PRMA on the next page (or the copy you printed out.) This self-assessment will take between 15 and 30 minutes to complete. You may want to share this exercise with your colleagues or your family. My clients really enjoy discussing their findings in pairs or small groups after they've filled them out. And, don't forget to write today's date somewhere on the document. That's important because as we've already learned, sources of restoration and depletion can and do change over time.

First, I'll coach you through the assessment. Then, I'll provide some examples and details. Start writing whenever you're ready – you can always go back and add details. Are we all set? Let's get started.

Fill In	Restorer 1	Restorer 2	Depleter 1	Depleter 2
Physical				
Social				
Cognitive				
Psychological				

Figure 3: Personal Resource Management Assessment   Reproduced with permission: Greenblatt, 2001

Take a moment to familiarize yourself with the form. You will need to identify and write down two reliably restorative scenarios and then two definitely depleting scenarios. These are the occasions that leave you either very much restored (energized, elated, enthusiastic, alert, sharp, balanced, whole) or very deeply depleted (exhausted, dull, upset, distracted, despondent, dysfunctional, burned out). To help get you started, here's an example of one of my restorative scenarios:

Skiing in Vail, Colorado with my local mountaineering friends is reliably restorative. It's a sunny, crisp day. It's cool enough to keep the two inches of fresh powder light but I'm warm in my comfy ski suit. My friends are all healthy and not processing any professional or personal catastrophes. They're all better skiers than I am but they've got nothing to prove and so are out for a leisurely tour rather than a death defying adventure. Some of the runs are a challenge for me but when it's difficult, they slow down or coach me through. We start at 8 am and end by 2 pm with no goal other than to spend a nice day outside that includes some great runs and a timely lunch break at the top of the mountain.

Notice that details are important here when describing your scenarios. That's because you'll use the details of these scenarios to help identify the distinguishing features that impact your personal resource levels. Learning the conditions and behaviors that increase or deplete your energy will help you improve the quality of your life and effectively increase your resilience.

Under Restorative Scenes 1 and 2

Think about two scenarios that reliably leave you feeling restored, rejuvenated, resilient, and mentally alert (exclude sleep since we know how that works). For the broadest impact, try to select one that is somehow related to

work. Now, think about them in excruciating detail and then jot down the summary in the boxes at the top of the appropriate column. (You can jot down the entire story on a separate piece of paper and then transfer the highlights to the form if you prefer.)

Under Depleting Scenes 1 and 2

Think about two scenarios that always leave you feeling rung out, drained, exhausted, pooped or burned out. Again, think of the specific conditions such as who and how many people are there, what it's like around you, what you feel like inside, what role you are playing. Then, jot down the summary of each in the boxes at the top of the appropriate depleter columns.

Create Your Personal Energy Profile (PEP)

Next, by answering the thought prompts in the section below, you'll find yourself describing the distinguishing features of your restorative and depleting scenarios. That will start to generate your PEP - a summary of what really impacts your personal resources. So, for each of the four energy categories, please read through the prompts and fill in each box. This approach to filling out the assessment is a bit like the inquiry style in Dr. Seuss' *Green Eggs & Ham*. For example: Do you do this in a house? Do you do this with a mouse?

The four categories are only there to help you capture a variety of information and they are not mutually exclusive. Sometimes you won't know which category a thought or feeling goes in. No problem. For example, if your ex-runway model secretary shows up at your 30th anniversary party, that affects both the social conditions and the psychological features of the event. In this case, it wouldn't matter if you wrote 'people I despise' under Social or 'emotionally charged'

under Psychological as long as the effect on you appeared somewhere on the page.

Physical

In this row, you'll focus on two kinds of distinguishing physical features: the external physical environment and your own physical experiences. Answering the following questions will help you define your scenarios. Are you indoors or out? What is the time of day? What's the climate like? Where are you located – city, countryside, lakeside, in a train, on a plane? What are the physical sensations you are experiencing? Do you hear music, people chatting, water flowing or traffic sounds? What do your other senses tell you? What is the physical environment like? Clutter or open vistas? Are you moving or stationary, sitting or standing, cramped or cramping up? Is this activity aerobic, anaerobic or sedentary? Are you tired, hungry, in pain, or practically perfect in every way?

Social

In the social row, you'll be describing the social conditions under which these scenarios take place. This means your situation vis-à-vis other people. Are you alone, in a pair, or with a group? What are your social roles and responsibilities? In this situation, are you responsible for the outcome? Are you a leader, team member, or follower? Are you a collaborator, antagonist or disinterested observer? How are people interacting — in person, on the phone, or virtually? How connected are you feeling to the earth, nature, spiritual powers, religious figures or ancestors? Are you able to engage fully with the people and the situation, or are you being interrupted and distracted by others, whether co-located or through messaging, emails, calls or errant thoughts?

Cognitive

Here, you should describe the cognitive or intellectual demands you face in this environment and the mental state you are in. Are you engaged in complex calculations or do you simply need to focus enough of your attention to avoid careening into a pine tree at 20 miles an hour? Do you need to forcefully concentrate in order to silence distractions or are you in flow – fully engaged and mentally alert? Are you being mindful of things around you or are you in a cognitive fog? Is your mind focused on solving big, complicated problems or managing urgent little daily life issues? Do the problems seem hard, easy or just challenging enough? What is your cognitive role during this activity – are you leading the problem-solving, reacting to others, mentally passive or disengaged from external concerns?

Psychological

For these characteristics, focus on the emotional or other set of psychological experiences that occur in this scenario. How do you feel – nervous, relaxed, elated, proud, self-conscious, frustrated, inadequate, calm, capable, loved, supported, happy, bashful, grumpy or dopey? What is your stress level? Do you feel pressured by time or other resource constraints? What is the emotional tenor of the occasion? Is there infectious enthusiasm, general dismay, unspoken fear, or collective calm? Are you or others actively managing their emotions or are people releasing their unprocessed delight, rage, frustration or glee into the shared space? How does that affect you?

LOOK FOR PATTERNS

Next, review what you've written looking for patterns that reveal distinguishing features of your Personal Energy Profile. First, look for similarities within the restorers and

within depleters. Do your restorative scenarios have any similar features? Perhaps they both involve sunlight and exercise? Maybe you do them both done alone or in environments absent any great performance pressures?

Next, what do you notice about your depleters? Do you see commonalities across these scenarios? Some of my clients, for example, have found that their most depleting scenarios all involved wasting time or loss of control. Draw boxes around the similar pairs.

Now, look for contrasts across the restorative and depleting examples. Circle the contrasting pairs: alone/many people, hot/cold, leading/following, etc... Roland, one of my clients, noticed that his depleters all had ambiguous outcomes, unattainable goals or lacked conclusive endings. He noticed that preparing presentations that were never presented and working diligently towards sales goals that were never going to be achieved frustrated him. In contrast, most of Roland's restorers, large and small, were activities that created an observable, finite outcome such as building model trains, sending the invoice at the end of a project, ironing his shirt in the morning, and running errands.

Finally, look at your boxes and your circles. What patterns do you see? Which similarities and contrasts could help you think about effectively energizing your days a bit? Roland realized that he could reduce his depletion by noticing what **was** completed even in long, complex projects and that he could also volunteer to manage a few shorter projects in the future.

USE YOUR PEP

What you have before you is a summary of conditions and behaviors that cause changes in your personal resources. This is your Personal Energy Profile. Now, to make it useful,

jot down here the patterns you've seen in your depleters and restorers.

Now, think about three easy things that you can do immediately to add some restorative characteristics to the scenarios that are currently depleting you. Similarly, think about some small changes you can make to improve the chances that you will more effectively restore. Jot your initial action plan down here.

If you were able to do all of this without an example to guide you, good. If not, don't fret. At this point, David was not quite sure what I meant so I showed him two examples. Yours are on the next pages. I have included only one exemplary restorer and one depleter from each of them. You, of course, will want to create two scenarios each (restorer and depleter) to generate a more precise PEP for yourself. See if these examples help you and then if you'd like go back and elaborate on your own form.

Example: Edy's PEP summary and action plan

Restorative Scenario 1

Skiing with friends in Colorado

Physical
Outdoors, aerobic activities, quiet, open vistas, nature, lots of movement, speed, lots of vestibular stimulation (turning, jumping), it is sunny, I'm warm.

Social
Done in a group, I am a follower, alive with others visiting casually while engaging in another activity. I'm in a friendly, encouraging, collaborative environment. Smart adults with capabilities well matched to the situation.

Cognitive
It is easy to get into flow. I am solving only physical movement challenges that I am more than capable of solving. Changing terrain is enjoyable and keeps me mindful and observant. Few critical decisions are necessary as long as I avoid hitting a tree.

Psychological
I'm happy, feel safe and competent. I experience a low level of responsibility for the group, low stress, serene. Companions are independent, happy, capable, enthusiastic, engaged and jovial. I don't have to worry about them.

Depleting Scenario 1

Writing articles at work

Physical:
Indoors, fluorescent lighting, sedentary, quiet or office buzz, looking at computer, makes me fidgety, chilly from air conditioning.

Social
Sitting alone or at least socially isolated from others. Interactions with others are all instrumental – i.e., can you help me get this done, turn down the ringer, etc. Feel unsupported.

Cognitive
Cognitive demands for creativity in short time frame very high. All problem solving done alone. All the answers that I need I must find inside my own head.

Psychological
Relatively high level of responsibility for outcome and impact on others. Some stress caused by time constraints. Often susceptible to anxiety, fear of failure, loneliness and self-criticism.

<u>Edy's PEP-based action plan</u>

- Edit hardcopy drafts by hand in a cafe where other people are around and I'm not looking at a computer screen
- Twice a week, try to write outdoors or by a big window
- Get up every 30 minutes to walk or run a quick errand

- Intentionally schedule my day to allow time for a quick workout halfway through writing
- Get others to be on call during the writing process in case I get mentally or emotionally stuck and need assistance
- Share drafts with colleagues and family often so I have someone with whom to think out loud
- Try to block out times in advance and vigilantly protect that time to reduce feeling time pressured
- Parse the work out so it can be reviewed by others to reduce my fear of surprise criticism
- Plan to eat at least one meal daily with others
- Share this PEP with the work team and ask for suggestions and support to better reach our shared goals

David's PEP summary and action plan

David's Restorative Scenario 1 (Summary)

Swimming Laps

- Outdoors, aerobic exercise, makes me breath deeply, I'm cool, it is quiet, lots of tactile and proprioceptive stimulation, endorphin buzz
- Accomplished alone. Even if others are present, I have no interaction or responsibility for them.
- Flow comes naturally, no problem solving involved, mind free to process other stuff. I have adequate skills not to drown.
- Zero level of stress and no time constraints within sufficiently allocated time (booked 1.5 hours for

workout). I feel peaceful, proud that I'm doing the right thing for myself. I feel deeply grateful.

David's Depleting Scenario 1 (Summary)

Family Functions at In-Laws' House

- Indoors, lots of people, LOUD talking, many distractions, dogs barking, sedentary
- Large group of agitated people out of their comfort zones. I'm responsible for outcome and the sole leader. Subject to many sequential and simultaneous person-to-person interactions
- No flow possible. I experience mental chaos from constant problem solving. Exposed to too many distractions and interruptions. No time to think through anything carefully.
- I feel responsible for everyone having a good time, highly pressured and stressed, a fear of failure and the need to optimize everything. I experience lots of emotional contagion from others' stressed out states. Doing lots of emotional labor not to scream in frustration.

David's PEP-based action plan

- Plan more family activities outdoors and away from the house
- Invite others to generate activities and perform tasks
- Lobby for activities that I enjoy
- Encourage others to plan with me
- Include friends at family events to help keep perspective and broaden the topics of conversation

- Take 15 minutes to meditate after lunch or during lulls
- Clarify actual family expectations and obligations
- Schedule a swim the days before and after family gatherings
- Share what depletes and restores me with the family and use that to start a conversation to design more restorative encounters for everyone for the next time

---

Note: If you have any trouble with this exercise, go to www.RestoreYourselfBook.com and, if what you need isn't posted, contact me directly through the site.

"Well, David, what do you think?" I asked. "Does it seem like you can change a few things that might increase your resilience?"

"I must tell you, Edy, I'm surprised," David said. I truly do think I can reduce what's exhausting me and restructure some tasks to make them more restorative. It's going to be a challenge, but I can do it. It'll require that I get clearer and more comfortable choreographing my work days and tasks. But, I'm willing to try."

"All that is to say, yes, Edy, I am going to try some of these things and I'm pretty sure they'll help me. Wow! When are you going to write a book on this stuff?" he asked.

A LITTLE MORE WORK WILL GO A LONG WAY

PRM is most effective when you fill out several of these worksheets so that all of the depleting and potentially restorative areas of your life become more obvious. Then, restoring yourself will simply be a matter of doing what you know needs doing. Believe me; a little work upfront now will go a long way later. Since you've already completed one worksheet, why not schedule a time in the next few weeks to

do another round so that you can move quickly to restore yourself?

By the way, you won't have to carry these worksheets around with you forever. After working with these tools a few times, the mechanics of PRM will become second nature and the corrective processes will occur naturally. Before you know it, your ability to spot problems before they occur will happen automatically.

In the next chapter, you'll discover that it is not only the behaviors and conditions under which you operate that cause you to burn out. How you schedule those tasks also significantly contributes to professional exhaustion. Now that you know what you're seeking out and avoiding, we can look at how you schedule that.

Up until now, we've avoided discussing time, a woefully scarce, shared resource for most of us. In the next chapter, however, I'll teach you how to use time and timing to your advantage in optimizing your personal resources. So what are you waiting for? Oh right, you're jotting down a few more of those nasty depleters so you can neutralize them a bit. Okay, when you're ready, I'll be waiting for you on the next page!

CHAPTER NINE

Strategic Sequencing

David looked at the circled behaviors and conditions on his PRMA, the beginnings of his PEP and his action planning notes.

"This is outstanding. Now I have a good idea of what affects my personal resources and some things I can do to have more energy. That's going to help me restore myself much more effectively," David remarked enthusiastically.

"What will you do differently, starting tomorrow?" I asked.

"In addition to what I jotted down earlier, I'm going to calendar in 60 minutes of undisturbed work time three mornings a week which will allow me to reduce my interruptions and maybe even get into flow. I'm also going to try telecommuting one day a week so I can have breakfast with my kids since that's a huge restorer for me, and will schedule my first phone meeting during my walk to work. That will get me 30 minutes more sleep and more sunlight every morning.

"Perfect," I said. "What else?"

"I'm going to have my co-CEO and our assistants either attend one of your workshops or, at minimum, sit down and take this assessment. Afterwards, we'll sit together and learn how we can use our differences to our advantage and how we can help each other be more restored while we help the company succeed," he responded.

"Outstanding," I complimented him. I was very happy

that the exercise had started him thinking in a new direction.

David paused to think for a moment. "I don't mean to seem ungrateful for an excellent tool but, I still have one concern. I'm hopeful your PRM has a solution for this, too. There are some tasks that deplete me that I simply must do. For example, there is no way to make firing someone any less than awful, is there?" David asked.

"None that I know of," I replied. "I think that even for the most naturally optimistic manager, firing someone is at least somewhat depleting. It's almost always a sad, difficult situation. However, I do have two tools that will help you make the occasions on which you have to fire someone less debilitating than they otherwise might be. One is using people's different personal rhythms to your advantage and the other I call *strategic sequencing*. In both cases, timing is everything," I finished.

PERSONAL RHYTHMS

PRM becomes an even more powerful tool when you use time and timing to your advantage. We can use variations in personal rhythms to be more efficient and as such, remain more resilient.

People naturally restore and deplete in predictable rhythms. Some patterns are common. For example, more people are alert at 8 am than they are at 11 pm. Physical performance is more likely to peak sometime shortly after eating a light, well-balanced meal than just before. Children in U.S. schools are more easily distracted and lethargic on November 1st after staying out late and eating too much candy on Halloween.

The idea of using time efficiently is nothing new. We all multi-task and schedule ourselves silly. Many time-based work/life balance approaches encourage us to simultaneously accomplish as many tasks as possible. That often backfires

since the benefits of multitasking are quite susceptible to overdose effects.

For many of us, doing two things at once can raise the cognitive load to an optimally restorative level: Listening to music while checking email, for example. Adding a third or fourth task can sometimes tip the scale into depletion from overdosing. No doubt you can recall a time when you found yourself doing so many things at once that you lost the capacity to do any of them well. Part of good timing is regulating when we should be doing certain tasks simultaneously and when we should be working sequentially.

"So, is my multitasking or failing to do so making me burn out or am I just not suited to being a co-CEO? Aren't some occupations just exhausting by nature?" David asked.

"Yes and no," I replied. I have found that in any organization and/or occupation, there are those who remain resilient longer than others. Part of that is most certainly a result of nature. But the other part is about strategies people use for keeping themselves from burning out – *strategic sequencing* in particular," I replied.

"What a relief," David admitted. "I was beginning to wonder if I need career counseling. Tell me about natural time advantages and strategic sequencing."

"First, let's talk about natural advantages and disadvantages," I suggested. "For example, those who really require only six hours of sleep each night can work or play 21 hours each week more than those who really need nine hours to function well. People who live from *latte* to *latte* are trying to use chemicals to keep up with those whose bodies simply allow them more productive waking hours than others. Not a good long term health strategy but for some in their current roles, a necessary evil for evening the playing field. (Plan to sleep extra on weekends and reconsider the long-term viability of this as a strategy if you currently live this way).

Similarly, there are those for whom a required set of occupational behaviors or organizational conditions are fundamentally restorative. Think about an extroverted greeter at Wal-Mart or a chocolate-loving candy maker and their introverted or sugar-allergic counterparts trying to be equally satisfied and content in those same roles.

"David, imagine that you and your business partner were required by law to switch roles every six months. What would happen?" I asked.

"I would have to schedule my one-month vacation immediately after I took his job because doing what he does would very nearly kill me!" he exclaimed.

"So, we agree that there are natural and personal tendencies that help people succeed in their careers. I'm not going to spend time here on the role of occupational fit. Let's instead talk about what **you** can do with time to make your current life work better for you," I suggested.

"If there are natural differences in how people work, use them. If your colleagues are good in the morning and you are good in the evening, stagger the work enough that you get to use people's strengths when they are strongest. When there is a slide deck that needs four eyes on it, give it to the night owl first and have it passed to the early riser in the morning for second review instead of allowing the review sequence to emerge randomly," I recommended.

As we go through our lives, our resource levels vary. The early riser often has more resources available earlier in the day than the night owl whose APRL peaks at night. Students are more susceptible to the flu during finals than in September. A clear understanding of how the four personal resource ranges work will help you hone your timing.

FOUR PERSONAL RESOURCE RANGES

Earlier in the book I spoke about direct strategies for

optimizing your personal resources, either by restoring more or by avoiding depletion. Indirect strategies for optimizing your personal resources involve modifications to the sequencing and timing of various tasks to raise your Average Personal Resource Level (APRL). These indirect strategies work because we operate at any given time in one of four particular APRL ranges shown in Figure 4. From highest to lowest, they are

- optimal range,
- normal range,
- reserve range, and
- burnout range

Your capacity to do quality work, the ease with which you operate and your ability to be your best all diminish as your APRLs descend into lower and lower ranges. And, in the burnout range, things go quickly from bad to worse.[36] That's why timing matters.

For example, imagine that first thing on Tuesday morning your boss drops a difficult, rush project on your desk that he needs completed within seven hours. You'll need to work straight through without any breaks to meet the crushing deadline. When you have completed the assignment, you go home, eat dinner and get lost on Facebook for a few hours before going to bed.

Now, if you rated your APRLs on a scale of 1-10 throughout the process, with 1 being about the worst a human can feel without being hospitalized and 10, alert and bouncing around like Winnie the Pooh's friend Tigger, your ratings would look like the Tuesday column on the next page.

If, instead, your boss showed up with the exact same demands on Thursday afternoon of a difficult week, you'd be starting out more depleted and so the same activity would

catalyze different APRL changes. Not only would the quality of your product likely be poorer, but your resilience would be dealt a significant blow in the process.

ACTIVITY	Tuesday AM APRL	Thursday PM APRL
Arrive at work	8	4
Start Project	7	3
Finish Project	3	1*
Get Home	4	1*
After Dinner	5	1*
Finish Facebooking	6	2
Wake Up Next Day	8	3

* Burnout

Notice how in the second scenario, the numbers got stuck down around one? That's because you started at a lower APRL on Thursday and dropped below your resilience threshold into burnout. My research shows that this happens because the APRL at which you start an activity can significantly change how that event affects you. Differing responses to stimuli occur because our sensitivity to resource changing events varies based on how depleted or restored we are at the time. It also points to a working definition of burnout.

BURNOUT AS ONE OF OUR FOUR RESOURCE RANGES

Look at Figure 4. Notice that on a given day, we can operate in any or all of four personal resource ranges. In each range, our capacity to perform varies. In the optimal range, we are able to be our best. In the normal range, we are, well, normal or average and can function pretty much the way we function on most similar days.

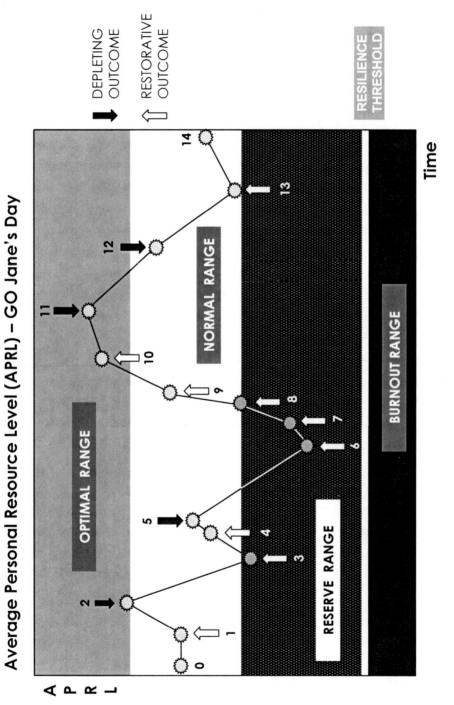

Figure 4: Strategic Sequencing

Reproduced with permission: Greenblatt, 2001

In the reserve range we are running on fumes and cannot respond as well or as quickly as usual. We often borrow from one energy system to fuel the next, much like using the cheering crowd to keep us running to the finish line. In this condition, you run a high risk of crashing through your resilience threshold and becoming burned out.

Burnout can by catalyzed by a singular, dramatic event, such as a personal loss, layoff, physical injury, or significant professional setback. However, more typically, a series of smaller resource depleting events steadily consumes our personal fuel until we can no longer function normally. And, because we also become unable to adequately replenish, we energetically collapse. This is how most of us become professionally exhausted. This is how we arrive in the burnout range. Once in the burnout range, we have almost no resilience at all and have lost the capacity to do some or all of our normal activities.

Burnout is an extreme case of personal resource depletion – a condition that occurs when the net sum of all depletion and restoration activities brings one's personal resource levels below minimum operating levels.

Arriving at very low resource levels is not the worst part of burning out. If we return to our car analogy from earlier, burnout is akin to running out of gasoline in a car with a catalytic converter. Of course, there are no resources left to fuel the car. But worse, adding fuel to the tank won't help because running out of gas damaged the system. You must make extra efforts and repair it before the system can optimally work again.

This is what happens to people's energy systems when they cross the *resilience threshold* into the burnout range. In the

burnout range, otherwise reliable restorative sources provide significantly less restorative effect and, otherwise insignificant sources of depletion cause more significant resource losses. That is, restorers lose their impact and depleters become supercharged.

It takes extra effort to replenish resources when in the burnout range. For example, a burned out employee who is typically restored by a weekend's rest and recreation might need an entire week's vacation in order to receive a comparable restorative effect. Similarly, a mildly critical comment to an employee in burnout range could have the same effect as a stinging rebuke.

Here's a less dramatic example. My even-tempered friend Gail, days before her medical school entrance exam, nearly lost her voice yelling at her husband because he wanted to wear an old green shirt to a party instead of the new white one they'd purchased together. For Gail under normal conditions, that minor social surprise would have been a small depletion blip. Because she was in burnout range, the impact of the disagreement with her husband was amplified, resulting in hours of emotional and cognitive losses from subsequent dickering.

That's why you never want to cross that line into burnout. The costs of getting back above the resilience threshold are so high, in fact, that we should always be mindful to make the relatively low investment necessary to stay above it. (Are you sensing that I am passionate about this point?)

STRATEGIC SEQUENCING

Fortunately, consciously manipulating task sequence can help avoid burnout. I call this approach *strategic sequencing*. Strategic sequencing minimizes the likelihood of falling into the burnout range by maximizing APRLs.

Figure 4, depicts how changes in circus GO Jane's APRL occurred over the course of a day. We'll use this typical Club Med day to exemplify how strategic sequencing can make or break your capacity to work. First, let's learn how the system works.

Recall, a person's APRL is an estimate of the relative amount of energy and ability available to them from all of their physical, social, cognitive and psychological/emotional resources at a given moment in time. As one's APRL varies over time, so does one's ability to accomplish a given task. A worker with a higher APRL simply has more to bring to his organization and personal stakeholders.

In Figure 4, each arrow represents a depleting or restorative outcome associated with a work-related event. Each event either increases or decreases Jane's resource level. For example, a complimentary phone call from a client would be depicted as an Up arrow because the recipient gains psychological resources in the form of increased self-esteem. A healthy breakfast or well-balanced workout would also register as an Up arrow. Similarly, reports of an impending economic depression would register as a Down arrow.

Vertical movements in the resource level represent the impact of a resource-changing event. The impact of any particular event, however, is not independent from the individual's personal circumstances at the time of the event. Rather, the impact depends on a number of factors, including the resource range in which the person is operating at the time. The heavy line at the bottom of the exhibit indicates the resilience threshold, the gateway to burnout.

USING STRATEGIC SEQUENCING TO MANAGE

"What should I do as a manager if I know this?" David asked me.

"I've found that project and task allocation decisions

that take into account the current personal resource levels of key workers are more likely to produce desired results than are those that assume a person's ability to perform remains constant over time," I replied. "Here's an example from my work with Club Med GO's that shows how organizationally designed strategic sequencing of work activities maintains a worker's personal resources at the highest possible levels," I shared with David.[37]

I pulled out GO Jane's daily APRL summary from the Club Med study and handed it to David (that's your Figure 4). Follow along and you'll see exactly how strategic sequencing works.

Jane is a circus GO who works teaching flying trapeze, trampoline and tumbling at a family village in North America. She starts her day in the upper end of her normal range (0) and walks to the main restaurant. Breakfast is a source of resource enhancement (1). By the end of the morning, her service duties (2) have depleted her such that when she leaves to lead participatory dancing by the pool she is running on reserves (3). Leading the Sun Dance begins to restore her (4), and lunch continues the process of returning her squarely back into normal range to start her afternoon work (5). Her service duties deplete her such that by the end of the afternoon, she is running purely on physical and psychological reserves (6). She is only able to carry on through the last hour because she feels the support of her team and the enthusiasm of a six-year-old guest with wondrous eyes who is jumping on the trampoline for the first time. Back in her room, a shower and a glance at a letter from home begin to revive her (7).

At the main bar, a guest buys Jane a drink and praises her talent, kindness, and beauty (8). She has dinner with his family (9) and by the time she leaves the main restaurant for the theater she feels like her enthusiastic self again. Her singing in the evening show and the audience's response to

her performance feel electrifying (10), and so by the end of the show, our GO Jane is rejuvenated. The music and dancing of the Macarena and similar participatory line dances top off Jane's resources. Later, an uninspiring late staff meeting (11) followed by duties to escort and register late arriving guests begin to deplete her (12). She goes to bed at a low, normal resource level (13). After six hours sleep, she awakens to begin her day within her normal resource range, albeit slightly lower than the morning before (14).

To demonstrate the potential impact of strategic sequencing on an individual's resources, note the hypothetical negative impact of changing the sequence of two mandatory work tasks. If management moved the Sun Dance (3) from before lunch to after dinner and changed the staff meeting from late at night to afternoon, (11), Jane would reach burnout levels by dinnertime. Since restorative events are less potent when someone is in the burnout range, Jane's' daily restorative activities alone would become insufficient to return her ability to perform effectively. As such, she would sink below the resilience threshold and become less productive, less satisfied, or both.

"Okay Edy," David said. "The story is compelling, not to mention the imagery of a good looking young woman flying on the trapeze, dancing, singing and having drinks with married men. Now, help me understand how this can be done in more traditional business settings."

"In most occupations, the individual can often effectively strategically sequence if they elect to do so," I said. For example, a resource-taxed administrative staff person whose key sources of depletion include constant interruptions to run errands, inadequate exposure to sunlight, and emotional exhaustion from managing interpersonal conflict, could organize her day to better enhance her resources. She could choose to run outdoor errands only twice a day–mid-

morning and mid-afternoon. She could then take her lunch outside away from her colleagues. This strategy exposes her to restorative daylight and provides respite from depleting interpersonal conflict. It provides revitalization well before her APRL has dropped into the reserve or burnout ranges."

"Similarly, an engineer whose key sources of depletion are long periods of time spent alone working on creative tasks, a sedentary lifestyle, and demanding supervisory responsibilities could use strategic sequencing to improve his APRL. Interspersing managerial interactions between long periods of lone research time could offset the potential depletion from working too long in isolation. Scheduling some managerial conversations while taking a walk could also restore resources. Emotional depletion from difficult conversations could be limited by scheduling them in between restorative research activities."

"Finally," I continued after sipping some water, "the home-based pharmaceutical salesperson whose 15-hour workday demands include both soliciting orders from new clients and doing housework can offset the depleting effects of successive failed closings by inserting a quickly-completed household chore between calls. Mixing ironing and folding laundry with intermittent work on a cognitively challenging sales projection could create a higher APRL day," I concluded.

HELPING RAISE TEAM APRLS

Team members can facilitate strategic sequencing to help each other. In my research, exemplary GO teams used their instinctive knowledge of strategic sequencing to create individual staffing schedules aimed at restoration. GOs who worked in more isolated or sedentary services that operated both day and night broke up their schedules with interactions that were dynamic, physical, and socially interactive. For example, boutique workers often rotated shifts to take

advantage of daytime breaks that enabled them to participate in sporting or artistic activities. Aware of her particular restoration needs, one successful manager agreed to be "sent jogging" by her direct reports when she became noticeably ineffective.

Outside of resort contexts, organizations can easily include strategic sequencing among their work assignment decision criteria. When determining which demands to make on employees at a given time, the decision criteria should include an estimate both of their current APRLs and the impact that the new demands will have on their ability to perform.

I have created and then helped teams prepare for engagements by assessing both the individual team members' PEPs as well as estimating the engagement's inherent sources of depletion. To get an idea of how that works, imagine a Boston-based professional service team assigned to help a small Western mining company cut its staff and reorganize both the company and its manufacturing processes. They could anticipate difficult travel schedules, separation from family, challenging physical working conditions, communication and other cultural challenges as well as the susceptibility to feeling the fear, resentment and anger of the workforce. By planning ahead, the team intentionally managed the flow of work, engagement norms, and the clients' expectations in a way that minimized these potential sources of depletion.

For team leaders, I have created a team and engagement-level assessment and taught managers to use this approach in their team kickoffs. This allows the team to collectively assess the likely sources and impact of various impending events to maximize resulting team members' APRLs. To increase its impact, the team needs to create and manage norms that encourage its members to discover and

use their collective resources optimally.

TAKE A BREAK

Frequently, workers unnecessarily deplete themselves because critical activities, mistakenly viewed as optional, quietly drop out of the work schedule. Many corporate cultures consider skipping breaks as a sign of commitment and a predictor of productivity. Unfortunately, this norm is counterproductive to optimizing personal resources. Taking a short call from home, sharing a joke in the hall, and taking one's full lunch break are mistakenly viewed as foregone work time. But just the opposite is true. In many cases, people replenish during these intermittent activities and time spent on them can increase overall productivity.

Some companies, among them high technology firms in Silicon Valley, have institutionalized systems, structures and values that support ongoing resource enhancement. They have done so by cultivating organizational cultures that compliment particular restoration needs. Non-traditional features of the workplace such as allowing pets, children, and amusements are intended to enable individuals to spontaneously insert restorative activities in their workday as needed. For many, there is an excellent fit between their needs and the type of work conditions these policies foster. For those people, the conditions and behaviors enabled by these non-traditional work environments helps them to maximize their contribution and optimize their personal resource levels thanks to strategic sequencing. For others, children, dogs and air hockey are disruptions. (Remember our musketeers.)

In short, it is within your control to mitigate the impact of many sources of exhaustion in your life, even at work. Even if you have not dutifully done the exercises in this book, you can learn what restores you and what depletes you by simply being on the lookout for clues and being mindful of how

things affect you. With the knowledge of strategic sequencing, you will also have a sense of how timing affects you. If either your boss or your organization supports ways in which you can strategically sequence your work, so much the better. But if not, remember that you do have control over certain aspects of your day that you can alter. Timing matters. Strategic sequencing matters. Most importantly, **you** matter.

So, before we get to the last chapter, write down the changes you are going to make to time and timing now that you know about strategic sequencing. And, why not summarize your **new energizing action plan** based on all we've covered so far? Now you know how to restore yourself! Jot down your action plans here!

_____

_____

_____

_____

_____

_____

_____

_____

_____

_____

_____

_____

CHAPTER NINE

Restore Yourself!

"Edy, this all sounds great and I'm truly optimistic." David adjusted his footrest and blanket. "In hindsight, it all seems so easy. What's the catch? I mean, how hard is it to make these changes? How far is the distance between understanding what needs to be done and implementation? Do many of your clients actually succeed? Can most people do this?" David asked in rapid succession.

In this chapter I will answer these questions and review what we covered in the book. To begin, the answer to David's questions are yes, many succeed and yes, most can do this. But this approach requires a change in how you view yourself and your world. Though we really do have some physical, cognitive, social and emotional limits, the good news is that we've always had those limits and can do a great deal to improve our energetic future nonetheless. Now, with the knowledge that you control more than you thought and the tools to do so, you'll be able to get more out of each day.

Just knowing you have the power to influence your personal resources will help you. For example, instead of presuming that you'll get a cold or the flu at the end of a stressful project or right after the big wedding you've planned, you can plan to mitigate or avoid that negative impact that known depleters will have. More importantly, through understanding and by practicing PRM regularly, you will find yourself choreographing your life to optimize your APRLs.

PRM will not only add to the quality of your life but it will improve the lives of those around you as well. That's because practicing PRM will have halted the downward spiral of professional exhaustion that once made you the one excusing performance failures by saying 'I left my Blackberry in the car last night,' or 'sorry I lost my temper because…' etc..

There are lots of tactics that experienced PRM users have discovered over the years and I've put some of them up at RestoreYourselfBook.com. I hope you'll visit our site and post yours as well.

A LITTLE HELP FROM MY FRIENDS

A powerful yet often underutilized aide in restoring yourself is enlisting the help of others. People, social structures and norms can go a long way in helping you keep your commitments and mobilize your resilience musketeers. A simple example of this is hiring a personal trainer. A personal trainer does more than show you which exercises to do. Engaging a personal trainer creates a financial and social contract. As such it is much more difficult to skip one's workout when you have a paid trainer who has gotten up at 5 am and driven 30 minutes to meet you at the gym than it is to just roll over promising yourself you'll workout tomorrow.

If you are positively influenced by social structures but are good at weaseling out of them, like I am, you can still create some very effective ones if you put your mind to it. For example, while finishing my dissertation I recognized that it was critical for me to exercise regularly to maintain my APRL in the highest possible range. I knew that would require me to focus on some greater good during the notoriously self-focused and grueling writing process. To create a social structure to help me exercise and finish writing the dissertation quickly, I registered to raise money for and then run in a marathon for AIDS Project Los Angeles (APLA).

To further encourage me when I felt tired and didn't want to train or write, I solicited donations to APLA from all of my friends and colleagues. My trick was that I not only promised to run the marathon as their sponsoree but also committed to work one hour on my dissertation for each dollar donated.

With more than $5000 in donations on the line, I had created what was for me, an unbreakable social contract that made the personal costs of not writing and not running so high that I could overcome any psychological or emotional barriers when my APRLs were low. The outcome was a win-win-WIN situation – the charity got money, sick people received necessary services, my friends got to contribute to a local and greater good, my dissertation got finished, I was supported in taking care of myself on many levels and we all got tax deductions.

USING OUR ENERGIZING DIFFERENCES

To most easily and effectively use PRM and integrate restorative characteristics into an otherwise regularly depleting professional environment, you will want to encourage your colleagues to use PRM. Many teams take the individual assessment and then discuss how to use the contrasts and complementarities in the team for collective advantage.

I worked with a group of architects who, after taking and comparing PRM profiles, discovered that they were all rather weak at problem solving from 4-6 pm and so they agreed to avoid scheduling problem-solving sessions during that time period when everyone was at his/her worst. They also discovered that two members loved to work at night whereas two loved to work early in the morning. They used these tendencies to get work done faster and easier when they had to do sequential revisions.

When your entire team becomes expert at identifying individual and collective sources of depletion and restoration, then, add in some group level strategic sequencing. Your entire team's APRLs, along with its productivity and satisfaction will soar!

RESTORE YOURSELF!

"Please return your seats to their full, upright, and locked position," announced the flight steward.

You've probably heard that phrase a hundred times. Every trip you take, whether by plane, train or taxi, ultimately reaches its destination. And, so it is with our journey. Before I say goodbye and leave you to a more resilient, restored and energized future, let's review the highlights from our trip hear together.

1. Work isn't always depleting and non-work isn't always restorative. Work/life balance is a fairy tale. You might wish it existed but reality tells us something different. Even though work/life balance is debilitating myth, you can still have a positive, energized, and satisfying life by managing your personal resources. The shortest path is to maximize restoration and minimize depletion of your energies using Personal Resource Management™ (PRM).

2. Effective PRM requires you to make and keep two commitments. First, you need to become expert at knowing what restores and depletes *you* and, second, you need to be mindful about managing the conditions and behaviors that affect your personal resource levels.

3. Use the three musketeers of resilience to assist you in your battle against depletion and burnout. Remember:

a) we differ in what restores and depletes each of us,

b) look behind the mask to find your true restoration and depletion triggers without being fooled by social tags, and

c) life changes us and so be mindful that your sources of restoration and depletion will also change over time.

4. Manage the four major personal resources to keep up your Average Personal Resource Level (APRL). Resource types interact with each other so don't be surprised when physical exhaustion compromises your patience or when a walk around the block makes you feel less tired and better able to concentrate.

5. Calendar in and protect time and opportunity for reliable restorers such as sleep, flow, movement and sensory integration.

6. Become vigilant about avoiding, minimizing and offsetting sneaky depleters like emotional labor, multi-tasking, interruptions and overdose effects.

7. Use strategic sequencing to prevent burnout by using time and timing to maintain your APRL's in the normal and optimal ranges.

8. Share what you've learned here with others. Create and then benefit from collaborating with these likeminded colleagues, family and friends. Together, use PRM to make our world a better and more energized place.

Don't worry if your understanding of what restores or depletes you is imperfect or incomplete at this moment. PRM is both a source of quick wins and lasting benefit. Trust me; over time the practices and mental models we've covered here will become second nature. Each time you review what you have learned in these chapters or choose a more restorative way to get your work done, your understanding of your needs and effective ways to avoid the hazards of professional exhaustion will become stronger and clearer.

Over time, your ability to identify opportunities to be and do your best will become a daily source of comfort. Using PRM, you will realize a better, happier, more productive you both in the short- and long-term.

I have shared with you with a powerful tool kit. It, together with your own magnificent brain will help you maneuver away from depletion and head toward restoration. I hope that these tools and techniques help you to not only survive but also to *thrive* on the great and on the challenging days of your life. PRM is the antidote for many of our cases of professional exhaustion. Please use it and share it with others. Our world needs more restored people who have the energy to do the right things and make the world a better place.

You are not alone from here out. You can join our fabulous on-line community by logging in at **www.RestoreYourselfBook.com** and if you want a quick boost, you can attend a Restore Yourself Workshop either live or virtually. You can also contact me directly through the website when you need more material or personal guidance.

Together we are building a better world. In it, there is enough room for life's necessary and most worthwhile endeavors. When next you feel overwhelmed by your job, family, latest crisis, passion overdose or others' demands, don't panic. You have the tools and the community to get you through it.

If you've reached this point in the book, it's clear you are a doer committed to creating good for yourself and others. And you know that the more you do, the more chances there are for unanticipated turbulence along the way. If you falter, you can get right back at it and *restore yourself!* With PRM, bluer skies are just up ahead.

———————————

"Well, I guess I'm not going to finish my novel." David said smiling.

"Sorry," I said.

"Don't be foolish," rebuked my companion. "This was extremely valuable for me. How can I repay the favor?"

"When things start going better and you have restored yourself, send some of that new found energy toward me. That will help me finish the book that I'm writing," I said.

"It's a deal. The pleasure will be all mine," David replied. "By the way, remember that *I Love Lucy* episode when she got drunk selling that Vitameatavegamin stuff? Maybe you should put that in the book."

"That's a great idea! Thank you. I think I might," I replied.

The cheery voice of the flight steward concluded its landing soliloquy: "…and have a great day in New York or at your final destination."

David turned on his phone and dialed.

"We just landed," David spoke into his phone as we taxied towards the gate. A few moments passed. "I'm actually feeling a little better. And, I have a plan to restore myself that I can't wait to tell you about."

Acknowledgments

Thousands of people have contributed to this book. I am not exaggerating. I cannot possibly sufficiently acknowledge all who have helped me achieve this very important goal. To everyone, named and unnamed here who has helped, please accept my guaranteed most sincere appreciation, recognition and gratitude. I've listed some of those people below (alphabetical order by first name). Thank you from the bottom of my heart to any who I have accidentally omitted[38] and of course, to the following:

Adina Wollner
Andy Nastase
Anja K. Redwood
Anne-Laure Lehman
Annie Shomron
Barbara Chase
Barbara Kataisto
Barbara Stern
Bentzion Wollner
Betty Merino
Brian Underhill
Bronwyn Fryer
Charlie Berg
Cindy Baily
Coca Greenblatt
Conrad Hernandez

Craig Singer
Dan Olivo
David Ager
David Wollner
Donna D'Amore
Drew Harris
Ed Lawler III
Elissa Ashwood
Ellen Langer
Emerson Hawley
Erin Lehman
Execu-Care Books
Execu-Care Coaching &
  Consulting
Frank Richardson
Gail Williams

Giselle Lehman
Gus Tolley
Harvard University
Helen Loser
Huber Family
J. Richard Hackman
Jan Grevsen
Janet Stark
Janet Stark
Jay Scanlan
Jesus Encinar
Joanna Barsh
Jordan Auslander
Josephine Mogelof
Joyce Tolley
Kate Barrett
Kate Rosloff
Kim Greenblatt
Kim Sanders' family
L.A. Balkan dancers
Laura Rubinstein
Leonard Pollara
Marcia Wollner
Margalit Wollner
Marshall Goldsmith
Michael Allan Kirk
Mike Buckley
Mike Moldoveanu
Monarch Design
Monica Higgins
Monica McGurk
Mustafa Narter
My dance buddies
My dance partners

My dance students
My family
My friends
Nitin Nohria
Optimists International
Oscar Cragwell
Phoenix Decorating
Pierre Giauque
Ramon Pabon
Rebecca Craske
Renee Frisbie
Rosanne Yu
Rosebowl Aquatics
Rusty Berg
Sherry Cochran Kirk
Stanard Evans
Steve Sakamoto
Susie Cranston
Teresa Amabile
Teresa Schwartz
Tom Stuart
Trapeze High, LLC
Upper Meadows Farm
USC Center for Effective
 Organizations
USC Center for Telecom
 Management
Warren Bennis
Zlatne Uste

About the Authors

EDY GREENBLATT, PH.D. is a motivational speaker, executive coach, entrepreneur, management consultant and scholar. She has founded and run her own professional services firm, was on the faculty at the Center for Effective Organizations at the University of Southern California, and has also had successful careers as a dance ethnologist, talk show host, performing artist and a circus peanut vendor. Through her speaking, coaching, writing and seminars, Dr. Edy is fast becoming the business world's *Energizer Bunny*.

Dr. Greenblatt earned her Ph.D. in the joint program in Organizational Behavior at Harvard University and Harvard Business School. Prior to that, she completed the required curriculum for an MBA and earned a master's degree in Psychology (both at Harvard), after earning a master's degree in Dance Ethnology and a B.S. in World Arts and Cultures at University of California at Los Angeles. Edy is the host of her own radio and television programs, *The Dr. Edy Shows* designed to help humans thrive in the modern workplace. In her free time she still dances, flies on the trapeze, swims and sleeps. There is more at www.EdyGreenblatt.com.

MICHAEL ALLAN KIRK was born into a large multicultural family and grew up in towns all over northwest Indiana including Gary, Black Oak and Merrillville. While still in his teens, he headed west to Los Angeles, anxiously

anticipating new adventures and exciting ways to channel his creative drive.

Michael became a dancer in his teens, choreographer in his twenties, poet, screenwriter and novelist in his thirties, and, now, is a freelance writer and photographer. Along the way he also tended bar, worked in healthcare, and produced large cultural events involving world music.

Michael's pragmatism, dry wit, and unique perspective on life have made him a great ally and source of humor and encouragement to a diverse set of professional colleagues, cyber fans and personal friends. He is a well-known podcaster operating under a pseudonym that shall, in this context, remain a pseudonym. He and his wife Sherry live in Pasadena, California with their two dogs Baby and Zeljko. He is currently writing a "dramedy" series for cable premium television.

ERIN V. LEHMAN, PH.D. is a Senior Researcher with the Center for Public Leadership at the John F. Kennedy School of Government, Harvard University. Prior to this appointment, Dr. Lehman worked for the Organization Practice at McKinsey & Company in Washington, D.C. and spent over 15 years with the Harvard Business School and the Department of Psychology at Harvard University.

Her academic research and publications have focused on leadership and teamwork, especially on self-governing and senior leadership teams. Dr. Lehman received a bachelor's degree in Economics from Wellesley College and a Ph.D. in Organizational Behavior from City University, London in the United Kingdom.

To reach any of our authors, please visit www.RestoreYourselfBook.com.

ENDNOTES

1 We'll talk about this in Chapter Five: Reliable Restorers

2 Bashevis Singer, Isaac. *Mazel and Shlamazel or the Milk of a Lioness.*

3 Vitameatavegamin episode of I Love Lucy, Desilu Productions, 1962

4 Op cit.

5 Work/Life Balance: Wisdom or Whining article in *Organizational Dynamics* by Edy Greenblatt, 2003)

6 See soon to be published work by Michnea Moldoveanu at Center for Integrative Thinking, Rotman School of Management, University of Toronto and Mobius Executive Leadership consulting and corporate training (Boston).

7 National Sleep Foundation Website, www.sleepfoundation.org.

8 Based on productivity, absenteeism and other US workforce data. Unpublished presentation Greenblatt, 2008.

9 See Ellen Langer's research and publications.

10 If you found this error, email us off the website.

11 From LeadershipNow.com article citing Bennis' and his use of Saul Bellows term First-Class-Noticer.

12 See the work of professors Blake Ashforth and Glen Kreiner.

13 Ashforth, B. E. & Kreiner, G. E. (1999). How can you do it?" Dirty work and the challenge of constructing a positive identity. *Academy Management Review*, 24, pp. 413-434.

14 Dutton, J. E., Debebe, G. & Wrzesniewski, A.. (1996). The revaluing of devalued work: The importance of relationships for hospital cleaning staff.

15 I discuss this specific situation later in the chapter on sneaky depleters.

16 Please go to www.RestoreYourselfBook.com to share your ideas with others.

17 Rosenthal, Norman. *Winter Blues.*

18 Avery, D. H.; Kizer D, Bolte MA, &Hellekson C. (2001). Bright light therapy of subsyndromal seasonal affective disorder in the workplace: morning vs. afternoon exposure. *Acta Psychiatrica Scandinavica* 103 (4): 267–274.

19 *Flow* by Mihaly Csikszentmihalyi

20 Op cit.

21 *A Paradox in Paradise*, Ph.D. dissertation by Edith Greenblatt (Harvard University, 2001), pg 157.

22 Center for Disease Control's website, October 2008 http://www.cdc.gov/

23 Op. cit.

24 A clear description of the process is in M.D. Herbert Benson's book *The Relaxation Response*

25 See Arly Hochschild's seminal work *The Managed Heart*

26 *A Paradox in Paradise*, Greenblatt 2001

27 *A Paradox in Paradise*, Greenblatt 2001

28 Vitamin D, in *Wikipedia,* October 2008.

29 "The Cost of Not Paying Attention: How Interruptions Impact Knowledge Worker Productivity," Jonathan B. Spira and Joshua B. Feintuch, Basex, 2005

30 Op cit.

31 For more information on emotional contagion, please see the work of Dr. Segal Barsade.

32 32 *A Paradox in Paradise*, Greenblatt 2001

33 The specifics of this process are outlined in "Work/life balance: Wisdom or Whining," Greenblatt 2003

34 Sometimes you reward the behavior and sometimes you don't so people keep up the activity hoping for reward. Slot machines are a great example of this. See any basic psychology book for more on intermittent positive reinforcement.

35 The idea of "Both And" Management comes from Dr. Wendy Smith's research. See Dr. Edy TV Show episode 2008 or search on Dr. Smith's research.

36 For details on these ranges, see Greenblatt, 2003.

37 The following example is from Greenblatt, 2003.

38 If you are not on this list and should be, please contact me and I will include you in the on-line errata and correct the omission the next edition. Thanks for your understanding.

Breinigsville, PA USA
12 January 2011
253207BV00005B/2/P